Natural Computing Series

Series Editors: G. Rozenberg
Th. Bäck   A.E. Eiben   J.N. Kok   H.P. Spaink

Leiden Center for Natural Computing

More information about this series at http://www.springer.com/series/4190

Susan Stepney • Steen Rasmussen • Martyn Amos
Editors

Computational Matter

 Springer

Editors
Susan Stepney
Department of Computer Science
University of York
York, UK

Steen Rasmussen
Department of Physics, Chemistry and Pharmacy
FLinT Center, University of Southern Denmark
Odense, Denmark

Martyn Amos
School of Computing, Mathematics
and Digital Technology
Manchester Metropolitan University
Manchester, UK

ISSN 1619-7127
Natural Computing Series
ISBN 978-3-030-09750-9   ISBN 978-3-319-65826-1   (eBook)
https://doi.org/10.1007/978-3-319-65826-1

This Springer imprint is published by the registered company Springer Nature Switzerland AG.
The registered company address is: Gewerbestrasse 11, 6330 Cham, Switzerland

Contents

1 Introduction 1
Susan Stepney, Steen Rasmussen, and Martyn Amos

Part I Mapping the UCOMP Territory

2 UCOMP Roadmap: Survey, Challenges,
Recommendations 9
Susan Stepney and Simon J. Hickinbotham

3 *In Materio* Computation Using Carbon Nanotubes 33
Julian F. Miller and Simon J. Hickinbotham

4 Computing by Non-linear Optical Molecular Response 45
Barbara Fresch, Tian-Min Yan, Dawit Hiluf, Elisabetta Collini,
Raphael D. Levine, and Françoise Remacle

5 Bioinspired Computing with Synaptic Elements 55
Göran Wendin

6 Microscopic Chemically Reactive Electronic Agents 81
John S. McCaskill

7 Cellular Computing and Synthetic Biology 93
Martyn Amos and Angel Goñi-Moreno

8 PhyChip: Growing Computers with Slime Mould 111
Andrew Adamatzky, Jeff Jones, Richard Mayne, James Whiting,
Victor Erokhin, Andrew Schumann, and Stefano Siccardi

9 Decoding Genomic Information 129
Giuditta Franco and Vincenzo Manca

Part II Delving into UCOMP Concepts

10 Philosophy of Computation 153
Zoran Konkoli, Susan Stepney, Hajo Broersma, Paolo Dini,
Chrystopher L. Nehaniv, and Stefano Nichele

**11 Computability and Complexity of Unconventional
Computing Devices** 185
Hajo Broersma, Susan Stepney, and Göran Wendin

**12 Encoding and Representation of Information Processing
in Irregular Computational Matter** 231
John S. McCaskill, Julian F. Miller, Susan Stepney, and
Peter R. Wills

13 BIOMICS: a Theory of Interaction Computing 249
Paolo Dini, Chrystopher L. Nehaniv, Eric Rothstein, Daniel
Schreckling, and Gábor Horváth

14 Reservoir Computing with Computational Matter 269
Zoran Konkoli, Stefano Nichele, Matthew Dale, and
Susan Stepney

15 Multivalued Logic at the Nanoscale 295
Barbara Fresch, M. V. Klymenko, Raphael D. Levine, and
Françoise Remacle

**16 Nanoscale Molecular Automata: From Materials to
Architectures** 319
Ross Rinaldi, Rafael Gutierrez, Alejandro Santana Bonilla,
Gianaurelio Cuniberti, and Alessandro Bramanti

List of Contributors

Andrew Adamatzky. Department of Computer Science, University of the West of England, Bristol, UK

Martyn Amos. School of Computing, Mathematics and Digital Technology, Manchester Metropolitan University, UK

Alessandro Bramanti. STMicroelectronics, Lecce, Italy

Hajo Broersma. Faculty of Electrical Engineering, Mathematics and Computer Science, and MESA+ Institute for Nanotechnology, University of Twente, Enschede, The Netherlands

Elisabetta Collini. Department of Chemical Science, University of Padova, Italy

Gianaurelio Cuniberti. Institute for Materials Science, Dresden University of Technology, Germany

Matthew Dale. Department of Computer Science, and York Cross-disciplinary Centre for Systems Analysis, University of York, UK

Paolo Dini. Royal Society Wolfson Biocomputation Research Lab, Centre for Computer Science and Informatics Research, University of Hertfordshire, Hatfield, UK

Victor Erokhin. CNR-IMEM, Parma, Italy

Giuditta Franco. Dipartimento di Informatica, Università di Verona, Italy

Barbara Fresch. Department of Chemical Science, University of Padova, Italy; and Department of Chemistry, University of Liege, Belgium

Angel Goñi-Moreno. School of Computing, Newcastle University, UK

Rafael Gutierrez. Institute for Materials Science, Dresden University of Technology, Germany

Simon J. Hickinbotham. Department of Computer Science, and York Cross-disciplinary Centre for Systems Analysis, University of York, UK

Dawit Hiluf. The Fritz Haber Center for Molecular Dynamics and Institute of Chemistry, The Hebrew University of Jerusalem, Israel

Gábor Horváth. Department of Algebra and Number Theory, Institute of Mathematics, University of Debrecen, Hungary

Jeff Jones. Department of Computer Science, University of the West of England, Bristol, UK

M. V. Klymenko. Department of Chemistry, University of Liege, Belgium

Zoran Konkoli. Department of Microtechnology and Nanoscience, Chalmers University of Technology, Gothenburg, Sweden

Raphael D. Levine. The Fritz Haber Center for Molecular Dynamics and Institute of Chemistry, The Hebrew University of Jerusalem, Israel; and Crump Institute for Molecular Imaging and Department of Molecular and Medical Pharmacology, David Geffen School of Medicine and Department of Chemistry and Biochemistry, University of California, Los Angeles, California, USA.

Vincenzo Manca. Dipartimento di Informatica, Università di Verona, Italy

Richard Mayne. Department of Computer Science, University of the West of England, Bristol, UK

John S. McCaskill. European Center for Living Technology, Ca' Foscari University, Venice, Italy

Julian F. Miller. Department of Electronic Engineering, University of York, UK

Chrystopher L. Nehaniv. Royal Society Wolfson Biocomputation Research Lab, Centre for Computer Science and Informatics Research, University of Hertfordshire, Hatfield, UK

Stefano Nichele. Department of Computer Science, Oslo Metropolitan University, Norway

Steen Rasmussen. Center for Fundamental Living Technology, University of Southern Denmark; and Santa Fe Institute, USA

Françoise Remacle. Department of Chemistry, University of Liege, Belgium

Ross Rinaldi. Department of Mathematics and Physics "E. De Giorgi", University of Salento, Lecce, Italy

Eric Rothstein. Department of Informatics and Mathematics, University of Passau, Germany

Alejandro Santana Bonilla. Institute for Materials Science, Dresden University of Technology, Germany

Daniel Schreckling. Department of Informatics and Mathematics, University of Passau, Germany

Andrew Schumann. University of Information Technology and Management, Rzeszow, Poland

Stefano Siccardi. Department of Computer Science, University of the West of England, Bristol, UK

Susan Stepney. Department of Computer Science, and York Cross-disciplinary Centre for Systems Analysis, University of York, UK

Göran Wendin. Applied Quantum Physics Laboratory, Microtechnology and Nanoscience, Chalmers University of Technology, Gothenburg, Sweden

James Whiting. Department of Engineering, Design and Mathematics, University of the West of England, Bristol, UK

Peter R. Wills. Department of Physics, University of Auckland, New Zealand

Tian-Min Yan. Department of Chemistry, University of Liege, Belgium; and Shanghai Advanced Research Institute, Chinese Academy of Sciences, China

Chapter 1
Introduction

Susan Stepney, Steen Rasmussen, and Martyn Amos

Abstract This chapter provides an introduction to the book *Computational Matter*, providing the historical background to the production of the book, and an overview of its scope and content.

1.1 Historical background

Stanislaw Ulam famously said that "using a term like non-linear science is like referring to the bulk of zoology as the study of non-elephant animals" (Campbell et al., 1985; Gleick, 1987): non-linear science actually forms the bulk of natural science. So we contend it is with *non-standard computing*, also referred to as *unconventional computing* (UCOMP): UCOMP actually forms the bulk of computational science.

UCOMP is the study of computation outside the standard model of conventional computing (which we refer to as *classical computation*, or CCOMP). By 'standard model' we mean the model underlying the implementation of almost all commercially available devices, and where the design of the devices make no special claims about their methods of computation. There is extensive territory outside this standard model, in terms both of theoretical models and of physical implementations, for UCOMP to occupy.

In order to help map out this territory, in 2009 the European Commission's Future and Emerging Technologies agency commissioned and published an Expert Consultation report on *Unconventional Formalisms for Computation* (European Commission, 2009), drafted by one of the editors of this book (SS).

Conventional (classical) computation may be baldly characterised as that of the Turing/von Neumann paradigm: based on the mathematical abstraction of Turing Machines (or equivalents) with exact provable results, and an implementation in terms of sequential program v data models. It has been incredibly successful. How-

© Springer International Publishing AG, part of Springer Nature 2018
S. Stepney et al. (eds.), *Computational Matter*, Natural Computing Series,
https://doi.org/10.1007/978-3-319-65826-1_1

ever, there is increasing argument that it encompasses only a small subset of all computational possibilities, and increasing evidence that it is failing to adapt to novel application domains. — (European Commission, 2009)

That report summarised the then-current state of UCOMP research, and made a recommendation:

> The recommendation of this consultation is for a funded programme in **advanced unconventional computation**, intended to take the discipline beyond its current state of relatively isolated individual topics: to fill the gaps, unify areas, break new ground, and build a unified discipline of computation as a whole. Individual projects funded in such a programme should clearly demonstrate how they intend to progress the field as a whole. — (European Commission, 2009)

In 2011 the agency opened the ICT FP7 Call 8 FET Proactive in Unconventional Computation[1], and for associated Coordination Actions. As a result, seven research projects were funded:

- BIOMICS: Biological and Mathematical Basis of Interaction Computing (Dini et al., 2012), www.biomicsproject.eu
- MICREAgents: MIcroscopic Chemically Reactive Electronic Agents (McCaskill et al., 2012), www.micreagents.eu
- MolArNet: Molecular Architectures for QCA-inspired Boolean Networks (Rinaldi et al., 2012), www.molarnet.eu
- Multi: Multi-Valued and Parallel Molecular Logic (Collini et al., 2012), www.multivalued.eu
- NASCENCE: NAnoSCale Engineering for Novel Computation using Evolution (Broersma et al., 2012), www.nascence.eu
- PhyChip: Growing Computers from Slime Mould (Adamatzky et al., 2012), www.phychip.eu
- SYMONE: SYnaptic MOlecular NEtworks for Bio-inspired Information Processing (Wendin et al., 2012), www.symone.eu

One coordination action was also funded:

- TRUCE: Training and Research in Unconventional Computation in Europe (Amos et al., 2012), www.truce-project.eu

The objectives of the TRUCE coordination action were (1) to formulate, develop and maintain a European vision and strategy for UCOMP; (2) to identify areas of importance in UCOMP, and help to focus research in these areas; (3) to provide a framework for the discussion and resolution of current issues in UCOMP; (4) to facilitate improvement in the quality, profile and applicability of European UCOMP research; (5) to encourage and support the involvement of students and early career researchers in UCOMP; (6) to facilitate industrial involvement with UCOMP (Amos et al., 2012).

---

[1] (Floeck, 2012), cordis.europa.eu/fp7/ict/fet-proactive/calls_en.html#previousfetproactive

This book, edited by TRUCE project leaders, comprises a distilled collection of outputs from the UCOMP projects, including a roadmap for Unconventional Computing (UCOMP) research and development in Europe and beyond, in order to identify new trends, challenges and opportunities.

1.2 Scope and content of the book

1.2.1 Roadmap: Mapping the UCOMP territory

Part I of the book comprises outputs from the TRUCE project's UCOMP roadmap activity. The resulting roadmap has been iteratively developed through information gathering from the literature, from specific experts, and from the wider community. The roadmap provides analyses of several specific UCOMP implementations, leading to a range of recommendations for the future of UCOMP research in Europe and beyond.

The chapters in Part I are:

- Chapter 2. UCOMP Roadmap: Survey, Challenges, Recommendations
- Chapter 3. *In materio* Computation Using Carbon Nanotubes
- Chapter 4. Computing by Non-linear Optical Molecular Response
- Chapter 5. Bioinspired Computing with Synaptic Elements
- Chapter 6. Microscopic Chemically Reactive Electronic Agents
- Chapter 7. Cellular Computing and Synthetic Biology
- Chapter 8. PhyChip: Growing Computers with Slime Mould
- Chapter 9. Decoding Genomic Information

1.2.2 Delving into UCOMP concepts

Part II of the book discusses certain aspects of UCOMP across the breadth of the domain, distilling findings from across the funded UCOMP projects. It covers: philosophy of UCOMP, computability and complexity of UCOMP devices, encoding and representing information in UCOMP devices, a theory of interactive computing, reservoir computing with unconventional material, multivalued logics in nanoscale materials, and molecular automata.

The chapters in Part II are:

- Chapter 10. Philosophy of Computation
- Chapter 11. Computability and Complexity of Unconventional Computing Devices
- Chapter 12. Encoding and Representation of Information Processing in Irregular Computational Matter

- Chapter 13. BIOMICS: A Theory of Interaction Computing
- Chapter 14. Reservoir Computing with Computational Matter
- Chapter 15. Multivalued Logic at the Nanoscale
- Chapter 16. Nanoscale Molecular Automata: From Materials to Architectures

Acknowledgements

We would like to thank our fellow TRUCE project partners, René Doursat and Francisco J. Vico, for their help in making the TRUCE coordination activity such a success, and a pleasure to work on. We thank all the members of the other UCOMP-funded projects, particularly for their enthusiasm for this book: their hard work is what made it possible. And we thank the European Commission, without whose funding the research described herein would not have happened.

We hope that this collected material will be of value to the entire UCOMP community, and more broadly to the computer science and related communities, gathering together common findings from the broadest disciplinary background.

References

Adamatzky, Andrew, Victor Erokhin, Martin Grube, Theresa Schubert, and Andrew Schumann (2012). "Physarum Chip Project: Growing Computers From Slime Mould". *International Journal of Unconventional Computing* 8(4):319–323.

Amos, Martyn, Susan Stepney, Rene Doursat, Francisco J. Vico, and Steen Rasmussen (2012). "TRUCE: A Coordination Action for Unconventional Computation". *International Journal of Unconventional Computing* 8(4):333–337.

Broersma, Hajo, Faustino Gomez, Julian Miller, Mike Petty, and Gunnar Tufte (2012). "Nascence Project: Nanoscale Engineering for Novel Computation Using Evolution". *International Journal of Unconventional Computing* 8(4):313–317.

Campbell, David, Jim Crutchfield, Doyne Farmer, and Erica Jen (1985). "Experimental mathematics: the role of computation in nonlinear science". *Commun. Assoc. Comput. Mach.* 28:374–384.

Collini, E., R.D. Levine, F. Remacle, S. Rogge, and I. Willner (2012). "Multi Project: Multi-Valued and Parallel Molecular Logic". *International Journal of Unconventional Computing* 8(4):307–312.

Dini, Paolo, Chrystopher L. Nehaniv, Attila Egr-Nagy, Maria J. Schilstra, Daniel Schreckling, Joachim Posegga, Gabor Horvath, and Alastair J. Munro (2012). "BIOMICS Project: Biological and Mathematical Basis of Interaction Computing". *International Journal of Unconventional Computing* 8(4):283–287.

European Commission (2009). "Unconventional Formalisms for Computation". *Expert Consultation Workshop*.

Floeck, Dagmar (2012). "European Support for Unconventional Computation". *International Journal of Unconventional Computing* 8(4):281–282.

Gleick, James (1987). *Chaos: Making a new science.* Viking Penguin.

McCaskill, John S., Gunter von Kiedrowski, Jurgen Ohm, Pierre Mayr, Lee Cronin, Itamar Willner, Andreas Herrmann, Steen Rasmussen, Frantisek Stepanek, Norman H. Packard, and Peter R. Wills (2012). "Microscale Chemically Reactive Electronic Agents". *International Journal of Unconventional Computing* 8(4):289–299.

Rinaldi, R., G. Maruccio, V. Arima, G.P. Spada, P. Samori, G. Cuniberti, J. Boland, and A.P. Bramanti (2012). "Molarnet Project: Molecular Architectures for QCA-Inspired Boolean Networks". *International Journal of Unconventional Computing* 8(4):289–299.

Wendin, G., D. Vuillaume, M. Calame, S. Yitschaik, C. Gamrat, G. Cuniberti, and V. Beiu (2012). "SYMONE Project: Synaptic Molecular Networks for Bio-Inspired Information Processing". *International Journal of Unconventional Computing* 8(4):325–332.

Part I
Mapping the UCOMP Territory

Chapter 2
UCOMP Roadmap: Survey, Challenges, Recommendations

Susan Stepney and Simon J. Hickinbotham

Abstract We report on the findings of the EU TRUCE project UCOMP roadmap activity. We categorise UCOMP along hardware and software axes, and provide a catalogue of hw-UCOMP and sw-UCOMP examples. We describe the approach we have taken to compiling the roadmap case studies in the remainder of Part I. We identify eight aspects of UCOMP to analyse the broad range of approaches: speed, resource, quality, embeddedness, formalism, programmability, applications, and philosophy. We document a range of challenges facing UCOMP research, covering hardware design and manufacture, software theory and programming, and applications and deployment. Finally, we list some recommendations for focussing future UCOMP research: scaling up hardware, software, and concepts; identifying killer apps; and unifying the UCOMP domain.

2.1 The EU TRUCE project roadmap

The EU TRUCE coordination action project (Amos et al., 2012) includes a task of scientific research roadmapping, with a final deliverable comprising a set of case studies, a survey of the domain, the challenges facing UCOMP, and a set of recommendations. The survey, challenges, and recommendations are summarised in this chapter; the case studies comprise the remaining chapters of Part I.

2.2 An atlas, not a roadmap

Unconventional computing (UCOMP) is a fundamental scientific domain, and there are challenges in mapping its scope and development. The act of

© Springer International Publishing AG, part of Springer Nature 2018
S. Stepney et al. (eds.), *Computational Matter*, Natural Computing Series,
https://doi.org/10.1007/978-3-319-65826-1_2

roadmapping such an emerging research domain contrasts with conventional technology roadmapping focussing on a specific technological need:

> Technology roadmapping is driven by a need, not a solution. It is a fundamentally different approach to start with a solution and look for needs. Technology roadmapping provides a way to identify, evaluate, and select technology alternatives that can be used to satisfy the need. (Garcia and Bray, 1997)

The UCOMP domain certainly encompasses and is driving many novel and exciting implementation technologies, but these cover only a part of the possible domain, not its entirety. Nevertheless, it is still necessary to describe and plan the current scope of development of UCOMP, in order to set out a work programme for the coming decades.

In order to distinguish this work from traditional technological roadmapping, we use the term *atlas* as a more appropriate term. A roadmap focusses on getting to a specific destination; an atlas maps out a whole terrain. 'Atlas' raises the idea of land masses, peninsulas, isolated islands, oceans, and uncharted regions. The distribution of research in UCOMP can be described via analogy with such an atlas.

In our UCOMP atlas, an 'ocean' may be an area of little interest in itself, that merely acts as a measure of the distance between land masses. Alternatively, it may be a region of theory which links together otherwise dissimilar UCOMP practices. Either way, it is important to declare whether these oceans have been charted sufficiently well, since there is a possibility that we might miss a significant technique otherwise.

There are two important 'continents' in UCOMP, namely Quantum Computing and ChemBioIT, each of which has recently had roadmaps commissioned and published (Calarco et al., 2010; Hughes et al., 2004; McCaskill et al., 2014), setting out the future of their topic over the next ten years or so.

Taking the analogy further, we might consider how CCOMP sits on the landscape just described. We consider CCOMP as the spread of *computational civilization* across the UCOMP landscape, exploiting resources and enriching its capabilities as it goes.

The TRUCE UCOMP research atlas thus provides (requirements adapted from Sloman (2007)):

- A specification of the problem domain (scope: the atlas as a whole)
- A breakdown into subdomains (structure: the macro-level organisation of the atlas)
- Potential routes to populating the domain (projects: case studies that illustrate the current and future range and status of UCOMP)

In this chapter we give a categorisation of the entire UCOMP landscape extracted from the literature and from a practitioner questionnaire (Stepney and Hickinbotham, 2015, App. A), and we discuss eight aspects of UCOMP that we use to analyse the case studies. We summarise the current state of

	hw-CCOMP	hw-UCOMP
sw-CCOMP	*CCOMP* • some simulations of UCOMP	*hw-only UCOMP* : eg • logic gates and TMs in unconventional substrates
sw-UCOMP	*sw-only UCOMP* : eg • some simulations of full UCOMP • AI/ALife algorithms	*full UCOMP* : eg • analogue computers • quantum computers • (postulated) hypercomputers • embodied unconventional algorithms

Fig. 2.1 UCOMP classified by whether it is hw-only UCOMP, sw-only UCOMP, or full UCOMP. Note that some UCOMP may be simulated in CCOMP.

UCOMP in terms of this classification, based on analysis of the detailed case studies. We provide some recommendations and guidance on where UCOMP research and development should be headed, based on analysis of the detailed case studies.

In the rest of Part I we present the contributed case studies.

2.3 Hardware-UCOMP and software-UCOMP

The simplest axes of classification from which we start are the conventional ones of *hardware* and *software*.

The *hardware* axis captures the physical or material substrate, suitably engineered, that is performing the computation. In CCOMP this is traditional silicon chips (substrate) with a von Neumann architecture (engineered configuration).

The *software* axis captures the abstract or mathematical model of the desired computation, and model of the hardware configuration needed to achieve this. The configuration includes a combination of both program and hardware architecture model; we do not explicitly separate these, since some unconventional approaches combine these components. In CCOMP this is the traditional Turing machine and Boolean logic model.

We classify the COMP landscape coarsely into four regions, depending on whether the hardware, or software, or both, are UCOMP, and give some typical examples, in Figure 2.1.

The boundary between UCOMP and CCOMP is diffuse and movable. Where do we draw the CCOMP/UCOMP line along the spectrum of single core through multi-core to massively parallel hardware (let alone exotic substrates)? Where do we draw it along the spectrum of stand-alone through real time to embedded software applications? However, here we are not concerned with this boundary region so much as the extremes of the spectrum, so arguments about its precise location is not important for our analysis.

Some, but by no means all, members of the UCOMP community require the substrate to be unconventional: they do not recognise sw-only UCOMP; some others recognise only full UCOMP (Stepney and Hickinbotham, 2015, A.2.1) Here we consider all three possibilities (sw-only UCOMP, hw-only UCOMP, and full UCOMP), as each has its interesting properties.

2.3.1 hw-UCOMP: unconventional substrates

Our classification of hw-UCOMP substrates is organised in the hierarchy below. The first level of the hierarchy identifies traditional academic disciplines: Engineering; Physics; Chemistry; Biochemistry; Biology. The next levels identify specific example substrates within that discipline. We identify some examples at this level, mentioned in the roadmap questionnaire responses, to indicate the diversity that exists; there is no attempt to be exhaustive, as novel computational materials are ever being posited and examined.

2.3.1.1 Engineering

Silicon transistors are used in the single classical chip set, and also in a variety of approaches to parallelism: massive multi-core systems, general purpose graphics processing (GPGPU), and field programmable gate arrays (FPGA).

More unconventional devices can be engineered at the nanoscale (the scale of atoms and molecules). Examples include superconducting qubit arrays, memristor arrays, and atomic switch networks.

A variety of media can be engineered to provide general purpose analogue computing. These include field programmable analogue arrays (FPAA), Łukasiewicz Logic Arrays (Mills et al., 1990), and Mills' 'foam' substrates (Mills et al., 2006).

There is a rich history of special purpose mechanical analogue devices, crafted to perform specific computations. These include such diverse devices as the orrery for planetary motions, Kelvin's tide-predictor, early curve integrators, rod and gear integrators, Babbage's clockwork difference and analytical engine, and the hydraulic MONIAC (Monetary National Income Analogue Computer).

2.3.1.2 Physics

A variety of physical processes are exploited for UCOMP.

Josephson junction circuits are used in quantum computing. Quantum dots, as well as being exploited in quantum computing, can be used for programmable matter.

Optical devices are used in both classical optical computers and in quantum-optics computers that exploit photons as qubits.

The technology of Nuclear Magnetic Resonance (NMR), which combines properties of nuclear spins, magnetic fields, and radio frequency pulses, can be used to perform classical computing (Roselló-Merino et al., 2010) and quantum computing (Gershenfeld and Chuang, 1997).

Complex physical materials have been repurposed for computation in several cases. These include liquid crystal (Harding and Miller, 2004; Harding and Miller, 2005; Harding and Miller, 2007), carbon nanotubes and amorphous substrates (Clegg et al., 2014), graphene, and non-linear magnetic materials.

2.3.1.3 Chemistry

In chemical computing, the computation exploits the chemical properties and reactions of the substrate.

Examples of chemical computing include chemical variants of field computing, and a range of reaction-diffusion systems (Adamatzky et al., 2005) such as Belousov–Zhabotinsky (B-Z) reaction systems (Stovold and O'Keefe, 2017).

Another popular form of chemical computing is droplet systems. The droplets themselves may be the units of computation, may package up and transport chemicals, and may host and interface local B-Z and other reaction-diffusion systems.

2.3.1.4 Biochemistry

Biomolecules including DNA and RNA can be induced to perform computation in a range of approaches.

The most obvious approach is to exploit DNA/RNA as an information-carrying material, and use this to program generic logic circuits (Carell, 2011) using gene expression.

An alternative approach is to exploit the stiffness of short strands of DNA as a construction material, and use this in concert with information carrying 'sticky ends' to self-assemble structures (Rothemund et al., 2004) using tiling theory.

2.3.1.5 Biology

Biology provides a very rich set of systems that can either be used directly for computation, or can provide inspiration for novel computational systems.

Biological systems and subsystems used in this way include neurons, plasmids, the immune systems, evolution, viruses, phages, single bacteria, synthetic biology, communicating bacteria, bacterial mats, mammalian cells, and slime moulds.

2.3.1.6 Hybrid systems that combine/compose more than one substrate

As with any engineering discipline, hw-UCOMP may combine a range of substrates into a computational system. Examples include: a conventional computer plus a UCOMP "co-processor"; electronics combined with chemicals; neurons attached to silicon; droplets interfacing reaction-diffusion chemicals; chemicals and bacteria in chemotaxis systems; optical and molecular systems; optical and bacterial systems engaged in phototaxis.

2.3.1.7 Other

There are several theoretical or conceptual substrates, which are used to illustrate an unconventional principle, and to explore limits, but are not implemented, beyond some toy cases. Such systems include spaghetti sorting (Dewdney, 1984); gravity sorting (Arulanandham et al., 2002); prisms for sorting with light frequencies (Schultes, 2006); soap film minimisation computers (Isenberg, 1976); elastic band convex hull computers (Dewdney, 1984); billiard ball computers (Fredkin and Toffoli, 1982); conjectured systems such as black holes and other exotic space-times (Earman and Norton, 1993).

2.3.2 sw-UCOMP: unconventional models

We provide the following classification of sw-UCOMP. Note that some examples can occur in more than one category. Some of these models are primarily theoretical, used to investigate aspects of computability and complexity. Others may be executed in CCOMP simulation (potentially with loss of efficiency), or may be executed in unconventional substrates to give full UCOMP.

Quantum models include: quantum circuit models; quantum annealing models, including adiabatic computing; quantum information; quantum communication.

Continuum models, and massively-parallel/spatial models, include: classical analogue computing; quantum analogue computing; field computing; ubiquitous computing; cellular automata.

Bio-inspired models include: population-based search algorithms (evolutionary, immune, swarm, etc); computational morphogenesis and developmental models; membrane-based models (brane-calculi, P-systems, etc); neural models (ANNs, reservoir computing); gene regulatory network models; metabolic network models; Artificial Life models (ALife).

Growth and self-assembly models include: Artificial Chemistries (AChems) and reaction networks; L-systems and other generative grammars; computational morphogenesis and developmental models; dynamical systems models, including reservoir computing; tiling models; self-modifying models.

Non-halting models include: process algebras; interaction computing.

Hypercomputing models include: Newtonian physics models; general relativistic models; infinite precision real number models.

2.3.3 Full UCOMP: unconventional models in unconventional substrates

Many of the unconventional substrates have been used to implement small CCOMP computations: logic gates or small circuits. Example systems that use unconventional substrates to implement sw-UCOMP models, to yield full UCOMP, include:

- analogue computers
- quantum computers, quantum communications
- evolution *in materio* computing
- reservoir computing *in materio*
- tile assembly of DNA tiles

Often there needs to be a careful choice of substrate and model, so that the computational model can exploit the properties of the substrate to perform its computation effectively.

2.3.4 Simulating UCOMP

Some practitioners require that true UCOMP not be efficiently simulable in CCOMP (to be super-Turing), but this seems overly restrictive: for one thing, it assumes a Turing model of computation; on the other hand it excludes simple logic circuits implemented in cells using synthetic biology.

We can categorise UCOMP approaches based on their simulability in CCOMP algorithms on CCOMP hardware as follows:

- Efficiently simulable models, possibly with a transfer of space resources in the model to time resources in simulation: for example, cellular automata.
- Super-Turing models, simulable in CCOMP, but not efficiently: for example, some quantum computing algorithms.
- Hypercomputing models, uncomputable in CCOMP and hence not simulable. Whether such models are physically implementable in UCOMP substrates is contentious (see Chapter 11).

Simulation is an important technology in UCOMP research, where expensive and specialised substrates can be difficult to obtain. Simulation allows UCOMP models to be explored and tested on conventional machines. Care needs to be taken when drawing detailed conclusions that may be true in simulation, but not carry over to physical substrates.

In addition to CCOMP clusters, silicon technologies such as GPUs and FPGAs may be suitable testbeds for simulating many UCOMP models and substrates, due to their potential for massively parallel computations.

2.4 Eight aspects of UCOMP

The roadmap questionnaire responses (Stepney and Hickinbotham, 2015, App. A), which fed into the above classification, reveal that UCOMP is a field that will continue to be dynamic for at least the next 25 years, and beyond. Current topics will either become accepted or discarded. New techniques will arise at the limits of what is conventionally possible or imaginable. Given this flux, the act of mapping UCOMP becomes more difficult, if we were to focus on particular techniques. Instead, we identify a set of computational properties, which we call *aspects*, and appraise the current and future development of particular techniques in light of these aspects.

Based on the roadmap questionnaire responses, and information from a literature review, and following on from the domain classification, we have identified eight aspects of UCOMP. Our goal was to select aspects that capture the range of potential of the entire UCOMP canon, which are in some sense independent of each other, and for which it is possible to get consensus on the potential of a UCOMP topic. Here we describe these eight aspects, and how they play out across the various UCOMP areas.

These aspects can be thought of as analogous to the DiVincenzo *promise criteria* used in the quantum computing roadmap (Hughes et al., 2004). The UCOMP aspects are:

1. Speed
2. Resource
3. Quality
4. Embeddedness

5. Formalism
6. Programmability
7. Applications
8. Philosophy

One of the uses for this atlas is to indicate the research areas which show the most promise as an augmentation of CCOMP, so UCOMP technologies should be considered on a scale relative to the current and 'best estimate' future state of CCOMP.

For each aspect, we have devised one or more 'prompting questions', which are intended to help the responders compile their case study descriptions consistently. One danger to be wary of is applying well-known conventional or practical CCOMP thinking to the UCOMP paradigm, and thereby missing the potential for a different way of thinking about the process of computation. We point out these risks as we describe each aspect.

Here, we describe each aspect, we mention how the aspect appears in CCOMP, and we summarise the UCOMP results as given in the case studies discussed in more detail in the following chapters.

2.4.1 Speed

Prompting question

Including programming and staging time, how fast is computation in your UCOMP research?

When assessing the utility of any computation, a key consideration is how much time it will take to obtain the output. In CCOMP, speed is usually a direct measure of the rate of processing. We can usually measure the absolute 'wall clock' time it takes to perform a computation, or we can measure the number of steps an algorithm takes and so obtain a speed estimate that is independent of the physical processor speed.

Other issues also need to be considered. There may be a trade-off between speed and accuracy for example. There may be no identifiable steps to count.

Speed is not merely related to the execution time of a UCOMP program. Because of the nature of the different strands of UCOMP, the execution time is only one part of the wider computational process. Writing or creating a computational algorithm can be a challenging process in itself. Setting up the algorithm, inputting the data, and extracting the outputs of the algorithm may be non-trivial in some applications. All of these should be considered when assessing the speed of a particular technique.

Given these observations, it becomes difficult to define what the potential offering of speed is for some UCOMP topics in a manner that allows direct comparison. Wherever difficulties arise, it should always be possible to measure the time between input and output. This time should then be used as the basis of a comparison of the merits of the technique and a CCOMP equivalent.

CCOMP

There is evidence that conventional chips have reached the limit of miniaturisation and the speed of processing may not improve much without replacing the current technology (Haron and Hamdioui, 2008). Assuming that it is not possible to simultaneously replace current transistorisation technology and increase processor speed, it is reasonable to suggest that processing speed in CCOMP will stay constant.

UCOMP

- There is a huge variation in 'clock speed' across materials, from femtosecond (10^{-15} s, physics/optical) and nanosecond (10^{-9} s, physics/electronic, logic gates and memristors), to seconds (chemistry), to minutes/hours (biology).
- In some cases with non-clocked models of computation (including certain analogue, continuous time evolution, and relaxation approaches), the effective speed may be unknown, and claims may be controversial.
- Most approaches benefit from massive parallelism.
- For embedded systems, the computation speed relative to the controlled system's timescales is the important factor. Absolute speed, or speed in comparison to CCOMP, is not the relevant metric.
- For hybrid systems, the relative computation speeds of the different substrates is an important factor; where they are very different, matching issues may exist.
- In some approaches, the hardware 'decays' (from quantum decoherence to biocell death), and so the important measure is how much computation can be done before the hardware is no longer usable.
- There are different aspects of speed:
    - hardware construction timescale: in CCOMP this is neglected, as the hardware is used repeatedly. However, this timescale is particularly significant in UCOMP for 'one-shot' devices where the computation destroys or consumes the device.
    - program loading timescale: in CCOMP this is generally neglected; in the Turing model the program is present on the tape at the start of the computation. However, this timescale can be significant in UCOMP if program loading corresponds to some slow configuration of the

substrate, or some slow search for the required configuration (as in *in materio* computing).

– input/output timescale: in CCOMP this is generally neglected; in the Turing model the input is present on the tape at the start of the computation, and the computation halts leaving the output present on the tape at the end. Communication applications are more concerned with I/O timescales, and transmission timescales; embedded applications with analogue-to-digital and digital-to-analogue conversion rates. These timescales can be significant in UCOMP if I/O requires significant data configuration and conversion.

2.4.2 Resource

Prompting question

How does the economic cost of the computational resource compare to the cost in CCOMP?

This aspect concerns the consumption of physical resource by the UCOMP process. In CCOMP where the main consumable is electrical power, this is an active area of research (ITRS, 2013). There is a wider range of resource use in UCOMP (Blakey, 2017). A benchmark of some utility is the economic cost of the resource: how easy is it to procure the resource, what are the by-products, and how easy is it to dispose of them. This allows the resource usage in a slime-mould computation, say, to be compared with electrical power consumption in CCOMP in a more objective manner.

Another facet of the resource aspect concerns the *scalability* of the technology. Costs should be considered per unit of computational resource, and by the total computational resource of however many units can reasonably be composed.

CCOMP

It is possible that processors which use less power than currently will be developed, whilst maintaining the symbolic nature of CCOMP.

UCOMP

• Most equipment is still highly specialist and expensive; but it is early days, and prices will come down.

- Some systems require expensive and power-hungry lasers; however research may be able to engineer some of these to run off less power hungry sources, and even sunlight instead.
- Some DNA-based systems require complex and slow laboratory synthesis processes; however, these resources will reduce as technology improves.
- Memristor memory may eventually be significantly cheaper than DRAM. Architectures based on data processing at the memristor memory level, avoiding processor-storage bottlenecks, have the potential to be much more energy efficient and faster than traditional CCOMP implementations.
- Some areas are non-comparable, such as synthetic biology, where there is not a meaningful CCOMP equivalent implementation.

2.4.3 Quality

Prompting question

Does your UCOMP research offer qualitatively different computation to CCOMP?

Quality is concerned with the manner in which a computation is carried out: precision; fit to underlying model (if the model is known); richness; stochasticity; repeatability. The quality of a UCOMP method concerns its potential to offer an analysis of the inputs that is different from a CCOMP analysis. For example, one could consider how the workings of an analogue computer can yield different results from a digital computer by virtue of its numerically continuous internal representation of the problem. The output might be a state of a physical system that could be interrogated at many different scales.

CCOMP

Since much of the definition of quality is relative to CCOMP, quality cannot progress much here. There is a potential for simulations on CCOMP platforms to emulate some unconventional processes.

UCOMP

- There are many novel models, offering benefits over, and differences from, CCOMP:

- various quantum models, with potential exponential speedup for a limited class of problems
- inherent massive parallelism, trading off time against space, avoiding traditional von Neumann bottlenecks
- analogue / continuous models, with continuous processing, and continuous input/ouptut
- 'sloppy', fuzzy, and probabilistic models, promising faster execution, but without a guaranteed or repeatable result
- stateful logic, e.g., memristors
- non-binary, and non-digital, encodings

- Some UCOMP substrates might not have any associated well-defined computational model; they are still being investigated for their potential. Search can be used to program devices despite there being no underlying model.
- Fit to the associated computational model varies across a spectrum. Physical hardware (especially quantum) tends to fit the associated model more closely than does biological wetware (where the intrinsic variability and noisiness of the wetware is often abstracted away in the associated model, despite the fact that biological systems may have evolved to exploit noise).
- An important difference is in hybrid devices exploiting multiple UCOMP substrates, and multiscale structures.
- There are issues around input and output for unconventional models; each might require significant data configuration and conversion, which might involve significant 'hidden' computational requirements.

2.4.4 Embeddedness

Prompting question

Can your UCOMP research be implemented within the process it is aimed at controlling/monitoring?

Embeddedness concerns the relationship between the performance of a computation, its output, and what the output is used for. How much does the computation rely directly on physical characteristics of the substrate, rather than only through an abstraction layer? Is the output useless unless it controls a system directly, rather than being abstractly read off and then fed into a system?

CCOMP

Embeddedness is never going to be high for CCOMP due to the highly abstract symbolic processing of data that it employs.

UCOMP

- Not all UCOMP devices are embedded; some are alternatives to standalone CCOMP devices.
- Even standalone unconventional substrates often have special purpose interface devices to link them to CCOMP kit: they are usually hybrid devices of UCOMP+CCOMP.
- For some UCOMP devices, being embedded is the *raison d'être* of the substrate choice; this tends to be certain chemical and biological devices designed to be embedded/embodied in chemical/biological systems.
- Embedded systems may suffer from the 'wiring problem', of moving data from one part of the processing to another – for example, signalling within or between cells – in a controlled and effective manner.
- Embeddedness can remove some of the input/output issues, by allowing a closer match between data formats in the controller and controlled system (cf the need for analogue-to-digital and digital-to-analogue converters in many embedded CCOMP devices). However, there is the complementary issue of programming the devices, which also needs I/O.

2.4.5 Programmability

Prompting question

How easy is it to write sophisticated programs in the computational substrate that you study?

This aspect concerns how UCOMP systems may be programmed. The ubiquity of CCOMP masks the challenges involved in organising an algorithm on a substrate. For example, in computation *in materio*, it is suggested that evolutionary search is the principal means of 'programming' the substrate (Miller et al., 2014).

CCOMP

This is well understood and there are myriad ways of writing, compiling and executing programs.

UCOMP

- There are existing quantum computing languages, both for digital and analogue devices.
- Some UCOMP systems use CCOMP-like approaches, such as gates and circuits.
- There are some multi-paradigm approaches for hybrid devices and multi-scale devices.
- In synthetic biology, there are high-level programming languages that 'compile' down to low-level components such as gene sequences, searching through databases to find suitable combinations of implementations.
- Evolution/search/learning is used where there is no good understanding or underlying model of the substrate (for example, *in materio* computing), and for non-modular complex emergent properties where classical decomposition approaches cannot be used.
- In some systems, the program is part of the substrate design: the system is application-specific, rather than reprogrammable.

2.4.6 Formalism

Prompting question

Does your UCOMP research topic have a formalism that augments/extends CCOMP formalism?

CCOMP systems have many formalisms that can be used to design algorithms etc. regardless of their hardware implementation. Few UCOMP systems have such a formalism, and most exist outside the standard Turing Machine model that underpins the formalisms of CCOMP.

Formalisms allow us to understand in abstract terms the expressiveness of a system, its limitations, and its relation to other systems and CCOMP. Whilst an over-reaching formalism for UCOMP may be desirable, it is equally desirable that UCOMP researchers foster development of formalisms for their own particular techniques.

CCOMP

Since CCOMP is purely symbolic and the underlying philosophy is well connected to the methods of implementation, it is reasonable to suggest that a rounded formalism exists for CCOMP.

UCOMP

- There is general purpose analogue computer formalism, but it is mostly in old literature, and underdeveloped.
- There are multiple quantum formalisms.
- There are substrate-inspired formalisms, such as membrane computing, reservoir computing, chemical swarm formalism, Boolean gene-regulatory networks.
- There are models based closely on the underlying physical substrate scientific models, such as on chemical kinetics.
- There are models based closely on the underlying biological substrate scientific models, such as Petri nets in systems biology.
- There are some special-purpose algebraical and category-theoretic formalisms.
- There are phenomenological and *ad hoc* formalisms, including using evolutionary search in place of a design technique.

2.4.7 Applications

Prompting question

Does your UCOMP research topic open up new applications?

The applications aspect gives a rating of a technology and its promise in terms of the range of its potential application.

UCOMP technologies are often assessed with respect to CCOMP paradigms, such as the construction of logic gates. Whilst this approach allows useful comparisons to be made between systems, it risks under-exploiting these emerging technologies. Conversely, it is almost impossible to assess the application of new technologies in new domains, because it is impossible to guarantee that all possible applications have been considered.

CCOMP

CCOMP is ubiquitous today, and this is likely to continue.

UCOMP

- Quantum applications are the most advanced, with emphasis on quantum communication and cryptography technologies, and quantum system simulation.

- Optical applications include ultrafast and massively parallel logic processing, imaging and sensing.
- Non-embedded devices often implement CCOMP benchmark problems to demonstrate their abilities.
- Many embedded/embodied applications exist or are proposed, particularly in synthetic biology, and chemical-electrical computing, providing localised programmable control of complex biological and chemical processes and sensors. Existing synthetic biology examples include clinical therapies, drug production and bio-fuel, with more examples emerging.

2.4.8 Philosophy

Prompting question

Does your UCOMP research have a non-CCOMP philosophy?

This aspect encapsulates the motivation for investigating UCOMP. A particular research area will work on extending the understanding of the field in general by reference to the philosophy of UCOMP.

CCOMP

The Church-Turing thesis / von Neumann architecture is well understood as underlying computation with symbols.

UCOMP

- Quantum computing certainly has a different and well-developed philosophy.
- UCOMP often identifies non-binary, non-symbolic, non-algorithmic aspects.
- UCOMP often exploits the physical properties of the substrate directly in order to perform computation, rather than implementing layers of abstraction in order to conform to a theoretical model; this can result in greater efficiency, but less flexibility. Universality is not necessarily a goal.
- Embedded/embodied computation is context-dependent, as opposed to CCOMP's black-box, general-purpose execution philosophy.
- Interaction models are opposed to CCOMP's 'ballistic' execution philosophy.

- The computational substrate can be dynamic, self-configuring, self-assembling, defined and built by the computation as it progresses, rather than being static and pre-defined.
- Hybrid systems can exploit multiple alternative computational philosophies.
- Hypercomputing has the non-CCOMP philosophy that Turing-uncomputable problems can be solved by some physical devices.
- Super-Turing philosophy has the non-CCOMP philosophy that some problems can be solved more efficiently (e.g., exponentially faster) by some physical devices than by a Turing machine. A form of exponential speedup has been demonstrated for a small class of quantum problems (although direct comparison is not straightforward), but not for NP-hard problems.
- Concepts such as abstraction, modularity, and separation of concerns are still important in UCOMP.

2.5 Challenges in UCOMP

The case study contributors were asked to identify specific challenges to developing their flavours of UCOMP. Their responses are summarised in this section.

2.5.1 Hardware: design and manufacture

- design and discovery – there is an issue with discovering and/or designing the relevant complex substrates: the search space of novel materials and compounds is huge, and the criteria not always well-characterised – designing hardware substrates with wetware characteristics.
- substrate engineering – novel substrates are not usually used 'raw', but instead have to be engineered into a suitable form – from atomic scale manufacture, to synthetic biology.
- input/output – interfacing novel substrates to input/output devices – detection of output signals from novel materials requires as much engineering as the substrate itself – detection of embedded processes that have no clear output signal (for example, in cells) is challenging .
- initialisation and reset – some materials are 'one shot', others can be reused, but resetting them to a known initial configuration may be challenging.
- accessing embedded devices – to embed, to program, to control, and to power.

- hybrid substrates – how to integrate functionality across multiple diverse substrates providing radically different classes of functionality, particularly hardware-wetware hybrids.
- scaling up in space and time – designing and building larger functional systems from complex components – keeping delicate substrates (from quantum to organisms) functioning for sufficient time – communication between components in a UCOMP device (sometimes known as "the wiring problem").

2.5.2 Software: theory and programming

- developing novel computational models and frameworks to exploit novel materials – this is needed both for using the devices, and for designing them initially.
- developing novel programming paradigms for encoding information and functional requirements in novel substrates.
- programming the UCOMP devices to carry out specific large scale tasks.
- simulation tools to explore the design space.

2.5.3 Use: applications and deployment

- identifying and realising suitable applications (finding "killer apps").
- safety and ethics – when embedding programmed cells in organisms, particularly humans.

2.5.4 Summary of challenges

Since the 2009 UCOMP report (European Commission, 2009), the technology has moved on. The challenges are more focussed: rather than 'playing' with substrates, the issues are how to build real devices from these substrates, how to conceptualise and perform programming in these new domains, and where the killer apps lie. In the latter case, there appear to be two radically different areas:

- Faster, better, bigger: providing hardware that can address the stalling of Moore's Law in CCOMP – for example, atomic switch networks, memristors, quantum computers, optical computers. Although these may need new programming paradigms, particularly for massive parallelism, the applications areas are roughly "more of the same", at least until more becomes different (Anderson, 1972).

- Different, other: providing systems that tackle novel problems, particularly embedding computation in material devices, moving from last century's industrial age, through today's information age, into the nascent 'BINC' age of integrated Bio-Info-Nano-Cogno capabilities (Andersen and Rasmussen, 2015).

2.6 Next Steps

The UCOMP community has identified the following items as significant next steps in the development of the discipline of UCOMP.

Novel paradigms

- Search as an engineering/programming approach
- Hybrids of substrates and their associated paradigms, including chemical computing, DNA computing, *in materio* computing, reservoir computing, membrane computing, swarm computing
- The complementary roles of *computation* and *construction*, especially dynamic construction and reconstruction of computational entities during and as part of computation – the fact that the computational substrate changes beyond mere reconfiguration

Scaling up

- Moving from single component to multiple networked component systems – including multi-cellular synthetic biology
- Ensuring that dynamic substrates (particularly cells) can remain active and suitably stable (given both death and evolution) for long periods

Programming and control

- Moving from gross behaviours demonstrated in the lab, to fine tuned very specific behaviours in applications

2.7 Recommendations

The main recommendations resulting from this community consultation and roadmapping exercise are for more interdisciplinary research and development in the following areas:

- **Scaling up hardware** from the current 'toy' existing systems to ones that can be deployed on realistic applications – from materials science to synthetic biology, including novel engineering approaches for multiscale and hybrid devices, I/O and interfacing.
- **Scaling up software** abstractions, paradigms and tools – including novel computational paradigms and how they relate to substrate properties, multiscale and hybrid devices.
- **Scaling up concepts** of computation – particularly to role of self-reconfiguration, self-construction, and reproduction in and of embodied 'BINC' systems.
- **Killer app** identification and realisation.

Overall, there is a need to unify the currently still somewhat fragmented domain of UCOMP. Coordination and Support Action efforts, such as those made in the TRUCE project, are an effective mechanism to support and encourage such unification.

References

Adamatzky, Andrew, Ben De Lacy Costello, and Tetsuya Asai (2005). *Reaction-Diffusion Computers*. Elsevier.

Amos, Martyn, Susan Stepney, Rene Doursat, Francisco J. Vico, and Steen Rasmussen (2012). "TRUCE: A Coordination Action for Unconventional Computation". *International Journal of Unconventional Computing* 8(4):333–337.

Andersen, Lene Rachel and Steen Rasmussen (2015). *The BINC Manifesto: An Emerging Technology Driven Global Transition?* flint.sdu.dk/index.php?page=technology-impact.

Anderson, P. W. (1972). "More Is Different". *Science* 177(4047):393–396.

Arulanandham, Joshua J., Cristian S. Calude, and Michael J. Dinneen (2002). "Bead-Sort: A Natural Sorting Algorithm". *The Bulletin of the European Association for Theoretical Computer Science* 76:153–162.

Blakey, Ed (2017). "Unconventional Computers and Unconventional Complexity Measures". *Advances in Unconventional Computing, vol 1*. Ed. by Andrew Adamatzky. Springer, pp. 165–182.

Calarco, T. et al. (2010). *QIPC Roadmap*. qurope.eu/content/qipc-roadmap.

Carell, Thomas (2011). "Molecular computing: DNA as a logic operator". *Nature* 469(7328):45–46.

Clegg, K. D., J. F. Miller, K. M. Massey, and M. C. Petty (2014). "Practical issues for configuring carbon nanotube composite materials for computation". *ICES 2014, International Conference on Evolvable Systems: From Biology to Hardware.* IEEE, pp. 61–68.

Dewdney, A.K. (1984). "On the spaghetti computer and other analog gadgets for problem solving". *Scientific American* 250(6):19–26.

Earman, John and John D. Norton (1993). "Forever Is a Day: Supertasks in Pitowsky and Malament-Hogarth Spacetimes". *Philosophy of Science* 60(1):22–42.

European Commission (2009). "Unconventional Formalisms for Computation". *Expert Consultation Workshop.*

Fredkin, Edward and Tommaso Toffoli (1982). "Conservative logic". *International Journal of Theoretical Physics* 21(3):219–253.

Garcia, M. L. and O. H. Bray (1997). *Fundamentals of Technology Roadmapping.* Tech. rep. SAND97-0665. East Lansing, Michigan: Sandia National Laboratories.

Gershenfeld, Neil A. and Isaac L. Chuang (1997). "Bulk Spin-Resonance Quantum Computation". *Science* 275(5298):350–356.

Harding, Simon L. and Julian F. Miller (2004). "Evolution in materio: a tone discriminator in liquid crystal". *Proc. CEC 2004.* Vol. 2, pp. 1800–1807.

Harding, Simon L. and Julian F. Miller (2005). "Evolution in materio : A real time robot controller in liquid crystal". *Proc. NASA/DoD Conference on Evolvable Hardware*, pp. 229–238.

Harding, Simon L. and Julian F. Miller (2007). "Evolution In Materio: Evolving Logic Gates in Liquid Crystal". *International Journal of Unconventional Computing* 3(4):243–257.

Haron, Nor Z. and Said Hamdioui (2008). "Why is CMOS scaling coming to an END?" *3rd International Design and Test Workshop (IDT), 2008*, pp. 98–103.

Hughes, Richard et al. (2004). *A Quantum Information Science and Technology Roadmap.* Advanced Research and Development Activity. URL: qist. lanl.gov/pdfs/rm_intro.pdf.

Isenberg, Cyril (1976). "The Soap Film: An Analogue Computer". *American Scientist* 64(5):514–518.

ITRS (2013). *International Technology Roadmap for Semiconductors, 2013 edition,Emerging Research Devices.* www.itrs.net/reports.html.

McCaskill, John S., Martyn Amos, Peter Dittrich, Steen R. Rasmussen, et al. (2014). *A Roadmap for Chemical and Biological Information Technology: ChemBioIT.* URL: www.cobra-project.eu/uploads/2/0/8/9/20895162/cobra_d2.3_draft_roadmap.pdf.

Miller, J. F., S. L. Harding, and G. Tufte (2014). "Evolution-in-materio: evolving computation in materials". *Evolutionary Intelligence* 7:49–67.

Mills, Jonathan W., M. Gordon Beavers, and Charles A. Daffinger (1990). "Lukasiewicz Logic Arrays". *Proc. 20th International Symposium on Multiple-Valued Logic, ISMVL 1990, Charlotte, NC, USA, May 1990*. IEEE Computer Society, pp. 4–10.

Mills, Jonathan W., Matt Parker, Bryce Himebaugh, Craig A. Shue, Brian Kopecky, and Chris Weilemann (2006). ""Empty space" computes: the evolution of an unconventional supercomputer". *Proc. Third Conference on Computing Frontiers, Ischia, Italy, May 2006*. ACM, pp. 115–126.

Roselló-Merino, Marta, Matthias Bechmann, Angelika Sebald, and Susan Stepney (2010). "Classical Computing in Nuclear Magnetic Resonance". *International Journal of Unconventional Computing* 6(3-4):163–195.

Rothemund, P. W. K., N. Papadakis, and E. Winfree (2004). "Algorithmic Self-Assembly of DNA Sierpinski Triangles". *PLoS Biol* 2(12):e424.

Schultes, Dominik (2006). "Rainbow Sort: Sorting at the Speed of Light". *Natural Computing* 5(1):67–82.

Sloman, Aaron (2007). *What's a Research Roadmap For? Why do we need one? How can we produce one?* www.cs.bham.ac.uk/research/projects/cosy/presentations/munich-roadmap-0701.pdf. Accessed: 2014-09-30.

Stepney, Susan and Simon Hickinbotham (2015). *A Roadmap for Unconventional Computing*. Tech. rep. www.truce-project.eu/uploads/4/9/9/2/49923679/d1.3_roadmap.pdf. TRUCE Deliverable D1.3.

Stovold, James and Simon O'Keefe (2017). "Associative Memory in Reaction-Diffusion Chemistry". *Advances in Unconventional Computing, vol 2*. Ed. by Andrew Adamatzky. Springer, pp. 141–166.

Chapter 3
In Materio Computation Using Carbon Nanotubes

Julian F. Miller and Simon J. Hickinbotham

Abstract All computing is physical, requiring a substrate in which to perform the computation. Conventional computation (CCOMP), based on the Church-Turing thesis and the von Neumann architecture, is built upon logical states that are engineered into the substrate. By contrast, *in materio* computation does not impose a computational model upon the substrate, but rather exploits a naturally-occurring computational property that it may have. New, unconventional models of computation are needed to exploit these naturally-occurring properties.

3.1 Overview

3.1.1 *In materio* **computing**

All computing is physical (Landauer, 1996), requiring a substrate in which to perform the computation. The distinction between *in materio* computation and CCOMP is that the latter engineers logical states in the substrate that are then used as the basis for executing processes based on the Church-Turing thesis via the von Neumann architecture. By contrast, *in materio* computation does not impose a computational model upon the substrate but rather exploits a naturally-occurring computational property that it may have.

The goal here is to find out simultaneously both what the computational power of the substrate might be and also how best to program it. An evolutionary search-based algorithm is usually employed to "exploit physical characteristics within the material without much concern as to how those characteristics could be formally understood or engineered" (Clegg et al., 2014b). This is appropriate when the system is not fully understood, as the

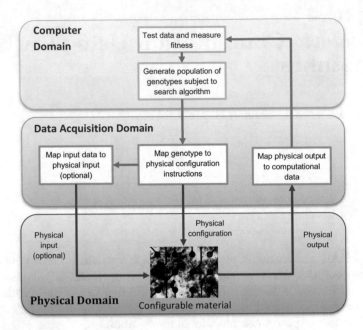

Fig. 3.1 Overview of *in materio* computing (Clegg et al., 2014a, Fig.1)

fitness of a configuration can be calculated without necessarily having knowledge of how the computation is performed. Indeed, this is often the great strength of the approach, as it raises the possibility of exploiting hitherto unknown properties of the computational substrate.

> "The concept of [*in materio* computing] grew out of work that arose in a sub-field of evolutionary computation called evolvable hardware [30, 38, 76, 104] particularly through the work of Adrian Thompson [86, 91]. In 1996, Thompson famously demonstrated that unconstrained evolution on a silicon chip called a Field Programmable Gate Array (FPGA) could utilize the physical properties of the chip to solve computational problems [85]." —(Miller et al., 2014)

An overview of the processes involved are shown in figure 3.1. There are three domains: the computer domain, which manages the evolutionary search; the data acquisition domain, which manages the I/O between the configurable material and the computer; and the physical domain, which generates the solution. The search commences in the lower box in the 'computer domain', by generating a set of genotypes to be evaluated. Each genotype specifies both the physical configuration of the substrate, and the input data for the computation that is presented to it. This gives maximum flexibility for searching the space of possible computations that can be performed on the input data. For each genotype, the material is reconfigured and the inputs are then processed and fed into the physical domain in which the substrate resides. The substrate is configured and processes the input data, and then produces out-

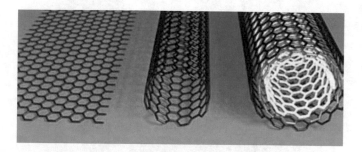

Fig. 3.2 Carbon nanotubes constructed from graphene sheets (Graham et al., 2005, Fig.1)

puts. The outputs are processed in the data acquisition domain and then used in a fitness evaluation of the genotype that specified the configuration.

The striking feature of this process is that there is a minimal requirement to understand the means by which the configurable material computes on the input data. Indeed, all that one needs to know about the material doing the computation that it is possible to configure it using a subset of the input channels. The inputs are usually electrical due to the fact that it is then straightforward to link the inputs to the genotype that is held on the classical computer, making the process much faster.

3.1.2 Carbon nanotubes

Carbon nanotubes are an integral part of the push towards further miniaturisation in classical semiconductor devices (ITRS, 2013).

"Carbon nanotubes (CNTs) were discovered by Iijima in 1991 while investigating the soot of an arc-discharge experiment used to create C 60 buckyballs [2]. From transmission electron microscope (TEM) images of periodic structures in the soot he speculated that concentric, graphene-based tubes had formed in the discharge zone. The basic forms of single-walled and multi-walled CNTs are shown in [Fig. 3.2 here] together with a planar graphene sheet. One year later Hamada et al. suggested that these tubes could be metallic or semiconducting from tight binding calculations [3]. In the same year Ebbesen and coworkers presented an optimization of the arc-discharge method that yielded large quantities of CNTs [4]. Despite this initial success, it took a further four years to purify the arc-discharge material sufficiently to enable devices to be created, starting with the first measurement by Ebbesen et al. on the resistance of multi-walled carbon nanotubes [5]. Two years later the first transistor was made [6] and ballistic transport in multi-walled CNTs was established [7]." —(Graham et al., 2005)

"The creation of a complete, functioning microelectronic system using only self-assembly and other nanotechnology methods is an enormous task requiring many

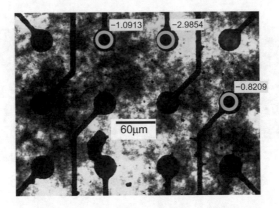

Fig. 3.3 Configurable carbon nanotube substrate embedded next to copper electrodes (Clegg et al., 2014b, Fig.2a)

different components to work together. Several important building blocks in this process have already been demonstrated, for instance selective bonding using DNA [8], but the ability to produce complex structures reliably seems a long way off. In particular, for microelectronics, it is important to reproduce the same device millions of times over almost flawlessly. For this reason a number of groups [. . .] are focusing on the selective integration of specific bottom up components into traditional top down microelectronics process flows to create hybrid systems with superior properties." —(Graham et al., 2005)

"Using carbon nanotubes as macromolecular electrodes and aluminum oxide as interlayer, isolated, non-volatile, rewriteable memory cells with an active area of   36 nm2 have been achieved, requiring a switching power less than 100 nW, with estimated switching energies below 10 fJ per bit [35]." —(Graham et al., 2005)

A key area of research in this domain is the challenge of reliability of the devices that are produced. Note however that the precision of devices is only applicable in CCOMP applications, and the UCOMP approach of *in materio* computation described in the previous section may provide an alternative route to exploiting these devices.

In (Clegg et al., 2014b), Clegg and Miller used a carbon nanotube assembly (Fig. 3.3) to solve simple instances of the Travelling Salesman Problem (TSP):

"Here one wishes to find the minimum length tour that visits a collection of cities. A solution can be represented by a permutation of the cities. Such a problem is easily mapped onto an electrode array. In this case there are no input electrodes, only output and configuration electrodes. One allocates as many output electrodes as there are cities. The objective is to obtain a set of output voltages which can be mapped into a permutation of cities." —(Clegg et al., 2014b).

In short, each electrode represents a city in the TSP, and the ranked set of voltages at each electrode describes the best tour that the salesman should take. Initially, the voltage-ranking is random, but through evolution, the voltages at the configuration electrodes affect the voltages at the output electrodes such that the correct solution emerges.

This methodology highlights some of the issues with this approach:

- It may be difficult and time-consuming to configure the device. The key design challenge of this approach is to find a convenient way of influencing the way the device processes the inputs.
- The device may not operate independently of its environment
- The substrate may have unwanted 'memory' of earlier events, which could influence the output of the current computation.
- Each implementation is a "one shot" solution: an evolved configuration on one device is not guaranteed to work on another.
- the result is merely a look-up table (although more sophisticated computations are in the pipeline).

However, the potential advantages should not be ignored (Miller et al., 2014):

- The response of the physical system does not have to be understood in depth.
- Unknown physical effects can be exploited, which may lead to new devices
- A solution can be found without any programming or design constraints, or limitations on human imagination and knowledge about the substrate.
- The substrate's computational capacity can potentially be exploited to the full.
- The amount of computation a small piece of material can do may be enormous.

3.2 Contribution to UCOMP aspects

3.2.1 Speed

In the TSP application (Clegg et al., 2014b), *measuring* the chip's output may be relatively slow, but the actual processing rate of a trained chip is nanoseconds, due to the massive parallelism inherent in the substrate. This means that the approach would be good for complex recognition tasks as part of a robot architecture for example.

The speed of configuring the device may seem slow, since one has wait until the evolutionary algorithm converges to a solution. However, in a strict sense, this comparison should be made with the time it takes a human programmer to write a program to run on a classical computer (repeatability notwithstanding).

3.2.2 Resources

Although the CN chip is a low-voltage device, further research is needed to discover the limit on how low a voltage would be needed to make the system operate reliably.

Embedding CNs in liquid crystal is an approach that might yield further efficiencies in this area. The nanotubes move in the liquid crystal according to the voltages on the configuration electrodes. If the configured arrangement could subsequently be 'fixed', then the circuit would work with virtually no power at all. This approach also has the potential to make the CN assemblage easier to program for more complex tasks.

3.2.3 Quality

Considered independently of the programming criteria, these devices are potentially unbounded in their ability to carry out non-conventional computation.

> "A strong theme in evolution-in-materio is the evolution of novel forms of computation. It appears to be a methodology that has promise in building new kinds of analogue computing devices. Evolution is used as the programming methodology. If unknown physical properties and interactions are to be utilized in a computer program, it is obvious that the the program cannot be designed in advance. An evolutionary algorithm together with a fitness function rewards those configurations of the system that provide the desired computational response. To some extent, we can see the program itself as 'emergent', since it is not known in advance and emerges during the evolutionary process."(Miller et al., 2014)

3.2.4 Embeddedness

Although the computational function of the substrate is non-classical, we can not currently embed the system in a native environment due to the requirement for electrical configuration signals to "program" the device. If it were possible to "fix" the program, such is in the liquid crystal approach discussed in the Resources aspect above, it may become possible to embed the computational material in a variety of devices that use carbon nanotubes.

3.2.5 Formalism

There is at present no formalism for the *in materio* approach other than the use of search algorithms for programming. The best match is Shannon's work on analogue computing. However, some of the pioneering work in the 50s etc. is not written up well. A lot of 'human in the loop' practises went on whilst training the systems. (See also work by John Mills/Lee Reubel in Indiana.)

3.2.6 Programming

Any stochastic search algorithm can be used to train *in materio*. This is because we don't know what the computational elements are. The process is analogous to training a neural network, with lots of back-propagation.

In terms of scalability, it may be possible to connect a number of slides together in a neural network like arrangement, using each CN chip as a hardware component. By this method, it may be possible to get some degree of programmability at a higher level.

> "We tentatively suggest that it will not be possible to construct computational systems of equivalent power to living organisms using conventional methods that employ purely symbolic methods. We argue that it will be advantageous for complex software systems of the future to utilize physical effects and use some form of search process akin to natural evolution." —(Miller et al., 2014)

> "According to Conrad this process leads us to pay 'The Price of Programmability' [21], whereby in conventional programming and design we proceed by excluding many of the processes that may lead to us solving the problem at hand. Indeed as Zauner notes, programmability is not a strict requirement for information processing systems since the enviable computing capabilities of cells and organisms are not implemented by programs. Artificial neural networks are also not programmable in the normal sense [103]." —(Miller et al., 2014)

3.2.7 Applications

In addition to the travelling salesman problem outlined above, *In materio* computation with carbon nanotubes has been used to develop solutions to function optimisation (Mohid et al., 2014b), machine learning (Mohid et al., 2014d), bin packing (Mohid et al., 2014c) and frequency classification (Mohid et al., 2014a).

At present it remains unclear what the best potential applications of this technology could be. It is anticipated that this should be revisited when some of the recommendations are implemented and challenges overcome.

3.2.8 Philosophy

Conrad criticizes traditional models of computing and he identifies that they
have a common feature: at most very limited context dependency (Conrad,
1999). The logic gates in conventional machines implement formally defined
input-output behaviours that are independent of the overall design of the
circuit. Turing machines read and write symbols on individual tape squares
in a manner that does not depend on the arrangement of symbols on the
tape. Whereas computation in physical systems (particularly biological) are
almost always context dependent.

3.3 Main achievements so far

As detailed above, the potential for carbon nanotubes as a computational substrate is promising, but constrained by the difficulties in producing complex
structures reliably. By using *in materio* computation methods, researchers are
able to use the material in configurations that can currently be manufactured
relatively cheaply. In summary:

- The core methodology has been proven
- Working hardware has been designed and engineered
- 'Software' (Implementation of TSP) has been tested and proven

3.4 What could be achieved in ten years?

Research in this area is focussed on demonstrating that devices can be programmed to solve complex problems faster – it is thought that this is reasonably feasible to do.

One way to prove this is to solve well known NP-hard problems. These
solutions would act as a benchmark for the process and allow comparison with
conventional CCOMP solutions. However, the focus on established CCOMP
test problems merely explores solutions to problems that are well-known to
be solvable by CCOMP devices. This is not necessarily the best application
for CN chips, but perhaps gives the clearest demonstration of their potential.

An alternative goal would be to do the same thing as Shaw's factorisation
of numbers on a quantum computer. The same potential exists here, but
is achieved via exploiting the massive parallelism of the CN chip. It must
be borne in mind that the 'true' application may be elsewhere – biological
emulation perhaps (due to similarities in the parallelism between biological
systems and the methodology described here).

There is also potential to apply the techniques in other areas. For example the evolution *in materio* principle could be used to evolve bacterial colonies sitting in meshed combs of electrodes. Thus we could develop interfacing methods in biology.

3.5 Current challenges

3.5.1 Substrate

It has been difficult to get a large number of electrodes in one nanotube array. The Norwegian team in the NASCENCE consortium are working on this. it might be possible to buy electrode arrays rather than manufacture them, but it is unclear what the best method is for putting nanotube material onto the chip. A significant investment needed to achieve this, but this is unlikely to be secured without a demonstration of the potential first. Unfortunately, it might not be possible to demonstrate the potential without a large electrode array. A method needs to be found to balance this risk.

Another problem is the sheer range of potential *in materio* devices: what materials should we try? What concentration? What insulator? Without knowledge of the properties and with a richer model of *in materio* computation, we are conducting a blind search of the material space.

"Harding et al. found that it was relatively easy to evolve a tone discriminator in liquid crystal, much easier than Thompson found it to be in silicon. Conceptually, we can understand this since most physical systems are likely to be endowed with many exploitable properties. We refer to this as *richness*. Silicon based electronic circuits have had the physics constrained as much as possible to implement Boolean logic and thus allow Turing computation. One way of possibly testing the relationship with richness and evolvability would be to attempt to evolve solutions to computational problems on a variety of FPGAs (say) with varying degrees of damage (perhaps by irradiating them). Experiments with radiation damaged FPTAs showed that evolutionary algorithms could make use of damaged parts of the chip [...]. It remains to be seen if such damage actually helps solve certain computational problems" — (Miller et al., 2014)

Maybe we should try to understand the simplest possible implementation of an *in materio* system, and use this to guide the choice of further systems that use those principles. There remains the possibility that *in materio* computing might 'invent' a new technology by guiding a search of the possible physical arrangement of substrate.

3.5.2 *Environmental effects, and the coherence problem*

"Ideally, the material would be able to be reset before the application of new configuration instructions. This is important as without the ability to reset the material it may retain a memory from past configurations, this could lead to the same configuration having different fitness values depending on the history of interactions with the material. " —(Miller et al., 2014)

3.6 Outlook and recommendations

"One of the difficulties of analogue computers was that they had to be set up by experts who could create analogues of specific systems in convenient physical devices. Using a search process running on a modern digital computer gives us a new way to "program" a physical device. It also gives us a methodology for the discovery of new computational devices that use physical effects for computation in ways that human ingenuity has thus far failed to invent. " —(Miller et al., 2014)

References

Clegg, K. D., J. F. Miller, K. M. Massey, and M. C. Petty (2014a). "Practical issues for configuring carbon nanotube composite materials for computation". *ICES 2014, International Conference on Evolvable Systems: From Biology to Hardware*. IEEE, pp. 61–68.

Clegg, K. D., J. F. Miller, K. Massey, and M. Petty (2014b). "Travelling Salesman Problem Solved *'in materio'* by Evolved Carbon Nanotube Device". *PPSN XIII, Parallel Problem Solving from Nature*. Vol. 8672. LNCS. Springer, pp. 692–701.

Conrad, M. (1999). "Molecular and evolutionary computation: the tug of war between context freedom and context sensitivity." *Biosystems* 52(1-3):99–110.

Graham, A.P., G.S. Duesberg, W. Hoenlein, F. Kreupl, M. Liebau, R. Martin, B. Rajasekharan, W. Pamler, R. Seidel, W. Steinhoegl, and E. Unger (2005). "How do carbon nanotubes fit into the semiconductor roadmap?" *Applied Physics A* 80(6):1141–1151.

ITRS (2013). *International Technology Roadmap for Semiconductors, 2013 edition,Emerging Research Devices*. www.itrs.net/reports.html.

Landauer, R. (1996). "The physical nature of information". *Phys. Lett. A* 217 :188–193.

Miller, J. F., S. L. Harding, and G. Tufte (2014). "Evolution-in-materio: evolving computation in materials". *Evolutionary Intelligence* 7:49–67.

Mohid, M., J. F. Miller, S. L. Harding, G. Tufte, O. R. Lykkebø, K. M. Massey, and M. C. Petty (2014a). "Evolution-In-Materio: A Frequency Classifier Using Materials". *Proceedings of the 2014 IEEE International Conference on Evolvable Systems (ICES): From Biology to Hardware.* IEEE Press, pp. 46–53.

Mohid, M., J. F. Miller, S. L. Harding, G. Tufte, O. R. Lykkebø, M. K. Massey, and M. C. Petty (2014b). "Evolution-in-materio: Solving function optimization problems using materials". *14th UK Workshop on Computational Intelligence (UKCI).* IEEE Press, pp. 1–8.

Mohid, M., J. F. Miller, S.L Harding, G. Tufte, O. R. Lykkebø, K. M. Massey, and M. C. Petty (2014c). "Evolution-In-Materio: Solving Bin Packing Problems Using Materials". *Proceedings of the 2014 IEEE International Conference on Evolvable Systems (ICES): From Biology to Hardware.* IEEE Press, pp. 38–45.

Mohid, Maktuba, Julian F. Miller, Simon L. Harding, Gunnar Tufte, Odd Rune Lykkebø, Mark K. Massey, and Michael C. Petty (2014d). "Evolution-In-Materio: Solving Machine Learning Classification Problems Using Materials". *PPSN XIII, Parallel Problem Solving from Nature.* Vol. 8672. LNCS. Springer, pp. 721–730.

Chapter 4
Computing by Non-linear Optical Molecular Response

Barbara Fresch, Tian-Min Yan, Dawit Hiluf, Elisabetta Collini,
Raphael D. Levine, and Françoise Remacle

Abstract Non-linear optical spectroscopies probe the dynamics of optically
active molecular systems interacting with a sequence of laser pulses. By encoding logical inputs into the allowed optical transitions, quantum dynamics
of populations and coherences implement logic processing in parallel and a
macroscopically readable output is obtained from the spectroscopic response.
The resulting hardware-based logic improves the potentialities of molecular
sized devices for computing applications. We introduce the basic concepts of
this molecular computing scheme and discuss its strengths and drawbacks
with respect to several performance indicators.

4.1 Introduction

Molecules are characterized by states of different nature (conformational,
vibrational, electronic to mention some) and a rich dynamics in response
to external stimuli. In addition, their sub-nanometer scale and the ability
to control molecular dynamics through chemical and spectroscopic means
makes molecules one of the most promising unconventional substrates for the
physical implementation of both conventional and unconventional paradigms
of computation.

This case study introduces and discusses the computational capabilities
of the molecular response to several weak laser pulses in the UV to visible
range. The logic that is implemented is classical, referring to the formalism
of Boolean algebra and its multivalued generalization. The power and the
unconventional character of the approach lie in the intrinsic parallelism that
characterizes the logic processing, stemming from the time evolution of the
molecular states and from the spatial decomposition of the signal emitted
by a macroscopic sample. Moreover, memory is naturally embedded in the

S. Stepney et al. (eds.), *Computational Matter*, Natural Computing Series,
https://doi.org/10.1007/978-3-319-65826-1_4

physical evolution of the molecular system enabling the implementation of finite state logic.

4.2 Overview

4.2.1 Non-linear optical molecular response

Non-linear optical spectroscopies use multiple ultrashort laser pulses to induce transitions between electronic excited states of molecules. In quantum mechanics, the state of the system and its time evolution triggered by the interactions with the laser fields are described by the density matrix, $\rho(t)$. This means that we do not describe only the populations of the accessible energy levels but also coherences between them. For a system with N energy levels involved in the dynamics, the density matrix has N^2 entries: diagonal elements are real, normalized and represent populations while the complex off-diagonal elements represent the coherences. A remarkable advantage of this representation is the quadratic scaling of the physical observables (and thus of the potential logical outputs) with the number of energy levels involved in the dynamics (Alhassid and Levine, 1978; Fresch et al., 2013). Figure 4.1a reports the experimental scheme used in Two-Dimensional Photon Echo Spectroscopy (Collini, 2013) (2D-PE) where three laser pulses are focused on a macroscopic sample of chromophores (=strongly light absorbing molecules) in solution. The three wave vectors of the laser pulses exciting the sample at times τ_1, τ_2, and τ_3 are denoted as $\mathbf{k}_1$, $\mathbf{k}_2$, and $\mathbf{k}_3$, respectively. At the microscopic level, each molecule develops a time dependent polarisation and emits a signal. Because of interference effects between the emitted signals, the macroscopic polarization is spatially resolved along a finite number of the so called "phase matching directions" given as linear combination of the wave vectors of the incoming lasers, $\mathbf{k}_l = \sum_{i=1}^{3} l_i \mathbf{k}_i$ where $\{l_i\}$ is a set of integers.

The photon-echo (PE) signal can be measured after the third laser–matter interaction as the molecular response in the particular phase-matching direction $\mathbf{k}_{PE} = -\mathbf{k}_1 + \mathbf{k}_2 + \mathbf{k}_3$ (i.e. $l = (-1, +1, +1)$), that is shown in Figure 4.1a. The photon echo depends on the three positive delay times between successive laser pulses: the coherence time, $\tau = \tau_2 - \tau_1$, the population time, $T = \tau_3 - \tau_2$, and the detection time, t. The 2D-PE spectrum is obtained as the double Fourier transform (FT) of the PE signal with respect to the coherence time ($\tau \to \omega_1$) and the detection time ($t \to \omega_2$). The 2D spectrum resolves the dynamics of the system along the excitation (ω_1) and the emission (ω_2) frequencies for each population time T. In Figure 4.1b we show an example of 2D spectra (absolute value) calculated for a molecular dimer: typically, diagonal ($\omega_1 = \omega_2$) and off-diagonal ($\omega_1 \neq \omega_2$) features are analysed and con-

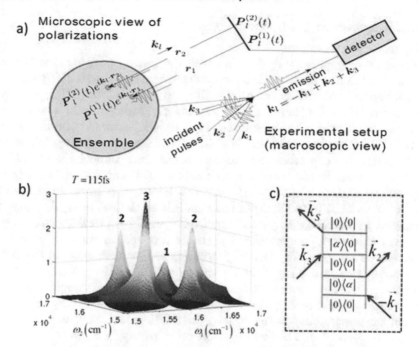

Fig. 4.1 a) schematic representation of the set-up for 2D photon echo spectroscopy; b) simulated absolute value spectrum of a molecular dimer; c) the Feynman diagram representing one of the process contributing to the third-order optical signal

nected to the system dynamics (Cho et al., 2005; Collini, 2013). To facilitate the analysis, the non-linear optical response along a particular direction can be decomposed in several contributions, each reflecting a possible sequences of laser induced transitions during the experiment. Each interaction with the laser field couples different elements of the density matrix according to the transition dipole of the molecular system, the history of the evolution of the state of the system during the whole experiment can be expressed through a set of possible paths, known in the spectroscopic community as "Feynman paths". Figure 4.1b shows one example of such a path, it represents the system starting in its ground state, $|0\rangle\langle 0|$, being excited in the coherence $|0\rangle\langle\alpha|$ by the first laser pulse, going back to the ground state under the action of the second pulse, and finally excited again in the $|\alpha\rangle\langle 0|$ by the third pulses. This path contributes to the signal in the diagonal position ($\omega_1 = \omega_\alpha, \omega_2 = \omega_\alpha$) since the coherences and both oscillate at the frequency ω_α.

4.2.2 Logic implementations

In a series of papers we discuss in detail the logic processing that is implemented in the non-linear optical response of a molecular system (Fresch et al., 2015; Fresch et al., 2013; Yan et al., 2015). In Fresch et al. (2013) we demonstrate that the evolution of the density matrix during the three weak lasers optical measurement implements the logic data structure known as "decision tree" (DT) (Falkowski and Stankovic, 2000) at the molecular level. The main idea is that we can trace the different paths that connect the initial state of the molecule to the spectroscopic readout. This enables us to relate each dynamical path to a path down a decision tree and, because more than one path connect the initial state of the molecule to the readouts, the computations are implemented in parallel. In the language of optical spectroscopy we can say that each computational path corresponds uniquely to a Feynman diagram as discussed for 2D-PE spectroscopy. All the branches of the DT are computed simultaneously since all the dynamical paths represented by the Feynman diagrams occur simultaneously in the molecular sample. The implementation of the molecular DT requires the capability of storing information about the previous inputs to correctly deduce the function value once the last input has been read. The history of the previous inputs is "imprinted" in the time evolution of the physical system. In the logic domain, the presence of a memory element is characteristic of a sequential logic circuit, whose output depends not only on the present inputs but also on the state (memory) of the machine. The molecular tree can thus be viewed as a logic machine that accepts several inputs and processes them by performing bilinear operations that are dependent on the input and on the state of the machine, as discussed in Fresch et al. (2013). The number of logical variables in a DT implemented by non-linear optical response corresponds to the number of light-matter interactions. Third order response implements a three level DT, increasing the number of pulses would increase the number of level of the DT (the so-called depth of the DT). The number of transitions simultaneously excited by the laser pulse defines the number of outgoing edges for each node of the tree (the so-called width of the DT). In other words, the number of different transitions triggered by each interaction with the external field defines the set of logical values that each variable can assume (i.e. the radix of the logic), so that the binary implementation presented in Fresch et al. (2013) can be easily generalized to multivalued logic.

The parallel implementation of a decision tree reflects the parallelism inherent in the time evolution of the different elements of the density matrix and it is realized in the signal emitted in each phase-matching direction. The spatial decomposition of the full polarization into directional components offers a further level of parallelisation provided that the signal can be simultaneously detected in different spatial positions (Yan et al., 2015).

4.3 Contribution to UCOMP aspects

4.3.1 Speed

In the implementations of computation by the non-linear optical response the inputs are given by the incoming laser fields. Light can be switched on or off much faster than an electrical voltage can. It takes roughly a nanosecond to switch an electrical signal and this is what determines the clock speed of modern computers. Light can be switched on or off up to a million times more quickly. The information processing by the system dynamics is in the femtosecond time-scale and massively parallel, so optical-based computing has great potentialities in terms of speed. In the case of non-linear optical response the processing of the spectroscopic signal is still a slow process but it can be made faster by the creation of dedicated optically active molecular units properly tested and calibrated for a precise logic implementation.

4.3.2 Resources

Currently the non-linear optical molecular response is studied by exciting the sample with high quality laser sources, which are both expensive and power consuming. We predict a big potential increase in future resources due to the possibility of triggering the molecular response with incoherent light sources such as the natural sunlight. Coherent two-dimensional electronic spectra measured using incoherent light have been experimentally obtained recently (Turner et al., 2013a). The spectra of model molecular systems using broadband spectrally incoherent light are similar but not identical to those expected from measurements using femtosecond pulses (Turner et al., 2013b). These developments suggest that a consistent gain in term of resources in likely to be realized in the future but further experimental and theoretical investigations are needed to fully exploit this possibility.

4.3.3 Quality

By computing with non-linear optical molecular response, the logic process-ing is implemented by the dynamical evolution of the system. This offers a qualitatively different approach to computation, in particular:

- inherent parallel processing
- embedded memory
- continuous time evolution, continuous signal
- multiscale in time and in space

In the implementations we discuss in Sect. 4.2.2 we take advantage of some of these aspects but we still refer to the framework of classical conventional logic for the interpretation of the input/output relation. Future implementations may depart from the conventional logic encoding.

4.3.4 Embeddedness

This aspect does not score high in optically-based computing. The output of massive parallel computations can be read at once but cascading the optical signal from one molecular unit to the next one intermolecularly is a problem that does not have a short-term solution. Cascading the signal intramolecularly is feasible and we are currently working on such implementations. This approach reduces the need for I/O and signal losses. Nonetheless, optical signal can well be the final output in imaging or sensing applications.

4.3.5 Formalism

In terms of formalism we bring together the theory of non-linear optical spectroscopy, including the ability of numerically simulating the output of the experiments, a Lie algebraic approach to analyse the quantum dynamics and notion from conventional logic like the decision tree and the decomposition of multivalued functions. Such a synergism between different theoretical frameworks constitutes the formalism underlying the approach of computing by non-linear optical molecular response.

4.3.6 Programming

The programming here consists in the rational design of the molecular optical properties together with the control of the light source set-up. The spectroscopic properties of a large array of organic dyes are already well-characterized and recent development on programmed self-assembly of nucleic acids offers the ability to scaffold secondary chromophore molecules at given locations (Teo and Kool, 2012), toward the realization of devices acting as light-harvesting antennas (Woller et al., 2013) or wires with custom optical properties (Dutta et al., 2011; Hannestad et al., 2008; Stein et al., 2011). The ability to incorporate not only standard organic dyes into these structures, but also fluorescent nanoparticles, is expected to enhance their energy transfer (ET) capabilities, especially within the context of multistep FRET (Foster Resonant Energy Transfer) cascades (Spillmann et al., 2013).

Important progresses in this area are expected in the near future thanks to fast developments in nanotechnologies. Moreover, it is natural to change the properties of the light sources (wavelength, polarization, etc...) as a mean of programming the logic unit.

4.3.7 Applications

Ultrafast and massively parallel logic processing, imaging and sensing. Since many molecular substrates are biologically compatible it is realistic to envisage possible future *in vivo* applications.

4.3.8 Philosophy

Computing by non-linear optical molecular response founds its conceptual foundation in the knowledge of molecular systems. It starts from the idea that such a substrate has more natural way of responding to external stimuli than acting as an on/off switching in analogy with conventional transistors. The resulting concept is a hardware-based logic that aims to fully exploit the potentialities of molecular devices.

4.4 Main achievements so far

The core methodology of computing in parallel by non-linear optical molecular response has been proven theoretically (Fresch et al., 2013; Yan et al., 2015) and a first experimental test has been successfully conducted by probing the third order laser-induced dynamics of populations and coherences in a Rhodamine dye mounted on a short DNA duplex (Fresch et al., 2015). Experimental measurements on multi-chromophoric system are currently performed for the 2D-PE configuration. Higher order spectroscopies (fifth order) has been also demonstrated (Zhang et al., 2013).

4.5 What could be achieved in ten years

At the experimental level, the third order response along two phase matching directions is currently measured (i.e. rephasing and non-rephasing signals). New instrumental set-up will be designed to fully exploit the parallelism stemming from the spatial decomposition of the molecular polarization (Yan et al., 2015). Research on specific logic implementations by non-linear response has been so far at the level of proof of concept. In the future such developments will acquire a more systematic character and a library of molecular units designed for specific logic purposes might be created. At the same time new logic implementations will be devised probably involving the coupling between electronic and vibrational molecular states.

4.6 Current challenges

Current technological challenges include the design of molecular units with targeted non-linear optical properties and the development of cheap and efficient and fast methodologies to detect and resolve the emitted signal in multiple spatial directions. At the conceptual level, the challenge of developing a framework to handle and turn at advantage the continuous nature of the output signal has to be faced.

References

Alhassid, Y. and R. Levine (1978). "Connection Between the Maximal Entropy and the Scattering Theoretic Analyses of Collision Processes". *Physical Review A* 18(1):89–116.

Cho, Minhaeng, Harsha M. Vaswani, Tobias Brixner, Jens Stenger, and Graham R. Fleming (2005). "Exciton Analysis in 2D Electronic Spectroscopy". *The Journal of Physical Chemistry B* 109(21):10542–10556.

Collini, Elisabetta (2013). "Spectroscopic Signatures of Quantum-Coherent Energy Transfer". *Chemical Society Reviews* 42(12):4932–4947.

Dutta, Palash K., Reji Varghese, Jeanette Nangreave, Su Lin, Hao Yan, and Yan Liu (2011). "DNA-Directed Artificial Light-Harvesting Antenna". *JACS* 133(31):11985–11993.

Falkowski, Bogdan J. and Radomir S. Stankovic (2000). "Spectral Interpretation and Applications of Decision Diagrams". *VLSI Design* 11(2):85–105.

Fresch, Barbara, Marco Cipolloni, Tian-Min Yan, Elisabetta Collini, R. D. Levine, and F. Remacle (2015). "Parallel and Multivalued Logic by the Two-Dimensional Photon-Echo Response of a Rhodamine–DNA Complex". *The Journal of Physical Chemistry Letters* 6(9):1714–1718.

Fresch, Barbara, Dawit Hiluf, Elisabetta Collini, R. D. Levine, and F. Remacle (2013). "Molecular Decision Trees Realized by Ultrafast Electronic Spectroscopy". *PNAS* 110(43):17183–17188.

Hannestad, Jonas K., Peter Sandin, and Bo Albinsson (2008). "Self-Assembled DNA Photonic Wire for Long-Range Energy Transfer". *JACS* 130(47):15889–15895.

Spillmann, Christopher M., Mario G. Ancona, Susan Buckhout-White, W. Russ Algar, Michael H. Stewart, Kimihiro Susumu, Alan L. Huston, Ellen R. Goldman, and Igor L. Medintz (2013). "Achieving Effective Terminal Exciton Delivery in Quantum Dot Antenna-Sensitized Multistep DNA Photonic Wires". *ACS Nano* 7(8):7101–7118.

Stein, Ingo H., Christian Steinhauer, and Philip Tinnefeld (2011). "Single-Molecule Four-Color FRET Visualizes Energy-Transfer Paths on DNA Origami". *JACS* 133(12):4193–4195.

Teo, Yin Nah and Eric T. Kool (2012). "DNA-Multichromophore Systems". *Chemical Reviews* 112(7):4221–4245.

Turner, Daniel B., Paul C. Arpin, Scott D. McClure, Darin J. Ulness, and Gregory D. Scholes (2013a). "Coherent multidimensional optical spectra measured using incoherent light". *Nat Commun* 4:2298.

Turner, Daniel B., Dylan J. Howey, Erika J. Sutor, Rebecca A. Hendrickson, M. W. Gealy, and Darin J. Ulness (2013b). "Two-Dimensional Electronic Spectroscopy Using Incoherent Light: Theoretical Analysis". *The Journal of Physical Chemistry A* 117(29):5926–5954.

Woller, Jakob G., Jonas K. Hannestad, and Bo Albinsson (2013). "Self-Assembled Nanoscale DNA–Porphyrin Complex for Artificial Light Harvesting". *JACS* 135(7):2759–2768.

Yan, Tian-Min, Barbara Fresch, R. D. Levine, and F. Remacle (2015). "Information processing in parallel through directionally resolved molecular polarization components in coherent multidimensional spectroscopy". *The Journal of Chemical Physics* 143:064106.

Zhang, Zhengyang, Kym L. Wells, Marco T. Seidel, and Howe-Siang Tan (2013). "Fifth-Order Three-Dimensional Electronic Spectroscopy Using a Pump–Probe Configuration". *The Journal of Physical Chemistry B* 117(49):15369–15385.

Chapter 5
Bioinspired Computing with Synaptic Elements

Göran Wendin

Abstract Unconventional computing (UCOMP) paradigms have been suggested to address and overcome a range of limitations of ordinary digital classical computers. In this case study we describe efforts to use nanoscale switching networks for digital and analogue/neuromorphic computing, with emphasis on synaptic networks based on various kinds of memristors.

5.1 Overview

On the road toward exa- and zettascale high-performance computing (HPC), unconventional computing (UCOMP) paradigms have been suggested to address and overcome a range of digital computing limitations. The European Commission (2009) consultation report states:

> Conventional digital Turing computation has been incredibly successful, but it encompasses only a small subset of all computational possibilities. Unconventional approaches to computation are currently less developed, but promise equally revolutionary results as they mature. Unconventional computing is a broad domain, covering hypercomputation, quantum computing, optical computing, analogue computing, chemical computing, reaction-diffusion systems, molecular computing, biocomputing, embodied computing, Avogadro-scale and amorphous computing, self-assembling and self-organising computers, unconventional applications, and more.

There are several reasons why unconventional paradigms are needed, e.g., to investigate and road-map opportunities for non-von Neumann computational paradigms, by designing application specific devices, or to perform embedded computation in situations where large-scale CMOS solutions cannot be used. Since the 1980s, analogue VLSI for neural systems (Mead, 1989) has been at the focus of brain-inspired analogue neuromorphic approaches to computing, optimisation and control. This has inspired UCOMP visions about using top-down fabricated or self-organised networks of nanoscale com-

© Springer International Publishing AG, part of Springer Nature 2018
S. Stepney et al. (eds.), *Computational Matter*, Natural Computing Series,
https://doi.org/10.1007/978-3-319-65826-1_5

ponents to mimic neural networks. The idea is that robust neuromorphic networks can be built from nanoscale components with highly variable properties.

In this case study we focus on this particular UCOMP area and describe efforts to use nanoscale switching networks for digital and analogue/neuromorphic computing, with emphasis on synaptic networks based on various kinds of memristors (Demming et al., 2013; Kuzum et al., 2013; Saïghi et al., 2015).

5.2 Information processing with memristor networks

The memristor (memory resistor) was invented by Chua in 1971 (Chua, 1971; Chua and Kang, 1976) and has recently been extensively investigated and exploited both experimentally and theoretically in applications for information processing[1].

The characteristic property of the memristor is that the resistance depends on a time-dependent state variable $x(t)$ and may itself be explicitly time dependent, $R(x, V, t)$, resistance changes being controlled/switched e.g. by voltages that exceed certain thresholds. This type of non-linear resistor actually already has a long history (Waser and Aono, 2007), but the recent interest in the useful memristor functionality has lead to an explosive development of memristor components; see e.g. Saïghi et al. (2015), Thomas (2013), Wikipedia (2016), and Yang et al. (2013) for overviews.

Quoting Saïghi et al. (2015):

Memristive devices present a new device technology allowing for the realization of compact non-volatile memories. Some of them are already in the process of industrialization. Additionally, they exhibit complex multilevel and plastic behaviors, which make them good candidates for the implementation of artificial synapses in neuromorphic engineering. However, memristive effects rely on diverse physical mecha-

---

[1] See Adam et al. (2016), Alibart et al. (2012a), Alibart et al. (2012b), Alibart et al. (2010), Alibart et al. (2013), Bichler et al. (2012), Bichler et al. (2013), Borghetti et al. (2010), Chang et al. (2011), DeSalvo et al. (2015a), DeSalvo et al. (2015b), Di Ventra and Pershin (2012), Garbin et al. (2015a), Garbin et al. (2015b), Georgiou et al. (2012), Gubicza et al. (2016), Guo et al. (2015), Hashem and Das (2012), Jo et al. (2010), Kataeva et al. (2015), Kim et al. (2016), Kim et al. (2012), Kumar et al. (2016), Lau et al. (2004), Medeiros-Ribeiro et al. (2011), Merrikh-Bayat et al. (2015), Nili et al. (2015), Oblea et al. (2010), Oskoee and Sahimi (2011), Pershin and Di Ventra (2010), Pershin and Di Ventra (2011), Pershin and Di Ventra (2012), Pickett et al. (2013), Prezioso et al. (2015a), Prezioso et al. (2016a), Prezioso et al. (2015b), Prezioso et al. (2016b), Prezioso et al. (2016c), Raghuvanshi and Perkowski (2014), Saïghi et al. (2015), Snider (2005), Stewart et al. (2004), Strachan et al. (2013), Strukov and Likharev (2007), Strukov et al. (2013), Strukov et al. (2008), Strukov and Williams (2009), Thomas (2013), Torrezan et al. (2011), Türel et al. (2004), Valov et al. (2011), Wang et al. (2017), Waser and Aono (2007), Wedig et al. (2016), Xia et al. (2009), Xu et al. (2016a), Xu et al. (2016b), Yakopcic et al. (2013), Yang et al. (2008), Yang et al. (2013), and Yi et al. (2016)

nisms, and their plastic behaviors differ strongly from one technology to another. ...they can be used to implement different learning rules whose properties emerge directly from device physics: real time or accelerated operation, deterministic or stochastic behavior, long term or short term plasticity. ...there is no unique way to exploit memristive devices in neuromorphic systems. Understanding and embracing device physics is the key for their optimal use

5.2.1 Stateful logic

The state of the memristor depends on its history, which can be used for implementation of Boolean conditional "stateful" logic (Adam et al., 2016; Borghetti et al., 2010; Raghuvanshi and Perkowski, 2014; Strukov et al., 2013), including reconfigurable logic (Huang et al., 2016; Mane et al., 2015; Rothenbuhler et al., 2013; Shin et al., 2011).

Adam et al. (2016) demonstrated experimentally a reliable multi-cycle multi-gate material implication logic operation and half-adder circuit within a three-dimensional stack of monolithically integrated memristors. Direct data manipulation in three dimensions enabled extremely compact and high-throughput logic-in-memory computing and, presenting a viable solution for the Feynman Grand Challenge of implementing an 8-bit adder at the nanoscale.

5.2.2 Neuromorphic networks

Memristors show properties similar to biological synapses, which means that they can be used for implementing and training neuromorphic networks (Alibart et al., 2012b; Alibart et al., 2013; Bichler et al., 2013; DeSalvo et al., 2015a; Garbin et al., 2015a; Garbin et al., 2015b; Pershin and Di Ventra, 2010; Pickett et al., 2013; Prezioso et al., 2015b; Saïghi et al., 2015). Combining CMOS and controllable two-terminal resistive memristors, the usual CMOS stack can be augmented with one or several crossbar layers, with memristors at each crosspoint (Prezioso et al., 2015b). The ambition is (Prezioso et al., 2015b) to provide comparable complexity to the human cortex while operating much faster and with manageable power dissipation, networks based on circuits

5.2.3 Spiking neuromorphic networks

The brain is working in a spiking mode, and the weight of the synapses is basically controlled via the relative timing of pre- and post-synaptic spikes, so called spike-time dependent plasticity (STDP); see e.g. Prezioso et al. (2016b) and Saïghi et al. (2015). The development of technologies for spiking neuromorphic networks is one of the main UCOMP HPC directions (Esser et al., 2016; Maass, 2016; Merolla et al., 2014).

5.2.4 Reservoir computing

An important recent UCOMP paradigm is reservoir computing (RC), involving dynamical complex systems based on recurrent neural networks (RNN) (involving feedback) of nonlinear nanoscale components (Appeltant et al., 2011; Büsing et al., 2010; Dale et al., 2017; Dambre et al., 2012; Hermans et al., 2015; Ju et al., 2013; Klampfl and Maass, 2010; Kudithipudi et al., 2016; Kulkarni and Teuscher, 2012; Larger et al., 2012; Lukosevicius and Jaeger, 2009; Maass, 2009; Manjunath and Jaeger, 2013; Merkel et al., 2014; Paquot et al., 2012). In usual neuromorphic paradigms, the network synaptic weights become adjusted and fixed as a result of a training/learning process. In reservoir computing (RC), however, one considers from the start a large synaptic network as a dynamic system in its own right, and only trains a relatively small synaptic readout layer. This has been suggested to be a model for how the brain may work (Yamazaki and Tanaka, 2007).

5.2.5 On the computational power of memristor-based synaptic networks

Computational complexity is defined in terms of different kinds of Turing machines (TM) providing digital models of computing. A universal TM can simulate any other TM (even quantum computers) and defines what is computable in principle, without caring about how long time it takes. Simply speaking, problems that can be solved by a deterministic TM (DTM) in polynomial time belong to class P, and are considered to be "easy", i.e. tractable. A DTM is a model for ordinary classical computers. A quantum TM, with a quantum processor and quantum tape (memory) is a model for a quantum computer. The class NP (non-deterministic polynomial) is defined by a non-deterministic TM (NTM) being able to provide an answer that can be verified by a DTM in polynomial time (but may take the DTM exponential time to compute from scratch). The NTM is not a real computer, but rather works as an oracle, providing an answer.

In the UCOMP literature, there are quite a few papers claiming to solve NP-hard problems by e.g. DNA-computing (Lipton, 1995), adaptive super-Turing procedures (Siegelmann, 1995) and, very recently, by memcomputing (Traversa and Di Ventra, 2017; Traversa et al., 2015). Most likely, however, fundamental principles of physics are such that no operationally meaningful systems can be constructed, even in principle: to efficiently solve NP-hard problems in time that grows polynomially with the input size will necessarily require exponential resources of other kinds (Aaronson, 2005; Aaronson, 2013). Nevertheless, not all instances of physical problems that belong to class NP are necessarily hard. That means that it is quite possible that computing in memory with synaptic networks might greatly speed up the time to solution compared to von Neumann type of digital HPC (Esser et al., 2016; Maass, 2016; Merolla et al., 2014), especially if one considers self-organised criticality in brain-like networks with ability for optimal information processing (Arcangelis and Herrmann, 2010; Kitzbichler et al., 2009; Levin et al., 2007; Nykter et al., 2008; Russo et al., 2014; Stepp et al., 2015; Stieg et al., 2012).

5.3 Contribution to UCOMP aspects

Computing with synaptic elements involves paradigms other than CCOMP. The performance of computation with UCOMP memristor-based devices involves a number of aspects: component switching speeds, hardware/architecture speed, programming and staging time, the time between input and output. In order to discuss performance, it is necessary to consider specific components, architectures and implementations. Here we discuss recent results pertaining to multi-level metal-oxide memristors with typical switching times in the nanosecond range. We consider (1) computing in memory with stateful logic, and (2) computing with spiking neuromorphic networks.

The analysis is formulated in terms of answers to a number of prompting question regarding: *Speed, Resource, Quality, Embeddedness, Programmability, Formalism, Applications, Philosophy.*

Speed: Including programming and staging time, how fast is the UCOMP considered? It should always be possible to measure the time between input and output (time-to-solution, TTS). This time should then be used as the basis of a comparison of the merits of the technique and a CCOMP equivalent.

Resource: How does the economic cost of the computational resource compare to the cost in CCOMP? Possible benchmarks are the economic cost of the resource, how easy it is to procure the resource, what the by-products are, and how easy is it to dispose of them. Another facet of the resource aspect concerns the scalability of the technology.

Quality: Does the UCOMP in question offer qualitatively different computation to CCOMP? Quality is concerned with the manner in which a computation is carried out: precision; fit to underlying model; richness; stochasticity; repeatability.

Embeddedness: Can the UCOMP in question be implemented within the process it is aimed at controlling/monitoring? This is related to issues of speed and resource in that the output may be useless unless it controls a system directly, rather than being abstractly read off and then fed into a system.

Programmability: How easy is it to write sophisticated programs in the computational substrate?

Formalism: Does the UCOMP research topic have a formalism that augments/extends CCOMP formalism? Formalisms allow us to understand in abstract terms the expressiveness of a system, its limitations, and its relation to other systems and CCOMP. Whilst an over-reaching formalism for UCOMP is desirable, it is equally desirable that UCOMP researches foster the development of formalisms for their own particular techniques.

Applications: Does the UCOMP research topic open up new applications?

Philosophy: Does the UCOMP research have a non-CCOMP philosophy? This aspect encapsulates the motivation for investigating UCOMP. A particular research area will work on extending the understanding of the field in general by reference to the philosophy of UCOMP.

5.3.1 Stateful logic

References to recent work: Adam et al. (2016), Borghetti et al. (2010), Huang et al. (2016), Mane et al. (2015), Rothenbuhler et al. (2013), Shin et al. (2011), and Strukov et al. (2013)

Speed: The HW speed is comparable to CMOS logic: the memristor switching speed is in the nanosecond or subnanosecond range (Medeiros-Ribeiro et al., 2011; Torrezan et al., 2011). The flexible implication logic should in principle admit faster software and shorter computing times.

Resource: Economic cost: metal-oxide memristors will have smaller footprints, and promise to be cheaper to fabricate than DRAM cells.

Quality: Architectures based on digital data processing at the memory level, with reconfigurable stateful logic, avoiding processor-storage bottlenecks, can be qualitatively different from traditional von Neumann type of CCOMP (Adam et al., 2016; Huang et al., 2016).

Precision: equivalent to CCOMP.

Fits underlying model.

Richness in principle unlimited.

Stochasticity: intrinsically non-stochastic.

Repeatability: Deterministic.

Embeddedness: Can be embedded and used for controlling and monitoring.

Programmability: Similar to CCOMP.

Formalism: There is a highly developed formalism (Adam et al., 2016; Borghetti et al., 2010; Raghuvanshi and Perkowski, 2014; Strukov et al., 2013).

Applications: There are a variety of models, systems and applications.

Philosophy: Architectures based on data processing at the memory level, with stateful logic, avoiding processor-storage bottlenecks, are qualitatively different from traditional von Neumann type of CCOMP.

5.3.2 Neuromorphic spiking networks

References to recent work: (Kataeva et al., 2015; Prezioso et al., 2015a; Prezioso et al., 2016b; Prezioso et al., 2016c; Saïghi et al., 2015)

Speed: The switching speed of the memristor synapses is comparable to CMOS switching speed (Medeiros-Ribeiro et al., 2011; Torrezan et al., 2011; Yakopcic ot al., 2013). The synapses are in a sense "instantaneous" and the time-to-solution (TTS) depends on network architecture, training and operation.

Resource: The economic cost of analog synaptic networks promises to be cheaper to fabricate than CMOS circuits.

Quality: Architectures based on analog neuromorphic data processing is qualitatively different from traditional von Neumann type of CCOMP.

Precision: Not well defined.

Fits underlying models.

Richness is limited/specific.

Stochasticity: Intrinsically stochastic (Gaba et al., 2014).

Repeatability: Non-deterministic.

Embeddedness: Can be embedded and used for controlling and monitoring.

Programmability: Supervised and unsupervised learning.

Formalism: There is a highly developed formalism (Adam et al., 2016; Bichler et al., 2012; Guo et al., 2015; Masquelier et al., 2008; Prezioso et al., 2015a; Prezioso et al., 2016a; Prezioso et al., 2015b; Prezioso et al., 2016b; Srinivasa and Cho, 2008).

Applications: There are a variety of models, systems and applications.

Philosophy: Architectures based on data processing at the memory level, with stateful logic, avoiding processor-storage bottlenecks, are qualitatively different from traditional von Neumann type of CCOMP.

5.4 Main achievements so far

In this section we broaden the scope to including systems with synapses simulated in software on CCOMP, or emulated in CMOS hardware.

5.4.1 Synapses in software

In the US, the DARPA SyNAPSE project (HRL Laboratories, 2015; IBM Cognitive, 2015; Neurdon, 2015; Srinivasa and Cho, 2008) has resulted, e.g., in TrueNorth (Esser et al., 2016; Merolla et al., 2014), a fully functional digital chip emulating convolutional networks for fast, energy-efficient neuromorphic computing, with 1 million spiking neurons and 256 million nonplastic synapses, based (2014) on a substrate of 5.4 billion transistors occupying $4.3\,cm^2$ area in Samsung's 28 nm process technology. TrueNorth's power density is $20\,mW\,cm^{-2}$, compared to 50–$100\,W\,cm^{-2}$ for a typical CPU. More recently (2016) TrueNorth provides 65 536 cores, 16 chips, and 16 million neurons, able to replicate the equivalent of 16 million neurons and 4 billion synapses while consuming only 2.5 W of power.

5.4.2 Synapses in CMOS hardware

Recent European examples are the EU FACETS (2015) and BrainScaleS (2015) projects, resulting in, e.g., the Heidelberg CMOS-based large-scale hardware simulator (Brüderle et al., 2011; Friedmann et al., 2017; Petrovici et al., 2016; Petrovici et al., 2014; Pfeil et al., 2013; Pfeil et al., 2016; Pfeil et al., 2012; Probst et al., 2015) implementing six networks on a universal neuromorphic computing substrate (Pfeil et al., 2013). Another recent project is the Blue Brain (2018) project at EPFL. These and other projects have converged into the current major European Flagship project, the Human Brain Project (2017).

5.4.3 Synapses in memristor hardware

There is now a wide variety of memristor components being actively researched and developed, and there is no obvious winning solution. Most likely there will be a whole menu of viable solutions for different purposes:

1. *Metal-oxide memristors:* TiO_2 (Borghetti et al., 2010; Kim et al., 2016; Lau et al., 2004; Medeiros-Ribeiro et al., 2011; Strukov et al., 2008; Wedig et al., 2016); TaO_x (Kumar et al., 2016; Torrezan et al., 2011; Wedig et al., 2016; Yi et al., 2016); HfO_x (Garbin et al., 2015a; Garbin et al., 2015b; Wedig et al., 2016)
2. *Silver-silicon memristors:* $W/SiO_xN_y:Ag/Cr:Pt$ (Wang et al., 2017); $Ag/Ag:Si/Ag$ (Jo et al., 2010)
3. *Silver-chalcogenide memristors:* $M/Ag_2S/M$ (Gubicza et al., 2016; Oblea et al., 2010; Stieg et al., 2012)

4. *Copper oxide memristors:* $Cu/Cu_xO/Cu$ (Xu et al., 2016b)
5. *Metal-organic memristors:* NOMFET (Alibart et al., 2012b)
6. *Organometal halide Perovskite memristors:* (Xu et al., 2016a)
7. *Electrochemical memristors:* OECT (Winther-Jensen et al., 2015); (Desbief et al., 2016; Giordani et al., 2016); (Shao et al., 2016)

5.4.4 Memristor/CMOS hybrids

Combinations of CMOS and nanoelectronic/molecular networks have been
clear alternatives for unconventional hybrid architectures for nearly two
decades (Huang et al., 2016; Husband et al., 2003; Jo et al., 2010; Prezioso
et al., 2015b; Reed et al., 2001; Sköldberg et al., 2007; Sköldberg and Wendin,
2007; Snider, 2005; Strukov and Likharev, 2007; Strukov and Williams, 2009;
Strukov and Likharev, 2011; Tour et al., 2002; Türel et al., 2004; Xia et al.,
2009), and are presently being commercialised (Crossbar, 2016) based on the
technology in Jo et al. (2010). Memristor crossbar structures have emerged
as viable approaches to computing in memory (Snider, 2005; Strukov and
Likharev, 2007; Strukov and Williams, 2009; Strukov and Likharev, 2011),
with stateful (Borghetti et al., 2010) or reconfigurable (Huang et al., 2016;
Xia et al., 2009) logic, or synaptic networks (Huang et al., 2016; Jo et al.,
2010; Molter and Nugent, 2016; Nugent and Molter, 2014; Prezioso et al.,
2015b).

5.4.5 Self-assembled memristor networks

The field is embryonic. To our knowledge, the only experimental implementation of a functional self-organized memristor network is that of Stieg et al.
(Stieg et al., 2012), based on a silver wire network and silver-sulfide mem-
risitve junctions. The original ideas of nano particle (NP)-molecule networks
with junctions with negative differential resistance (NDR) (Husband et al.,
2003; Tour et al., 2002) and hysteretic NDR characteristics (Konkoli and
Wendin, 2014; Sköldberg et al., 2007; Sköldberg and Wendin, 2007; Wendin
et al., 2012) remain to be achieved due to the difficulty to create NDR and
memristor characteristics in NP-molecule nanoscale junctions. However, recently strong NDR and non-volatile memory has been found in hybrid redox
organic/nanoparticle devices (Zhang et al., 2015). Also note the recent work
by Bose et al. (Bose et al., 2015) exploiting the rich behaviour emerging from
a network of interconnected metal nanoparticles, acting as strongly non-linear
single-electron transistors, find that the network can be configured in situ into
any Boolean logic gate.

5.4.6 Commercial memristor-based computing efforts

Hewlett-Packard (HP)

Researchers have been working for 10 years on unconventional memory for high-performance computing (Borghetti et al., 2010; Green et al., 2007; Lau et al., 2004; Strukov et al., 2008; Xia et al., 2009). The single-memristor technology was successful, demonstrating sub-nanosecond switching of a tantalum oxide memristor (Torrezan et al., 2011). HP expressed in 2014 a commitment (Morgan, 2014) to develop large-scale memristor memories and to put "memristors at the heart of a new machine" based on computing with large-scale multi-level memory. Being ahead of its time (Mellor, 2016; Simonite, 2015), the "Machine" project is now turned into a long-term research project on memory-driven computing (Hewlett Packard Enterprise, 2018).

Knowm

Knowm (2015) is a startup company that makes use of memristors for machine learning based on a working memristor technology (Oblea et al., 2010), and perceptron nodes with Anti-Hebbian and Hebbian (AHaH) plasticity rules (Molter and Nugent, 2016; Nugent and Molter, 2014). The memristors used by Knowm (Oblea et al., 2010) are sized 100–200 nm but can be scaled down. Thermodynamic RAM (kT-RAM) (Molter and Nugent, 2016) is a neuromemristive co-processor design based on the theory of AHaH computing and implemented via CMOS and memristors.

5.4.7 Quantum networks

A quantum information processor (QIP) is in principle a coherent piece of matter (network) where some components can be externally (classically) controlled while maintaining coherence of the quantum system (Wendin, 2017). It is an artificial coherent collection of quantum objects (natural ones would be e.g. molecules and solids). The simplest possible network is a coherent collection of coupled qubits (two-level systems). Simply viewed, a QIP is a coherent memory register where the quantum memory bits (qubits) can be addressed, manipulated, coupled, entangled, and read out via external (classical) gate operations ("the program"). Fundamentally, a QIP is a combination of memory and processor, performing reversible computation in memory.

Quantum neural networks (QNN) have been raising considerable interest for the last twenty years; see the review by Schuld et al. (2014). The idea of QNN is to introduce quantum coherent components into the network and perform training in ways similar to classical ANNs, especially in terms of the concepts of Deep Learning and Machine Learning. With the advent of classical memristor technology, there is recent work extending the memristor concept to quantum memristors (Pfeiffer et al., 2016; Salmilehto et al., 2017).

Here we choose to discuss QNNs in terms "synaptic" weights not connected with new types of quantum memristor components. Rather, in a quantum network, the synaptic weights can either be multi-state quantum nodes (qubits, qutrits, qudits, ...), or qubit couplings with tunable strength. The qubit-qubit coupling strengths can be tuned in a number of ways: by varying the frequency difference between the qubits; or by controlling the strength of the physical coupling element. In this way one can build physical qubit networks described by Ising spin Hamiltonians with controllable interactions, connected with an energy landscape. This is precisely what corresponds to the cost function in ANNs.

In classical ANN classifiers, the synaptic weights are tuned by training in order for the network to become represented by an energy landscape where the minima correspond to the desired patterns to be recognised. The tuning of the coupling strengths (synaptic weights) is achieved by classical feedback systems.

In the case of quantum networks, the largest system (D-Wave, 2016) consists of > 2000 short-lived qubits in a crossbar structure with tunable coupling elements (Bunyk et al., 2014; Harris et al., 2010). With a fully coherent system one could in principle perform Quantum Adiabtic Optimisation (QAO) (an analogue version of quantum computing) with quantum speedup, finding the ground state of a given Hamiltonian, e.g. an Ising Hamiltonian with fixed coupling parameters, representing the physical problem one wants to solve. The present D-Wave case rather performs Quantum Annealing (QA), making use of quantum tunneling and some local entanglement to find the minima in the energy landscape when the temperature is lowered. No quantum speedup has been found so far; see Wendin (2017) for more discussion and references.

Nevertheless, one can expect quantum coherent technologies to develop quite dramatically during the next 5 10 years, there is much theoretical work being developed for quantum neural networks in terms of quantum deep learning and quantum machine learning (Amin et al., 2016; Wiebe et al., 2015a; Wiebe et al., 2015b; Wiebe et al., 2015c).

5.5 What could be achieved in ten years?

5.5.1 Scalable solid-state technologies

New nonvolatile ReRAM resistive memory crossbar technologies have reached a certain maturity (Crossbar, 2016), and will certainly play important roles in emerging fields of application, such as neuromorphic circuits, to save energy and increase performance (Alibart et al., 2012b; Alibart et al., 2013; DeSalvo et al., 2015a; Garbin et al., 2015a; Garbin et al., 2015b; Kuzum et al., 2013; Pickett et al., 2013; Saïghi et al., 2015). Recent examples involve large-scale energy efficient neuromorphic systems based on ReRAM as stochastic-binary synapses with demonstration of complex visual- and auditory-pattern extraction using feedforward spiking neural networks.

In ten years, one can expect a paradigm shift in high-performance computing.

5.5.2 Solid-state-organic technologies

The liquid gate organic electrochemical transistor (OECT) (Desbief et al., 2016; Giordani et al., 2016; Shao et al., 2016; Winther-Jensen et al., 2015) is an example of an emerging technology, showing good progress at the level of fundamental research and small-scale applications. It has strong potential for sensor technologies and for integration with biological systems.

In ten years, one can expect arrays with a variety of sensors interacting with ANNs to detect a a variety of biological markers in, e.g., a blood test, and be trained to diagnose various diseases.

5.5.3 Self-assembled memristor networks

The field (Konkoli and Wendin, 2014; Wendin et al., 2012) is embryonic. To start with, it remains to demonstrate how to produce memristive links in a nanocell network. Nanoparticle-molecule networks have great potential for sensor technologies and for integration with biological systems.

In ten years, one can expect nanoparticle-molecule networks to provide programmable interfaces to biological systems.

5.5.4 Quantum networks

In ten years on can expect quantum simulators and computers to be able to solve relevant and important problems that cannot be handled by classical computers, e.g. the electronic structure of large molecules, of importance for designing catalyzers and enzymes.

5.6 Current challenges

In general: To understand the computational power of memcomputing in relation to the complexity of problems addressed. To understand and exploit the computational power of reservoir computing

5.6.1 Scalable solid-state technologies

To develop computing-in-memory systems along the lines of the HP Machine and Knowm.

5.6.2 Solid-state-organic technologies

To develop memristive OECT sensors, for a variety of markers, that can be nodes in neural networks.

5.6.3 Self-assembled networks

The immediate challenge is to demonstrate how to produce switchable memristive links in a self-assembled nanocell network. Another challenge is to demonstrate some functionality for information processing, e.g. in the form of reservoir computing, with non-switchable but strongly non-linear links, e.g. of NDR type. Another outstanding challenge would be to investigate nanocell interfaces to living biological matter.

To develop intelligent sensors: e.g. self-assembled synaptic memristor networks combined with sensors and CMOS, forming dynamical sensor RC systems.

5.6.4 Quantum networks

To build and entangle coherent quantum networks with thousands of qubits.

5.7 Outlook and recommendations

1. *Scalable solid-state technologies:* should be strongly supported via collaborative projects involving industry and academia.

2. *Solid-state-organic technologies:* represent a fundamental UCOMP mission and should be supported within the FET program.

3. *Self-assembled nanoparticle-molecule networks:* represent a fundamental UCOMP mission and should be strongly supported within the FET program.

4. *Quantum networks:* The field is going to be supported by an EU FET Flagship on *Quantum Technologies* during 2019–2029.

Acknowledgement

This project has received funding from the European Union's Horizon 2020 research and innovation programme under grant agreement No 664786, as well as from SYMONE (ICT-FP7 318597), and from Chalmers University of Technology.

References

Aaronson, S. (2005). "NP-complete problems and physical reality". *ACM SIGACT News* 36(1):30–52.

Aaronson, S. (2013). "Why Philosophers Should Care About Computational Complexity". *Computability: Gödel, Turing, Church, and Beyond.* Ed. by B. J. Copeland, C. J. Posy, and O. Shagrir. MIT Press.

Adam, G. C., B. D. Hoskins, M. Prezioso, and D. B. Strukov (2016). "Optimized stateful material implication logic for three-dimensional data manipulation". *Nano Research* 9(12):3914–3923.

Alibart, F., L. Gao, B. D. Hoskins, and D. B. Strukov (2012a). "High precision tuning of state for memristive devices by adaptable variation-tolerant algorithm". *Nanotechnology* 23(7):075201.

Alibart, F., S. Pleutin, O. Bichler, C. Gamrat, T. Serrano-Gotarredona, B. Linares-Barranco, and D. Vuillaume (2012b). "A memristive nanoparticle/organic hybrid synapstor for neuro-inspired computing". *Adv. Funct. Mater.* 22(3):609–616.

Alibart, F., S. Pleutin, D. Guerin, Ch. Novembrev, S. Lenfant, K. Lmimouni,
C. Gamrat, and D. Vuillaume (2010). "An organic nanoparticle transistor
behaving as a biological spiking synapse". *Adv. Funct. Mater.* 20(2):330–
337.

Alibart, F., E. Zamanidoost, and D. B. Strukov (2013). "Pattern classification
by memristive crossbar circuits using *ex situ* and *in situ* training". *Nature
Communications* 4:2072.

Amin, M. H., E. Andriyash, J. Rolfe, B. Kulchytskyy, and R. Melko (2016).
Quantum Boltzmann Machine. eprint: arXiv:1601.02036v1[quant-ph].

Appeltant, L., M.C. Soriano, G. Van der Sande, J. Danckaert, S. Massar,
J. Dambre, B. Schrauwen, C.R. Mirasso, and I. Fischer (2011). "Informa-
tion processing using a single dynamical node as complex system". *Nature
Communications* 2:468.

Arcangelis, L. de and H. J. Herrmann (2010). "Learning as a phenomenon
occurring in a critical state". *PNAS* 107(9):3977–3981.

Bichler, O., D. Querioz, S. J. Thorpe, J.-P. Bourgoin, and C. Gamrat (2012).
"Extraction of temporally correlated features from dynamic vision sensors
with spike-timing-dependent plasticity". *Neural Networks* 32:339–348.

Bichler, O., W. Zhao, F. Alibart, S. Pleutin, S. Lenfant, D. Vuillaume, and
C. Gamrat (2013). "Pavlov's dog associative learning demonstrated on
synaptic-like organic transistors". *Neural Computation* 25(2):549–556.

Blue Brain (2018). bluebrain.epfl.ch.

Borghetti, J., G. S. Snider, P. J. Kuekes, J. J. Yang, D. R. Stewart, and R. S.
Williams (2010). "'Memristive' switches enable 'stateful' logic operations
via material implication". *Nature* 464:873–876.

Bose, S.K., C.P. Lawrence, Z. Liu, K.S. Makarenko, R.M.J. van Damme,
H.J. Broersma, and W.G. van der Wiel (2015). "Evolution of a designless
nanoparticle network into reconfigurable Boolean logic". *Nature Nanotechnology* 10:1048–1052.

BrainScaleS (2015). brainscales.kip.uni-heidelberg.de.

Brüderle, D., M. A. Petrovici, B. Vogginger, M. Ehrlich, T. Pfeil, S. Millner,
A. Grübl, K. Wendt, E. Müller, M.-O. Schwartz, D. Husmann de Oliveira,
S. Jeltsch, J. Fieres, M. Schilling, P. Müller, O. Breitwieser, V. Petkov, L.
Muller, A. P. Davison, P. Krishnamurthy, J. Kremkow, M. Lundqvist, E.
Muller, J. Partzsch, S. Scholze, L. Zühl, C. Mayr, A. Destexhe, M. Diesmann, T. C. Potjans, A. Lansner, R. Schüffny, J. Schemmel, and K. Meier
(2011). "A comprehensive workflow for general-purpose neural modeling
with highly configurable neuromorphic hardware systems". *Biol. Cybern.*
104:263–296.

Bunyk, P. I., E. Hoskinson, M. W. Johnson, E. Tolkacheva, F. Altomare,
A. J. Berkley, R. Harris, J. P. Hilton, T. Lanting, and J. Whittaker (2014).
"Architectural considerations in the design of a superconducting quantum
annealing processor". *IEEE Trans. Appl. Superconductivity* 24(4):1700110.

Büsing, L., B. Schrauwen, and R. A. Legenstein (2010). "Connectivity, Dynamics, and Memory in Reservoir Computing with Binary and Analog Neurons". *Neural Computation* 22(5):1272–1311.

Chang, T., S. H. Jo, and W. Lu (2011). "Short-Term Memory to Long-Term Memory Transition in a Nanoscale Memristor". *ACS NANO* 5(9):7669–7676.

Chua, L. (1971). "Memristor, the missing circuit element". *IEEE Trans. Circuit Theory* 18(5):507–519.

Chua, L. and Kang (1976). "Memristive devices and systems". *Proc. IEEE* 64(2):209–223.

Crossbar (2016). www.crossbar-inc.com.

Dale, M., J. F. Miller, and S. Stepney (2017). "Reservoir Computing as a Model for *In Materio* Computing". *Advances in Unconventional Computing*. Ed. by A. Adamatzky. Vol. 1. Springer 2017, pp. 533–571.

Dambre, J., B. Schrauwen D. Verstraeten and, and S. Massar (2012). "Information Processing Capacity of Dynamical Systems". *Scientific Reports* 2 :514.

Demming, A., J. K. Gimzewski, and D. Vuillaume (2013). "Synaptic electronics". *Nanotechnology* 24(38):380201.

DeSalvo, B., E. Vianello, D. Garbin, O. Bichler, and L. Perniola (2015a). "From Memory in our Brain to Emerging Resistive Memories in Neuromorphic Systems". *2015 IEEE Int. Memory Workshop (IMW)*, pp. 193–198.

DeSalvo, B., E. Vianello, O. Thomas, F. Clermidy, O. Bichler, C. Gamrat, and L. Perniola (2015b). "Emerging resistive memories for low power embedded applications and neuromorphic systems". *2015 IEEE Int. Symp. Circuits and Systems (ISCAS)*, pp. 3088–3091.

Desbief, S., M. di Lauro, S. Casalini, D. Guerin, S. Tortorella, M. Barbalinardo, A. Kyndiah, M. Murgia, T. Cramer, F. Biscarini, and D. Vuillaume (2016). "Electrolyte-gated organic synapse transistor interfaced with neurons". *Organic Electronics* 38:21–28.

Di Ventra, M. and Y. V. Pershin (2012). "Biologically inspired electronics with memory circuit elements". *Advances in Neuromorphic Memristor Science and Applications*. Ed. by Kozma R., Pino R., and Pazienza G. Springer, pp. 15–36.

Esser, S. K., P. A. Merolla, A. S. Cassidy J. V. Arthur and, R. Appuswamy, A. Andreopoulos, D. J. Berg, J. L. McKinstry, T. Melano, D. R. Barch, C. di Nolfo, P. Datta, A. Amir, B. Taba, M. D. Flickner, and D. S. Modha (2016). "Convolutional networks for fast, energy-efficient neuromorphic computing". *PNAS* 113(41):11441–11446.

European Commission (2009). *Unconventional Formalisms for Computation*.

FACETS (2015). facets.kip.uni-heidelberg.de.

Friedmann, S., J. Schemmel, A. Gruebl, A. Hartel, M. Hock, and K. Meier (2017). "Demonstrating Hybrid Learning in a Flexible Neuromorphic

Hardware System". *IEEE Trans. Biomedical Circuits and Systems* 11(1) :128–142.

Gaba, S., P. Knag, Z. Zhang, and W. Lu (2014). "Memristive Devices for Stochastic Computing". *2014 IEEE Int. Symp. Circuits and Systems (IS-CAS)*, pp. 2592–2595.

Garbin, D., E. Vianello, O. Bichler, M. Azzaz, Q. Rafhay, P. Candelier, C. Gamrat, G. Ghibaudo, B. DeSalvo, and L. Perniola (2015a). "On the impact of OxRAM-based synapses variability on convolutional neural networks performance". *2015 IEEE/ACM Int. Symp. Nanoscale Architectures (NANOARCH)*, pp. 193–198.

Garbin, D., E. Vianello, O. Bichler, Q. Rafhay, C. Gamrat, G. Ghibaudo, B. DeSalvo, and L. Perniola (2015b). "HfO2-Based OxRAM Devices as Synapses for Convolutional Neural Networks". *IEEE Trans. Electron Devices* 62(8):2494–2501.

Georgiou, P. S., M. Barahona, S. N. Yaliraki, and E. M. Drakakis (2012). "Device Properties of Bernoulli Memristors". *Proc. IEEE* 100(6):1938–1950.

Giordani, M., M. Di Lauro, M. Berto, C. A. Bortolottia, D. Vuillaume, H. L. Gomes, M. Zoli, and Fabio Biscarini (2016). "Whole organic electronic synapses for dopamine detection". *Proc. SPIE 9944, Organic Sensors and Bioelectronics IX*, 99440P.

Green, J.E., J.W. Choi, A. Boukai, Y. Bunimovich, E. Johnston-Halperin, E. DeIonno, Y. Luo, B.A. Sheri, K. Xu, Y.S. Shin, H.-R. Tseng, J.F. Stoddart, and J.R. Heath (2007). "A 160-kilobit molecular electronic memory patterned at 1011 bits per square centimetre". *Nature* 445:414–417.

Gubicza, A., D. Zs. Manrique, L. Pósa, C. J. Lambert, G. Mihály, M. Csontos, and A. Halbritter (2016). "Asymmetry-induced resistive switching in Ag-Ag2S-Ag memristors enabling a simplified atomic-scale memory design". *Scientific Reports* 6:30775.

Guo, X., F. Merrikh-Bayat, L. Gao, B. D. Hoskins, F. Alibart, B. Linares-Barranco, L. Theogarajan, C. Teuscher, and D.B. Strukov (2015). "Modeling and Experimental Demonstration of a Hopfield Network Analog-to-Digital Converter with Hybrid CMOS/Memristor Circuits". *Frontiers in Neuroscience* 9:488.

Harris, R., M. W. Johnson, T. Lanting, A. J. Berkley, J. Johansson, P. Bunyk, E. Tolkacheva, E. Ladizinsky, N. Ladizinsky, T. Oh, F. Cioata, I. Perminov, P. Spear, C. Enderud, C. Rich, S. Uchaikin, M. C. Thom, E. M. Chapple, J. Wang, B. Wilson, M. H. S. Amin, N. Dickson, K. Karimi, B. Macready, C. J. S. Truncik, and G. Rose (2010). "Experimental investigation of an eight-qubit unit cell in a superconducting optimization processor". *Phys. Rev. B* 82:024511.

Hashem, N. and S. Das (2012). "Switching-time analysis of binary-oxide memristors via a nonlinear model". *Appl. Phys. Lett.* 100:26210.

Hermans, M., M. C. Soriano, J. Dambre, P. Bienstman, and I. Fischer (2015). "Photonic Delay Systems as Machine Learning Implementations". *J. Machine Learning Res.* 16:2081–2097.

Hewlett Packard Enterprise (2018). *The Machine: our vision for the future of computing.* URL: www.labs.hpe.com/the-machine.

HRL Laboratories (2015). www.hrl.com/laboratories/ISSL.

Huang, P., J. Kang, Y. Zhao, S. Chen, R. Han, Z. Zhou, Z. Chen, W. Ma, M. Li, L. Liu, and X. Liu (2016). "Reconfigurable Nonvolatile Logic Operations in Resistance Switching Crossbar Array for Large-Scale Circuits". *Adv. Mater.* 28:9758–9764.

Human Brain Project (2017). EU Flagship Project. www.humanbrainproject.eu.

Husband, C. P., S. M. Husband, J. S. Daniels, and J. M. Tour (2003). "Logic and memory with nanocell circuits". *IEEE Trans. Electron Devices* 50(9):1865–1875.

IBM Cognitive (2015). www.research.ibm.com/cognitive-computing.

Jo, S. H., T. Chang, I. Ebong, B.B. Bhadviya, P. Mazumder, and W. Lu (2010). "Nanoscale Memristor Device as Synapse in Neuromorphic Systems". *Nano Letters* 10:1297–1301.

Ju, H., J.-X. Xu, E. Chong, and A. M. J. VanDongen (2013). "Effects of synaptic connectivity on liquid state machine performance". *Neural Networks* 38:39–51.

Kataeva, I., F. Merrikh-Bayat, E. Zamanidoost, and D. Strukov (2015). "Efficient Training Algorithms for Neural Networks Based on Memristive Crossbar Circuits". *Proc. IJCNN 2015.* IEEE, pp. 1–8.

Kim, K. M., J. Zhang, C. Graves, J. J. Yang, B. J. Choi, C. S. Hwang, Z. Li, and R. S. Williams (2016). "Low-Power, Self-Rectifying, and Forming-Free Memristor with an Asymmetric Programing Voltage for a High-Density Crossbar Applications". *Nano Letters* 16:6724–6732.

Kim, Y., A. N. Morozovska, A. Kumar, S. Jesse, E. A. Eliseev, F. Alibart, D. B. Strukov, and S. V. Kalinin (2012). "Ionically-mediated electromechanical hysteresis in transition metal oxides". *ACS Nano* 6(8):7026–7033.

Kitzbichler, M. G., M. L. Smith, S. R. Christensen, and E. Bullmore (2009). "Broadband Criticality of Human Brain Network Synchronization". *PLoS Comput Biol.* 5(3):e1000314.

Klampfl, S. and W. Maass (2010). "A theoretical basis for emergent pattern discrimination in neural systems through slow feature extraction". *Neural Computation* 22(12):2979–3035.

Knowm (2015). knowm.org.

Konkoli, Z. and G. Wendin (2014). "On Information Processing with Networks of Nano-Scale Switching Elements". *Int. J. Unconv. Comp.* 10(5–6):405–428.

Kudithipudi, D., Q. Saleh, C. Merkel, J. Thesing, and B. Wysocki (2016). "Design and Analysis of a Neuromemristive Reservoir Computing Architecture for Biosignal Processing". *Frontiers in Neuroscience* 9:502.

Kulkarni, M. S. and C. Teuscher (2012). "Memristor-based Reservoir Computing". *2012 IEEE/ACM Int. Symp. Nanoscale Architectures*, pp. 226–232.

Kumar, S., C. E. Graves, J. P. Strachan, E. M. Grafals, A. L. D. Kilcoyne, T. Tyliszczak, J. Nelson Weker, Y. Nishi, and R. S. Williams (2016). "Direct Observation of Localized Radial Oxygen Migration in Functioning Tantalum Oxide Memristors". *Adv. Mat.* 28(14):2772–2776.

Kuzum, D., S. Yu, and H.-S. P. Wong (2013). "Synaptic electronics: materials, devices and applications". *Nanotechnology* 24:382001.

Larger, L., M. C. Soriano, D. Brunner, L. Appeltant, J. M. Gutierrez, L. Pesquera, C. R. Mirasso, and I. Fischer (2012). "Photonic information processing beyond Turing: an optoelectronic implementation of reservoir computing" *Optics Express* 20(3):3241–3249.

Lau, C. N., D.R. Stewart, R.S. Williams, and M. Bockrath (2004). "Direct observation of nanoscale switching centers in metal/molecule/metal structures". *Nano Lett.* 4:569.

Levin, A., J.M. Herrmann, and T. Geisel (2007). "Dynamical Synapses Causing Self-Organized Criticality in Neural Networks". *Nature Phys.* 3:857–860.

Lipton, R. J. (1995). "DNA solution of hard computational problems". *Science* 268(5210):542–545.

Lukosevicius, M. and H. Jaeger (2009). "Reservoir computing approaches to recurrent neural network trainings". *Computer Science Review* 3(3):127–149.

Maass, W. (2009). "Liquid state machines: motivation, theory, and applications". *Computability in context: computation and logic in the real world.* Ed. by B. Cooper and A. Sorbi. World Scientific, pp. 275–296.

Maass, W. (2016). "Energy-efficient neural network chips approach human recognition capabilities". *PNAS* 113(41):11387–11389.

Mane, P., N. Talati, A. Riswadkar, R. Raghu, and C. K. Ramesha (2015). "Stateful-NOR based reconfigurable architecture for logic implementation". *Microelectronics Journal* 46(6):551–562.

Manjunath, G. and H. Jaeger (2013). "Echo State Property Linked to an Input: Exploring a Fundamental Characteristic of Recurrent Neural Networks". *Neural Computation* 25:671–696.

Masquelier, T., R. Guyonneau, and S. J. Thorpe (2008). "Spike Timing Dependent Plasticity Finds the Start of Repeating Patterns in Continuous Spike Trains". *PLoS ONE* 1:e1377.

Mead, C. (1989). *Analog VLSI and Neural Systems.* 1st ed. Addison-Wesley.

Medeiros-Ribeiro, G., F. Perner, R. Carter, H. Abdalla, M. D. Pickett, and R. S. Williams (2011). "Lognormal switching times for titanium dioxide bipolar memristors: origin and resolution". *Nanotechnology* 22:095702.

Mellor, Chris (2016). "RIP HPE's The Machine product, 2014-2016: We hardly knew ye". *The Register.* URL: www.theregister.co.uk/2016/

11 / 29 / hp_labs_delivered_machine_proof_of_concept_prototype_but_machine_product_is_no_more.

Merkel, C., Q. Saleh, C. Donahue, and D. Kudithipudi (2014). "Memristive Reservoir Computing Architecture for Epileptic Seizure Detection". *Procedia Computer Science* 41:249–254.

Merolla, P. A., J. V. Arthur, R. Alvarez-Icaza, A. S. Cassidy, J. Sawada, F. Akopyan, B. L. Jackson, N. Imam, C. Guo, Y. Nakamura, B. Brezzo, I. Vo, S. K. Esser, R. Appuswamy, B. Taba, A. Amir, M. D. Flickner, W. P. Risk, R. Manohar, and D. S. Modha (2014). "A million spiking-neuron integrated circuit with a scalable communication network and interface". *Science* 345:668–673.

Merrikh-Bayat, F., B. Hoskins, and D.B. Strukov (2015). "Phenomenological modeling of memristive devices". *Applied Physics A* 118(3):770–786.

Molter, T. W. and M. A. Nugent (2016). "Machine Learning with Memristors via Thermodynamic RAM". *CNNA 2016, 15th International Workshop on Cellular Nanoscale Networks and their Applications*, pp. 1–2. eprint: 1608.04105v1[cs.ET].

Morgan, T. P. (2014). "HP Puts Memristors At The Heart Of A New Machine". *EnterpriseTech*. URL: www.enterprisetech.com/2014/06/12/hp-puts-memristors-heart-new-machine.

Neurdon (2015). www.neurdon.com.

Nili, H., S. Walia, A.E. Kandjani, R. Ramanathan, P. Gutruf, T. Ahmed, S. Balendhran, V. Bansal, D.B. Strukov, O. Kavehei, M. Bhaskaran, and S. Sriram (2015). "Donor-induced performance tuning of amorphous SrTiO3 memristive nanodevices: Multistate resistive switching and mechanical tunability". *Adv. Funct.Mat.* 25:3172–3182.

Nugent, M. A. and T. W. Molter (2014). "AHaH Computing-From Metastable Switches to Attractors to Machine Learning". *PLoS ONE* 9(2):e85175.

Nykter, M., N. D. Price, A. Larjo, T. Aho, S. A. Kauffman, O. Yli-Harja, and I. Shmulevich (2008). "Critical Networks Exhibit Maximal Information Diversity in Structure-Dynamics Relationships". *Phys. Rev. Lett.* 100 :058702.

Oblea, A. S., A. Timilsina, D. Moore, and K. A. Campbell (2010). "Silver Chalcogenide Based Memristor Devices". *Proc. IJCNN 2010*. IEEE.

Oskoee, E. N. and M. Sahimi (2011). "Electric currents in networks of interconnected memristors". *Phys. Rev. E* 83:031105.

Paquot, Y., F. Duport, A. Smerieri, J. Dambre, B. Schrauwen, M. Haelterman, and S. Massar (2012). "Optoelectronic Reservoir Computing". *Scientific Reports* 2:287.

Pershin, Y. V. and M. Di Ventra (2010). "Experimental demonstration of associative memory with memristive neural networks". *Neural Networks* 23(7):881–886.

Pershin, Y. V. and M. Di Ventra (2011). "Solving mazes with memristors: A massively parallel approach". *Phys. Rev. E* 84:04670.

Pershin, Y. V. and M. Di Ventra (2012). "Neuromorphic, Digital, and Quantum Computation With Memory Circuit Elements". *Proc. IEEE* 100(6):2071–2080.

Petrovici, M. A., J. Bill, I. Bytschok, J. Schemmel, and K. Meier (2016). "Stochastic inference with spiking neurons in the high-conductance state". *Phys. Rev. E* 94:042312.

Petrovici, M. A., B. Vogginger, P. Müller, O. Breitwieser, M. Lundqvist, L. Muller, M. Ehrlich, A. Destexhe, A. Lansner, R. Schüffny, J. Schemmel, and K. Meier (2014). "Characterization and Compensation of Network-Level Anomalies in Mixed-Signal Neuromorphic Modeling Platforms". *PLoS ONE* 9(10):e108590.

Pfeiffer, P., I. L. Egusquiza, M. Di Ventra, M. Sanz, and E. Solano (2016). "Quantum Memristors with Superconducting Circuits". *Scientific Reports* 6:29507.

Pfeil, T., A. Grübl, S. Jeltsch, E. Müller, P. Müller, M. A. Petrovic, M. Schmuker, D. Brüderle, J. Schemmel, and K. Meier (2013). "Six networks on a universal neuromorphic computing substrate". *Frontiers in Neuroscience* 7:11.

Pfeil, T., J. Jordan, T. Tetzlaff, A. Grübl, J. Schemmel, M. Diesmann, and K. Meier (2016). "The effect of heterogeneity on decorrelation mechanisms in spiking neural networks: a neuromorphic-hardware study". *Phys. Rev. X* 6:021023.

Pfeil, T., T. C. Potjans, S. Schrader, W. Potjans, J. Schemmel, M. Diesmann, and K. Meier (2012). "Is a 4-bit synaptic weight resolution enough? - constraints on enabling spike-timing dependent plasticity in neuromorphic hardware". *Frontiers in Neuroscience* 6:90.

Pickett, M. D., G. Medeiros-Ribeiro, and R. S. Williams (2013). "A scalable neuristor built with Mott memristors". *Nature Materials* 12:114–117.

Prezioso, M., I. Kataeva, F. Merrikh-Bayat, B. Hoskins, G. Adam, T. Sota, K. Likharev, and D. Strukov (2015a). "Modeling and Implementation of Firing-Rate Neuromorphic-Network Classifiers with Bilayer Pt / Al2O3 / TiO2-x / Pt Memristors". *Proc. IEDM 2015*. IEEE, pp. 17.4.1–17.4.4.

Prezioso, M., F. Merrikh-Bayat, B. Chakrabarti, and D. Strukov (2016a). "RRAM-Based Hardware Implementations of Artificial Neural Networks: Progress Update and Challenges Ahead". *Proc. SPIE 9749, Oxide-based Materials and Devices VII*, p. 974918.

Prezioso, M., F. Merrikh-Bayat, B. D. Hoskins, G. C. Adam, K. K. Likharev, and D. B. Strukov (2015b). "Training and operation of an integrated neuromorphic network based on metal-oxide memristors". *Nature* 521:61–64.

Prezioso, M., F. Merrikh-Bayat, B. Hoskins, K. Likharev, and D. Strukov (2016b). "Self-Adaptive Spike-Time-Dependent Plasticity of Metal-Oxide Memristors". *Scientific Reports* 6:21331.

Prezioso, M., Y. Zhong, D. Gavrilov, F. Merrikh-Bayat, B. Hoskins, G. Adam, K. Likharev, and D. Strukov (2016c). "Spiking Neuromorphic Networks with Metal-Oxide Memristors". *IEEE Int. Symp. Circuits and Systems (ISCAS 2016)*, pp. 177–180.

Probst, D., M. A. Petrovici, I. Bytschok, J. Bill, D. Pecevski, J. Schemmel, and K. Meier (2015). "Probabilistic inference in discrete spaces can be implemented into networks of LIF neurons". *Frontiers in Compututational Neuroscience* 9:13.

Raghuvanshi, A. and M. Perkowski (2014). "Logic Synthesis and a Generalized Notation for Memristor-Realized Material Implication Gates". *IEEE/ACM Int. Conf. Computer-Aided Design (ICCAD 2014)*, pp. 470–477.

Reed, M. A., J. Chen, A. M. Rawlett, D. W. Price, and J. M. Tour (2001). "Molecular random access memory cell". *Appl. Phys. Lett.* 78:3735.

Rothenbuhler, A., T. Tran, E. H. B. Smith, V. Saxena, and K. A. Campbell (2013). "Reconfigurable Threshold Logic Gates using Memristive Devices". *J. Low Power Electron. Appl.* 3(2):174–193.

Russo, R., H. J. Herrmann, and L. de Arcangelis (2014). "Brain modularity controls the critical behavior of spontaneous activity". *Scientific Reports* 4:4312.

Saïghi, S., C. G Mayr, T. Serrano-Gotarredona, H. Schmidt, G. Lecerf, J. Tomasa, J. Grollier, S. Boyn, A. Vincent, D. Querlioz, S. La Barbera, F. Alibart, D. Vuillaume, O. Bichler, C. Gamrat, and B. Linares-Barranco (2015). "Plasticity in memristive devices for Spiking Neural Networks". *Frontiers in Neuroscience* 9:51.

Salmilehto, J., F. Deppe, M. Di Ventra, M. Sanz, and E. Solano (2017). "Quantum Memristors with Superconducting Circuits". *Scientific Reports* 7:42044.

Schuld, M., I. Sinayskiy, and F. Petruccione (2014). "The quest for a Quantum Neural Network". *Quantum Information Processing* 13:2567–2586.

Shao, Feng, Yi Yang, Li Qiang Zhu, Ping Feng, and Qing Wan (2016). "Oxide-based Synaptic Transistors Gated by Sol-Gel Silica Electrolytes". *ACS Appl. Mater. Interfaces* 8:3050–3055.

Shin, S., K. Kim, and S.-M. Kang (2011). "Reconfigurable Stateful NOR Gate for Large-Scale Logic-Array Integrations". *IEEE Trans. Circuits and Systems II: Express Briefs.* 58(7):442–446.

Siegelmann, H. (1995). "Computation beyond the Turing limit". *Science* 268(5210):545–548.

Simonite, Tom (2015). "Machine Dreams". *MIT Technology Review*. URL: www.technologyreview.com/s/536786/machine-dreams.

Sköldberg, J., C. Önnheim, and G. Wendin (2007). "Nanocell devices and architecture for configurable computing with molecular electronics". *IEEE Trans. Circuits and Systems I* 54(11):2461–2471.

Sköldberg, J. and G. Wendin (2007). "Reconfigurable logic in nanoelectronic switching networks". *Nanotechnology* 18(48):485201.

Snider, G. (2005). "Computing with hysteretic resistor crossbars". *Appl. Phys. A* 80:1165–1172.

Srinivasa, N. and Y. Cho (2008). "Unsupervised discrimination of patterns in spiking neural networks with excitatory and inhibitory synaptic plasticity". *Front. Comput. Neurosci.* 8:159.

Stepp, N., D. Plenz, and N. Srinivasa (2015). "Synaptic Plasticity Enables Adaptive Self-Tuning Critical Networks". *PLoS Comput. Biol.* 11(1) :e1004043.

Stewart, D. R., D. A. A. Ohlberg, P. A. Beck, Y. Chen, R. S. Williams, J. O. Jeppesen, K. A. Nielsen, and J. Fraser Stoddart (2004). "Molecule-independent electrical switching in Pt/organic monolayer/Ti devices". *Nano Lett.* 4:133–136.

Stieg, A. Z., A. V. Avizienis, H. O. Sillin, C. Martin-Olmos, M. Aono, and J. K. Gimzewski (2012). "Emergent Criticality in Complex Turing B-Type Atomic Switch Networks". *Adv. Mater.* 24:286.

Strachan, J. P., J. J. Yang, L. A. Montoro, C. A. Ospina, A. J. Ramirez, A. L. D. Kilcoyne, G. Medeiros-Ribeiro, and R. S. Williams (2013). "Characterization of electroforming-free titanium dioxide memristors". *Beilstein J. Nanotechnol.* 4:467–473.

Strukov, D. B. and K. K. Likharev (2007). "Defect-Tolerant Architectures for Nanoelectronic Crossbar Memories". *J. Nanosci. Nanotechnol.* 7:151–167.

Strukov, D. B., A. Mishchenko, and R. Brayton (2013). "Maximum Throughput Logic Synthesis for Stateful Logic: A Case Study". *Reed-Muller 2013 Workshop.*

Strukov, D. B., G. S. Snider, D. R. Stewart, and R. S. Williams (2008). "The missing memristor found". *Nature* 453:80–83.

Strukov, D. B. and R. S. Williams (2009). "Four-dimensional address topology for circuits with stacked multilayer crossbar arrays". *PNAS* 106:20155–20158.

Strukov, Dmitri B. and Konstantin K. Likharev (2011). "All-NDR Crossbar Logic". *11th IEEE International Conference on Nanotechnology*, pp. 865–868.

Thomas, A. (2013). "Memristor based neural networks". *J. Phys. D: Appl. Phys.* 46:0930018.

Torrezan, A. C., J. P. Strachan, G. Medeiros-Ribeiro, and R. S. Williams (2011). "Sub-nanosecond switching of a tantalum oxide memristor". *Nanotechnology* 22:485203.

Tour, J. M., W. L. Van Zandt, C. P. Husband, S. M. Husband, L. S. Wilson, P. D. Franzon, and D. P. Nackashi (2002). "Nanocell logic gates for molecular computing". *IEEE Trans. Nanotechnol.* 99(2):100–109.

Traversa, F. L. and M. Di Ventra (2017). "Polynomial-time solution of prime factorization and NP-hard problems with digital memcomputing machines". *CHAOS* 27:023107.

Traversa, F. L., C. Ramella, F. Bonani, and M. Di Ventra (2015). "Memcomputing NP-complete problems in polynomial time using polynomial resources and collective states". *Science Advances* 1(6):e1500031.

Türel, Ö., J. H. Lee, X. L. Ma, and K. K. Likharev (2004). "Neuromorphic architectures for nanoelectronic circuits". *Int. J. Circ. Theory App.* 32 :277–302.

Valov, I., R. J. R. Jameson, and M. N. Kozicki (2011). "Electrochemical metallization memories—fundamentals, applications, prospects". *Nanotechnology* 22:254003.

Wang, Z., S. Joshi, S. E. Savel'ev, H. Jiang, R. Midya, P. Lin, M. Hu, N. Ge, J. P. Strachan, Z. Li, Qing Wu, M. Barnell, G.-L. Li, H. L. Xin, R. S. Williams, Q. Xia, and J. J. Yang (2017). "Memristors with diffusive dynamics as synaptic emulators for neuromorphic computing". *Nature Materials* 16:101–108.

Waser, R. and M. Aono (2007). "Nanoionics-based resistive switching memories". *Nature Materials* 6:833–840.

Wedig, A., M. Luebben, D.-Y. Cho, M. Moors, K. Skaja, V. Rana, T. Hasegawa, K. K. Adepall, B. Yildiz, R. Waser, and I. Valov (2016). "Nanoscale cation motion in TaO_x, HfO_x and TiO_x memristive systems". *Nature Nanotechnology* 11:67.

Wendin, G. (2017). "Quantum information processing with superconducting circuits: a review". *Reports on Progress in Physics* 80:106001.

Wendin, G., D. Vuillaume, M. Calame, S. Yitzchaik, C. Gamrat, G. Cuniberti, and V. Beiu (2012). "SYMONE Project: Synaptic Molecular Networks for Bio-Inspired Information Processing". *Int. J. Unconv. Comp.* 8(4):325–332.

Wiebe, N., A. Kapoor, C. E. Granade, and K. M. Svore (2015a). *Quantum Inspired Training for Boltzmann Machines.* eprint: arXiv:1507.02642v1[cs.LG].

Wiebe, N., A. Kapoor, and K. M. Svore (2015b). "Quantum algorithms for nearest-neighbor methods for supervised and unsupervised learning". *Quantum Inf. Comput.* 15(3-4):316–356.

Wiebe, N., A. Kapoor, and K. M. Svore (2015c). *Quantum Deep Learning.* eprint: arXiv:1412.3489v2[quant-ph].

Wikipedia (2016). *Memristor.* URL: en.wikipedia.org/wiki/Memristor.

Winther-Jensen, B., B. Kolodziejczyk, and O. Winther-Jensen (2015). "New one-pot poly(3,4-ethylenedioxythiophene): poly(tetrahydrofuran) memory material for facile fabrication of memory organic electrochemical transistors". *APL Materials* 3:014903.

Xia, Q., W. Robinett, M.W. Cumbie, N. Banerjee, T.J. Cardinali, J.J. Yang, X. Li, W.Wu, W.M. Tong, D.B. Strukov, G.S. Snider, G. Medeiros-Ribeiro, and R.S. Williams (2009). "Memristor/CMOS hybrid integrated circuits for reconfigurable logic". *Nano Lett.* 9:364.

Xu, W., H. Cho, Y.-H. Kim, Y.-T. Kim, C. Wolf, C.-G. Park, and T.-W. Lee (2016a). "Organometal Halide Perovskite Artificial Synapse". *Adv. Mater.* 28(5916-5922).

Xu, W., Y. Lee, S.-Y. Min, C. Park, and T.-W. Lee (2016b). "Simple, Inexpensive, and Rapid Approach to Fabricate Cross-Shaped Memristors Using an Inorganic-Nanowire-Digital-Alignment Technique and a One-Step Reduction Process". *Adv. Mater.* 28(527-532):3914–3923.

Yakopcic, C., T.M. Taha, G. Subramanyam, and R.E. Pino (2013). "Memristor SPICE model and crossbar simulation based on devices with nanosecond switching time". *Proc. IJCNN 2013*, p. 7.

Yamazaki, T. and S. Tanaka (2007). "The cerebellum as a liquid state machine". *Neural Networks* 20:290.

Yang, J. J., M. D. Pickett, X. Li, D. A. A. Ohlberg, D. R. Stewart, and R. S. Williams (2008). "Memristive switching mechanism for metal/oxide/metal nanodevices". *Nature Nanotechnology* 3:429.

Yang, J. J., D. B. Strukov, and D. S. Stewart (2013). "Memristive devices for computing". *Nature Nanotechnology* 8:13.

Yi, W., S. E. Savel'ev, G. Medeiros Ribeiro, F. Miao, M.-X. Zhang, J. J. Yang, A. M. Bratkovsky, and R. S. Williams (2016). "Quantized conductance coincides with state instability and excess noise in tantalum oxide memristors". *Nature Communications* 7:11142.

Zhang, T., D. Guerin, S. Lenfant, D. Vuillaume, F. Alibart, K. Lmimouni, A. Yassin, M. Ocafrain, J. Roncali, and P. Blanchard (2015). "Negative differential resistance and non-volatile memory in hybrid redox organic/ nanoparticle devices". *11th International Conference on Organic Electronics, Paris, 2015*.

Chapter 6
Microscopic Chemically Reactive Electronic Agents

John S. McCaskill

Abstract This case study considers MICREAgents (MIcroscopic Chemically Reactive Electronic Agents), composed of free-floating CMOS "*lablets*" in aqueous solution, which can control the chemistry of their immediate vicinity and thereby also their interactions with one-another, as a substrate for unconventional computing. Such *lablets* at the space scale of $100\,\mu\text{m}$ are being fabricated and investigated in the EU project MICREAgents (McCaskill et al., 2012).

6.1 Overview

There are several compelling reasons that such a novel computational medium may be interesting. We first consider general features. Firstly, chemical systems can master the massively parallel, autonomous and efficient construction and evolution of complex material structures, devices and systems including living systems, while serial digital electronic information systems have proven to be efficient for human programming – so a combination of both worlds may allow us to reap the advantages of both. Secondly, chemical systems are ultimately also based on a molecular form of reconfigurable electronic information processing, so that this combination is more natural than might appear at first sight. Thirdly, the use of digital electronic systems to control and record features of chemical systems shares several key aspects with the use of genes to encode proteins and features of their dynamical interactions in biochemical systems: (i) a general basis for copying and editing information, (ii) the possibility of a translation apparatus to convert electronic/genetic information into chemical/protein information, (iii) the possibility of using an electronic system to facilitate the copying of a broad class of chemical systems, and (iv) the possibility of artificial cells which couple together the two types of system in self-reproducing entity.

© Springer International Publishing AG, part of Springer Nature 2018
S. Stepney et al. (eds.), *Computational Matter*, Natural Computing Series,
https://doi.org/10.1007/978-3-319-65826-1_6

Fig. 6.1 MICREAgents concept: self-assembling MICREAgent lablets (reproduced from McCaskill et al. (2012)), with electrodes (black), reaction chambers (grey), shallow chemical IO channels (white), electronics and supercapacitor layers (translucent). *Lablets* self-assemble reversibly via specific DNA-mediated recognition in pairs to form *gemlabs*, enabling pairwise communication with one another in series. They can also communicate with the docking station – an array of electronically interconnected *lablets* forming a chip with a power and communication interface to external computers. *Lablets* control their own docking to one another and are completely autonomous when free in solution.

One can also consider the motivation of MICREAgents as residing in the desire for and requirement of a new level of autonomy in experimentation. Whereas chemical experiments proceed typically with comparatively low information content control of macroscopic physical boundaries (mixing chemicals, separating chemical by passage through filters or columns, changing global temperature etc.), there is an increasing call for microscopic and local experimentation, especially in biochemistry. The need to conduct very large numbers of experiments on combinatorially complex systems has called for automation and the vision of a robot scientist, able to autonomously "compute" and carry out experiments to achieve certain goals of system understanding and/or utilization. This development has been accompanied by the transition from liquid handling robots to microfluidic systems for integrating such experiments, followed by the realization that most lab-on-a-chip systems are more like chip-in-a-lab systems, requiring major macroscopic support equipment in the lab for successful operation. The problem here is that the interfacing of microscopic chemical systems, both in terms of control (e.g. electronic wires or pneumatic channels for valve control) and chemicals (capillary tubes) is a complex bottleneck. Wireless electronics can help only a little here, being still restricted to relatively large scales e.g. by antennae needs, and material scavenging chemistry is still in its infancy. Autonomous microscopic agents that can simply be poured into a chemical system like chemicals, and that are able to conduct experiments, i.e. perturb a chemical system locally and record and communicate the results, would change this situation radically as well as allow an information rich interaction with inaccessible chemical systems (such as inside organisms).

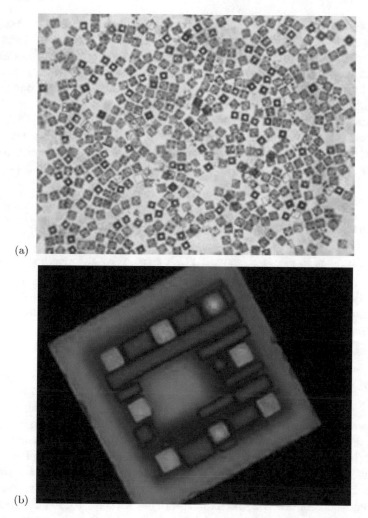

(a)

(b)

Fig. 6.2 MICREAgents lablets (100 μm across). (a) First structured metallic lablets in solution. (b) Gold electrodes on separated CMOS lablets. The CMOS lablets were designed in a collaboration between RUB-AIS (D. Funke, P. Mayr, J. Oehm) and RUB-BioMIP (T. Maeke, P. Wagler, J.S. McCaskill). [Reproduced from McCaskill (2014)]

More practically, current technology for the first time enables us to attempt such a transformation to autonomous microscale experimentation. Firstly, silicon integration is now at a scale to support significant memory and processing capability in microscopic particles, making it an attractive possibility now to begin to interact locally with chemical processes. Developments in microscopic power sources such as supercaps and microbatteries make it conceivable that microscopic electronic particles can operate on timescales up to an hour using locally stored resources. Thirdly, our control of self-assembly

processes is reaching a level where it is conceivable to replace global broad-
casting communication by pairwise communication between objects based
on reversible self-assembly, avoiding the space requirements of aerials, and
hence create a novel "chemical" architecture based on local communication
for dealing with both system internal communication needs and our needs to
communicate with and program such systems.

In the following case study we will explore several aspects of MICREAgents
as a form of unconventional computing, especially considering the special
opportunities and challenges raised by this novel type of system. See also
COBRA roadmap (topic 4e) (McCaskill et al., 2014; McCaskill et al., 2012).

6.2 Contribution to UCOMP aspects

This section discusses the eight aspects of UCOMP for *MICREagents* computing. Note that the interpretation of these aspects shows specific features
to the type of and target of computation in MICREAgents. Other aspects
that would be relevant to MICREAgents would be autonomy, sustainability,
constructability (McCaskill et al., 2014).

6.2.1 Speed

The speed of MICREAgents operation is fundamentally limited by the speed
of relevant chemical reactions, rather than by the electronics component.
Most relevant chemical reactions occur well below 50 Hz on the timescale of
seconds. The communication frequency between chemistry and electronics is
limited by the relatively large capacitances of microelectrodes in electrolyte
solutions and comparatively weak currents associated with ion diffusion: usually to values significantly below 1 MHz, but still faster than most chemical
reactions of interest. The electronic component technology is typically optimized for high frequency operation, i.e. 100 MHz or more, and this creates
significant problems in terms of wasted energy and resources to achieve com-
mensurately slow process control. Special ultra low power slow electronic
clocks (below 1 kHz) are being developed to allow energy efficient electronic
circuitry to control chemical processes locally on appropriate time scales (Mc-
Caskill, 2014). So speed is an issue: with matching more important than an
extreme value.

6.2.2 Resources

The resources utilized by MICREAgents are diverse, including silicon hardware, power sources and chemicals. Silicon wafers can be turned into microparticles by thinning and wafer sawing or reactive ion etching, with millions of microparticles (100 µm scale) generated from a single wafer, with these numbers increasing quadratically with decreasing microparticle size. The footprint of silicon gates e.g. in 65 nm CMOS allows 4-bit microprocessors to be integrated on single 100 µm scale lablets with a couple of 100 words of memory, while currently employed 180 nm technology supports only bit serially programmed extended finite state machines. The power consumption of 180 nm resolution CMOS can be pinned back to an average of about 2 nA, allowing a 2 µF supercapacitor to run the device autonomously for 1000 s. Local chemical concentrations in solution in the µM to mM range can readily be changed by surface reactions, if local compartments (thin films) are separated off from the main solution for local processing. Dilute chemicals in the bulk solution can be concentrated by lablets through electronic membranes: acting a little like the filter feeders known in marine biology (usually much smaller than whales).

6.2.3 Quality

The quality of MICREAgents computation lies primarily in the quality of the achieved programmable link between electronics and chemistry, and should be judged accordingly. It is not important how much computation is going on in the electronics, but how accurately information can be transferred back and forth between the electronic and chemical systems. Initial devices are expected to be limited but a clear roadmap of increasing accuracy will allow increasingly complex structures to be produced dynamically by the joint action of electronics and chemistry in MICREAgents.

6.2.4 Embeddedness

MICREAgents are fully embedded and designed to run autonomously without external power. They do not need to be programmed externally, but can also in principal receive an electronic program in a communication process with another lablet. The CMOS lablet components are pre-fabricated, and in this sense may be regarded as restricting the general open-endedness of construction in these systems. However, the chemical functionality can be largely dictated by the (emergent) chemical post processing of lablet coatings, and the programs of the electronics communicated by other lablets, so

that the CMOS chips can be treated increasingly like an environmental resource than a very specific external control mechanism, extending the system
to full chemical embodiment.

6.2.5 Formalism

The chemical swarm formalism (McCaskill et al., 2014) may be applied to certain aspects of collective lablet functionality. A formalism for the emergence of
translation systems has been investigated by Wills, McCaskill and colleagues
(Sharma et al., 2015; Straczek et al., 2016) and is being further developed
as a platform for understanding the bootstrapping of MICREAgents systems
capable of translating electronic to chemical information and back. Physical
and chemical simulation formulations include the integration of electrochemistry, chemical kinetics and physical processes such as the self-assembly of
lablets and electrokinetics.

6.2.6 Programming

The programming of MICREAgents involves several levels:

1. the programming of lablet geometries and hardware properties (e.g.
   microelectrode patterning and lablet shapes, 3D profiles and material
   coatings
2. The programming of electronic FSMs or microcontrollers in individual
   lablets. The only unconventional features requiring consideration are the
   real world real-time embedding, requiring considerations of timing, power
   consumption, noise control, and the avoidance of damage traps
3. the programming of surface electrochemistry, including (possibly multilayer) initial patterning of microelectrodes and the assignment of voltage
   levels and timing parameters to allow digital combinatorial control
4. the programming of bulk solution chemistry, which may interface with
   DNA Computing for example to allow the deployment of complex combinatorial molecular processes in conjunction with lablets

Various learning (e.g. neural) or evolutionary algorithms are being explored
may prove effective in programming lablets automatically, rather than by
rational design, especially in the light of incomplete knowledge of complex
chemistry and ionic interaction sat surfaces. Another type of programming
considers lablets as a reconfigurable hardware system, with self-modifying
capabilities: and formalisms from both these areas can potentially help in
programming lablet systems. Finally, insights from the field of evolutionary
design of experiments and autonomous experimentation will prove useful in

linking the programming of MICREAgents to one of the main application areas in autonomous experimentation.

6.2.7 Applications

The potential applications of MICREAgents are primarily to microscopic real-world embedded (immersed) systems. These include experimentation with chemical systems and biochemical systems such as cells, local control of technical chemical and biochemical systems such as biopower systems, water treatment systems, energy scavenging systems, remote sensing systems, environmental, agricultural, epidemic monitoring and diverse medical systems. They may ultimately acquire a pivotal role in taking the step to artificial life systems for applications in these areas. The interaction of MICREAgents with natural cells will play an increasing role in future applications, especially as the size of MICREAgents decrease towards average eukaryotic cell sizes (e.g. $10\,\mu m$).

6.2.8 Philosophy

Firstly, MICREAgents follows the dualistic von Neumann philosophy of coupled computation and construction originally exemplified in his studies of self-reproducing automata: the chemical subsystem does limited computation and strong construction, while the electronic subsystem does strong computation with limited reconstruction (replaced by some reconfigurability and a generic architecture).

Secondly, MICREAgents relates to the computational philosophy of artificial life and synthetic biology, exploring the computational power of alternative embedded systems capable of construction control. In particular, the target to approach a technical electronic implementation of a cell, capable of autonomous resource acquisition, metabolism, homeostasis, self-reproduction and evolution guides some of the design decisions in MICREAgents.

MICREAgents, as with many embedded systems, also highlights the benefits and challenges associated with strong context dependence of hardware operation, cf. the case study of *in Materio Computing*, Chapter 3.

6.3 Main achievements so far

The first MICREAgents have been produced at the $100\,\mu m$ scale, and shown to support specific chemical reactions at their surfaces (Sharma et al., 2015).

A smart docking interface has been developed to allow the interaction with lablets (Straczek et al., 2016). A major step towards powering has been taken with bipolar chemistry in external global electric fields. Chemistry has been developed to allow the control of local ion concentrations (Freage et al., 2015), the reversible self-assembly of lablets (Liu et al., 2015) and on-board super-capacitors (Sharma et al., 2016). A concept of the gemlabic code has been developed to guide the bootstrapping of translation between electronic and chemical information (Wills et al., 2015). A swarm chemical architecture of simulating agent properties of lablets has been developed (Tangen et al., 2015) and a physical model of electroosmotic lablet locomotion developed (Sharma and McCaskill, 2015). First steps in the interactions between lablets and other soft-matter containers such as droplets and cells have been realized (Sarvašová et al., 2015). A conceptual study of a nanomorphic cell has been published (Zhirnov and Cavin III, 2011), that aims at the $10\,\mu m$ scale. In 2016–2017 an improved fabrication of lablets was achieved, supported by the EON Seed Grant.

6.4 What could be achieved in ten years?

In 10 years, MICREAgents could become a mainstream technology for chemical and biochemical experimentation, harnessing local on-particle electronic computation in the control of chemical processes. The size scale of MICRE-Agents could progress rapidly down to the scale of cells and begin to incorporate more complex topologies (e.g. involving interior channels, membranes and pores). The beginnings of a generic translation system relating electronic to chemical information might be achievable in 10 years, and allow an unprecedented biotechnology-type explosion of applications of MICREAgents in the following decade. MICREAgents may acquire many of the properties of cells and represent a first convincing artificial life form.

6.5 Current challenges

6.5.1 Manufacturing

Current lablet fabrication involves conventional CMOS processing, followed by wafer scale post-processing. While this process is moderately efficient, the interface between high throughput production constraints of CMOS and the requirements for custom post-processing harbors several limitations. Lablets will need to take advantage of 3D-silicon processing, to allow dual-sided functionality and a better separation of powering and operation, but access to this technology is limited. This situation could improve radically with improved funding and a strategic alliance between CMOS producers and post-processing clean-rooms. In addition, the packaging of interior solutions required for supercap operation is still a challenge. The thinning and separation of lablets works at the scale of $100\,\mu m$ but will need significant extensions if we are to go down to the scale of $10\,\mu m$. As the resolution of CMOS gets higher, the losses in conventional circuitry begin to dominate, and more radical departures from conventional design constraints are required.

6.5.2 Lablet power

Although supercaps can provide appropriate power levels, the low voltage range of many power sources (e.g. sugar battery) limit their application to MICREagents. Achieving encapsulated lablet power is still a difficult technical challenge, but one within the reach of current technology.

6.5.3 Buoyancy, locomotion and reversible self-assembly

Despite major achievements in the current project, bringing the integrated status of these processes up to the level of separately achieved functionalities is a considerable challenge.

6.5.4 Information encoding for chemical functionality

The exploration of mechanism of encoding chemical information in time dependent electrochemical and electrokinetic signals on microelectrodes is a large area of research and a major challenge. Connections with electrochemistry and neuro-electronic coupling strategies will both be useful in achieving future progress. The completion of a proof of principle of boot-strapping an encoding will be a major milestone.

6.6 Outlook and recommendations

The move to combine electronics and chemistry to create programmable autonomous microparticles (later nanoparticles) capable of controlling chemical construction has already begun and holds the final promise of providing a pourable digital platform for chemical construction, regulation and interaction. This platform will be able to both interact with biological cells and emulate many of their complex chemical functions, including self-reproduction (dependent on a naked electronically functional substrate). This resource dependence is actually a feature, not a limitation, allowing us to fully control the proliferation of such smart devices should they acquire the ability to self-reproduce. Combinations with DNA computing, in materio computation, reservoir computing, membrane computing, swarm computing are possible and probably rewarding. The central issue of bootstrapping a code between electronic and chemical processing is certainly a grand challenge for this technology, and one on a similar footing to the realization of a universal translation machinery (the ribosome and its free components) for proteins.

The overall recommendation stemming from this work is that unconventional computation needs to focus more strongly on the complementary roles of computation and construction, and deal more strongly with systems that like chemistry, to manage dynamic construction and reconstruction of information entities, well beyond the framework of evolvable hardware and reconfigurable computation.

Acknowledgements

This work was supported by the European Commission under Grant#318671. This publication was also made possible through the support of a grant from the John Templeton Foundation provided through the Earth-Life Science Institute of the Tokyo Institute of Technology. The opinions expressed in this publication are those of the author(s) and do not necessarily reflect the views of the John Templeton Foundation or the Earth-Life Science Institute.

References

Freage, Lina, Alexander Trifonov, Ran Tel-Vered, Eyal Golub, Fuan Wang, John S. McCaskill, and Itamar Willner (2015). "Addressing, amplifying and switching DNAzyme functions by electrochemically-triggered release of metal ions". *Chemical Science* 6(6):3544–3549.

Liu, Shaohua, Pavlo Gordiichuk, Zhong-Shuai Wu, Zhaoyang Liu, Wei Wei, Manfred Wagner, Nasser Mohamed-Noriega, Dongqing Wu, Yiyong Mai, Andreas Herrmann, Klaus Müllen, and Xinliang Feng (2015). "Patterning two-dimensional free-standing surfaces with mesoporous conducting polymers". *Nature Communications* 6:8817.

McCaskill, John S. (2014). "MICREAgents – Electronics meets Chemistry in Autonomous Computation (abstract)". *TRUCE workshop, UCNC 2014, Ontario, Canada.*

McCaskill, John S., Martyn Amos, Peter Dittrich, Steen R. Rasmussen, et al. (2014). *A Roadmap for Chemical and Biological Information Technology: ChemBioIT.* URL: www.cobra-project.eu / uploads / 2 / 0 / 8 / 9 / 20895162 / cobra_d2.3_draft_roadmap.pdf.

McCaskill, John S., Guenter von Kiedrowski, Juergen Oehm, Pierre Mayr, Lee Cronin, Itamar Willner, Andreas Herrmann, Steen Rasmussen, František Štěpánek, Norman H. Packard, and Peter R. Wills (2012). "Microscale Chemically Reactive Electronic Agents". *International Journal of Unconventional Computing* 8(4):289–299.

Sarvašová, Nina, Pavel Ulbrich, Viola Tokárová, Aleš Zadražil, and František Štěpánek (2015). "Artificial swarming: Towards radiofrequency control of reversible micro-particle aggregation and deposition". *Powder Technology* 278:17–25.

Sharma, A., D. Funke, T. Maeke, P. Mayr, P. F. Wagler, O. Anamimoghadan, L. Cronin, J. Oehm, and J. S. McCaskill (2016). *Integrating a supercapacitor for autonomous electrochemistry on microscopic electronic particles (lablets).* (preprint).

Sharma, A. and J. S. McCaskill (2015). "Autonomous lablet locomotion and active docking by sensomotory electroosmotic drive". *European Conference on Artificial Life 2015, York, UK.* MIT Press, pp. 456–462.

Sharma, A., P. F. Wagler, T. Maeke, D. Funke, J. Oehm, and J. S. McCaskill (2015). *Bipolar electrochemical charging of active CMOS microparticles (lablets) in external electric fields.* (in preparation).

Straczek, L., T. Maeke, D. A. Funke, A. Sharma, J. S. McCaskill, and J. Oehm (2016). "A CMOS 16k microelectrode array as docking platform for autonomous microsystems". *2016 IEEE Nordic Circuits and Systems Conference (NORCAS)*, pp. 1–6.

Tangen, U., H. Fellermann, and S. R. Rasmussen (2015). "MICREAgents (presentation)". *TRUCE workshop, ECAL 2015, York, UK.*

Wills, Peter R., Kay Nieselt, and John S. McCaskill (2015). "Emergence of Coding and its Specificity as a Physico-Informatic Problem". *Origins of Life and Evolution of Biospheres* 45(1–2):249–255.

Zhirnov, Victor V. and Ralph K. Cavin III (2011). *Microsystems for Bioelectronics: the nanomorphic cell.* Elsevier.

Chapter 7
Cellular Computing and Synthetic Biology

Martyn Amos and Angel Goñi-Moreno

Abstract Synthetic biology is an emerging, rapidly growing research field in which engineering principles are applied to natural, living systems. A major goal of synthetic biology is to harness the inherent "biological nanotechnology" of living cells for a number of applications, including computation, production, and diagnosis. In its infancy, synthetic biology was mainly concerned with the construction of small-scale, proof-of-principle computational devices (cellular computing), along the lines of simple logic gates and circuits, but the state-of-the-art now uses multicellular complexes and engineered cell-cell communication. From its practical origins around the turn of the century, the field has grown into a global scientific market predicted to be worth tens of billions of dollars by 2020. Anticipated applications include tissue engineering, environmental remediation, *in situ* disease detection and treatment, and even the development of the first fully-synthetic organism. In this chapter we review the timeline of synthetic biology, describe its alignment with unconventional computation, and, drawing on quotations from leading researchers in the field, describe its main challenges and opportunities.

7.1 Overview

Synthetic biology is a growing research area which is concerned with the application of engineering principles to the rational redesign of living (cellular)

Sections of this material are adapted from Amos (2014). Further bibliography items not cited in the main body of the chapter, but considered a foundational or otherwise useful reference, are: Becskei and Serrano (2000), Benner and Sismour (2005), Bray (2009), Church and Regis (2012), Dorrian et al. (2013), Douglas and Stemerding (2014), Forster and Church (2006), Goñi-Moreno and Amos (2012), Goodwin (1965), Monod (1971), Noireaux and Libchaber (2004), Pohorille and Deamer (2002), Rasmussen et al. (2003), Ruoff et al. (1999), and Serrano (2007).

systems. As well as generating fundamental insights into natural processes, a primary aim of synthetic biology is to obtaining useful (human-defined) behaviour in living systems. This might include the production/delivery of drugs, bioengineering, environmental monitoring/remediation, sensing, and biofuel production. The field has rapidly developed over the past 15 years, from initial conceptual studies to a major area of interest, with significant funding support and the accompanying infrastructure of international conferences, journals and professional societies.

For many, the emerging field of synthetic biology is a natural progression of "traditional" genetic engineering (Amos, 2006). As Purnick and Weiss (2009) observe,

> Conventional genetic engineering approaches for solving complex problems typically focus on tweaking one or a few genes. Synthetic biology, by contrast, approaches these problems from a novel, engineering-driven perspective that focuses on wholesale changes to existing cellular architectures and the construction of elaborate systems from the ground up. ... Whether addressing an existing problem or creating new capabilities, effective solutions can be inspired by, but need not mimic, natural biological processes. Our new designs can potentially be more robust or efficient than systems that have been fashioned by evolution.

Although biological and electronic systems operate along very different principles (analogue versus digital, asynchronous versus clocked, and so on), and employ very different substrates, they share an inherent hierarchical structure, whereby each later corresponds to a specific level of organization. At the bottom of the hierarchy we have the simplest components, which form the initial building blocks for subsequent layers. As we move from layer to layer, in a "bottom up" fashion, the system grows in complexity, but in an inherently *modular* fashion (Wall et al., 2004). Andrianantoandro et al. (2006) make this link explicit, and in Figure 7.1, we present an augmented version of their scheme.

At the lowest level of computer architecture (the *physical layer*), we have fundamental *components*, such as transistors and resistors. In synthetic biology, these components may be represented by basic elements such as *promoters* (regions of DNA that initiate the transcription of a gene) and *repressors* (proteins which inhibit gene transcription) (Purnick and Weiss, 2009). These may then be connected to form *devices*, such as Boolean logic gates (akin to biochemical reactions in synthetic biology). In the early days of synthetic biology, these devices were pieced together to form *modules* to achieve specific tasks, such as *switching*, *pulse generation* and *oscillation*. A landmark "first wave" paper (Elowitz and Leibler, 2000) demonstrated the "repressilator"; an oscillator based on a circuit of gene transcription *repressors*. This demonstrated the feasibility of integrating, in a rational, engineered manner, a non-trivial number of fundamental components (i.e., repressors, promoters) together into a single module (as opposed to making modifications to existing structures, or inserting single genes). New modules quickly followed; around the same time that the repressilator work appeared, a number of other im-

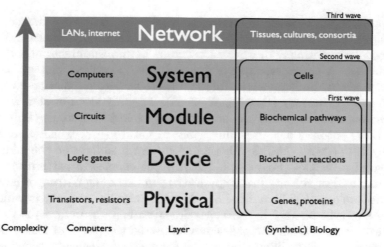

Fig. 7.1 Hierarchical mapping between existing layers of abstraction for both computer engineering and synthetic biology, showing both the mapping between them, and the "waves" of activity in the latter area (adapted from Andrianantoandro et al. (2006)).

portant "first wave" experiments were published. In the same issue of *Nature*, Gardner et al. (2000) demonstrated a genetic "toggle switch", which allowed external control of a bi-stable (two state) circuit engineered into *E. coli*. According to the authors, toggle switching had not yet been "demonstrated in networks of non-specialised regulatory components." That is to say, at that point nobody had been able to construct a toggle switch using genes that hadn't already been selected by evolutionary processes to perform that specific task.

Fundamental to the success of both projects was the use of *mathematical modelling*. As Hasty et al. (2002) observe,

> As in the case of the toggle switch, a mathematical model was instrumental in the process of designing the repressilator. Although the ring network architecture is theoretically capable of sustaining oscillations, not all parameter choices give rise to oscillatory solutions. The modelling work indicated that oscillations were favoured by high protein synthesis and degradation rates, large cooperative binding effects, and efficient repression. These theoretical conclusions led to specific design choices . . .

We now consider the subsequent ("second wave") work, in which modules were brought together to form larger scale *systems*. As Likic et al. (2010) point out (by highlighting O'Malley and Dupré (2005) in the context of *systems biology*), the basic notion of what constitutes a biological "system" can be hard to capture. We define a synthetic biological system as a *set of modules* which interact to produce some coherent behaviour(s). These modules may be confined to a single cell, or (as is becoming increasingly common) they may be *distributed* over a number of different cells.

We distinguish "systems" from "networks" by measuring their capacity for *information transmission*; within systems we generally observe relatively low rates of transmission, whereas networks have much higher "bandwidth" capabilities. A classic example of "second wave" synthetic biology concerns the engineering and connection of modules to achieve population-level coordination of behaviour (Basu et al., 2005). The formation of *spatiotemporal patterns* is a fundamental property of many biological systems (Ball, 1999), and these patterns are often functional in nature (e.g., when protecting a colony from a pathogen). Synthetic biology can shed light on the underlying biological principles (Payne et al., 2013), but *engineered* pattern formation may also find significant future applications in tissue engineering or biological nanotechnology (Khalil and Collins, 2010). Controlling the way in which collections of cells interact to form specific patterns (or structures) is therefore of great interest. Basu and colleagues harnessed the power of bacterial communication to effect differential spatial responses. Specifically, they used the bacterial *quorum sensing* (QS) mechanism (Atkinson and Williams, 2009), which is used by certain species to assess cellular concentrations, and thus coordinate gene expression (the idea being that a specific response, such as producing light, may only be "worthwhile" or feasible if there is a sufficient number – or *quorum* – of individuals present in a particular region).

Other notable examples of multiple module systems include a set of genetic clocks, synchronised using QS (Danino et al., 2010), a logic evaluator that operates in mammalian cells (Rinaudo et al., 2007), an edge detector (Tabor et al., 2009), a synthetic predator-prey ecosystem (Balagaddé et al., 2008) and a bistable ("push on, push off") switch (Lou et al., 2010). What all of these implementations have in common is the importance of computational / mathematical modelling; either to understand the behaviour of the system, to find the best molecular sequences to use in specific situations, or to "fine tune" system parameters. However, engineering and computer science may also *inform* the development of the *next* wave of synthetic biology, through the adoption and application of basic principles.

As Heinemann and Panke (2006) point out, the idea of *abstraction* (as used in its engineering context) is already fundamental to the field. The notion of *distributed computing* will allow us to construct large-scale *networked* synthetic biology systems. In computer science, distributed systems are characterised by several features, including (1) *asynchrony*, that is, the lack of a global "clock", (2) *local failure* of components, without global failure, and (3) *concurrency*. that is, components work in parallel (Attiya and Welch, 2004). As biological systems share all of these features, the model may provide useful guidance for future synthetic biology implementations.

However, biological molecules and systems present additional scientific and engineering challenges, compared to relatively well-understood semiconductor-based substrates. As Purnick and Weiss (2009) observe,

... engineering biological systems probably requires both new design principles and the simultaneous advance of scientific understanding. ... Beyond typical circuit design issues, synthetic biologists must also account for cell death, crosstalk, mutations, intracellular, intercellular and extracellular conditions, noise and other biological phenomena. A further difficult task is to correctly match suitable components in a designed system. As the number of system components grows, it becomes increasingly difficult to coordinate component inputs and outputs to produce the overall desired behaviour.

This problem is elaborated by Macía et al. (2012), who point out that

> In contrast to standard electronics, every wire needs to be a different molecule to properly connect different elements or cells. Inside a cell or in culture media the spatial insulation of wires that is assumed in electronics is no longer satisfied. As a consequence, the chemical diversity of constructs rapidly grows.

The complex and dynamic environment of the cell restricts the complexity of engineered units that may be introduced via synthetic biology methods: "... inside a cell, the cables need to have a different implementation: different proteins must be used for each different pair. Additionally, because of the intrinsic difficulties of implementing them, the resulting constructs are usually specific for the given problem and cannot be reused afterwards" (Macía et al., 2012). This problem has motivated the search for *multi-cellular* solutions, based on bacterial consortia (Brenner et al., 2008; Solé and Macia, 2013). These are made up of *multiple* populations of microbes, each of which may interact and share information with the other groups. The benefits of using such mixed populations in synthetic biology include: (1) the ability to perform complex tasks that are impossible for individual strains; (2) robustness to environmental perturbation; (3) the ability to use communication to facilitate a division of labour; (4) biological insight that can be derived from engineering consortia (Brenner et al., 2008). These benefits map nicely onto the features of distributed computer systems listed above, and it is clear that engineered microbial consortia "... represent an important new frontier for synthetic biology" (Brenner et al., 2008).

The issue of addressable "wiring" has been approached in a number of ways. One solution (Regot et al., 2011) uses engineered yeast cells as building blocks for the evaluation of logical functions. Each cell type implements a specific logic function; by combining cells together, the authors were able to evaluate a large number of complex circuits (including a multiplexer and an adder) using a relatively small "library". A similar, distributed approach is taken by Tamsir et al. (2011), who describe the construction of a multicellular NOR gate, using quorum sensing molecules as "wires". They demonstrate how their NOR gates may be combined in order to evaluate other functions, including the notoriously difficult XOR. In an accompanying commentary article, Li and You (2011) describe the benefits of both approaches: (1) *encapsulation*: the notion that each logic gate, when engineered into a cell, may be considered to be a "black box", with implementation details hidden from the designer (that is, the designer need only concern themselves with module interfacing issues), (2) the facility for module *reuse* (which derives naturally from encapsulation): modules are general-purpose, and may be used multiple times, in different parts of a circuit, and (3) *noise suppression*: the use of circuit layers containing a sub-population of cells allows erroneous individual cell responses to be filtered out.

Although computation using distributed cellular populations is still relatively new, researchers are looking to augment the range of communication schemes available. Reliance on signalling molecules (such as those employed in quorum sensing) leads to a natural restriction on both bandwidth and message variety (that is, they are restricted to a single message per channel, and they tend to have a relatively narrow range of responses) (Ortiz and Endy, 2012). One possible way around these limitations may be to "... establish an information channel that is capable of transmitting arbitrary messages encoded via a common format" (Ortiz and Endy, 2012). They propose the exchange of *genetic material*, rather than simple signalling molecules, as this offers the capability of transmitting *arbitrary* messages. This "DNA messaging" protocol uses bacterial *transduction*, the transfer of DNA from one cell to another by a virus (in this case, M13). The three success criteria defined for their system are (1) *decoupling*: the ability to transmit different messages in a "reusable" fashion (see the "reuse" benefit in the previous paragraph), (2) *flexibility*: the ability to transmit messages of different length, and messages that specify different functional outcomes, and (3) *specificity*: the ability to target messages to particular cell types in a mixed population. All three criteria were met in a series of experiments; moreover, Ortiz and Endy (2012) also demonstrated the ability to extend the range of their messaging scheme by harnessing the power of bacterial *chemotaxis* (the ability of cells to move in response to chemical gradients). This allowed them to achieve DNA messaging at the centimetre scale. An alternative messaging scheme was also proposed by Goñi-Moreno et al. (2013), which uses bacterial *conjugation*, transfer of DNA during direct cell-cell contact, which has been likened to "bacterial sex" (Llosa et al., 2002).

7.2 Contribution to UCOMP aspects

7.2.1 Speed

"The general consensus now is that DNA computing will never be able to compete directly with silicon-based technology" (Parker, 2003)

Although the quotation above concerns molecular-based (DNA) computing, comparisons are still often made between cell-based devices and silicon computers. For example, "Every living cell within us is a hybrid analog–digital supercomputer that implements highly computationally intensive non-linear, stochastic, differential equations with 30 000 gene–protein state variables that interact via complex feedback loops" (Sarpeshkar, 2014). Although the comparison may be valid in terms of broad metaphors, early work on DNA computing claimed significant speed benefits, due to massive inherent parallelism of operations on solutions of molecules. However, these are quickly outweighed by the inherent space trade-off that is required to achieve them (Amos, 2006). Although there is, of course, always a risk of appearing foolish when making such predictions, at least in the short- to medium-term we expect that cell-based computational devices will provide no competition for existing substrates *on their "home turf"*. Rather, such devices will find specific application niches, in which *they might well outperform traditional silicon-based machines* (for example, in the biosensing or medical device domains). In these types of situation, "speed" becomes a relatively meaningless metric.

7.2.2 Resources

"Synthetic biology is still in its early stages of development. If we stick with the comparison to the microchip industry and consider that the first transistor was developed in 1947, then we are now at about 1960" (Way et al., 2014)

Synthetic biology, as its name suggests, requires significant resource in terms of the synthesis of DNA. The main limiting factor here is, therefore, the cost of DNA synthesis (and the associated person-hours required to piece together vectors. As Way et al. (2014) explain,

although there is an ongoing evolution toward outsourcing DNA constructions, graduate students and postdocs still spend much of their time making plasmids. The real transition will come when DNA synthesis is so cheap that a graduate student no longer needs to ask an advisor for permission to build a new microbial genome or an entire plant chromosome, for example.

Jovicevic et al. (2014), reporting on attempts to construct synthetic yeast by the end of this decade, argue that

By then, it is expected that the cost of synthetic DNA will have decreased by orders of magnitude, especially if innovations in constructing synthetic DNA directly from printed oligo arrays continue. Considerably, lower costs will make it likely that chromosome synthesis and genome re-design will be within the reach of the average research group by 2020.

However, if we consider an individual cell in terms of its computational resource requirements, the picture looks slightly more favourable. Sarpeshkar (2014) states:

The average 10 μm human cell performs these amazing computations with 0.34 nm self-aligned nanoscale DNA–protein devices, with 20 kT per molecular operation (1 ATP molecule hydrolysed), approximately 0.8 pW of power consumption (10 M ATP s^{-1}) and with noisy, unreliable devices that collectively interact to perform reliable hybrid analog–digital computation. Based on a single amino acid among thousands of proteins, immune cells must collectively decide whether a given molecule or molecular fragment is from a friend or foe, and if they err in their decision by even a tiny amount, autoimmune disease, infectious disease, or cancer could originate with high probability every day. Even at the end of Moore's law, we will not match such performance by even a few orders of magnitude.

7.2.3 Quality

"Nature is not purely digital. While molecules are discrete and digital, all molecular interactions that lead to computation, e.g. association, transformation and dissociation chemical reactions, have a probabilistic analog nature to them. Depending on one's point of view, computation in a cell is owing to lots of probabilistic digital events or owing to continuous analog computation with noise. Both views are equivalent" (Sarpeshkar, 2014).

To date, the majority of synthetic biology implementations have been based on the Boolean circuit model of gene regulation. As Goñi-Moreno (2014) points out,

There is still some opposition to the use of digital abstractions to describe molecular processes. Some people argue that, for example, the expression of a protein is a very noisy process that cannot be compared to the perfect 1 or 0 values of the signal coming from digital devices. However, it is important to note that the typical perfect-world-based digital signal is just an abstraction used for the conceptualization of reality. In fact, electronic signals rarely attain perfect values due to voltage drops and circuitry-based stochasticity.

Sarpeshkar argues that analog(ue) computation in cells is advantageous in terms of energy, part count or number of molecules (ie. space), below a specific threshold for precision. However, this does still not allow us to transcend the circuit metaphor; for this, we will need to consider the capabilities of cellular *consortia*, heterogenous mixtures of large numbers of cells. Khalil and Collins (2010) state

The future of translational synthetic biology is dependent on and limited by the development of reliable means for connecting smaller functional circuits to realize higher-order networks with predictable behaviours.

7.2.4 Embeddedness

"Mammalian cells engineered with programmable genetic devices performing arithmetic calculations with similar precision, robustness and predictability to those of their digital electronics counterparts may enable the assembly of tissue-like biocomputers that could allow the design of complex human-machine interfaces and provide diagnostic information and therapeutic interventions in future gene-based and cell-based treatment strategies" (Ausländer et al., 2012).

Although most synthetic biology applications are currently executed *in vivo*, the potential application domains, e.g., biomedical engineering, bioremediation, drug delivery (Khalil and Collins, 2010; McDaniel and Weiss, 2005), naturally lend themselves to embedding of solutions in native environments, such as the human body, or in oil spills, for example. Advances in mammalian synthetic biology will facilitate the former (Lienert et al., 2014; Rinaudo et al., 2007), although, of course, there are still significant legal, ethical and safety concerns to be addressed (Church et al., 2014).

7.2.5 Formalism

"At the systems level, synthetic biology is beginning to design and to implement systems that are several layers of abstraction above the raw sequence of DNA. Formalized design can help by decomposing complex desired functions into manageable components, potentially aided by computational automation" (Slusarczyk et al., 2012).

Mathematical modelling has been fundamental to synthetic biology since its inception (Elowitz and Leibler, 2000; Gardner et al., 2000). Of course, the Boolean logic formalism of gene regulation was already well-established in microbiology, prior to the emergence of syn bio. The field is inherently amenable to novel formalisms, or the application of existing formalisms to a new domain. Existing examples of how well-understood systems may be applied to synthetic biology include Petri nets (Heiner et al., 2008), P-systems (Romero-Campero et al., 2009) and markup languages (Endler et al., 2009). Recent work has included formal methods for the analysis and design of biosystems using model checking (Konur and Gheorghe, 2015), rule-based modelling (Wilson-Kanamori et al., 2015) and design communication (Galdzicki et al., 2014).

7.2.6 Programming

"Another important consideration for biological design is the limited ability of humans to manage the details of increasingly complex systems. Although it is reasonable to expect a designer of small synthetic systems to choose and keep track of all genetic components (such as ribosome-binding sites, degradation tails and regulatory regions in promoters), this is not feasible for larger systems. To manage complexity, biological system designers must be able to create bioprograms using intuitive high level abstractions" (Purnick and Weiss, 2009)

Following on from formalism, the notion of programmability is well-established in synthetic biology. Marchisio and Stelling (2009), Pedersen and Phillips (2009), Purnick and Weiss (2009), and Umesh et al. (2010) all provide snapshots of several programming models and languages that automatically "compile" high-level programs down to the level of low-level components such as gene sequences. Beal et al. (2011) and Beal et al. (2012) describe a detailed workflow for designing biological networks from a program-based specification. Importantly, this has been validated in the laboratory, using a simple sensor-reporter program in *E. coli*, and recent work presents a CAD-based automated circuit design methodology (Huynh et al., 2013). Additionally, tools have recently emerged to support the automated design of multi-cellular consortia (Ji et al., 2013). However, despite these developments, Church et al. (2014) note that

> Synthetic biology is less like highly modular (or 'switch-like') electrical engineering and computer science and more like civil and mechanical engineering in its use of optimization of modelling of whole system-level stresses and traffic flow.

7.2.7 Applications

> "With an expected global market of $10.8 billion by 2016, synthetic biology will play an important role in the bioeconomy" (Kelley et al., 2014)

There are many existing applications of synthetic biology, including the domains of clinical therapies, drug production and bio-fuel. Where the field lags behind is in the area of mammalian synthetic biology, where are are, so far, relatively few applications. Recent "success stories" include the efficient production of anti-malarial drugs (Paddon and Keasling, 2014; Paddon et al., 2013), and the replacement of petrochemicals (Schirmer et al., 2010). Several recent discussion papers summarise existing and emerging synthetic biology applications in the biomedical domain (Folcher and Fussenegger, 2012; Weber and Fussenegger, 2012), industrial microbiology (Zhu et al., 2012), the environment (Schmidt, 2012) and translational medicine (Ruder et al., 2011).

7.2.8 Philosophy

> "In sum, the original guiding principles conceptualized for synthetic biology a decade ago have permeated a widespread, diverse community, but it remains to be seen which elements merit adoption as research becomes more translational" (Way et al., 2014).

Although by no means universally accepted, the following principles define much current activity in synthetic biology (Way et al., 2014):

1. **Design to meet specifications set in advance.** Specifications should ideally be quantifiable in terms of biological variables such as switching rate, cell type, doubling time, etc.

2. **Separate design from fabrication**. Using the hardware/software analogy from traditional computer engineering, the hardware is concerned
   with the production of DNA, RNA and/or proteins, while the software
   aspect concerns itself with the design of constructs.
3. **Use biological "parts"**. An emphasis on modularity can help to drive
   the application of engineering principles in synthetic biology, although
   the boundaries between modules are often more fuzzy than in traditional
   electronic engineering. One example of a part specification system is the
   well-known BioBricks standard.
4. **Abstract wherever possible**. Abstraction is a useful tool in terms of
   ignoring unnecessary detail and focussing on the essential function of a
   component, but it is important to take care to ensure that this is not
   performed prematurely, while there is still room for further characteriza-
   tion/engineering of components.
5. **Use well-defined "chassis" organisms**. The use of a standardised
   (perhaps minimal) cell could potentially remove unknown factors inherent to a "natural" cell. This may be achieved by either systematically
   removing genes from an existing cell, or by synthesising entirely new organisms.

7.3 Main achievements so far

Cameron et al. (2014) give a timeline of the main milestones in synthetic biology to date. We list key highlights from this, ordered by year of publication
/ development:

- 2000: First synthetic circuits (toggle switch and repressilator).
- 2001: First cell–cell communication circuit engineered, based on quorom
  sensing.
- 2002: Combinatorial synthesis of genetic networks.
- 2003: Engineering of artemisinin precursor pathway in *E. coli*.
- 2004: First international conference for synthetic biology; first iGem competition.
- 2005: Bacterial "photography" – light-sensing circuit engineered into *E.
  coli*; engineered multicellular pattern formation.
- 2006: Bacteria engineered to invade cancer cells.
- 2007: Engineered phage for biofilm dispersal.
- 2008: RNA-based devices for performing logical operations; biofuel production.
- 2009: Gibson DNA assembly; MAGE (Multiplex Automated Genomic
  Engineering); counting circuit; edge-detector.
- 2010: Bacterial cell with synthetic genome; synchronised genetic clock for
  population-based oscillatory waves.

- 2011: Complete set of Boolean logic gates in *E. coli.*
- 2012: Multiple input logic cascade.
- 2013: Commercial production of anti-malarial drug using engineered yeast.

7.4 What could be achieved in ten years?

Some key possible achievements over the next decade include (Church et al., 2014):

- First fully synthetic organism.
- Programmed mammalian cell lines.
- Synthetic gene circuit therapies in humans (e.g., skin, gut microbial, neurotherapies).
- Spatiotemporal programming and pattern formation applied to tissue engineering and regenerative medicine.

7.5 Current challenges

The following quotations, taken from (Church et al., 2014), from leading figures in synthetic biology describe some possible challenges over the next decade or so (emphasis ours):

> What is critically lacking, however, with respect to mammalian synthetic biology (an area that my laboratory is currently most focused on), are 'real-world' applications. We must now make an effort to transition from developing 'toy' applications to creating actual applications for cancer therapies, vaccination and engineered tissues that society can directly benefit from. **Arguably, the main challenge here is how to safely deliver synthetic circuits into mammalian organisms**. I predict that the development of RNA-based delivery methods could be a game changer in overcoming the regulatory hurdles and required safety guarantees associated with traditional gene therapy. [Ron Weiss]

> [S]ynthetic biology remains extremely primitive owing both to technical challenges and, even more, to fundamental inadequacies in our understanding of biological circuit design. On the technical side, **synthesizing genetic circuits and transferring them into cells remains far too slow and idiosyncratic, especially in animal cells**. However, several new methods, such as those based on the CRISPR system, are extremely encouraging. On the fundamental side, we still have little understanding of how circuit designs can function effectively in cells and tissues and much to learn from natural examples. In particular, one of the greatest challenges is to move synthetic biology from circuits operating in individual microorganisms to circuits that function in a truly multicellular fashion, for example, circuits sufficient to implement self-patterning of cells. If successful, we may be able to understand multicellular development from a totally new point of view that could inform tissue engineering and regeneration. [Michael B. Elowitz]

One big challenge in the field remains to develop **measurement technologies** that enable the high-throughput, non-invasive quantification of activities that are not encoded in fluorescent reporter proteins. As the field has shifted towards favouring design approaches that generate diversity within the genetic programmes, there has not been a corresponding emphasis on the development of technologies that enable the characterization of the resulting diversity of genetic designs. As such, the shift towards a 'design smarter' approach (versus a 'design more' approach) is limited by our inability to learn from current design approaches. [Christina Smolke]

One of the challenges in applications is **harnessing cells to build complex functional materials**. Cells are natural atomic architects and we already exploit this, as many in?use materials are from biology. The examples above are all relatively simple chemicals, natural products or individual proteins. Obtaining more complex products will require synthetic gene circuits and the ability to control many, possibly hundreds, of genes simultaneously. [Christopher Voigt]

Of course there are also significant legal, ethical and safety considerations inherent to the field; this will require a reassessment of how risks are categorized, and how new products are regulated (Church et al., 2014). One of the major challenges for synthetic biology will be to contribute to and drive the development of new regulatory structures that are set up to cope with engineered organisms for use in the body or in the field. Another key challenge is that of avoiding "hype", and ensuring that the mistakes of Genetic Modification are not repeated with synthetic biology (Kaebnick et al., 2014).

7.6 Outlook and recommendations

The previous sections outline key recommendations/challenges/opportunities. The following is a personal take on the future of synthetic biology, and should not be interpreted as exhaustive.

We anticipate an emerging "third wave" of synthetic biology, in which attention is moving from single cell solutions, towards "networked", multicellular approaches. Such models will allow us to transcend the inherent limitations of isolated cells, and enable the full potential of biological "wetware". As Bacchus and Fussenegger (2013) argue,

The move from intracellular to intercellular communication systems is a major tool that will enable future advances in synthetic biology. These intercellular systems are likely to out-perform any intracellular counterpart. The future will require greater processing capacity, as more complex networks and circuits are being established, which will dramatically increase performance characteristics. Therefore, the division of metabolic workload of the overall system between cells is crucial, as one cell is unlikely to be sufficient. Just as computers are assembled using different standardized electrical hardware coupled in a rational way to increase a system's overall performance, the assembly of distinct biological cellular machineries will be achieved in a similar manner.

Of course, this transition is not without its difficulties, and some of the major future challenges include (1) how to ensure long-term maintenance of homeostasis in engineered consortia, (2) how to account for (or even harness) horizontal gene transfer between population members, (2) how to engineer "non-standard" organisms that offer new and useful functionalities, and (4) how to "fine tune" the behaviour of multiple interacting microbial populations (Brenner et al., 2008). Computational modelling and simulation will provide central contributions to addressing these, and the ongoing development of software tools (see Slusarczyk et al. (2012) for a recent list) will continue to enable fruitful collaborations between biologists, mathematicians, computer scientists and engineers.

References

Amos, M. (2006). *Genesis Machines: The New Science of Biocomputing*. Atlantic Books.

Amos, M. (2014). "Population-based microbial computing: A third wave of synthetic biology?" *International Journal of General Systems* 43(7):770–782.

Andrianantoandro, E., S. Basu, D. K. Karig, and R. Weiss (2006). "Synthetic biology: new engineering rules for an emerging discipline". *Molecular Systems Biology* 2(1):0028.

Atkinson, S. and P. Williams (2009). "Quorum sensing and social networking in the microbial world". *Journal of the Royal Society Interface* 6(40):959–978.

Attiya, H. and J. Welch (2004). *Distributed Computing: Fundamentals, Simulations and Advanced Topics*. John Wiley and Sons.

Ausländer, S., D. Ausländer, M. Müller, M. Wieland, and M. Fussenegger (2012). "Programmable single-cell mammalian biocomputers". *Nature* 487(7405):123–127.

Bacchus, W. and M. Fussenegger (2013). "Engineering of synthetic intercellular communication systems". *Metabolic Engineering* 16:33–41.

Balagaddé, F. K., H. Song, J. Ozaki, C. H. Collins, M. Barnet, F. H. Arnold, S. R. Quake, and L. You (2008). "A synthetic *Escherichia coli* predator-prey ecosystem". *Molecular Systems Biology* 4(1):187.

Ball, P. (1999). *The Self-Made Tapestry: Pattern Formation in Nature*. Oxford University Press.

Basu, S., Y. Gerchman, C. H. Collins, F. H. Arnold, and R. Weiss (2005). "A synthetic multicellular system for programmed pattern formation". *Nature* 434(7037):1130–1134.

Beal, J., T. Lu, and R. Weiss (2011). "Automatic compilation from high-level biologically-oriented programming language to genetic regulatory networks". *PLoS One* 6(8):e22490.

Beal, J., R. Weiss, D. Densmore, A. Adler, E. Appleton, J. Babb, and F. Yaman (2012). "An end-to-end workflow for engineering of biological networks from high-level specifications". *ACS Synthetic Biology* 1(8):317–331.

Becskei, A. and L. Serrano (2000). "Engineering stability in gene networks by autoregulation". *Nature* 405(6786):590–593.

Benner, S. A. and A. M. Sismour (2005). "Synthetic biology". *Nature Reviews Genetics* 6(7):533–43.

Bray, D. (2009). *Wetware: A Computer in Every Living Cell.* Yale University Press.

Brenner, K., L. You, and F. H. Arnold (2008). "Engineering microbial consortia: A new frontier in synthetic biology". *Trends in Biotechnology* 26(9):483–489.

Cameron, D. E., C. J. Bashor, and J. J. Collins (2014). "A brief history of synthetic biology". *Nature Reviews Microbiology* 12(5):381–390.

Church, G. M., M. B. Elowitz, C. D. Smolke, C. A. Voigt, and R. Weiss (2014). "Realizing the potential of synthetic biology". *Nature Reviews Molecular Cell Biology* 15:289–294.

Church, G. and E. Regis (2012). *Regenesis: How Synthetic Biology will Reinvent Nature and Ourselves.* Basic Books.

Danino, T., O. Mondragón-Palomino, L. Tsimring, and J. Hasty (2010). "A synchronized quorum of genetic clocks". *Nature* 463(7279):326–330.

Dorrian, H., J. Borresen, and M. Amos (2013). "Community structure and multi-modal oscillations in complex networks". *PLOS ONE* 8(10):e75569.

Douglas, C. M. and D. Stemerding (2014). "Challenges for the European governance of synthetic biology for human health". *Life Sciences, Society and Policy* 10(1):1–18.

Elowitz, M. B. and S. Leibler (2000). "A synthetic oscillatory network of transcriptional regulators". *Nature* 403(6767):335–338.

Endler, L., N. Rodriguez, N. Juty, V. Chelliah, C. Laibe, C. Li, and N. Le Novère (2009). "Designing and encoding models for synthetic biology". *Journal of the Royal Society Interface* 6:S405–S417.

Folcher, M. and M. Fussenegger (2012). "Synthetic biology advancing clinical applications". *Current Opinion in Chemical Biology* 16(3):345–354.

Forster, A. C. and G. M. Church (2006). "Towards synthesis of a minimal cell". *Molecular Systems Biology* 2(1):45.

Galdzicki, M., K. P. Clancy, E. Oberortner, M. Pocock, J. Y. Quinn, C. A. Rodriguez, and H. Sauro (2014). "The Synthetic Biology Open Language (SBOL) provides a community standard for communicating designs in synthetic biology". *Nature Biotechnology* 32(6):545–550.

Gardner, T. S., C. R. Cantor, and J. J. Collins (2000). "Construction of a genetic toggle switch in *Escherichia coli*". *Nature* 403:339–342.

Goñi-Moreno, A. (2014). "On genetic logic circuits: forcing digital electronics standards?" *Memetic Computing* 6:149–155.

Goñi-Moreno, A. and M. Amos (2012). "A reconfigurable NAND/NOR genetic logic gate". *BMC Systems Biology* 6(1):126.

Goñi-Moreno, A., M. Amos, and F. de la Cruz (2013). "Multicellular computing using conjugation for wiring". *PLOS ONE* 8(6):e65986.

Goodwin, B. C. (1965). "Oscillatory behaviour in enzymatic control processes". *Advances in Enzyme Regulation, Vol. 3.* Ed. by G. Weber. Pergamon Press, pp. 425–438.

Hasty, J., D. McMillen, and J. J. Collins (2002). "Engineered gene circuits". *Nature* 420:224–230.

Heinemann, M. and S. Panke (2006). "Synthetic biology—putting engineering into biology". *Bioinformatics* 22(22):2790–2799.

Heiner, M., D. Gilbert, and R. Donaldson (2008). "Petri nets for systems and synthetic biology". *Formal Methods for Computational Systems Biology.* Springer, pp. 215–264.

Huynh, L., A. Tsoukalas, M. Köppe, and I. Tagkopoulos (2013). "SBROME: a scalable optimization and module matching framework for automated biosystems design". *ACS Synthetic Biology* 2(5):263–273.

Ji, W., J. Zheng, H. Shi, H. Zhang, R. Sun, J. Xi, and Q. Ouyang (2013). "A formalized design process for bacterial consortia that perform logic computing". *PLOS ONE* 8(2):e57482.

Jovicevic, D., B. A. Blount, and T. Ellis (2014). "Total synthesis of a eukaryotic chromosome; Redesigning and SCRaMbLE-ing yeast". *Bioessays* 36(9):855–860.

Kaebnick, G. E., M. K. Gusmano, and T. H. Murray (2014). "The Ethics of Synthetic Biology: Next Steps and Prior Questions". *Hastings Center Report* 44(S5):S4–S26.

Kelley, N. J., D. J. Whelan, E. Kerr, A. Apel, R. Beliveau, and R. Scanlon (2014). "Engineering biology to address global problems: Synthetic biology markets, needs, and applications". *Industrial Biotechnology* 10(3):140–149.

Khalil, A. S. and J. J. Collins (2010). "Synthetic biology: Applications come of age". *Nature Reviews Genetics* 11(5):367–379.

Konur, S. and M. Gheorghe (2015). "A property-driven methodology for formal analysis of synthetic biology systems". *IEEE/ACM Transactions on Computational Biology and Bioinformatics* 2:360–371.

Li, B. and L. You (2011). "Division of logic labour". *Nature* 469(4):171–172.

Lienert, F., J. J. Lohmueller, A. Garg, and P. A. Silver (2014). "Synthetic biology in mammalian cells: next generation research tools and therapeutics". *Nature Reviews Molecular Cell Biology* 15(2):95–107.

Likic, V. A., M. J. McConville, T. Lithgow, and A. Bacic (2010). "Systems biology: The next frontier for bioinformatics". *Advances in Bioinformatics* 2010:268925.

Llosa, M., F. X. Gomis-Rüth, M. Coll, and F. D. L. Cruz (2002). "Bacterial conjugation: a two-step mechanism for DNA transport". *Molecular Microbiology* 45(1):1–8.

Lou, C., X. Liu, M. Ni, Y. Huang, Q. Huang, and L. Huang (2010). "Synthesizing a novel genetic sequential logic circuit: A push-on push-off switch". *Molecular Systems Biology* 6:350.

Macía, J., F. Posas, and R. V. Solé (2012). "Distributed computation: The new wave of synthetic biology devices". *Trends in Biotechnology* 30(6):342–349.

Marchisio, M. A. and J. Stelling (2009). "Computational design tools for synthetic biology". *Current Opinion in Biotechnology* 20(4):479–485.

McDaniel, R. and R. Weiss (2005). "Advances in synthetic biology: On the path from prototypes to applications". *Current Opinion in Biotechnology* 16(4):476–83.

Monod, J. (1971). *Chance and Necessity*. Alfred A. Knopf.

Noireaux, V. and A. Libchaber (2004). "A vesicle bioreactor as a step toward an artificial cell assembly". *PNAS* 101(51):17669–17674.

O'Malley, M. A. and J. Dupré (2005). "Fundamental issues in systems biology". *BioEssays* 27:1270–1276.

Ortiz, M. E. and D. Endy (2012). "Engineered cell-cell communication via DNA messaging". *Journal of Biological Engineering* 6(1):16.

Paddon, C. J. and J. D. Keasling (2014). "Semi-synthetic artemisinin: a model for the use of synthetic biology in pharmaceutical development". *Nature Reviews Microbiology* 12(5):355–367.

Paddon, C. J., P. J. Westfall, D. J. Pitera, K. Benjamin, K. Fisher, D. McPhee, ..., and J. D. Newman (2013). "High-level semi-synthetic production of the potent antimalarial artemisinin." *Nature* 496(7446):528–532.

Parker, J. (2003). "Computing with DNA". *EMBO Reports* 4(1):7–10.

Payne, S., B. Li, Y. Cao, S. Schaeffer, M. D. Ryser, and L. You (2013). "Temporal control of self-organized pattern formation without morphogen gradients in bacteria". *Molecular Systems Biology* 9:697.

Pedersen, M. and A. Phillips (2009). "Towards programming languages for genetic engineering of living cells". *Journal of the Royal Society Interface* 6(Suppl 4):S437–S450.

Pohorille, A. and D. Deamer (2002). "Artificial cells: Prospects for biotechnology". *Trends in Biotechnology* 20(3):123–128.

Purnick, P. E. and R. Weiss (2009). "The second wave of synthetic biology: From modules to systems". *Nature Reviews Molecular Cell Biology* 10(6):410–422.

Rasmussen, S., L. Chen, M. Nilsson, and S. Abe (2003). "Bridging nonliving and living matter". *Artificial Life* 9(3):269–316.

Regot, S., J. Macia, N. Conde, K. Furukawa, J. Kjellén, T. Peeters, S. Hohmann, E. de Nadal, F. Posas, and R. Solé (2011). "Distributed biological computation with multicellular engineered networks". *Nature* 469(7329):207–211.

Rinaudo, K., L. Bleris, R. Maddamsetti, S. Subramanian, R. Weiss, and Y. Benenson (2007). "A universal RNAi-based logic evaluator that operates in mammalian cells". *Nature Biotechnology* 25(7):795–801.

Romero-Campero, F. J., J. Twycross, M. Camara, M. Bennett, M. Gheorghe, and N. Krasnogor (2009). "Modular assembly of cell systems biology models using P systems". *International Journal of Foundations of Computer Science* 20(3):427–442.

Ruder, W. C., T. Lu, and J. J. Collins (2011). "Synthetic biology moving into the clinic". *Science* 333(6047):1248–1252.

Ruoff, P., M. Vinsjevik, C. Monnerjah, and L. Rensing (1999). "The Goodwin oscillator: On the importance of degradation reactions in the circadian clock". *Journal of Biological Rhythms* 14(6):469–479.

Sarpeshkar, R. (2014). "Analog synthetic biology". *Philosophical Transactions of the Royal Society A* 372(2010).

Schirmer, A., M. A. Rude, X. Li, E. Popova, and S. B. del Cardayre (2010). "Microbial biosynthesis of alkanes." *Science* 329:559–562.

Schmidt, M. (Ed.) (2012). *Synthetic Biology: Industrial and Environmental Applications*. John Wiley and Sons.

Serrano, L. (2007). "Synthetic biology: Promises and challenges". *Molecular Systems Biology* 3:158.

Slusarczyk, A. L., A. Lin, and R. Weiss (2012). "Foundations for the design and implementation of synthetic genetic circuits". *Nature Reviews Genetics* 13(6):406–420.

Solé, R. V. and J. Macia (2013). "Expanding the landscape of biological computation with synthetic multicellular consortia". *Natural Computing* 12(4):485–497.

Tabor, J. J., H. M. Salis, Z. B. Simpson, A. A. Chevalier, A. Levskaya, E. M. Marcotte, C. A. Voigt, and A. D. Ellington (2009). "A synthetic genetic edge detection program". *Cell* 137(7):1272–81.

Tamsir, A., J. J. Tabor, and C. A. Voigt (2011). "Robust multicellular computing using genetically encoded NOR gates and chemical 'wires'". *Nature* 469(7329):212–5.

Umesh, P., F. Naveen, C. U. M. Rao, and A. S. Nair (2010). "Programming languages for synthetic biology". *Systems and Synthetic Biology* 4(4):265–269.

Wall, M. E., W. S. Hlavacek, and M. A. Savageau (2004). "Design of gene circuits: Lessons from bacteria". *Nature Review Genetics* 5(1):34–42.

Way, J. C., J. J. Collins, J. D. Keasling, and P. A. Silver (2014). "Integrating biological redesign: Where synthetic biology came from and where it needs to go". *Cell* 157:151–161.

Weber, W. and M. Fussenegger (2012). "Emerging biomedical applications of synthetic biology". *Nature Reviews Genetics* 13(1):21–35.

Wilson-Kanamori, J., V. Danos, T. Thomson, and R. Honorato-Zimmer (2015). "Kappa rule-based modeling in synthetic biology". *Computational Methods in Synthetic Biology*. Springer, pp. 105–135.

Zhu, L., Y. Zhu, Y. Zhang, and Y. Li (2012). "Engineering the robustness of industrial microbes through synthetic biology". *Trends in Microbiology* 20(2):94–101.

Chapter 8
PhyChip: Growing Computers with Slime Mould

Andrew Adamatzky, Jeff Jones, Richard Mayne, James Whiting, Victor Erokhin, Andrew Schumann, and Stefano Siccardi

Abstract Slime mould *Physarum polycephalum* is a large single cell capable of distributed sensing, concurrent information processing, parallel computation, and decentralised actuation. The ease of culturing and experimenting with Physarum makes this slime mould an ideal substrate for real-world implementations of unconventional sensing and computing devices. In the last decade Physarum has become a popular inspiration for mathematical and algorithmic models and philosophical concepts of unconventional computing: give the slime mould a problem and it will solve it. We provide a concise summary of computing and sensing operations implemented with live slime mould and evaluate the feasibility of slime mould-based computing.

8.1 Overview

Research in unconventional, or nature-inspired, computing aims to uncover novel principles of efficient information processing and computation in physical, chemical and biological systems, to develop novel non-standard algorithms and computing architectures, and also to implement conventional algorithms in non-silicon, or wet, substrates. This emerging field of science and engineering is predominantly occupied by theoretical research, e.g. quantum computation, membrane computing and dynamical systems computing.

8.1.1 Why slime mould computers?

Despite the profound potential offered by unconventional computing, only a handful of experimental prototypes are reported so far, for example gas-discharge analog path finders; maze-solving micro-fluidic circuits; geomet-

© Springer International Publishing AG, part of Springer Nature 2018

S. Stepney et al. (eds.), *Computational Matter*, Natural Computing Series,

https://doi.org/10.1007/978-3-319-65826-1_8

111

Fig. 8.1 Slime mould *P. polycephalum.*

rically constrained universal chemical computers; specialized and universal chemical reaction–diffusion processors; universal extended analog computers; maze-solving chemo-tactic droplets; enzyme-based logical circuits; spatially extended crystallization computers for optimization and computational geometry; molecular logical gates and circuits.

A weak representation of laboratory experiments in the field of unconventional computers could be explained by technical difficulties, costs of prototyping of novel computing substrates, and also psychological barriers. Chemists and biologists do not usually aspire to experiment with unconventional computers because such activity diverts them from mainstream research in their fields. Computer scientists and mathematicians would like to experiment but are scared of laboratory equipment. If there was a simple to maintain substrate, which requires minimal equipment to experiment with and whose behaviour is understandable by and appealing to researchers from all fields of science, then progress in designing novel computing devices would be much more visible. We offer slime mould *Physarum polycephalum* for a role of such a 'universal' computing substrate.

8.1.2 Concept

Physarum polycephalum belongs to the species of order Physarales, subclass Myxogastromycetidae, class Myxomycetes, division Myxostelida. It is commonly known as a true, acellular or multi-headed slime mould. Plasmodium is a 'vegetative' phase, a single cell with a myriad of diploid nuclei. The plasmodium is visible to the naked eye. The plasmodium looks like an amorphous yellowish mass with networks of protoplasmic tubes (Fig. 8.1). The plasmod-

ium behaves and moves as a giant amoeba. It feeds on bacteria, spores and
other microbial creatures and micro-particles (Stephenson et al., 1994).

The unique features of *P. polycephalum* are, following Adamatzky (2010):

- Physarum is a living, dynamical reaction-diffusion pattern formation
  mechanism.
- Physarum may be considered as equivalent to a membrane bound sub
  excitable system (excitation stimuli provided by chemo-attractants and
  chemo-repellents).
- The complex patterning (reticulate networks, dendritic patterns) is equivalent to parts of the continuum of Turing structure patterns.
- Physarum efficiently exploits — or outsources — external computation
  by the environment via the sensing and suppression of nutrient gradients
- Physarum may be regarded as a highly efficient and living micro-manipu-
  lation and micro-fluidic transport device
- The induction of pattern type is determined partly by the environment,
  specifically nutrient quality and substrate hardness, dryness, etc.
- Physarum is thus a computational material based on modification of pro-
  toplasm transport by presence of external stimuli.
- Physarum is sensitive to illumination and AC electric fields and therefore
  allows for parallel and non-destructive input of information
- Physarum represents results of computation by configuration of its body.

In our PhyChip project we designed and fabricated a distributed biomorphic computing device built and operated by the slime mould. A Physarum
chip is a network of processing elements made of the slime mould's protoplasmic tubes coated with conductive substances; the network is populated by
living slime mould. A living network of protoplasmic tubes acts as an active
non-linear transducer of information, while templates of tubes coated with
conductor act as fast information channels.

The Physarum chip has parallel inputs (optical, chemo- and electro-based)
and outputs (electrical and optical). The Physarum chip solves a wide range
of computation tasks, including optimisation on graphs, computational geometry, robot control, logic and arithmetical computing. The slime mould-
based implementation is a bio-physical model of future nano-chips based on
biomorphic mineralisation.

We envisage that research and development centred on novel computing
substrates, as self-assembled and fault-tolerant fungal networks will lead to
a revolution in the bio-electronics and computer industry. Combined with
conventional electronic components in a hybrid chip, Physarum networks
will radically improve the performance of digital and analog circuits.

8.2 Contribution to UCOMP aspects: critical analysis

In terms of classical computing architectures, the following characteristics
can be attributed to Physarum chips:

- Massive parallelism: there are thousands of elementary processing units,
  oscillatory bodies, in a slime mould colonised in a Petri dish;
- Homogeneity: Compared to classical computing devices, the components
  of the Physarum computing plasmodium are remarkably uniform. The
  complexity of Physarum computation occurs as an emergent property of
  their local interactions, rather than complex features of individual units;
- Massive signal integration: Membrane of plasmodium is able to integrate
  massive amounts of complex spatial and time-varying stimuli to effect
  local changes in contraction rhythm and, ultimately, global behaviour of
  the plasmodium;
- Local connections: micro-volumes and oscillatory bodies of cytoplasm
  change their states, due to diffusion and reaction, depending on states
  of, or concentrations of, reactants, shape and electrical charges in their
  closest neighbours;
- Parallel input and output: Physarum computers by changing its shape,
  can record computation optically; Physarum is light sensitive, data can
  be input by localised illumination;
- Fault tolerance: being constantly in a shape changing state, Physarum
  chip restores its architecture even after a substantial part of its protoplasmic network is removed.

8.2.1 Speed

Speed of PhyChip depends on the mode of functioning and scale. In the
growing mode, e.g when we need to develop wires or memristive elements or
oscillators, the PhyChip's architecture develops with the speed 2–5 mm/hour.

Speed of sensors (Adamatzky, 2013c) and oscillatory logic components
(Whiting et al., 2014a) is typically by oscillation frequency which is 0.01–
0.03 Hz (Adamatzky, 2014).

Physarum microfluidic gates (Adamatzky and Schubert, 2014) are slow (it
might take 120 seconds to compute a logical function), their speed is an order
of seconds, much slower than silicon gates.

However, slime mould frequency based and microfluidic gates are self-
growing and self-repairing and can be incorporated in a hybrid wetware-
hardware devices for sensing and analysing of non-lethal substances, and
detection of molecules or certain types of living cells.

The Physarum microfluidic gates could form a basis for disposable biocompatible mechanically controlled devices, as embedded fluidic controllers and

circuits in bio-inspired robots or memory arrays embedded into soft-bodied robots.

When talking about memristive properties of slime, we are more optimistic about speed: the switching of conductivity could occur in less than a second (Gale et al., 2013).

8.2.2 Resource: space

Collision-based logical gates are limited from below by wave-length of the active growing zone, i.e. c. 1–2 mm, thus a minimum size of e.g. $x \wedge \bar{y}$ gate would 4 mm^2. Frequency based gates are, in principal, limited by wave-length of a calcium wave, i.e. about 0.01 mm. Micro-fluidic gates offer a high-density of basic logical elements to be implemented on a planar substrate. Assuming that every junction of protoplasmic tubes can be utilised as a logical element we can estimate that there will be c. 10–20 elementary computing units on 1 mm^2 of planar substrate. This is indeed lower than a typical density of logical elements in modern VLSI, however quite a high value for non-silicon wetware circuits.

8.2.3 Quality: accuracy

When computing circuits are implemented using a collision-based computing approach, where on non-nutrient substrate the plasmodium propagates as a travelling localisation, in the form of a compact wave-fragment of protoplasm; this Physarum-localization travels in its originally predetermined direction for a substantial period of time, even when no gradient of chemo-attractants is present. Gates can be constructed in lab conditions $G_1(x, y) = \langle x \wedge y, x \vee y \rangle$ and $G_2(x, y) = \langle x, \bar{x} \vee y \rangle$. Accuracy of experimental laboratory prototypes of gate $G_1(\cdot)$ was over 69% and of $G_2(\cdot)$ over 59% (Adamatzky, 2012). In Frequency-based Boolean logical gates (Whiting et al., 2014a) implemented with Physarum (based on frequencies of oscillations) have the following upper margins of accuracy as follows (Whiting et al., 2014a): OR, NOT 90% accuracy, AND, NAND 78%, NOT 92%, XOR, XNOR 71%, 2-4 Decoder 57%, half-adder 65%, full-adder 59%.

8.2.4 Embeddeness: modularity and interconnections

Physarum chip prototype devices – including optically-coupled (Mayne and Adamatzky, 2015a), frequency-based (Whiting et al., 2014a) and microfluidic logic gates (Adamatzky and Schubert, 2014) – aim to reduce modularity where possible to increase computational efficiency. A single plasmodium is a discrete computing device in its own right, but larger devices, e.g. combinatorial logic circuits, currently require several individual Physarum computing devices to be linked together. Current designs aim to achieve this by physically connecting each device to conventional computer hardware which will automatically read the result of the computation performed and collate these accordingly.

As such, the major constraint imposed by this system is that no direct communication between two individual Physarum plasmodia can occur and must go through an intermediary computer interface. Direct plasmodium-plasmodium communication via the creation of artificial synapses is currently under investigation. This modularity does have a major benefits, however, including comparative ease of tracing errors to individual components and rapid removal and replacement of faulty units.

8.2.5 Programmability

Physarum devices are programmed by configurations of attractants and repellents. Almost all tasks solved in experimental laboratory conditions demonstrate our success in programming the Physarum Chips. We analysed families of formal languages to be used in Physarum computers. We shown that ladder diagrams, Petri nets, and transition systems allow us for enabling programming the Physarum machines (Pancerz and Schumann, 2014; Schumann and Pancerz, 2014b). We focus our research on implementation of operations based on the π-calculus (Milner et al., 1992) model of processes and extension of the programming platform to the agent-oriented programming language for computation with living plasmodium.

8.2.6 Time scales and energy

A frequency based logical gate can be implemented using a single oat flake (c. 6 mg) and the gate can function for several days. Thus energy consumed by a single Physarum gate can be approximated as 0.005 kcal per hour.

8.2.7 Anticipated computer interface with Physarum

The Physarum chip computer interface will be a device capable of receiving and interpreting biological signals from the living slime mould within the chip.

It will be suitably accurate with a high sampling rate (several per second). The projected primary medium of Physarum signal to be interpreted by the interface will be bioelectrical potential as measured at the external membrane of the Physarum plasmodium. Each chip will have several electrodes, each of which will be monitored by the interface.

Current designs are based on an FPGA (field-programmable gate array) model, a user-programmable multi-use digital circuit which is able to monitor the input from several electrodes (up to 40) in prototype Physarum chips. As FPGAs are necessarily digital devices, separate circuits which digitalize the signal are required: this is achieved with a voltage comparator circuit which detects the oscillations in membrane potential associated with plasmodial shuttle streaming by comparing the Physarum input with a user-defined reference voltage. External power supplies are required to amplify the Physarum bioelectrical signals and empower the digitalization circuit. The FPGA receives this digital input and relays it to a computer via a USB connection.

Future devices will be far more accessible and adaptable. For example, certain Physarum chip architectures intended for lower-specification computation, portability and/or harsh environments will be based on cheap, self-contained, commercially available USB-powered microcontroller chips, whereas chips designed for static use with higher necessity for accuracy and speed will be readily transferable with microelectrode array apparatus based on RS-232/serial/other high-speed ports. Effort will also be expended in reducing the modularity and physical size of these interfaces.

Furthermore, future interfaces will enable two-way communication which will allow direct Physarum-machine correspondence: bespoke computer programs written for the interface will automatically interpret patterns of Physarum behaviour and respond by supplying stimulation to the living slime mould, e.g. electrical innervation, illumination.

We have done scoping experiments on developing the interface between slime mould and hardware (Mayne et al., 2015). Through a range of laboratory experiments, we measured plasmodial membrane potential via a non-invasive method and used this signal to interface the organism with a digital system. This digital system was demonstrated to perform predefined basic arithmetic operations and is implemented in a FPGA. These basic arithmetic operations, i.e. counting, addition, multiplying, use data that were derived by digital recognition of membrane potential oscillation and are used here to make basic hybrid biological artificial sensing devices. The low-cost, energy efficient and highly adaptable platform designed in our scoping experments can be used for developing next-generation machine-organism interfaces.

8.2.8 Formalism

The computational power of implementations of conventional spatial algorithms like Kolmogorov-Uspensky machines on the *Physarum polycephalum* medium is low. The point is that not every computable function can be simulated by plasmodium behaviors: first, the motion of plasmodia is too slow (several days are needed to compute simple functions such as 5-bit conjunction, 3-bit adder, etc., but the plasmodium stage of *Physarum polycephalum* is time-limited, therefore there is not enough time for realizations, e.g., of thousands-bit functions); second, the more attractants or repellents are involved in designing computable functions, the less accuracy of their implementation is, because the plasmodium tries to be propagated in all possible directions and we will deal with indirected graphs and other problems; third, the plasmodium is an adaptive organism that is very sensitive to environments, therefore it is very difficult to organize the same laboratory conditions for calculating the same k-bit functions, where k is large.

To formalize Physarum computing under the negative conditions mentioned above we define a kind of simple actions of labeled transition systems which cannot be atomic; consequently, their compositions cannot be inductive (Schumann, 2015b). Their informal meaning is that in one simple action we can suppose the maximum of its modifications. Such actions are called hybrid. The formalism of this extension of labelled transition systems can be regarded as an extension of concurrent games. This new theory is called theory of context-based games on hybrid actions. In this theory we can propose some extensions of formal theories: non-linear group theory and non-linear Boolean algebra (Schumann, 2015b). The group theory proposed by us can be used as the new design method to construct reversible logic gates on plasmodia (Schumann, 2014a). In this way, we should appeal to the so-called non-linear permutation groups. These groups contain non-well-founded objects such as infinite streams and their families.

In the object-oriented programming language for simulating the plasmodium motions we are based on context-based games (Schumann and Pancerz, 2014a; Schumann et al., 2014). So, we consider some instructions in Physarum machines in terms of process algebra like: add node, remove node, add edge, remove edge. Adding and removing edges can change dynamically over time. So, in any experiment with the slime mould we deal with attractants which can be placed differently to obtain different topologies and to induce different transitions of the slime mould. If the set A of attractants, involved into the experiment, has the cardinality number $p-1$, then any subset of A can be regarded as a condition for the experiment such as "Attractants occupied by the plasmodium". These conditions change during the time, $t = 0, 1, 2, \ldots$, and for the infinite time, we obtain p-adic integers as values of fuzzy (probability) measures defined on conditions (properties) of the experiment. This space is a semantics for p-adic valued logic we constructed for describing the propagation of the slime mould (Schumann, 2014b; Schumann and Adamatzky,

2015). This logic can be extended to a p-adic valued arithmetic. Within this logic we can develop a context-based game theory (Schumann et al., 2014). All these logical tools can be implemented on plasmodia by conventional and unconventional reversible logic gates (Schumann, 2014a; Schumann, 2015a).

8.2.9 Philosophy

Plasmodia do not strictly follow spatial algorithms like Kolmogorov-Uspensky machines, but perform many additional actions. We can say that plasmodia have 'free will' and can choose between different possible courses of action. In order to define and simulate ways of plasmodium rationality we have proposed a bio-inspired game theory on plasmodia (Schumann and Pancerz, 2015; Schumann et al., 2014), i.e. an experimental game theory, where, on the one hand, all basic definitions are verified in the experiments with *Physarum polycephalum* and *Badhamia utricularis* and, on the other hand, all basic algorithms are implemented in the object-oriented language for simulations of plasmodia (Schumann and Pancerz, 2014b). The theory of reflexive games (Schumann, 2014c) is a generalization of bio-inspired game theory on plasmodia.

In our experiments, we follow the following interpretations of basic entities:

- Attractants as payoffs;
- Attractants occupied by the plasmodium as states of the game;
- Active zones of plasmodium as players;
- Logic gates for behaviors as moves (available actions) for the players;
- Propagation of the plasmodium as the transition table which associates, with a given set of states and a given move of the players, the set of states resulting from that move.

Thus, we have designed the zero-sum game between plasmodia of *Physarum polycephalum* and *Badhamia utricularis* (Schumann and Pancerz, 2015; Schumann et al., 2014). To simulate Physarum games, we have created a specialized software tool. It is a part of the larger platform developed, using the Java environment. The tool works under the client-server paradigm. The server window contains:

- a text area with information about actions undertaken,
- a combox for selecting one of two defined situations,
- start and stop server buttons.

Communication between clients and the server is realized through text messages containing statements of our object-oriented programming language (Schumann and Pancerz, 2014b). The locations of attractants and repellents are determined by the players during the game. At the beginning, origin points of *Physarum polycephalum* and *Badhamia utricularis* are scattered randomly on the plane. During the game, players can place stimuli. New veins of plasmodia are created. The server sends to clients information about the current configuration of the Physarum machine (localization of origin points of *Physarum polycephalum* and *Badhamia utricularis*, localization of stimuli as well as a list of edges, corresponding to veins of plasmodia, between active points) through the XML file.

Hence, our bio-inspired game theory on plasmodia (Schumann and Pancerz, 2015; Schumann et al., 2014) explains some features of plasmodium behaviour from the viewpoint of philosophy: what is rational for plasmodia, how do plasmodia make decisions, which strategies do they choose under different conditions, etc.

8.3 Main achievements so far

8.3.1 Computing with living raw Physarum

We developed a range of computing circuits including stimuli counters interfaces with field-programmable arrays, micro-fluidic living logical gates and memory devices based on Physarum response to tactile stimuli, optically coupled Physarum Boolean gates. We have also progressed towards understanding of Physarum computing at the intracellular level and developed graph-based representations of actin and tubulin cytoskeletal devices with potential information processing properties; within this medium, a wide array of energetic events may be considered as data, ranging from electrical potential to solitons to substance/organelle trafficking.

8.3.2 Building hybrid devices

We analysed conductive properties of living Physarum wires and demonstrated that protoplasmic tubes can be integrated (and function for a substantial period of time) in conventional electronic circuits. We developed techniques for increasing conductivity of the Physarum wires by loading and/or coating protoplasmic tubes with functional nano-particles. We developed techniques for programmable routing of Physasum wires with configurations of attractants and repellents and proposed a range of biocompatible insulators for Physarum wires. We also coated the slime mold with conductive polymers by specially tailor biocompatible techniques and growing the slime mold on conductive polymer surfaces. Using these techniques we manufactured novel prototypes of slime mould based memristors, sensors and transistors, which can be tuned by an intensity and geometry of Physarum interacting with conducting polymer.

8.3.3 Verification of computational tasks

We developed models of Physarum chip implementing lateral inhibition in neural networks, discovered indicators of halting computation in dynamics of Physarum chip (on a range of argraph optimisation and computational geometry tasks) in terms of compressibility of two-dimensional configurations of protoplasmic tubes, and imitated a cortical response of the human visual system in Physarum chip.

8.3.4 Solving computational problems

We solved the following problems on Physarum chip: generation of spline curves, computation of centroid, approximation of outline perimeter of convex hull and interior area of concave full, path planning in dynamically changing environment and approximation of statistical data.

8.3.5 Nonsymbolic interfaces

We developed Physarum-based model of creativity as contra-play between cognitive control versus schizotypy and uncovered morphological meanings of Physarum-based terms creativity in topologies of growing protoplasmic networks. The concept was formalised in a model of growing beta-skeletons. The slime mould as a stimulant of human creativity was analysed in terms of colour spectrum of Kolmogorov-Uspensky machines, growing geometries, Physarum-inspired computer games and competitions between two species of slime mould. We produced a range of physical and simulated musical devices incorporating slime mould: Physarum oscillators in sound-generating electrical circuits, sonification of Physarum electrical activity, and generation of sound tracks based on multi-agent models of the slime mould's protoplasmic movements. We delivered a range of multi-media presentations in art festivals and exhibitions, developed interacting atlas of slime mould computing.

8.4 Current challenges

Longevity of PhyChip functioning is the main challenge. We are overcoming this challenge with two approaches: (1) supporting the living slime mould by making its condition comfortable and (2) immortalizing the slime mould by with additives.

8.4.1 Keeping slime mould alive

A 'raw' living slime mould can function in a humid environment for days and sometimes weeks. The resilience to environmental factor can be increased (and electrical properties kept unchanged) by insulating slime mould with silicon gum. In our experiments with slime mould wires we have shown that a protoplasmic tube covered by 2–5 mm layer of silicon can function as wire and even conduct oscillations between two blobs of Physarum for several weeks (Adamatzky, 2013a).

8.4.2 Making a cyborg

Slime mould cannot function for 50+ years as silicon computer chip do. Such longevity might be not necessary, cause a practical way could be to make disposable computers from slime mold. However, if we were to make 'proper' computing devices we must find an artificial substitute for the slime. Such substitutes do not exist and may be never will. Therefore, we are considering to make hybrid architectures where living slime mould co-function with its 'dead' yet functionalised components. Two routes could be explored: loading slime mould by functional nanoparticles and coating the slime mould with polymers. Let us consider example of how these approaches can be implemented.

In laboratory-based experiments presented in Mayne and Adamatzky (2015b) we developed a nanoscale artificial circuit components by encouraging slime mould to internalize a range of electrically active nanoparticles, assemble them in vivo and distribute them around the plasmodium. We found that they hybridized plasmodium is able to form biomorphic mineralized networks inside the living plasmodium and the empty trails left following its migration, both of which facilitate the transmission of electricity. Hybridization also alters the bioelectrical activity of the plasmodium and likely influences its information processing capabilities. It was concluded that hybridized slime mould is a suitable substrate for producing functional unconventional computing devices.

Another example. In Tarabella et al. (2015) we developed a hybrid bio-organic electrochemical transistor by interfacing an organic semiconductor, poly(3,4-ethylenedioxythiophene) doped with poly(styrene sulfonate), with the Physarum. The system shows unprecedented performances since it could be operated both as a transistor, in a three-terminal configuration, and as a memristive device in a two terminal configuration mode. The system was studied by a full electrical characterization using a series of different gate electrodes, namely made of Ag, Au and Pt, which typically show different operation modes in organic electrochemical transistors.

8.4.3 Fast prototyping

Experiments with living creatures are inherently time consuming. Designing a new architecture with slime mould requires months and months of work. To speed up the prototyping we must develop a very accurate Physarum model in software. Substantial progress has been made. Jeff Jones designed a unique particle based model, which predicts almost all behavioural trains of the slime mould, see e.g. Jones (2015b) and Jones et al. (2017). His unique book (Jones, 2015a) tells the a detailed account on how the model was developed and what the model can do in terms of unconventional computing and soft robotics applications.

The purpose of Jones' particle model is to understand how Physarum – an organism with no nervous system – can generate its complex behaviours using simple, homogeneous component parts. By constraining the model to use equally simple components (in the form of program instructions) we can explore the generation of emergent second-order quasi-physical behaviour (for example morphological adaptation and minimisation) seen in Physarum. We can then explore external means of influencing the behaviour of this virtual Physarum in order to perform useful spatially represented computation. Furthermore, we can also use the model to explore and explain how simple homogeneous and *unorganised* systems such as Physarum may implement functionality that has hitherto only been explained in terms of hardwired neural systems (Jones, 2015c).

The study of the external inputs to the model (and its response) can both inform the work of, and take guidance from, the physical experiments in the Phychip project on providing inputs to Physarum (chemical, light, tactile etc.). From a computing perspective we are contributing to the nascent field of morphological computation by devising mechanisms by which the virtual Physarum can be used to tackle classical computing tasks in a spatially represented manner, including results on combinatorial optimisation (TSP), computational geometry (proximity graphs, Voronoi diagrams), data smoothing (1D data smoothing, path planning, noisy estimation, 2D image smoothing, spline curve approximation).

We believe that, using this modelling approach, it is important not to just to simply replicate classical logic devices but also to explore new means of spatially representing, programming, executing and reading the 'output' of computations embodied within distributed computing – and indeed robotic – substrates.

Another subtle, yet important, implication of this model of Physarum is the relationship between modelling, classical computation and unconventional computation. To facilitate TRUCE it is necessary to communicate the distinctions and similarities between classical and unconventional devices. Occasionally, however, these distinctions may be slightly muddied. For example, Jones' model of Physarum is executed on a classical PC (natively compiled Java code on a Windows platform, to be precise). Can such a model be truly classed as an unconventional computing substrate?

Previous experience (for example, with cellular automata which are also commonly implemented on classical devices, rather than dedicated hardware platforms) suggests yes. This is true if we include the lower-level mechanisms (classical programs) which are used to create the UCOMP 'universe' (or virtual *material*, in this case) as a computational *given* and interact only with the emergent behaviours embodied within in the UCOMP material itself. Such interactions were earlier proposed by Stepney (2008) as the application of external 'fields' to a material computing substrate. In the case of this model the fields are simulated concentration gradients of attractants and repellents, and the simulated exposure to light irradiation. The model follows Stepney's prescription in that the embodied dynamics of the substrate (the emergent network formation and minimisation) are what actually performs the computation. The results of the computation can then be 'read' by examining the state of the substrate. As previously noted, in the model Physarum both problem input and result output are represented as spatial patterns. However the notion of a final (halting) output as seen in classical computing may not be as readily attainable in UCOMP systems and relatively steady states must often suffice.

Note that this mechanism of computation (exploiting second-order emergent behaviours) is qualitatively (and, potentially, quantitatively) different from the *metaphorical* application of natural systems as abstracted and implemented in classical computing algorithms. As examples we might include the application of evolutionary computation mechanisms (mutation and crossover) as implemented in binary strings in genetic algorithms, or the phenomena of pheromone deposition and evaporation in Ant Colony Algorithms. Although it would be churlish to compare bottom-up emergent computation as implemented in classical systems with abstracted natural systems (also implemented in classical systems as more traditional programs), it is reasonable to ask whether abstracted natural systems – as implemented in classical algorithms – can capture the richness of physically implemented mechanisms, even if these physical mechanisms reside within (or rather upon) classical computing devices. Or more simply put: does the actual implementation of, for example, spatial pheromone evaporation and diffusion result in a more complex output when compared to its non-spatial numerical evaluation? One challenging ongoing task for TRUCE is to explore the differences, advantages, disadvantages when comparing actual implementation of emergent mechanisms in natural systems to relatively simple abstractions. The differences are likely to include trade-offs between speed, accuracy, repeatability and the technical challenges of interfacing with more exotic computing substrates.

8.4.4 Solving hard computational tasks

Slime mould computers can solve a wide variety of tasks, from computational geometry to logic and arithmetic. However, an ocean of challenging problems remains unsolved. Take for example, Shor factorisation (Shor, 1997). Classical efficient algorithms are proposed for quantum computers. Their time complexity is bounded by a polynomial in the input size of integers to be factored. Blakey (2014) proposed to implement the Shor factorisation on the slime mould. His approach employed periodic oscillations of the Physarum. He posed a question: "...whether a period can equally well be imparted not via regular pulses, but via more general periodic functions—for example via stimulus intensity varying sinusoidally with time, or even varying with time as a function with unknown period (whence the organisms not merely retain the period, but in a sense compute it)". He speculated that if oscillation parameters can be tuned by a non-linear function imposed this will lead to a non-quantum implementation of Shor's algorithm. We have done first steps by managing to control frequency, and sometimes amplitude of oscillations, by chemical (Whiting et al., 2014b), electrical (Whiting et al., 2015) and mechanical stimuli (Adamatzky, 2013b). However, we did not achieve any programmable dynamics of oscillations.

8.4.5 Moving to nano-scale and quantum

Computation with slime mould at meso- and macro-scales is slow. To overcome the speed restriction we consider moving to a nano-level and focus on implementation of computation with Physarum cyto-skeleton networks, which we have argued to be an intracellular data network that provides information structuring and sensorimotor coupling to the organism (Mayne et al., 2014). The feasible way of doing so would be to employ propagation locations (voltage solitons, defects, kinds) along actin filaments and implementation of computation in interaction between the travelling localisations. In our pioneer theoretical studies (Adamatzky and Mayne, 2014) we design actin automata model and shown that a wide range of interactions between localisation can be achieved by tuning inter-relations between subunits in actin filaments. Further, we have shown that by adopting a quantum interpretation of actin unit states (spatial configurations of negative and positive charges) we can implement logical gates and binary arithmetical circuits (Siccardi and Adamatzky, 2015). Addressing individual actin units and reading their states remains the key experimental challenge.

8.5 Outlook and recommendations

We have demonstrated that the slime mould *P. polycephalum* is a unique living substrate capable to solve a wide range computational problems. We admit that a scope of practical applications are limited because of low speed of growing computing architectures in slime, and low speed of implementing computational operations at meso- and macro-scales. We propose to focus on intra-cellular computation with the slime mould and to develop computing architectures based on interaction of travelling localisations in the networks of actin filaments.

References

Adamatzky, Andrew (2010). *Physarum machines: computers from slime mould*. World Scientific.

Adamatzky, Andrew (2012). *Slime mould logical gates: exploring ballistic approach*. eprint: arXiv:1005.2301[nlin.PS].

Adamatzky, Andrew (2013a). "Physarum wires: Self-growing self-repairing smart wires made from slime mould". *Biomedical Engineering Letters* 3(4):232–241.

Adamatzky, Andrew (2013b). "Slime mould tactile sensor". *Sensors and actuators B: chemical* 188:38–44.

Adamatzky, Andrew (2013c). "Towards slime mould colour sensor: Recognition of colours by Physarum polycephalum". *Organic electronics* 14(12):3355–3361.

Adamatzky, Andrew (2014). "Slime mould electronic oscillators". *Microelectronic Engineering* 124:58–65.

Adamatzky, Andrew and Richard Mayne (2014). *Actin automata: Phenomenology and localizations*. eprint: arXiv:1408.3676[cs.ET].

Adamatzky, Andrew and Theresa Schubert (2014). "Slime mold microfluidic logical gates". *Materials Today* 17(2):86–91.

Blakey, Ed (2014). "Towards Non-Quantum Implementations of Shor's Factorization Algorithm". *IJUC* 10(5–6):339–352.

Gale, Ella, Andrew Adamatzky, and Ben de Lacy Costello (2013). "Slime mould memristors". *BioNanoScience* 5(1):1–8.

Jones, Jeff (2015a). *From Pattern Formation to Material Computation: Multi-agent Modelling of Physarum Polycephalum*. Springer.

Jones, Jeff (2015b). "Mechanisms Inducing Parallel Computation in a Model of *Physarum polycephalum* Transport Networks". *Parallel Processing Letters* 25(1):1540004.

Jones, Jeff Dale (2015c). "Towards Lateral Inhibition and Collective Perception in Unorganised Non-neural Systems". *Computational Intelligence, Medicine and Biology*. Ed. by Pancerz K. and Zaitseva E. Springer, pp. 103–122.

Jones, Jeff, Richard Mayne, and Andrew Adamatzky (2017). "Representation of shape mediated by environmental stimuli in *Physarum polycephalum* and a multi-agent model". *International Journal of Parallel, Emergent and Distributed Systems* 32(2):166–184.

Mayne, R. and A. Adamatzky (2015a). "Slime mould foraging behaviour as optically coupled logical operations". *International Journal of General Systems* 44(3):305–313.

Mayne, R., A. Adamatzky, and J. Jones (2014). "On the role of the plasmodial cytoskeleton in facilitating intelligent behaviour in slime mould *Physarum polycephalum*". *Communicative and Integrative Biology* 7(1):e32097.

Mayne, Richard and Andrew Adamatzky (2015b). "Toward Hybrid Nanostructure-Slime Mould Devices". *Nano LIFE* 5(1):1450007.

Mayne, Richard, Michail-Antisthenis Tsompanas, Georgios Ch. Sirakoulis, and Andrew Adamatzky (2015). "Towards a slime mould-FPGA interface". *Biomedical Engineering Letters* 5(1):51–57.

Milner, Robin, Joachim Parrow, and David Walker (1992). "A calculus of mobile processes, I". *Information and computation* 100(1):1–40.

Pancerz, Krzysztof and Andrew Schumann (2014). "Principles of an object-oriented programming language for Physarum polycephalum computing". *DT 2014, International Conference on Digital Technologies*. IEEE, pp. 262–269.

Schumann, Andrew (2014a). "Non-Linear Permutation Groups on Physarum Polycephalum". *Proc. ICSAI 2014*. IEEE, pp. 246–251.

Schumann, Andrew (2014b). "p-Adic Valued Fuzzyness and Experiments with Physarum Polycephalum". *Proc. FSKD 2014*. IEEE, pp. 466–472.

Schumann, Andrew (2014c). "Payoff cellular automata and reflexive games". *Journal of Cellular Automata* 9(4):287–313.

Schumann, Andrew (2015a). "Reversible Logic Gates on Physarum Polycephalum". *AIP Conference Proceedings* 1648:580011.

Schumann, Andrew (2015b). "Towards context-based concurrent formal theories". *Parallel Processing Letters* 25(1540008):1–15.

Schumann, Andrew and Andrew Adamatzky (2015). "The Double-Slit Experiment with Physarum Polycephalum and p-Adic Valued Probabilities and Fuzziness". *International Journal of General Systems* 44(3):392–408.

Schumann, Andrew and Krzysztof Pancerz (2014a). "Timed Transition System Models for Programming Physarum Machines: Extended Abstract". *Proc. CSandP 2014*. IEEE, pp. 180–183.

Schumann, Andrew and Krzysztof Pancerz (2014b). "Towards an Object-Oriented Programming Language for Physarum Polycephalum Computing: A Petri Net Model Approach". *Fundamenta Informaticae* 133(2–3) :271–285.

Schumann, Andrew and Krzysztof Pancerz (2015). "Interfaces in a Game-Theoretic Setting for Controlling the Plasmodium Motions". *Proc. International Conference on Bio-inspired Systems and Signal Processing – Volume 1: BIOSIGNALS*, pp. 338–343.

Schumann, Andrew, Krzysztof Pancerz, Andrew Adamatzky, and Martin Grube (2014). "Bio-Inspired Game Theory: The Case of Physarum Polycephalum". *Proc. BICT 2014*. ICST, pp. 1–8.

Shor, P. W. (1997). "Polynomial-time algorithms for prime factorization and discrete logarithms on a quantum computer". *SIAM Journal of Computing* 26:1484–1509.

Siccardi, S. and A. Adamatzky (2015). "Actin quantum automata: Communication and computation in molecular networks". *Nano Communication Networks* 6(1):15–27.

Stephenson, Steven L, Henry Stempen, and Ian Hall (1994). *Myxomycetes: a handbook of slime molds*. Timber Press, Portland, Oregon.

Stepney, Susan (2008). "The neglected pillar of material computation". *Physica D: Nonlinear Phenomena* 237(9):1157–1164.

Tarabella, Giuseppe, Pasquale D'Angelo, Angelica Cifarelli, Alice Dimonte, Agostino Romeo, Tatiana Berzina, Victor Erokhin, and Salvatore Iannotta (2015). "A hybrid living/organic electrochemical transistor based on the Physarum polycephalum cell endowed with both sensing and memristive properties". *Chemical Science* 6(5):2859–2868.

Whiting, James G. H., Ben P. J. de Lacy Costello, and Andrew Adamatzky (2014a). "Slime mould logic gates based on frequency changes of electrical potential oscillation". *Biosystems* 124:21–25.

Whiting, James G. H., Ben P. J. de Lacy Costello, and Andrew Adamatzky (2014b). "Towards slime mould chemical sensor: Mapping chemical inputs onto electrical potential dynamics of Physarum Polycephalum". *Sensors and Actuators B: Chemical* 191:844–853.

Whiting, James G. H., Ben P. J. de Lacy Costello, and Andrew Adamatzky (2015). "Transfer function of protoplasmic tubes of *Physarum polycephalum*". *Biosystems* 128:48–51.

Chapter 9
Decoding Genomic Information

Giuditta Franco and Vincenzo Manca

Abstract Genomes carry the main information generating life of organisms and their evolution. They work in nature as a marvellous operative system of molecular (reading, writing and signal transmission) rules, orchestrating all cell functions and information transmission to cell daughters. As long polymers of nucleotides, they may be seen as a special book which reports in its own sequence all developments it had passed through during evolution. All fragments which were mutated, duplicated, assembled, silenced are still present in the genomic sequence to some extent, to form genomic dictionaries.

Here we outline some trends of research which analyse and interpret (i.e., decode) genomic information, by assuming the genome to be a book encrypted in an unknown language, which has still to be deciphered, while directly affecting the structure and the interaction of all the cellular and multicellular components. We focus on an informational analysis of real genomes, which may be framed within a new trend of computational genomics, lying across bioinformatics and natural computing. This analysis is performed by sequence alignment-free methods, based on information theoretical concepts, in order to convert the genomic information into a comprehensible mathematical form and to understand its complexity.

After a nutshell of the state of the art, given as a brief overview of approaches in the area, we present our viewpoint and results on genomic wide studies, by means of mathematical distributions and dictionary-based analysis inspired by information theory, where normalized multiplicities of genomic words are frequencies defining discrete probability distributions of interest. The definition, computation, and analysis of a few informational indexes have highlighted some properties of genomic regularity and specificity, which may be a basis for the comprehension of evolutional and functional aspects of genomes.

© Springer International Publishing AG, part of Springer Nature 2018   129
S. Stepney et al. (eds.), *Computational Matter*, Natural Computing Series,
https://doi.org/10.1007/978-3-319-65826-1_9

9.1 Introduction

Science has many important challenging open problems. Some of the approaches to solve them are still intractable using conventional computing, which may be briefly identified with the Turing/von Neumann paradigm. Even if processors become faster and more compact, and memory storage larger, standard computer science has clear limits of miniaturization, speediness, and parallelism scalability. Moreover, only a specific model of computation is investigated (albeit on a massive scale), with well known intrinsic limits (of decidability, of complexity) which cannot be overcome by any technological advancement (Conrad, 1988).

Research in *Unconventional Computing* (UCOMP) takes a different view, in exploring alternative computational approaches (with properties such as massive parallelism, approximation, non-determinism, adaption, redundancy, robustness, learning, self-organization, reproduction, competition), in order to increase the range and power of computation available to us.

A main difference between the two worlds is the (digital) data format. In conventional computing it consists of strings of digits, or formal languages, while in unconventional/biological computing data populations or multisets of strings (e.g., molecules, bacteria) are processed by the computation (Manca, 2013). Beside a redundant and undefined number of copies for each string, different notions arise of unconventional complexity (Almirantis et al., 2014; Lynch and Conery, 2003) with specific properties of uniformity and confluency of solutions (Păun, 2016).

UCOMP is often assumed to be any way to compute that is different from Turing's model. Crucial aspects of Turing Machines, which are missing in many unconventional computing approaches, are the existence of a global clock, and of a program to execute as a list of instructions. Some examples of a different approach, where the computation program is not centralised, include: distributed, cloud, network computing (namely VPN: virtual private network), machine learning in the context of artificial intelligence (e.g., computer learning games), evolutionary computing (including genetic algorithms), light/optical and quantum computing (also exhibiting an unconventional means to store information), molecular computing (employing unconventional means and instructions to compute).

Bioalgorithms with interesting massive parallel strategies have been developed in the context of DNA computing recently, for example Ratner et al. (2013) and Rothemund et al. (2004), while laboratory biotechniques have been improved in terms of computation precision and efficiency (Franco, 2005; Franco and Manca, 2011a; Manca and Franco, 2008). Network-based algorithms, for example simulating metabolism (Castellini et al., 2011; Franco and Manca, 2011b; Manca et al., 2013) or immunological processes (Castellini et al., 2014; Franco et al., 2008; Franco and Manca, 2004), have been developed in the context of systems biology and membrane/cell computing, to better understand natural processes, as well as to formulate new computational models. As attested by numerous dedicated series of books, international conferences, and journals, UCOMP includes *bioinformatics* (bio-computer science), which is the "closest upper envelope of the computability inspired by biology" (Păun, 2016).

In search of solutions for current (often urgent) questions, for example from the bio-medical area, (applied) mathematics and computer science often develop and provide *ad hoc* models, techniques, and tools to tackle problems. This approach is related to *mathematical biology*, where mathematical modelling and simulation are applied to biological, biomedical and biotechnology research.

A marvellous operative system working in nature is the genome, carrying the main information generating life of organisms and their evolution, and having a system of molecular (reading, writing and signal transmission) rules, orchestrating all cell functions and information transmission to cell daughters. Most of these rules and especially the ways they cooperate are unknown. This is a problem of great scientific and medical interest, due mainly to currently incurable genetic diseases.

After the revolutionary human genome sequencing project, and the subsequence decade-long joint project ENCODE, involving 440 scientists from 32 laboratories around the world[1], sequences of genes, chromosomes, and whole genomes from numerous species are downloadable by freely accessible databases[2]. Also, the ENCODE project has systematically mapped regions of transcription, chromatin structure, transcription factor association, and histone modification, providing new insights into the mechanisms of gene regulation (Neph et al., 2012; Spivakov et al., 2012), and a biological annotation of the human genome (for more details, see for example Dunham et al. (2012) and Franco (2014)). However, such an avalanche of data would be difficult to handle and understand without the use of powerful mathematical and computational tools.

Our work here outlines and follows some trends of research which analyze and interpret (i.e., decode) genomic information, by assuming the genome to be a book encrypted in an unknown language. This analysis is performed by sequence alignment-free methods, based on information theoretical concepts, in order to convert the genomic information into a comprehensible mathematical form and understand its complexity (Almirantis et al., 2014; Lynch and Conery, 2003; Vinga, 2013).

Sections of this chapter are adapted from Bonnici and Manca (2016), Castellini et al. (2012), Franco (2014), Manca (2015), and Manca (2016), to be considered foundational references of the bibliography, while relevant related papers which pursue genomics investigations by the same aim are Chor et al. (2009), Fofanov et al. (2008), Li et al. (2016), Sadovsky et al.

---

[1] at MIT, Harvard, Stanford, and SUNY in the USA, and at universities in Germany, the UK, Spain, Switzerland, Singapore, China, and Japan

[2] such as the NCBI at www.ncbi.nlm.nih.gov/sites/genome, UCSC at hgdownload.cse.ucsc.edu/downloads.html, and EMBL-EBI at www.ebi.ac.uk/genomes/

(2008), Sims et al. (2009), Vinga (2013), Zhang et al. (2007), Zheng et al. (2017), and Zhou et al. (2008). After a nutshell of the state of the art given as a brief overview of approaches in the area, we present our viewpoint and results on genomic wide studies by means of mathematical distributions and dictionary-based analysis inspired by information theory, that we call *Infogenomics*.

9.2 Overview

The role and the contribution of Shannon information theory to the development of molecular biology has been the object of stimulating debates during the last fifty years (Gatlin, 1966). The concept of information itself, if viewed in a broader perspective, is very pervasive and far from being completely defined (just like the concept of energy in physics (Manca, 2013)), while classical information theory has been conceived at a high technical level (Fabris, 2002; Thomas and Cover, 1991). The concept of information (and complexity (Almirantis et al., 2014; Lynch and Conery, 2003)) in biology is still a debated problem, so the application of information theory has often to be adapted to the context, namely when outside of standard computer science (Vinga, 2013).

Information science was born with Norbert Wiener from a philosophical viewpoint, with John von Neumann from a more pragmatic viewpoint, and finally with both Claude Shannon, who defined a mathematical measure of information (in the processes of representation, communication, and transmission), and Alan Turing, who set down its famous mathematical model of computation machine in terms of data storing and program execution.

Information is related to probability (an event is as informative as it is rare to happen), and establishes mathematical relationships between digital and probabilistic concepts definable over strings. Here we work on formal languages or codes, composed by words appearing on a given genome, then we develop (genome-wide) information theoretic methods along the perspective of alignment-free methods of genome analysis (Vinga, 2013; Vinga and Almeida, 2003).

Genomes are sequences of nucleotides from hundreds to billions of base pairs long. As sequences of symbols they determine dictionaries, that is, formal languages constituted by words occurring in them. They encode the language of life, as dictating the functioning of all the organisms we consider living beings. A main open problem in science is to find any key to understand such an encrypted language, which directly effects the structure and the interaction of all the cellular and multicellular components. It is like having a book in an undeciphered language (Manca, 2013; Manca, 2015; Manca, 2016; Mantegna et al., 1994; Percus, 2007; Searls, 2002). A genome is however a special book, being diachronic (rather than synchronic): it reports in its own sequence all developments it had passed through during evolution. All fragments which were mutated, duplicated, assembled, or silenced are still present in the genomic sequence to some extent, and could tell us the paths which evolution has followed to generate modern organisms.

We focus on genome-wide numerical properties, by computing, analyzing, and comparing informational indexes, with the aim to discover which of them can be relevant to identify characteristics of genomes that are of biological or clinical interest. Related previous dictionary-based studies of genomes may be found in Crochemore and Vérin (1999) and Vinga and Almeida (2007), where entropy measures are employed to estimate the randomness or repeata-bility of DNA sequences (Holland, 1998; Kong, W.-L. Fan, et al., 2009), even in function of their different 'biological complexity' (Annaluru et al., 2014; Castellini et al., 2015; Deschavanne et al., 1999; Franco and Milanese, 2013; Spivakov et al., 2012).

In the post-genomic era, several attempts are emerging to understand genomic complexity. Works on modelling biological sequences by means of formal languages have been proposed, along with an extensive investigation (Searls, 2002), including a linguistic semantics inspired approach (Mantegna et al., 1994; Neph et al., 2012; Searls, 2002). A recent development is the introduction of context-free grammars formalizing design principles for new genetic constructs, by starting from a library of genetic parts already orga-nized according to their biological function (Cai et al., 2007).

In general, the definition, computation, and analysis of a few informational indexes have highlighted some properties of genomic regularity and specificity that may be a basis for the comprehension of evolutional and functional aspects of genomes.

9.2.1 Dictionary based indexes

A *genomic dictionary* is a set of strings occurring in a given genome G. We denote by $D_k(G)$ the dictionary of all k-mers occurring in G. A word α may occur in G many times, and we call *multiplicity* of α its number of occurrences. It is easy to verify that the number of occurrences of k-mers (factors of length k) in G corresponds to the maximum cardinality reachable by a dictionary of k-mers within genomes of the same length, and that the multiplicities average decreases with the k-value.

A word with multiplicity greater than one is called a *repeat* of G, whereas a word with multiplicity equal to one is called a *hapax*. This term is used in philological investigation of texts, but it is also adopted in document in-dexing and compression (Giancarlo et al., 2009; Sadovsky et al., 2008). A nullomer (Hampikian and Andersen, 2007) or forbidden word is a sequence that does not appear in the genome. Franco and Milanese (2013) propose a bioinformatic investigation on genomic repeats that occur in multiple genes, of three specific genomes, thus providing non-conventional graph based methods to abstractly represent genomes, gene networks, and genomic languages. By normalising multiplicities one obtains frequencies, and a consequent discrete probability distribution over genomic words.

Recent approaches may be pointed out, based on the empirical frequencies of DNA k-mers in whole genomes (Chor et al., 2009; Wang et al., 2015; Zhou et al., 2008). However, any set of words (factors) occurring in a genome provides a genomic dictionary, and some indexes related to characteristics of dictionaries may be defined on genomes. For example, MRL(G) is the length of the longest repeat of G; MRL is the minimum length such that k-mers in the dictionary with k greater than MRL are all hapaxes; MHL(G) is the minimal length for hapaxes in the genome G; MFL(G) is the minimal forbidden length, that is, minimal length of words that do not occur in G (Fici et al., 2006; Herold et al., 2008).

When genomic complexity is considered, it cannot be easily measured by parameters such as genome length, number of genes, CG-content, basic repeatability indexes, or their combinations. An information theoretical line of investigation based on k-mer dictionaries and entropies may be found for example in Chor et al. (2009), Fabris (2002), Holland (1998), Kong, W.-L. Fan, et al. (2009), Sims et al. (2009), and Zhang et al. (2007), which is aimed at defining and computing more complex informational indexes for a representative set of genomes. In this context, it is natural to assume that the complexity of a genome increases with its distance from randomness (Bonnici and Manca, 2016; Manca, 2017), as identified by means of a suitable comparison between the genome under investigation and random genomes of the same length. The identification of appropriate genomic distributions is crucial for looking at the genomic information.

9.2.2 Genomic distributions

For any numerical index I_k with parameter k, the distribution $k \mapsto I_k$ can be defined on a genome, and its classical statistical parameters (mean, standard deviation, median, mode, etc.) may be derived as further indexes (Castellini et al., 2012; Manca, 2016).

Word distribution in a genome may be represented along a graphical profile, which measures the number of k-words having a given number of occurrences. We call such curves the multiplicity-cardinality k-distribution of a genome, having the same information of a rank-multiplicity Zipf map as usually employed to study word frequencies in natural languages (Mantegna et al., 1994); see Figure 9.1. Several other nice representations of genomic frequencies may be found in the literature, for example by means of images; in Deschavanne et al. (1999) distance between images results in a measure of phylogenetic proximity, especially to distinguish eukaryotes and prokaryotes.

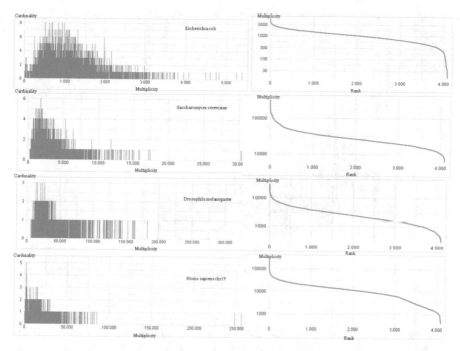

Fig. 9.1 Multiplicity-cardinality and rank-multiplicity Zipf distributions of some organisms are reported. [Reproduced by courtesy of the authors of (Castellini et al., 2012)]

An intriguing genomic distribution, called the recurrence distance distribution (RDD), has been computed for several genomic sequences by Bonnici and Manca (2015b). For a given word α (say a 3-mer or a 6-mer), RDD associates a distance-value n to the number of times that α occurs at distance n from its previous occurrence in G. The well-known peak 3-periodicity has been confirmed by Bonnici and Manca (2015b), and is easily visualized by means of RDD plots; see a simple example in Figure 9.2. The same periodicity has been observed in bacteria whole genomes, human protein coding exon regions, and exons of ncRNAs (non-protein coding RNA). More interestingly, a connection has been established between distance peaks (on k-mers with $k > 3$) and (approximate) repetitive elements between the corresponding recurrent k-mers.

9.3 Contribution to UCOMP aspects

Our topic focuses on an informational analysis of real genomes, and may be framed within a new trend of computational genomics, lying across bioinformatics and natural computing, depending on which type of methods are

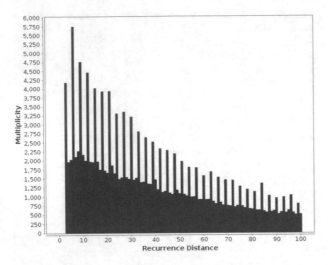

Fig. 9.2 RDD related to the word AGA, computed on the human exome. [Reproduced by courtesy of the authors of (Bonnici and Manca, 2015b)]

employed, both to analyze high-throughput biotechnology genomic data and to develop a mathematical modelling of basic laws underlying information structured in genomes. This approach enters the field of UCOMP, as it is outside the standard model of conventional computing that underlies the implementation of commercially available devices. Conventional computation, as nowadays implemented by parallel algorithms and parallel architectures for big data mining, are important in that they need to be employed to simulate our data-driven mathematical models, as data rich information sets or genomic databases. In terms of traditional computing architectures, big data and massive parallelism will be involved and developed alongside research lines based on infogenomic interests.

9.3.1 Speed

One of the current challenges is to find good genome representation to speed up the analysis of interest. However, distributed and parallel computing will be necessary to successfully handle big volumes of variable data in practice, and the capabilities of existing big-data frameworks should be combined with bringing the computation as close as possible to the data (Computational Pan-Genomics Consortium, 2018).

Advantages of k-mer-based representations include simplicity, speed and robustness (Wang et al., 2015; Zhou et al., 2008). Among alternative indexing methods, we mention as an example the Burrows–Wheeler based approaches, which append the extracted contexts around variations to the reference genome.

9.3.2 Resource(s)

The advent of rapid and cheap next-generation sequencing technologies since 2006 has turned re-sequencing into one of the most popular modern genome analysis workflows. An incredible wealth of genomic variation within populations has already been detected, permitting functional annotation of many such variants, and it is reasonable to expect that this is only the beginning.

9.3.3 Quality

Next-generation short-read sequencing has contributed tremendously to the increase in the known number of genetic variations in genomes of many species. However, the inherent limitations often provide us with error prone and uncertain data.

The most promising developments in sequencing technology involve single-molecule real-time sequencing of native DNA strands, which is widely used for variation discovery and genome assembly. The MinION device (Oxford Nanopore Technologies) provides even longer reads of single DNA molecules, but has been reported to exhibit GC biases. Data generated on the MinION platform have been successfully used for assembly of small genomes and for unravelling the structure of complex genomic regions.

Despite this progress, sequencing reads are not yet sufficiently long to traverse and assemble all repeat structures and other complementary technologies are necessary to investigate large, more complex variation (Computational Pan-Genomics Consortium, 2018).

One of the computational (and modelling) current challenges is indeed to find the know-how dealing with data uncertainty propagation through the individual steps of analysis pipelines (Castellini et al., 2011; Cicalese, 2016), which need to be able to take uncertain data as input and to provide a level of confidence for the output made.

9.3.4 Embeddedness

Clear applications of the above approach may be identified for metagenomics (i.e., the genomic composition of microorganisms sampled from an environment) and viruses (which are notoriously mutation executors), apart than on human genetic diseases, as cancer. Besides, metagenomics can be applied as well to gain insights on human health and disease.

Personalized medicine is one the main goals (Ginsburg and Willard, 2017), having a notable social and economical impact, while political and ethical/privacy issues should be discussed and regulated for (genomic) data sharing.

9.3.5 Programmability

Ad hoc developed methods to analyse genomes belong to a computing model that is universal (in the Turing sense). Even when a biological substrate is the input object (Consortium, 2001), sequencing algorithms are applied to get the final genome by means of powerful software developed for the scope.

Although traditional programmability is necessary to process (massive) biological data, the aim for the future points to a closer integration between computation and life, namely by agents able to solve problems by means of their own mechanisms typical of evolutionary systems. Such an approach would result in a trade-off between programmability and evolvability, as in Bonnici and Manca (2016) and Conrad (1988).

9.3.6 Formalism

Infogenomics employs information theoretical analysis of well-characterized genomic features, such as indices, distributions, entropies, representations (and visualizations). The main formalisms for this approach, and in general for computational genomics, are:

- Algorithms on strings and related structures (suffix arrays, hash tables, dictionaries, multisets of strings) and efficient massive computation (Bonnici and Manca, 2015a; Cicalese, 2016; Cicalese et al., 2011; Fici et al., 2006; Herold et al., 2008; Lothaire, 1997);
- Strings representation and reconstruction, dictionaries, factorization, localization, articulation and assembly, variability, similarity, networks (Bonnici and Manca, 2015b; Castellini et al., 2015; Franco and Milanese, 2013; Li et al., 2016; Manca, 2013; Manca, 2017; Percus, 2007);
- Discrete probability (probability distributions, random variables, purely random processes, Monte Carlo methods) (Fofanov et al., 2008; Li et al., 2016; Sims et al., 2009; Zhang et al., 2007);
- Information theoretic concepts (information sources, codes, entropy, entropic divergences, mutual information) (Fabris, 2002; Manca, 2015; Manca, 2016; Manca, 2017; Sadovsky et al., 2008; Thomas and Cover, 1991);

- Specialized software, that is a computational platform for massive computations of genomic informational indexes. For example, an open-source suite for the informational analysis of genomic sequences has been developed (Bonnici and Manca, 2015b) and proposed in Bonnici and Manca (2015a).

9.3.7 Applications

Recent experiments on minimal bacteria (Gibson et al., 2010; Gibson et al., 2014; Venter et al., 2016) are based on the search for genome sequences obtained by manipulating and reducing some real genomes. It has been proved that after removing some parts of the *M. mycoides* genome, the resulting organism (with 531 kilobase pairs, 473 genes), is able to survive and has a genome smaller than that of any autonomously replicating cell found in nature (very close to *M. genitalium*). In this manner a better understanding of biological basic functions is gained, which directly relates to the investigated genome (removing essential portions results in life disruption).

On the basis of this principle, Bonnici and Manca (2016) consider *M. genitalium* and remove some portions of its genome through a greedy exploration of the huge space of possibilities. At every step of their genome modifications (of many different types), they check the validity of their genomic laws, and the number of genes to be possibly eliminated (by keeping the holding of the laws) is comparable with the actual recent experiment in the lab (Venter et al., 2016). This is an example about the applicability of computational experiments, based on informational indexes and laws (possibly after suitable improvements to support and complement the development of genome synthesis and analysis), in the spirit of emergent trends in synthetic biology.

The InfoGenomics project aims at proving an innovative systematic approach for analysis of genomic diseases, and comparative analysis between "ill" and "healthy" genomes, and between species. Other areas commonly face the challenge of analyzing rapidly increasing numbers of genomes, such as microbiology and virology. Identification of genomic markers takes to the development of individual pharmagenetics as well as the so-called personal(ised) and precision genomics and medicine (Ginsburg and Willard, 2017).

Genomic rearrangements and structural variants are of fundamental importance in medicine, namely chromosomal rearrangements and structural variations do in chromotripsis. If we think of cell receptors, of antibody equipment, of viral loads, of genomic variations in microRNA, as bags of words to be designed or analysed, then we may see that computational genomics is an important part of future medicine.

9.3.8 Philosophy

The computer is a digitalisation of mathematics, as DNA is a digitalisation of life. Computational genomics aims/points at extracting principles of organisation and phenomena of regularity in genomic sequences, by means of algorithms, information theoretic concepts, and formal language notions. This perspective is a modelling attitude typical of physicists, with some important differences. The mathematics underlying this approach is mainly of discrete nature (Lothaire, 1997; Manca, 2013); the goal of the investigations is focused on the discovery of general principles of aggregation, and well-formedness of genomic structures, rather than on the determination of equations or invariants of temporal dynamics. Evolution is an essential characteristic of genomes, but there is no specific interest in the predictive analysis of genome evolution; rather, a crucial research perspective is how random processes and mechanisms of structural control in genomes can cooperate to ensure evolvability and programmability. Understanding the interplay of these two apparently conflicting aspects is one of the most difficult conundrums emerging in all the cases where new notions of calculus are considered, especially inspired by natural systems.

A classical computing agent is neutral with respect to the program that is called to execute, and remains unaffected by the computations that it performed in the past. Natural systems, however, especially in situations of great complexity, have an intrinsic relationship with their historical background. Nevertheless, many processes are realised with perfect uniformity, and the individual variability of some natural agents performing computation does not compromise the precision; rather it often enriches the ability to reformulate problems and find solutions (adaptivity, typical of biological systems). The computational and mathematical analysis of these competences, starting from genomes, which are a kind of "operating system" of cells, has a deep relevance not only for genomics and its applications, but also for suggesting new perspectives in the extension of classical paradigms of calculus.

9.3.9 Scaling up

Simply scaling up established bioinformatics pipelines will not be sufficient for leveraging the full potential of such rich genomic data sets. Instead, novel, qualitatively different computational methods and paradigms are needed.

9.4 Main achievements so far

The analysis of genomes by means of strings of length k occurring in the genomes, that is by means of genomic dictionaries of k-mers, has provided important insights into the basic mechanisms and design principles of genome structures (Bonnici and Manca, 2015b; Castellini et al., 2012; Chor et al., 2009; Franco, 2014; Li et al., 2016; Manca, 2013; Sims et al., 2009; Wang et al., 2015; Zheng et al., 2017; Zhou et al., 2008).

Castellini et al. (2012) individuates a relevance in the distinction of hapaxes (once-occurring words) versus repeats (multi-occurring words). Hapax/repeat ratio, minimal length of non-appearing factors, maximal repeat length, and repeat distributions, with respect to their lengths, are defined, and specific genome characters are investigated by means of them. In general, a methodology based on dictionaries has been discussed, where k-mer distributions are integrated with specific features depending on the internal organisation of genome structure.

Many studies have approached the investigation of genomes by means of algorithms, information theory and formal languages, and methods have been developed for genome wide analysis. Dictionaries of words occurring in genomes, distributions defined over genomes, and concepts related to word occurrences and frequencies, have been useful to characterise some genomic features relevant in biological contexts (Bonnici and Manca, 2015b; Castellini et al., 2015; Chor et al., 2009; Fofanov et al., 2008).

Bonnici and Manca (2016) and Manca (2017) propose the proper choice of the value k for applying information theoretic concepts that express intrinsic aspects of genomes. The value $k = \lg_2(n)$, where n is the genome length, allows the definition of some indexes based on information entropies, helpful to find some informational laws (characterizing a general informational structure of genomes) and a new informational genome complexity measure. Bonnici and Manca (2016) compute this by a generalised logistic map that balances entropic and anti-entropic components of genomes, which are related to their evolutionary dynamics. Figure 9.3 shows the localisation of some organisms according to such a numerical complexity.

Figure 9.4 shows a chart of the main informational indexes investigated by Bonnici and Manca (2016) over seventy different genomes. The two quantities EC and AC correspond to informational measures of evolvability (a random component) and programmability (order conserved during evolution) (Conrad, 1988).

We refer to Bonnici and Manca (2016) and Manca (2017) for a formal definition of EC, AC and of the related indexes of Figure 9.4. However, $EC(G)$ is the difference $E_{\lg_2 n}(G) - \lg_4 n$, where n is the length of the genome G and $E_{\lg_2 n}(G)$ is the logarithmic entropy of the genome computed for k-mers with $k = \lg_2 n$. The index $AC(G)$ is given by $\lg_2 n - E_{\lg_2 n}(G)$, which is always positive because $\lg_2 n$ is an upper bound of any empirical entropy of the genome, essentially coinciding with the maximum entropy reachable

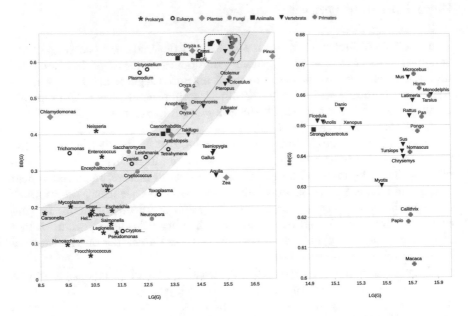

Fig. 9.3 Biobit computed for seventy genomes from different species. [Reproduced by courtesy of the authors of (Bonnici and Manca, 2016)]

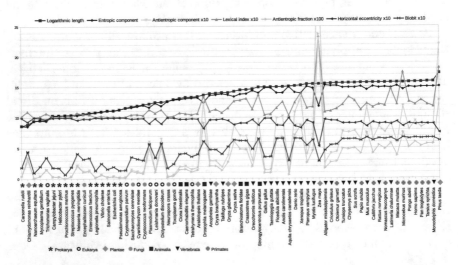

Fig. 9.4 A chart main informational indexes computed over seventy genomes. [Reproduced by courtesy of the authors of (Bonnici and Manca, 2016)]

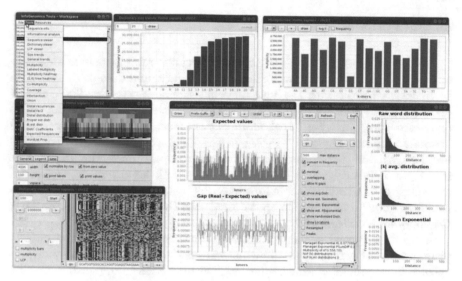

Fig. 9.5 IGtools software interface. [Reproduced by courtesy of the authors of (Bonnici and Manca, 2015a)]

by a random genome of length n. Of course, EC + AC = $\lg_4 n$ (we omit the explicit mention of G) and this value is an index denoted by LG. Three other indexes are EH = EC − AC, AF = AC/LG, and LX that is the average multiplicity of the logarithmic k-mers of the genome. Finally, a more complex index BB is defined by means of Euler's beta function $\beta(\mathrm{AF}, a, b)$ for two suitable parameters a, b; see Bonnici and Manca (2016) and Manca (2017) for the motivation of this definition. The interest of these indexes is given by some informational laws (Bonnici and Manca, 2016; Manca, 2017) expressed by means of them. These laws have been tested over hundreds of genomes, including prokaryotes, algae, amoebae, fungi, plants, and animals of different types.

The specific software IGtools (Bonnici and Manca, 2015a) has been developed for extracting k-dictionaries, computing on them distributions and set-theoretic operations, and for evaluating empirical entropies and our informational indexes, for different and very large values of k-mers. IGtools is a suite (also open to developers) made on top of well-established data structures and algorithms (suffix trees and suffix arrays), adapted for real genomic sequences, and equipped by interactive graphical interfaces and CLI (for batch analyses). Figure 9.5 illustrates some computation for different genomic representations by the IGtools interface.

9.5 Current challenges

Current challenges in computational genomics undoubtably include the development of new algorithms to process genomic data, and data structures able to efficiently handle with the huge mole of genomic variability. These should allow dynamic updates of stored information without rebuilding the entire data structure, including local modifications and dealing adequately with genomic variants. Especially owing to the huge size of generated sequencing data, extreme heterogeneity of data and complex interaction of different levels, we definitively need hybrids that offer both large public repositories as well as computational tools for analyzing genomes in the context of personalized interpretations (Computational Pan-Genomics Consortium, 2018; Ginsburg and Willard, 2017).

A first conceptual challenge is the search of suitable representation and visualization of genomes, at different scale and with multidimensional perspectives, by providing easy frameworks within which to organize and think about genomic data.

An interesting current challenge is the definition and computation/extraction of specific genomic dictionaries, giving both the key to compare different genomes and individual genomes of the same species (that would mean to be able to efficiently dominate the species variants).

Specific analysis in this respect could focus on computation of dictionary intersections, to systematically find evolutionarily conserved motifs among genomes (UCE) (Franco, 2014).

In conclusion, this field still expects considerable progress in both algorithmic and software engineering aspects, to face questions about efficient data structures, algorithms and statistical methods to perform complex and integrated bioinformatic analyses of genomes.

More related to the Infogenomics project, a current challenge is to apply informational indexes as biomarkers in specific pathological situations, and suitable distributions in order to discriminate genome regions and their internal organization.

9.6 What could be achieved in ten years

Evolution is the secret of life and the genomic perspective provides a more precise formulation of Darwinian theory of natural selection. However, even though this theory is a cornerstone in the interpretation of life phenomena, it remains a qualitative theory. A challenge of inestimable importance for a deep comprehension of life is the discovery of quantitative principles regulating biological evolution. Computational genome analyses where specific informational concepts are massively investigated could unravel the internal logic of genome organization, where rigorous mechanisms and chance are mixed together to achieve the main features that are proper of living organisms.

It is not easy to tell now what are the detailed steps of this path, but surely such a kind of enterprise will shed a new light in the interplay between chance and computation and new computing paradigms will emerge that are inherently involved in the deepest mechanisms of natural evolution. One example of quantitative analysis related to this scenario is the "Fundamental Theorem of Natural Selection" proved by Ronald Fisher (Fisher, 1958). Informally, this theorem tells us that the evolutionary change of a population is directly related to the degree of gene variability within the population. This explains in rigorous terms why nature introduces mechanisms of genomic variability within species: the more the individuals present genomic variability, the more rapidly the species can evolve. This theorem is an example of mathematical analysis explaining biological evidence.

In the genomic era, mathematical rigour will be conjugated with genomic data and with the computational power of bioinformatics. We could hope for the achievement of important results that not only will explain to us some secrets of life, but will suggest to us new computational mechanisms with abilities typical of living organisms and of the evolution directing them. This would naturally have spin-offs in biotechnology, health science, synthetic biology, and all the life sciences. We can then expect to witness amazing development in the understanding of the nature of evolution in the mid-term future (Computational Pan-Genomics Consortium, 2018).

References

Almirantis, Y., P. Arndt, W. Li, and A. Provata (2014). "Editorial: Complexity in genomes". *Comp. Biol. Chem.* 53:1–4.

Annaluru, N., H. Muller, L. A. Mitchell, et al. (2014). "Total synthesis of a functional designer eukaryotic chromosome". *Science* 344(6186):816.

Bonnici, V. and V. Manca (2015a). "Infogenomics tools: a computational suite for informational analysis of genomes". *Bioinform. Proteomics Rev.* 1(1):7–14.

Bonnici, V. and V. Manca (2015b). "Recurrence distance distributions in computational genomics". *Am. J. Bioinformatics and Computational Biology* 3(1):5–23.

Bonnici, V. and V. Manca (2016). "Informational laws of genome structures". *Nature Scientific Reports* 6:28840.

Cai, Y. et al. (2007). "A syntactic model to design and verify synthetic genetic constructs derived from standard biological parts". *Briefings in Bioinformatics* 23(20):2760–2767.

Castellini, A., G. Franco, and V. Manca (2012). "A dictionary based informational genome analysis". *BMC Genomics* 13(1):485.

Castellini, A., G. Franco, V. Manca, R. Ortolani, and A. Vella (2014). "Towards an MP model for B lymphocytes maturation". *Unconventional Computation and Natural Computation (UCNC)*. Vol. 8553. LNCS. Springer, pp. 80–92.

Castellini, A., G. Franco, and A. Milanese (2015). "A genome analysis based on repeat sharing gene networks". *Natural Computing* 14(3):403–420.

Castellini, A., G. Franco, and R. Pagliarini (2011). "Data analysis pipeline from laboratory to MP models". *Natural Computing* 10(1):55–76.

Chor, B., D. Horn, N. Goldman, et al. (2009). "Genomic DNA k-mer spectra: models and modalities". *Genome Biology* 10:R108.

Cicalese, F. (2016). *Fault-tolerant search algorithms: reliable computation with unreliable information*. Springer.

Cicalese, F., P. Erdös, and Z. Lipták (2011). "Efficient reconstruction of RC-equivalent strings". *IWOCA 2010*. Vol. 6460. LNCS. Springer, pp. 349–62.

Computational Pan-Genomics Consortium (2018). "Computational pan-genomics: status, promises and challenges". *Briefings in Bioinformatics* 19(1):118–135.

Conrad, M. (1988). *The price of programmability. The Universal Turing Machine A Half-Century Survey*. Oxford University Press.

Consortium, International Human Genome Sequencing (2001). "Initial sequencing and analysis of the human genome". *Nature* 409:860–921.

Crochemore, M. and R. Vérin (1999). "Zones of low entropy in genomic sequences". *Computers & chemistry* 23:275–282.

Deschavanne, P.J., A. Giron, J. Vilain, G. Fagot, and B. Fertil (1999). "Genomic Signature: Characterization and Classification of Species Assessed by Chaos Game Representation of Sequences". *Mol. Biol. Evol.* 16(10):1391–1399.

Dunham, I., A. Kundaje, S. Aldred, and the ENCODE Project Consortium (2012). "An integrated encyclopedia of DNA elements in the human genome". *Nature* 489:57–74.

Fabris, F. (2002). "Shannon information theory and molecular biology". *J. Interdisc Math* 5:203–220.

Fici, G., F. Mignosi, A. Restivo, et al. (2006). "Word assembly through minimal forbidden words". *Theoretical Computer Science* 359:214–230.

Fisher, R.A. (1958). *The Genetical Theory of Natural Selection*. 2nd edn. Dover.

Fofanov, Y., Y. Luo, C. Katili, et al. (2008). "How independent are the appearances of n-mers in different genomes?" *Bioinformatics* 20(15):2421–2428.

Franco, G. (2005). "A polymerase based algorithm for SAT". *ICTCS*. Vol. 3701. LNCS. Springer, pp. 237–250.

2277

5555

a23e646e525e

Franco, G. (2014). "Perspectives in computational genome analysis". *Discrete and Topological Models in Molecular Biology*. Ed. by N. Jonoska and M. Saito. Springer. Chap. 1, pp. 3–22.

Franco, G., N. Jonoska, B. Osborn, and A. Plaas (2008). "Knee joint injury and repair modeled by membrane systems". *BioSystems* 91(3):473–88.

Franco, G. and V. Manca (2004). "A membrane system for the leukocyte selective recruitment". *Membrane Computing*. Vol. 2933. LNCS. Springer, pp. 181–190.

Franco, G. and V. Manca (2011a). "Algorithmic applications of XPCR". *Natural Computing* 10(2):805–819.

Franco, G. and V. Manca (2011b). "On Synthesizing Replicating Metabolic Systems". *ERCIM News 85 - Unconventional Computing Paradigms*. Ed. by Peter Kunz. European Research Consortium for Informatics and Mathematics. Chap. 21, pp. 21–22.

Franco, G. and A. Milanese (2013). "An investigation on genomic repeats". *Conference on Computability in Europe – CiE*. Vol. 7921. LNCS. Springer, pp. 149–160.

Gatlin, L. (1966). "The information content of DNA". *J. Theor Biol* 10(2):281–300.

Giancarlo, R., D. Scaturro, and F. Utro (2009). "Textual data compression in computational biology: a synopsis". *Bioinformatics* 25(13):1575–86.

Gibson, D. G. et al. (2010). "Creation of a bacterial cell controlled by a chemically synthesized genome". *Science* 329(5987):52–56.

Gibson, D. G. et al. (2014). "Synthetic Biology: Construction of a Yeast Chromosome". *Nature* 509:168–169.

Ginsburg, G. S. and H. F. Willard, eds. (2017). *Genomic and Precision Medicine – Foundations, Translation, and Implementation*. 3rd edn. Elsevier.

Hampikian, G. and T. Andersen (2007). "Absent sequences: nullomers and primes". *Pacific Symposium on Biocomputing* 12:355–366.

Herold, J., S. Kurtz, and R. Giegerich (2008). "Efficient computation of absent words in genomic sequences". *BMC Bioinformatics* 9(5987):167.

Holland, J. H. (1998). *Emergence: from chaos to order*. Perseus Books.

Kong, S. G., H.-D. Chen W.-L. Fan, et al. (2009). "Quantitative measure of randomness and order for complete genomes". *Phys Rev E* 79(6):061911.

Li, Z., H. Cao, Y. Cui, and Y. Zhang (2016). "Extracting DNA words based on the sequence features: non-uniform distribution and integrity". *Theoretical Biology and Medical Modelling* 13(1):2.

Lothaire, M. (1997). *Combinatorics on Words*. Cambridge University Press.

Lynch, M. and J. S. Conery (2003). "The origins of genome complexity". *Science* 302:1401–1404.

Manca, V. (2013). *Infobiotics – Information in Biotic Systems*. Springer.

Manca, V. (2015). "Information Theory in genome analysis". *Conference on Membrane Computing (CMC)*. Vol. 9504. Lecture Notes in Computer Science. Berlin, Germany: Springer, pp. 3–18.

Manca, V. (2016). "Infogenomics: genomes as information sources". *Emerging Trends in Applications and Infrastructures for Computational Biology, Bioinformatics, and Systems Biology.* Ed. by Q. N. Tran and H. R. Arabnia. Elsevier. Chap. 21, pp. 317–323.

Manca, V. (2017). "The principles of informational genomics". *Theoretical Computer Science* 701:190–202.

Manca, V., A. Castellini, G. Franco, L. Marchetti, and R. Pagliarini (2013). "Metabolic P systems: A discrete model for biological dynamics". *Chinese Journal of Electronics* 22(4):717–723.

Manca, V. and G. Franco (2008). "Computing by polymerase chain reaction". *Mathematical Bioscience* 211(2):282–298.

Mantegna, R.N. et al. (1994). "Linguistic Features of Noncoding DNA Sequences". *Physical Review Letters* 73(23):3169–3172.

Neph, S., J. Vierstra, A. Stergachis, et al. (2012). "An expansive human regulatory lexicon encoded in transcription factor footprints". *Nature* 489 :83–90.

Păun, G. (2016). "Looking for Computers in the Biological Cell. After Twenty Years". *Advances in Unconventional Computing, volume 1: Theory.* Ed. by A. Adamatzky. Springer, pp. 805–853.

Percus, J. K. (2007). *Mathematics of Genome Analysis.* Cambridge University Press.

Ratner, T., R. Piran, N. Jonoska, and E. Keinan (2013). "Biologically Relevant Molecular Transducer with Increased Computing Power and Iterative Abilities". *Chemistry & Biology* 20(5):726–733.

Rothemund, P. W. K, N. Papadakis, and E. Winfree (2004). "Algorithmic Self-Assembly of DNA Sierpinski Triangles". *PLoS Biology* 2(12):2041–2053.

Sadovsky, M., J.A. Putintseva, and A. S. Shchepanovsky (2008). "Genes, information and sense: Complexity and knowledge retrieval". *Theory in Biosciences* 127(2):69–78.

Searls, D. B. (2002). "The language of genes". *Nature* 420:211–217.

Sims, G. E., S.R. Jun, G. A. Wu, and S.H. Kim (2009). "Alignment-free genome comparison with feature frequency profiles (FFP) andoptimal resolutions". *PNAS* 106(8):2677–2682.

Spivakov, M., J. Akhtar, P. Kheradpour, et al. (2012). "Analysis of variation at transcription factor binding sites in Drosophila and humans". *Genome Biology* 13:R49.

Thomas, A. and T. M. Cover (1991). *Elements of Information Theory.* John Wiley.

Venter, C. et al. (2016). "Design and synthesis of a minimal bacterial genome". *Science* 351:6280.

Vinga, S. (2013). "Information theory applications for biological sequence analysis". *Briefings in Bioinformatics* 15(3):376–389.

Vinga, S. and J. Almeida (2003). "Alignment-free sequence comparison—a review". *Bioinformatics* 19(4):513–523.

Vinga, S. and J. Almeida (2007). "Local Renyi entropic profiles of DNA sequences". *BMC Bioinformatics* 8:393.

Wang, D., J. Xu, and J. Yu (2015). "KGCAK: a *k*-mer based database for genome-wide phylogeny and complexity evaluation". *Biol direct* 10(1):1–5.

Zhang, Z.D., A. Paccanaro, Y. Fu, et al. (2007). "Statistical analysis of the genomic distribution and correlation of regulatory elements in the ENCODE regions". *Genome Res.* 17(6):787–797.

Zheng, Y., H. Li, Y. Wang, et al. (2017). "Evolutionary mechanism and biological functions of 8-mers containing CG dinucleotide in yeast". *Chromosome Research* 25(2):173–189.

Zhou, F., V. Olman, and Y. Xu (2008). "Barcodes for genomes and applications". *BMC Bioinformatics* 9:546.

Part II
Delving into UCOMP Concepts

Chapter 10
Philosophy of Computation

Zoran Konkoli, Susan Stepney, Hajo Broersma, Paolo Dini,
Chrystopher L. Nehaniv, and Stefano Nichele

Abstract Unconventional computation emerged as a response to a series
of technological and societal challenges. The main source of these challenges
is the expected collapse of Moore's law. It is very likely that the existing
trend of building faster digital information processing machines will come
to an end. This chapter provides a broad philosophical discussion of what
might be needed to construct a theoretical machinery that could be used
to understand the obstacles and identify the alternative designs. The key
issue that has been addressed is simple to formulate: given a physical system,
what can it compute? There is an enormous conceptual depth to this question
and some specific aspects are systematically discussed. The discussion covers
digital philosophy of computation, two reasons why rocks cannot be used
for computation are given, a new depth to the ontology of number, and the
ensemble computation inspired by recent understanding of the computing
ability of living cell aggregates.

10.1 Introduction

Given a physical system, what can it compute? In broad philosophical terms
this question is normally referred to as *the implementation problem*. This
seemingly practical question has a surprising conceptual depth: Any attempt
to formalize a rigorous answer (e.g. in pure mathematical terms) is bound to
end in paradoxes. To illustrate the types of paradoxes that usually emerge,
consider Hilary Putnam's answer to this question. As a critique of the thesis
of computational sufficiency in cognitive science Putnam, in the appendix of
his book (Putnam, 1988), suggested a construction, or a recipe, that can be
used to turn any object into a device that can implement any finite state
automaton with input and output.

In brief, the thesis of computational sufficiency states that the human brain can be modelled as an abstract automaton, and that the different states of mind are simply the different states of the automaton (Von Eckardt, 1995). In somewhat simplistic terms, should this be the case, then this would explain to a large extent what the mind is. Note a particular focus on computation in this context. Here the mind is strongly related to the ability to compute.

Putnam's agenda was to show that the notion of computation is simply too broad to be used to define what mind is. His goal was to show that every material object has an intrinsic ability to compute. Namely, for Putnam's construction to work the object that the procedure is being applied to must have a set of rather generic properties (e.g. the system should not be periodic), that are naturally realized in existing objects. Thus a corollary of Putnam's construction is that any object can implement any finite state automaton. Note that the statement does not read "some objects can implement any automaton", or "every object can implement some automaton". It was precisely this corollary that was the key motivation behind the construction. Putnam wished to illustrate that the ability to compute is something that is intrinsic to every object, and that this ability *per se* cannot be used to define what a mind is. According to this corollary, a rock can compute anything, and it should have a mind of its own. This statement is clearly a paradox, since it contradicts our intuition regarding what computing means. This illustrates the first type of paradoxes one can encounter when aiming for a formal (mathematically rigorous) answer to the implementation problem.

The second type of a paradox is as follows. Given that every simple object, even a rock, can be turned into a computing device, the information processing engineers that are exploring various devices for information processing applications should achieve their goals with much less efforts than they are obviously investing in finding new device designs. This is clearly another paradox. To describe it, the term *the natural computability paradox* has been coined (Konkoli, 2015). Note the key difference between the two types of paradoxes: the implementation problem emphasizes the existence of computation, while the natural computability problem emphasizes the use of the device.

The paradoxes that have just been presented indicate that such generic philosophical-computing-oriented questions should not be taken too lightly. A seemingly rather intuitive and straightforward question that deals with the philosophy of computation can have an immense depth. Our main goal in this chapter is to provide a structured exposé of how such questions could be asked, point to the paradoxes that are arising in the process, and discuss ways of resolving such paradoxes.

This chapter is organized on the following principles. Two approaches are exploited to present the material. (i) The traditional way is to define a class of systems and then investigate their expressive power (e.g. the standard models of computation like Turing Machines). We cover that angle for completeness, simply to help a reader versed in digital computation who perhaps wishes to understand the unconventional computation better. While doing so, some philosophical aspects are emphasized, in addition to the usual emphasis on the expressive power and complexity of computation. (ii) We present a palette of philosophical ideas and frame them as thought experiments. Each thought experiment deals with a given system for which we consider the task of turning it into a useful information processing device. In the process, we discuss the key philosophical questions we wish to address. These discussions are organized into separate sections where each section contains a structured and rigorous set of statements describing what a computation might be in a well-defined context, addressing either a class of systems (emphasizing the model of computation context), or a particular fixed (e.g. dynamical) system.

The above principles are implemented as follows. For completeness, a few key ideas of the digital computation paradigm are reviewed first, in Sect. 10.2. It is implicitly understood that the reader has an elementary understanding of the Turing machine concept. Accordingly, this concept is not covered in detail. The section emphasizes some philosophical aspects of the Turing machine construct, since it is the standard answer to the questions of what computing is and what computing means in the context of digital computation. The following sections extend the discussion towards unconventional computation. We begin these discussions by addressing the first thought experiment in Sect. 10.3: what would it take to turn a rock into a computer? Sect. 10.3.1 and Sect. 10.3.2 address the question from two related yet distinct ways. Obviously, we are trying to justify from a theoretical point of view that a rock cannot compute.[1] Philosophical relation between systems and control mechanisms is discussed in Sect. 10.4. In Sect. 10.5 an intimate relationship between the concepts of number and state is discussed, and how these concepts are related to finite state automata and permutation-reset automata. Sect. 10.6 addresses the problem of instantiating computing systems that behave as living cells do: they multiply, process information, aggregate into complex structures, and eliminate redundant computational units when they are no longer needed, all while being affected by their environment. Sect. 10.7 contains a brief summary of the topics covered.

10.2 Philosophy of digital computation

What is digital computation? In this section we are going to explain what we mean by digital computation. Our concept of digital computation is based on an abstract model of this type of computation due to Alan Turing that has been around since the 1930s (Turing, 1936), and an outline of a machine to perform this type of computation described by John von Neumann in 1945.

---

[1] Note that due to Putnam's construction this question has a surprising depth to it. Arguing that a rock cannot compute is not as easy as it sounds.

All our modern digital computers are based on this model of Turing and its implementation by von Neumann.

Turing's aim of defining computation the way he did, was to give an abstract description of the simplest possible device that could perform any computation that could be performed by a human. His purely abstract definition of computation raises a number of controversial philosophical and mathematical problems we will encounter. Moreover, it can be argued that computation, understood in the abstract terms of Turing, is too far removed from the physical implementation of computation. There are quite a few other models of digital computation around, and we mention several of them briefly. We focus on the Turing model because it is a reasonably simple model, and has the same computational power. We explain what we mean by this.

Moreover, the Turing model has been instrumental in the development of the theory of computational complexity, a very active area within computer science and mathematics. We explain this relationship in Chapter 11 of this volume. Even taking into account the controversial nature of Turing's abstract model and its implementation, the great success story of digital computation is based on his ideas, together with the invention and continuing miniaturization of the transistor since 1947. Transistors are the fundamental building blocks of all modern electronic devices, including our supercomputers, PCs, laptops, mobile phones and other gadgets. We shortly explain the impact of what is known as Moore's Law on the advancement of nanotechnology and the further miniaturization of our digital equipment.

10.2.1 Turing machines

Just like any type of computation, digital computation is always dealing with or considered to be computing something. For a general discussion on the philosophical issues related to central common notions like data, representation and information, we refer to Sect. 10.3.2. In fact, the philosophy of information has become an interdisciplinary field in itself, intimately related to the philosophy of computation. Here, for digital computation in particular, we assume that any data and necessary information for the computation at hand is represented at the abstract level by strings of zeros and ones, and at the implementation level in a von Neumann setting by clearly distinguishable low (for a zero) and high (for a one) currents or voltages, determining the switch state of transistors (zero for Off and one for On).

Based on the above assumption, we are now turning our attention to the abstract model of a computational device due to Turing, that is widely known as a Turing machine (not *the* Turing machine, as there are many variations on the basic concept).

10.2.2 The basic version of a Turing machine

What we describe next is usually referred to as the standard deterministic Turing machine.

A Turing machine (TM) is a so-called finite-state automaton combined with an unlimited storage medium usually referred to as a tape. It is called a finite-state automaton because at any moment during a computation it can be in one of a finite number of internal states. The TM has a read/write head that can move left and right along the (one-sided infinite) tape. Initially, the TM is in its start state and the head is at the left end of the tape. The tape is divided into cells, each capable of storing one symbol, but cells can be empty as well.

For simplicity and in the light of the above remarks, we can think of the symbols as zeros and ones, and that there is an additional symbol that represents a blank cell (in most text books λ is used for this purpose). Furthermore, in its simplest form the TM has a transition function that determines whether the read/write head erases or writes a zero or a one at the position of the current cell, and whether the head moves one cell to the left or right along the tape (but not passing the left end of the tape). In addition to these operations, the TM can change its internal state based on the transition function and the symbol in the current cell on the tape. Hence, the transition function determines instructions of the form: if the TM is in state s, the head of the TM points to cell c, and the TM head reads a zero, one, or λ from c, then it writes a zero, one or λ into cell c, moves its head one cell to the left or right, and changes to state s' (or stays in state s).

In fact, the behaviour of the TM is completely determined by the transition function (that can be a partial function): the TM starts in its start state with its head at the left end of the tape, and operates step by step according to the transition function. The TM halts (stops moving its head or changing states or erasing/writing symbols) if the transition function for the current state and cell content is undefined; otherwise it keeps operating. In principle, it could go on forever.

If the TM halts on a particular binary input string w that is initially written on the tape, we can interpret the resulting binary string on the tape as the output of the TM on input w. This way, we can interpret the operations of a (halting) TM as a mapping from input strings to output strings, hence as the computation of a (partial or total) function. Using this interpretation, one can define Turing computable functions as those that can be computed on a TM in the above sense. The subsequent operations of the TM can then be seen as an algorithmic procedure or program to compute the output for any given input of a Turing computable function. For these reasons, TMs are a model for computability, although they do not model the physical processes of a real computer or the command lines of programming languages directly. In fact, Turing invented his abstract model in a time real computers as we know them today did not exist yet. His intention was to formalize the notion of what is sometimes referred to as 'intuitively computable' or 'effectively computable'. We come back to this later.

We know – in fact, Turing already knew – that there exist many functions that are not Turing computable. There are simple counting arguments to show that such functions must exist, but there are also easy tricks to actually construct examples of such functions. From a philosophical point of view, the interesting question here is: are such functions not computable at all because they are inherently non-computable? Or do there exist more powerful devices or alternative models for computation that can compute some functions that are not Turing computable? Perhaps surprisingly, up to now all known alternatives are equally powerful, in the sense that they can compute exactly the same functions. Note that we are not talking about computation time, complexity issues and memory usage here, only about the ability to compute the output value(s) of a function for all possible input values. Interestingly, it was Turing himself who claimed that any effectively computable function could be computed on a TM. In the next sections we gather supporting evidence for his claim.

There exist several alternative paradigms for (digital) computation, like for instance models based on RAM, λ-calculus, While programs, and Goto programs. We will not give any details on such models here, but just mention that all the existing models are, in some sense, equivalent to the Turing model.

10.2.3 The Church-Turing thesis

As we have seen, the investigations about computability have led to a number of approaches to actually try to get our hands on what it means for something to be computable. The earliest attempt was based on the seminal work of Turing, who defined when functions are computable in terms of his abstract model of computation. We have called these functions Turing computable. It turns out that all other notions of computability based on existing alternative approaches are equivalent: the computation of a function in any of these approaches can be simulated in any of the other approaches. In other words, a function is computable in any of these known approaches if and only if it is Turing computable. In this light, it is widely accepted among computer scientists that it is likely that any notion of effective or intuitive computation is equivalent to Turing computation. This is known as the Church-Turing thesis for computable functions.

Church-Turing Thesis I *A function f is effectively computable if and only if there is a TM that computes f.*

It should be clear that the above statement is not a theorem, but more like a working hypothesis. A possible proof for the statement would require a precise mathematical definition of what we mean by an effective computation. That would mean being back at square one. Due to the existing supporting evidence, one could consider taking the statement of the Church-Turing thesis as a definition of what we mean by effectively computable functions, with the risk that one day someone might turn up with a more powerful model or device for computation.

For the purpose of explaining what the existing theory of computational complexity based on TMs entails, we now focus on decisions problems. These are problems for which we require a Yes or No answer for any instance of the problem. Solving such problems is in a way closely related to computation, and requires only a slight adaptation of the abstract model of TMs. As a consequence, the above Church-Turing thesis also has a counterpart for decision problems.

10.2.4 Decision problems and (un)decidability

To be able to decide whether a specific instance of a decision problem is a Yes instance or a No instance, any algorithm for solving this problem has to reach one of the two conclusions, for any instance of the problem. Therefore, it is intuitively clear that we need to extend our TM model by defining which of the halting states should correspond to a Yes answer and which should not. For this purpose a subset of the states of the TM is designated and called the set of accepting states.

Assuming that the instances of the decision problem are encoded as input strings on the tape of the TM, we now consider the set of instances as a language over an alphabet. A language L over an alphabet (for simplicity, think again of a set of strings of zeros and ones) is said to be recognized by the TM if for all strings $w \in L$ ($w \notin L$) the computation of the TM halts in an accepting state (does not halt in an accepting state or does not halt at all); L is decided by the TM if, subject to this, the TM halts on all $w \notin L$. If there exists a TM that decides a language L, then L is called decidable. In fact, L is decidable if its characteristic function is Turing computable (outputting 1 or 0 when halting in an accepting or non-accepting state, respectively).

The counterpart of the Church-Turing thesis for decision problems is as follows.

Church-Turing Thesis II *A decision problem P can be solved effectively if and only if there is a TM that decides the language corresponding to an encoding of P.*

As in the case of computability, also here we have no formal description of what we mean by effectively solving a decision problem.

We know that there are undecidable problems like there are non-computable functions. Again, from a philosophical point of view, the interesting question here is: are such problems not decidable at all because they are inherently undecidable?

10.3 Why rocks do not compute

The material presented in the previous section focused on digital computation. It can be seen as a way to answer the question what computing means, and how it can be realized using digital devices. There are many systems in nature that process information and do not resemble digital devices. Such digital devices can be used to simulate existing systems (e.g. fluid dynamics software packages or chemical reactions simulators, or ultimately, various software packages that can be used to simulate living cells). However, the converse is not necessarily true. For example, it is hard to judge whether the living cells performs digital computation since the dynamics of the living cell hardly resembles anything digital, at least not in an obvious way.[2] There is a plethora of systems that are being investigated for information processing applications, that are far from being digital, e.g. this whole book addresses the possibility of using amorphous materials. The question is, to what extent can we extrapolate our understanding of digital devices to understand unconventional computation? How large is the step that is needed to bridge between the two to gain a unified understanding of both?

Clearly these issues are extremely complex and very broad. Very likely, any attempt to obtain a systematic answer is likely to end in failure. Accordingly, as an illustration, in this and following section Putnam's paradox is discussed in the context of unconventional computation. This is done in the form of a thought experiment. Assume that, against all odds, the goal is to turn a rock into a computer. Can we tell, in any rigorous mathematical way, why rocks do not compute? The following two subsections argue that they, indeed, cannot from two different but still related perspectives.

10.3.1 Powerful computation with minimal equipment

Putnam's construction has been criticized in several ways and there have been numerous responses to Putnam's work (Brown, 2012; Chalmers, 1996; Chrisley, 1994; Copeland, 1996; Godfrey-Smith, 2009; Horsman et al., 2014; Joslin, 2006; Kirby, 2009; Ladyman, 2009; Scheutz, 1999; Searle, 1992; Shagrir, 2012). The most common argument is that the auxiliary equipment that would be needed to turn a rock into an automaton would perform actual computation. Such arguments contain an implicit assumption that there

---

[2] Gene expression networks behave as digital switches, but intrinsically they are not constructed using digital components, their collective behaviour appears such.

is an intention to actually use the device. Here the natural question to ask
is: what type of computation is performed most naturally by the rock?

10.3.1.1 Finding the right balance

In this thought experiment, the goal is to have a simple device consisting
ideally of rock and nothing else. Since this is clearly not possible, the question
is what is the minimal amount of equipment that should be used to achieve
the information processing functionality (of some automaton), and what is
the automaton? This line of reasoning has been formalized in depth in Konkoli
(2015).

Namely, assume that the goal is to compare the computing abilities of
two physical systems, which are fixed, but otherwise arbitrary. This can be
done by simply investigating how hard or easy it might be to use the systems
for computation. Clearly, each of the two systems might be suitable for a
particular type of computation, and this might be guessed in some cases,
but we wish to ask the question in a generic way: is there a procedure for
identifying the most suitable computation for a given system?

As an example, Putnam's construction indicates that both a single bacterial cell and the human brain have the same computing power. However, there
is an intuitive expectation that it should be much easier to use the human
brain for computation, provided it would be ethically justifiable to use the
human brain in this way. We also have a rather good intuitive understanding
of what each of these systems could compute (e.g. one could use bacteria for
relatively simple sensing purposes, while the human brain could be used to
play a game of chess). What is this expectation based on? Is it possible to
formalize this implicit intuition about their respective computing powers?

This rather extreme example shows that a way to understand what a given
system can compute best (and possibly distinguish it from other systems in
terms of their computing power) is to analyze how to actually use the system
to perform computation. For example, it would be very hard to force bacteria
to play a game of chess, this is simply not practical. Thus the ease of use of
a given object (for information processing tasks) is a good starting point for
understanding which information processing tasks it can perform naturally.

The reasoning in the above has been formalised mathematically in Konkoli
(2015). The mathematical formalisation is reviewed in here briefly, Thereafter
it is applied to the issue of the computing rock.

10.3.1.2 The mathematics of balances

The first question one must address is how to measure the "amount" of
auxiliary equipment that needs to be used to turn a system into a computer.
Given that a suitable definition can be found, the amount should be as small

as possible, since we wish the system to perform the computation (and not the equipment).

The amount of the auxiliary equipment can be "measured" by quantifying the complexity of the computation performed by the auxiliary equipment L while implementing an automaton A. The complexity can be measured using the concept of the logical depth (Bennett, 1988), which is a measure of the length of the digitized description of the automaton. Thus given the description of the interface L and the automaton A being implemented, there is a procedure to evaluate the complexity of the computation it performs, $H(L|A)$. The least costly implementation L_* is such that $H(L|A) > H(L_*|A)$ for every conceivable equipment (interface) L. This complexity should be compared with the complexity of the automaton A being implemented by the device, which is denoted by $H(A)$.

The balance between the two is the most important concept. The most natural automaton implemented by the device is the one that appears with the largest complexity $H(A)$ and the lowest cost of implementation $H(L_*|A)$. In less mathematical terms, we are asking the question: what is the most complex computation that a given device can compute most naturally (with the least costly interface)?

This balance between the complexity of the interface and the complexity of the computation achieved can be expressed in many ways, e.g. as

$$F(A) = H(A) - H(L_*|A) \tag{10.1}$$

or by using the ratio $F(A) = H(A)/H(L_*|A)$. Then the most natural implementation A_* can be identified by maximizing the above expression(s) with regard to A, i.e. $F(A_*) > F(A)$ where A is any imaginable automaton.

The formula (10.1) suggest that even the most trivial automaton, the one that does nothing, A_0, is a natural implementation. No interface is needed to implement such an automaton and both logical depths are balanced in some sense. A similar type of balance can occur for more complex automata. Presumably, there is a whole range of automata with roughly identical F values. However, this trend is broken at some point, which can be used to define the natural computation performed by the system.

10.3.1.3 The case of a rock

Finally, returning to the rock, the key question at this stage is how can one use the construct in (10.1) to analyze what a rock can compute? Given that a rock is given, the whole range of automata should be investigated. These automata occur with a varying degree of complexity, and one has to look at the trends in the $F(A)$, and find the automaton for which the complexity of the function being computed per the complexity of interface implementation is the largest. After such point on the complexity scale the complexity of

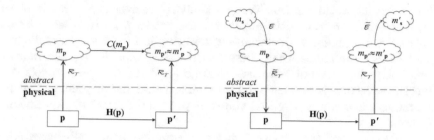

Fig. 10.1 (a) A sufficiently commuting diagram: the physical evolution **H** and the abstract evolution C give the same result, as viewed through a particular representation $\mathcal{R}$. (b) A computation: prediction of the abstract evolution C through instantiation, physical evolution, and representation. (Adapted from Horsman et al. (2014))

the interface simply explodes. The reason why the rock does not compute is that the values for $H(L_*|A)$ grow very fast for any automaton that starts deviating from the null automaton A_0. The null automaton represents the natural computation performed by the rock.

10.3.2 Abstraction/representation theory

Classical computer science regards computations, and often computers, as mathematical objects, operating according to mathematical rules. However, every computer, whether classical or unconventional, is a physical device, operating under the laws of physics. That computation depends in some way on the laws of physics is demonstrated by the existence of quantum computing, which results in a different model from classical computing, because it operates under different physical laws. Classical computation implicitly assumes Newtonian physics.

Unconventional computational matter, from carbon nanotubes to slime moulds and beyond, raise the question of distinguishing a system simply evolving under the laws of physics from a system performing a computation. Abstraction/representation theory (Horsman et al., 2014; Horsman, 2015; Horsman et al., 2018; Horsman et al., 2017a; Horsman et al., 2017b; Kendon et al., 2015) has been developed specifically to answer the question: 'when does a physical system compute?'

Consider a physical system **p** evolving under the laws of physics **H(p)** to become **p′** (Figure 10.1(a)). Let this system **p** in the physical world be represented by a model $m_\mathbf{p}$ in the abstract world, via some representation relation $\mathcal{R}_\mathcal{T}$, where the representation is relative to some theory $\mathcal{T}$. Note that $\mathcal{R}_\mathcal{T}$ is not a mathematical relation, since it relates physical world objects to their abstract world models. We can similarly represent the result of the physical evolution, $\mathbf{p}'$, as the abstract world model $m_{\mathbf{p}'}$. Now let C be our abstract world model of the evolution, resulting in $m_{\mathbf{p}}'$. We say the diagram (sufficiently) *commutes* when these two resulting models $m_{\mathbf{p}}'$ and $m_{\mathbf{p}'}$ are sufficiently close for our purposes. Finding good theories and models such that the substrate is well-enough characterised that the diagram sufficiently commutes for a range of initial states of $\mathbf{p}$, is the subject of experimental science.

Now assume we have such a commuting diagram for some well-characterised substrate $\mathbf{p}$. We can use this to compute, in the following way. We encode our abstract problem $m_{\mathbf{s}}$ into an abstract computational model $m_{\mathbf{p}}$ (for example, via computational refinement). We then instantiate this model $m_{\mathbf{p}}$ in some physical system $\mathbf{p}$ (Figure 10.1(b)). Note that this instantiation relation is a non-trivial inversion of the representation relation, and has connections with engineering (see Horsman et al. (2014) for details). We allow the physical system to evolve under its laws, then represent the resulting state back in the abstract realm as $m_{\mathbf{p}'}$. Since the diagram sufficiently commutes, this observed result $m_{\mathbf{p}'}$ is a sufficiently good prediction of the desired computational result $m_{\mathbf{p}}'$. This computational result can then be decoded back into the problem result $m_{\mathbf{s}}'$.

Hence the physical system has been used to compute the result of the abstract evolution C. This gives the definition: *physical computing is the use of a physical system to predict the outcome of an abstract evolution.*

Note that the physical computation comprises three steps: instantiation of the initial system, physical evolution, and representation of the result. Computation may be 'hidden' in the initial instantiation and final representation steps, and needs to be fully accounted for when assessing the computational power of the physical device. Such hidden computation may include steps such as significant image processing to extract a pattern representing the result from a physical system, or the need to initialise or measure physical variables with unphysically realisable precision.

This definition allows the same abstract computation to be realised in multiple diverse physical substrates, using different instantiation and representation relations (Figure 10.2). Note that if a particular substrate $\mathbf{q}$ is not well-characterised, so that the result $m_{\mathbf{q}'}$ is being compared against some other computed result $m_{\mathbf{p}'}$ in order to check that it is correct, then $\mathbf{q}$ is *not* being used to compute: rather, the substrate $\mathbf{q}$ is being used to perform experiments, possibly in order to characterise it. Computation requires prediction of a result, not of checking a result against some alternative derivation.

This definition applies to multiple substrates being used to perform a computation together. There are two conceptually different approaches (Horsman, 2015), although they can be combined. Figure 10.3(a) shows a hybrid computing system: the problem is decomposed in the abstract domain, and part of it is performed in one substrate, part in another, and the separate abstract results are combined. Figure 10.3(b) shows heterotic computing (Hors-

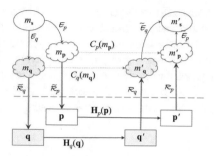

Fig. 10.2 Alternative realisations of the same computation in different physical systems, using different instantiation and representation relations.

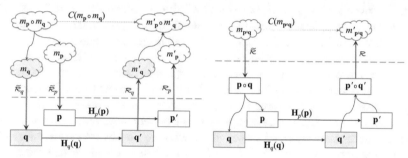

Fig. 10.3 Multiple substrate computing: (a) hybrid computing; (b) heterotic computing. (Adapted from Horsman (2015))

man, 2015; Kendon et al., 2015). Here the decomposition happens in the physical domain, and the instantiation and representation relations apply to the composed physical system as a whole. This potentially allows the composed physical system to have computational capability greater than the sum of its individual parts.

This definition of physical computing demonstrates why a rock does not compute, does not implement any finite state automaton (Horsman et al., 2018). The rock's purported computation is actually occurring entirely in the representation relation being used to interpret the result, not in the rock itself. And the specific computation (specific choice of representation relation) is being imposed *post hoc*, using some previous computation of the answer; it is not a *prediction*.

The definition of physical computation talks of a physical system "being used". This "user" is the *representational entity* (*computational entity* in Horsman et al. (2014)), There is no need for this entity to be conscious, sentient, or intelligent (Horsman et al., 2017b). However, it must exist; see Horsman et al. (2014) for details of why this is the case. This requirement can summarised as "no computation without representation" (Horsman, 2015). This in turn demonstrates why the entire universe is not a computer. Unlike the case of the rock, where representation is everything, here there is no representational activity at all: everything is in the physical domain, and there is no corresponding abstract computation being performed. Clearly representational entities may instantiate and represent part of the universe to perform their computations, but the entire universe is 'merely' a physical system.

10.4 On the requisite variety of physical systems

In the previous sections, the examples of a Turing machine and a rock have been presented with the purpose of clarifying what can compute and what can be computed. Turing machines are ideal models and make use of an arbitrary number of internal states. Rocks (hypothetically) make use of arbitrary complex interfaces, i.e. auxiliary equipment to the computational automaton. In order for a physical system to compute, some problem inputs have to be encoded in a way that is "understood" by the computational substrate. In other words, the inputs have to have an effect on the internal state of the computational medium. The computational system itself can hold (represent) a certain number of internal states. If we want to be able to observe any kind of computation, some result has to be read from the physical system and decoded by some kind of output apparatus, i.e. interface.

If a physical system can represent a certain number of internal states, the computational complexity of the problems that can be computed by such system is bounded by the number of output states that can be distinguished. Computational matter exploits the underlying physical properties of materials as a medium for computation. As such, the internal theoretical number of states in which the material can be, e.g. state of each of the molecules composing the material system, is several orders of magnitude higher than what can be practically decoded (unless we use particle collider detectors as reading apparatus, colliding particles as computational material and quarks as units of information). What can we compute with a physical system then? The available computational power is bounded by the number of states that are available to the observer, e.g. electric apparatus or any apparatus that measures any interesting physical property of the material.

Such philosophical relation between systems and control mechanisms has been rigorously formalized within the field of cybernetics by Ross Ashby, a pioneer British cyberneticist and psychiatrist. Ashby, recognized as one of the most rigorous thinkers of his time, formulated his law of requisite variety (Ashby, 1956) which states, in a very informal way, that in order to deal correctly with the diversity of problems, a (control) system needs to have a repertoire of responses which is at least as many as those of the problem. Ashby described the systems under his investigation as heterogeneous, made of a big collection of parts, great richness of connections and internal interactions. Even if Ashby proposed the concept of relative variety in the context of biological regulation, i.e. organisms' adaptation to the environment, it has been adopted and reformulated in a large number of disciplines. Some examples include Shannon's information theory (Shannon, 1948), structure and management of organizations and societies (Beer, 1984), behavior-focused design (Glanville et al., 2007), and computational systems in general.

In the following sections we review the concept of variety and give a formulation of Ashby's law of requisite variety in the context of computation. We describe some philosophical issues related to variety, computation and complexity, such as the intrinsically incorrect variety of physical computational systems.

10.4.1 Variety

Consider the set of elements $S = \{a, b, c, a, a, d\}$; its variety is the number of elements that can be distinguished. As such, the variety of S is 4. In many practical cases, the variety may be measured logarithmically (if base 2, then measured in *bits*). If a set is said to have no variety, it has all elements of one type and no distinctions can be made. If logarithmically measured, the variety of a set with only elements of one kind is $\log_2 1 = 0$.

10.4.2 Law of requisite variety

Let O be the set of outcomes of a system, D the set of disturbances that can deteriorate the outcomes and R the set of regulations available to a regulator (control mechanisms) to counterbalance the disturbances and maintain the functionality of the system. Let us denote V_O, V_D and V_R the varieties of the sets O, D and R, respectively. If the varieties are measured logarithmically, the minimal value of V_O (numerically) is $V_D - V_R$. If the value of V_D is given and fixed, V_O's minimum can be lessened only by a corresponding increase in V_R. Only variety in R can force down variety in D, "only variety can destroy variety".

Glanville (2004) describes two types of possible system controllers, one in the form of a regulator (the kind of control that "allows us to stay upright when skiing, stable in the face of perturbations", the skiing control) and one in the form of a restriction ("in a classroom the variety of the teacher is much lower than the variety of the class but some Victorian teachers used to handle the situation by restricting the variety of the students" (Robinson, 1979), restrictive control).

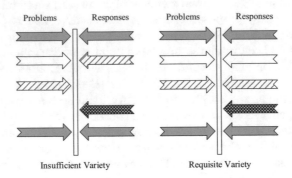

Fig. 10.4 Graphical representation of the law of requisite variety. On the left the variety of responses is insufficient or incorrect, on the right there is requisite variety (at least enough variety) of responses.

Now, for the sake of creating a more realistic analogy, let us consider a physical system D that is supposed to perform some sort of computation, O is the set of possibly incorrect (or unwanted) outcomes of the systems (if the result is read and interpreted correctly, O has minimum variety) and R is the system's controller (e.g. reading apparatus, interface or output mapping). In the ideal case, the variety of R would be as much as the variety of D and the variety of O would be minimized.

Figure 10.4 shows a simple graphical representation of the original formulation of the law of requisite variety as initially proposed by Ashby. In practice, the number of available responses of the system has to match the possible problems to be solved in order to have requisite variety. Otherwise the variety is said to be insufficient or incorrect.

10.4.3 Insufficient variety of physical systems

In the context of a physical computational system, requisite variety may be considered at two different stages:

1. the number of internal states of the systems has to code (represent) at least the number of possible input instances of the problem under investigation;
2. the number of responses that can be read has to have at least the variety of the possible number of states represented by the systems.

While the first point is intimately connected to the fact that rocks cannot compute, the latter raises a deeper concern. The number of states that a physical system can represent is typically higher than the number of states that can be decoded. Hence, the variety of complex physical systems is not well defined. The way we have been able to control systems of increasing computational complexity has relied by far on Moore's law: building better controllers of continuously increasing variety. Bremermann (1962) postulated that any unit of matter has a finite computing capacity, according to the Laws of Physics. He calculated the computational capacity of a gram of matter and called this number Bremermann's constant, which is equal to 10^{47} bits per second. With this number, Ashby derived the computational capacity of the whole universe as 10^{100} bits. (It is not our intention to argue this calculation, as few orders of magnitude here do not make any difference.) It is possible to think of systems with greater variety than the computational power of the universe. Imagine a screen with 50×50 pixels than can be either black or white. Its variety is 2^{2500}. Thus, no control system with such variety can be built, no matter if Moore's law still holds or not. From a practical perspective, this implies that the complexity of the problems that can be solved is bounded by the number of states (and the scale) of the input/output interface used for decoding and reading the result.

10.4.4 Variety as complexity, new computational models?

Variety is a synonym of complexity. Cybernetics has studied systems independently of the substrate in which computation may happen (Wiener, 1961) and the same set of concepts is suitable for formalizing different kinds of systems. To paraphrase Ashby, one of the "peculiar virtues of cybernetics is that it offers a method for the scientific treatment of the system in which complexity is outstanding and too important to be ignored", and again, "variety, a concept inseparable from that of information". Shannon used information as measure of uncertainty (read complexity). If a message is predictable, it carries little information as there are few states that are very probable and information content may be derived from a probability distribution. On the other hand, if all the states have same probability of occurrence, the information cannot be predicted beforehand. Ashby added that "it must be noticed that noise is in no intrinsic way distinguishable from any other form of variety". Shannon's Theorem 10 (Shannon, 1948) is formulated in terms of requisite variety as "if noise appears in a message, the amount of noise that can be removed by a correction channel is limited to the amount of information that can be carried by that channel". Bar-Yam (2004) uses variety as synonym of complexity and proposed the law of requisite complexity. In the context of matter that computes, it can be reinterpreted as "the controller (input/output apparatus) for a complex system needs to be at least as complex as the system it attempts to control".

If computation is to be embedded into physical matter systems, a different computational model that goes beyond the standard Turing mechanistic model may be needed, as material computers are devices that interact with the physical world. Dodig-Crnkovic and Burgin (2011) describe the mechanistic world by the following principles:

1. The ontologically fundamental entities of physical reality are [space-time and matter (mass-energy)] defining physical structures and motion (or change of physical structures);
2. All the properties of any complex physical system can be derived from the properties of its components;
3. Change of physical structures is governed by laws.

It may be argued that Turing models (Turing, 1936), which consist of an isolated computing machine that operates on an input tape of atomic symbols, are mechanistic models. The assumption of a mechanistic model is that the laws of conservation of energy, mass, momentum, etc. hold, i.e. the system is isolated from the environment. Computational matter is hard to model mechanistically because of its inherent complexity. If Ashby's law of requisite variety is considered, in order for a computational model to be well defined it has to match the complexity of its environment. Physical systems exhibit a much higher complexity than Turing machines. Hence, it may be necessary to have more powerful models than Turing machines in order to represent matter that computes.

More than 20 years after Ashby's law of requisite variety was formulated, new (second-order) cybernetics (Foerster, 2007; Maruyama, 1963) started to give more importance to the positive side of requisite variety instead of the negative ones: "Give up trying to control, [...] gain access to enormous amounts of variety, [...] a potential source of creativity". von Neumann, while working with self-replicating automata, postulated a lower complexity threshold under which the system would degenerate, but above which would become self-reproducing. Ashby himself wrote a note on this, saying that a good regulator, i.e. controller, should account for emergence in the variety. The emergence of new functionality in a system should add to the variety of the regulator as to be able to cope with unexpected disturbances.

Requisite variety is an ideal condition and physical systems should aspire to have a variety as well defined as possible (or at least enough for the kind of computational problems one may want to solve).

10.5 On the ontology of number and state

In order to perform a computation, an abstract mathematical model requires a physical substrate or system that changes its physical state in a corresponding manner. This suggests that the Numbers of computations and the States of the physical systems they represent are intimately connected. Although this observation is already sufficient to motivate ontological questions such as 'what is a state?' and 'what is a number?', the question of the relationship between them investigated in this section arose from a different perspective on the representation problem. Namely, can the time-evolution of a physical system be used to "guide" a computation, or to define or enable a specific *type* of computation?

10.5.1 Motivation

The correspondence of the time evolution of an electronic system with certain mathematical operations was exploited by the analogue computers of the 1950s. For example, different arrangements of circuit elements (resistors, capacitors, etc.) connected to one or more operational amplifiers yield algebraic or analytical relationships between the input and output voltages that correspond to addition, subtraction, integration, differentiation, and so forth.

In digital computers there is no such connection, by design. The 'general-purpose' digital computer was developed precisely to abstract from the details of the physical system so as to be able to perform any kind of computation. This has been largely successful, but as mentioned above there are some computations that classical computers cannot do and that require quantum computers. Similarly, we expect some biological systems to "compute" in a very different way from what the current von Neumann architecture does, or even from the Turing Machine model described in Sect. 10.2. Thus, one of the current research questions in unconventional computing is whether such biological systems afford any properties for the computational systems they implement that may be deemed desirable or interesting from an anthropocentric point of view. Self-healing and self-organizing computing systems are typical examples of such desirable properties.

At this point the problem splits in two. On the one hand, a biological system can be seen as a computational device that executes the functions it evolved for. A typical example is the ability of slime mould to find food by growing around obstacles of different topologies (Adamatzky, 2010). In other words, this view is based on regarding physical behaviour as a form of computation, and is likely to benefit from a clarification of the link between State and Number.

On the other hand, the other perspective aims to develop computing systems that satisfy human needs and requirements, but that embody some of the dynamical characteristics of biological systems, such as self-healing and self-organization. In this view, we could argue for a three-tier model:

- At the lowest level is a general-purpose digital computer, which we can assume to be classical. At this level (the physical system of Sect. 10.3.2) the voltages of the logic gates can be identified with the binary number system and related operations.

- At an intermediate level we have a subset of the computations that are possible at the lowest level. Such computations are consistent with constraints derived from biological systems, so in some sense this level is able to emulate different biological systems, or some of their properties.
- At the top level (the representation level of Sect. 10.3.2) 'normal' computations are performed on variables that are meaningful to human users. However, since these computations are implemented by the intermediate level, they rely on an evolution of the physical system that in some sense emulates the behaviour of a biological system.

This framework underpins the type of biocomputing that is discussed next, and motivated the search for any fundamental properties or 'primitives' that could make the formalization of the biological constraints into the intermediate layer easier or more natural. Seeking a better understanding of the ontology of Number and State is part of this exploration.

10.5.2 Interaction computing

The BIOMICS project[3] is exploring the idea to leverage the self-organizing properties of biological systems to achieve 'self-organizing computing systems' through the concept of 'interaction computing' (Dini et al., 2013), some of whose properties and implications are discussed in Sect. 10.6. The idea of Interaction Computing is inspired by the observation that cell metabolic/regulatory systems are able to self-organize and/or construct order dynamically, through random interactions between their components and based on a wide range of possible inputs. The emphasis on ontogenetic rather than phylogenetic processes was partly motivated by Stuart Kauffman's observation that natural selection in biological evolution does not seem powerful enough to explain the order construction phenomena we see in nature (Kauffman, 1993, Preface).

The expectation of the three-tier model above is that it is *more* powerful than the Turing machine model, in spite of the fact that the intermediate layer performs a *subset* of the computations that the physical system at the lowest layer can support. This idea has been around for a long time and was well-argued by Peter Wegner almost 20 years ago (Wegner, 1997), but could probably be summarized most simply by noticing that the computation results from the interaction of multiple machines which, like the molecules in a biochemical mixture, do not always know which inputs will arrive next and which other machines they will interact with next. Whether the different machines are implemented as separate von Neumann computers or are emulated

---

[3] www.biomicsproject.eu

in the intermediate layer by a single von Neumann machine is inconsequential. In the vision of Interaction Computing their interactions are constrained in the same way. Interestingly, the original concept for this kind of computation can also be ascribed to Alan Turing, in the same paper where the TM was introduced (Turing, 1936). Turing did not provide a formal model, but only briefly described the 'Choice Machine', i.e. a machine that could be interrupted by external inputs during the execution of an algorithm. Rhodes provides an abstract formalization of this concept in the form of a generalization of a sequential machine (Rhodes, 2010).

The achievement of self-organizing computational systems, therefore, appears to depend on the ability to express and formalize architectural and dynamical properties of biological – and in particular biochemical – systems as constraints on binary general-purpose digital computing systems. Whereas the encoding between the two is generally achieved through the semantics of programming languages, it is worth asking whether some structural or algebraic properties of biological systems might give rise to desirable computational properties, thereby in essence "modulating" the encoding achievable by programming languages, compilers, and so forth.

One of the first questions that arose in this line of thinking sought to establish whether there are any "primitive" properties of physical systems that could be related directly to similarly "primitive" properties in computational systems. This is the main motivation behind the exploration of the relationship between the concept of State and the concept of Number.

10.5.3 Algebraic automata theory

The first step in constructing the link between the concepts of State and Number is to associate a physical or biological system with its approximation as a finite-state automaton. The second step is to recognize that a finite-state automaton can be seen mathematically as a set of states acted upon by a semigroup of transformations (including an identity transformation, so technically a monoid).

The idea of connecting the states of such a 'transformation semigroup' to the concept of number is due to Rhodes (Rhodes, 2010) and is based on the interpretation of the Krohn-Rhodes decomposition of a transformation semigroup into a cascade of simpler machines through the 'prime decomposition theorem' (Krohn and Rhodes, 1965).[4] The simpler machines in the cascade play the same role as the different digits of a number expressed as a posi-

---

[4] The appellative 'prime' derives from the fact that, since the simpler machines have irreducible semigroups (the irreducible 2-state reset automata with identity (flip-flops), prime order counters, or simple non-abelian groups (SNAGs)), they cannot be decomposed further and so are analogous to prime numbers in integer decomposition.

tional expansion.[5] The manner in which the component machines depend on each other is uni-directional ('loop-free') in the same way as the carry bit in regular addition. In other words, the expansion of an automaton into a cascade of machines means that each ("global") state of the automaton can be expanded into an ordered tuple of ("positional") states analogous to the expansion of a number in a given positional number system (with variable base).[6] And the change of state caused by the receipt of an input symbol is mathematically analogous to addition in a positional number system, with the effect of positional state changes in the upper layers in the cascade on the lower layers through 'dependency functions' being mathematically identical to the effect of the carry bit on the positions to the left of any given digit in the positional expansion of any given number. Through this representation state changes of automata can be seen as generalizations of the addition of numbers: State 1 + Input Symbol = State 2.

A few years after the Krohn-Rhodes theorem was proved, Zeiger (1967) proved a variant whose statement is somewhat easier to understand. The holonomy theorem says that any finite-state automaton can be decomposed into a cascade product of certain permutation-reset automata. The permutation automata involved are 'sub-machines' of the original automaton whose states are *subsets* of the original state set X and whose semigroups are permutation groups (which include an identity map) permuting these subsets, and these are augmented with all possible resets to yield the permutation-reset automata of the decomposition.[7]

This idea is explained in some detail by Dini et al. (2013), but the gist can probably be communicated well enough by Figure 10.5. The figure shows an example of the converse of what is stated above because it is easier to understand. Namely, a 4-bit binary number can be seen as a cascade of 4 binary counters. Each counter, in turn, is isomorphic to a cyclic group of order 2 (C_2). In this idealized example each level of the decomposition only has (reversible) groups, there are no irreversible resets (flip-flops).

Permutation-reset automaton.

To explain what a permutation-reset automaton is, Figure 10.6 shows different types of actions that can be induced on a set of six states by the elements of a semigroup S. Let's call one such element $s \in S$. In Case 10.6a, s per-

---

[5] A positional expansion (in a constant base) is a representation of a number into a string of digits each of whose position from the right end of the string corresponds to the power of the base -1 times which that digit should be multiplied.

[6] Furthermore, at each level in the cascade more than one machine could be present, but this is not important for this conceptual discussion.

[7] Holonomy decomposition was implemented within the past few years as the SgpDec package (Egri-Nagy et al., 2014) in the GAP (GAP Group, 2014) computational algebra language.

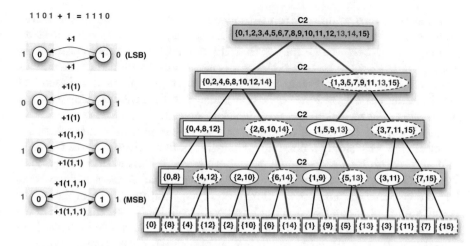

Fig. 10.5 (Left) Binary positional notation for non-negative integers < 16 expressed as a composition of binary counters, with dependency conditions (carry bit) shown explicitly. (Right) Corresponding group coordinatization in decimal notation.

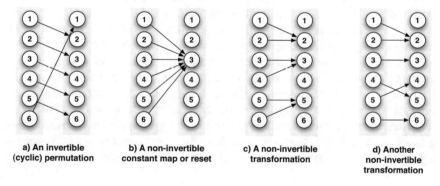

a) An invertible (cyclic) permutation

b) A non-invertible constant map or reset

c) A non-invertible transformation

d) Another non-invertible transformation

Fig. 10.6 Different kinds of transformations of 6 states (after Maler (Maler, 2010))

mutes the states and so is a member of a group that is a subgroup of S; in Case 10.6b, s is a constant map, which is non-invertible; the remaining two cases are other examples of non-invertible transformations. A permutation-reset automaton has elements that can only be like Case 10.6a (including the identity permutation) or Case 10.6b. In Cases 10.6b, 10.6c, and 10.6d, s cannot belong to a group action that permutes the states. At the same time, in Case 10.6b the degree of non-invertibility is maximum. Thus, permutations and resets could be regarded as "mutually orthogonal" in the sense that no combination of one type can yield a member of the other type. In other words, permutation groups and identity-reset semigroups are analogous to a generalized basis into which an automaton can be decomposed.

As in the more complex Krohn-Rhodes decomposition, also in the holonomy decomposition the way the permutation-reset automata are wired together is 'loop-free', which means that the dependence is unidirectional. As above, this is a generalization of the carry rule in normal addition. The various levels must be wired in a loop-free manner, setting up particular dependencies from higher-level to lower-level components so that the resulting 'cascade product' is able to emulate the original automaton.

As above, the cascade of machines can also be seen from a more abstract point of view as yielding a possible "expansion" of any given state of the original automaton into a positional "number" system. This is best understood by realizing that the notion of a number is actually an abstract concept that has many possible "implementations" or representations: we can choose to count a flock of sheep by an equal number of pebbles, or we can write down a number in positional decimal notation like 89. We could also express 89 in binary notation as 1011001, which is also positional, or in Roman numerals as LXXIX, which is not (and therefore much less useful in both practical and mathematical terms). Writing '89' on a piece of paper is easier and more practical than carrying around 89 pebbles, or 89 beans, etc.

However, notice an interesting fact: whereas with numbers we are much more familiar with their (decimal) expansion, to the point that we have to make an effort to notice that '89' is not the "essence" of this number but just one of its possible representations, the opposite is true for an automaton: we are quite familiar with the fact that an automaton is at all times in one of its states, which we can easily visualize, but we have a really hard time thinking about the "expansion" of such a state into a positional notation of some form. This is not just because the base of such an expansion is far from clear and, even if it were clear, in general it changes between positions (levels of the cascade), but because we don't really know what to *do* with such an expansion until we become familiar with using it.

Reconciling algebra and physics.

A potentially confusing aspect of the holonomy decomposition of an automaton concerns the relationship between its algebraic structure and the physical behaviour of the system it models. The action of any groups that may be present in the decomposition on (sub)sets of states is generally described in terms of permutations of the state set upon which any such group is acting; thus, it is *parallel*. By contrast, a physical system will visit a *sequence* of its states, one at a time. These two views can be reconciled by noting that a permutation should be seen as an (invertible) function from the state set to itself. Thus, a physical state change corresponds, for each level of the expansion of the corresponding state in the automaton, to one evaluation of one such function at one state, to obtain another state. And a sequence of physical states in general corresponds, at each level where there is a group, to the sequential evaluation of *different* elements of that group acting on a sequence of states from the same set (where the output of one evaluation is the input of the next).

In other words, the algebraic description is meant to capture the structure of a cascade that emulates the original automaton, i.e. all its possible computations (input sequences and state traces). Whether any group structure that results has a deeper physical or computational significance is not immediately clear and requires further thought. Indeed, the group structure of modulo n counters in the base n expansion of the real numbers is essential, but could seem mysterious at first sight given the fact that the numbers have no elements of finite order n at all!

From a physics perspective the presence of groups is appealing because it implies the presence of conserved quantities.[8] Conserved quantities that are relevant in physics are conserved along the time-evolution of the system, implying that the state changes of a physical system that conserves some quantity can be expressed as the elements of a group. An example of such an invariant is, trivially, the constant of integration obtained when a differential system is reduced to quadrature and that corresponds more generally to a level set of a 'first integral' of the system. It appears that such conserved quantities and groups correspond to the top level of the holonomy decomposition, because the top-level group acts on the whole state set. If there are groups at lower levels the expectation is that they correspond to some further aspect of the physical quantity being conserved.

In many cases we can see what is being conserved by groups at the various levels of the decomposition, but it often takes great effort to understand this kind of correspondence. However, the development of the mathematical theories is proceeding, as discussed in the next section. From a computational point of view, the challenge is to understand the meaning of the intermediate levels of the decomposition. If the top layer represents global transformations that affect the whole state set and the lowest layer the encoded action on singleton states, the intermediate layers encode the action on subsets of states, also known as 'macrostates' in computer science. Such a hierarchy amounts to a 'coordinatisation' of the original automaton that becomes increasingly more fine-grained the lower one goes in the levels. It is very interesting that such a coordinatisation should emulate the behaviour of the original automaton, but it may still seem very difficult to imagine "programming" in such an environment, i.e. where each instruction is coordinatised across multiple levels, within each of which it acts as either a constant map on a subset of states or a permutation thereof. Therefore, the expectation is that progress will be made first by relying on the algebra to understand the biology, and then by

---

[8] Paraphrasing Ian Stewart, a symmetry is an invertible transformation that leaves some aspect of the structure of a mathematical object invariant. The set of all such symmetries always forms a group. The converse is also true: the presence of a group implies the presence of an invariant of some kind or other.

relying on the biology to gain new insights into the very unconventional kind of computation it appears to implement.

10.6 Interaction and dynamically deployable computational structure in ensembles

Unlike traditional computing using a pre-circumscribed state- and phase-space where all the possible configurations are in principle limited at the outset to some fixed structure, natural systems like differentiated multicellular organisms can grow from one or a few cells to fill and create dynamic structures. It is clear that such systems perform a myriad of information processing tasks. For example, consider the case of evolving embryo where cells have to differentiate into specific types and further have to be positioned properly in a rather robust way. Is this type of computing intrinsically different from the computation performed in more stable environments? Below we address some topics that might be helpful for reasoning around this question from a rather broad conceptual point of view.

10.6.1 Growing and changing computational structures

Resources may be allocated or released as cells proliferate or die away in the course of development in interaction with the external environment, including other individuals (West-Eberhard, 1989). Multiple asynchronous parallel processes are created and branch, or terminate, depending on interaction. The nature of this interaction may be impossible to circumscribe at the outset, not only in terms of its detailed content, but also even in terms of what channels of interaction exist. While Turing computation can be regarded as 'off-line' and computation involving interaction as 'on-line' (Wegner, 1997) (through a fixed interface) making the latter qualitatively different in terms of what algorithms can be carried out, but we are speaking here of something beyond merely adding interactivity. Beyond static state spaces, pre-circumscribed computation, and even beyond augmenting traditional models with interaction, we refer to something much more like what living systems do as they grow, change and reproduce: *the capacity to change structure in the course of interaction in ways that are dynamically defined during the unfolding of the time course of interaction with whatever entities may come and go in the external environment.* Here interaction itself takes place through dynamically changing structures. These changes affect the nature of interactions internally and externally, as well as re-structuring the internal dynamic (often recursive hierarchical) constituent components and the dynamic interaction topologies connecting their activity. *Interaction machines* (Nehaniv et al., 2015) and related formalisms allows us to treat discrete or continuous constructive dynamical systems whose structure, constituents, state spaces, and capacities vary dynamically over the course interaction.

10.6.2 Ensembles

Furthermore, a key idea for us is that the ensemble of computational resources deployed at any given moment may include *multiple copies* or *instances* of computational 'cells' from a lineage that has experienced various different trajectories in their interaction with the environment (*ensembles*), as is the case with living cells in a multicellular body, or living in close proximity in a colony. These multiple instances can be viewed as the 'same' individual experiencing multiply time-lines, and responding in multiple ways. This viewpoint allows us then to apply the methods of algebra (Nehaniv et al., 2015) that facilitate the use of such ensembles to maintain natural subsystems as pools of reversible computation in which actions or reversible. The permutations we referred to in the previous section now explicitly map not single states, but are operators that permute an ensemble of states. Even relatively simple systems that we find in living cells (like the p53-mdm2 genetic regulatory control pathway) can achieve *finitary universal computation*, i.e. the capacity to realize any mapping $f \colon X^n \to X^m$ from every finite set X when harnessed in multiple copies (Nehaniv et al., 2015). This may be the case with genetic regulatory control in cells.

10.6.3 Recurrence and differentiation

Dynamic re-engagement with recurring scenarios of such computational ensembles could lead to robustness and more adaptive choice – as in the case of Darwinian evolution (Nehaniv, 2005; Pepper, 2003) or interaction history learning (Nehaniv et al., 2013) – compare also F. Varela's ideas on principles of biological autonomy (Varela, 1979) and recurrence in cycles of dependent origination (Varela et al., 1991).

With further differentiation between types of cells – i.e. ensembles not of heterogeneous cells but organized structurally to reflect different functions in a division of labour – even more is possible in terms of exploiting dynamic organizational structure, including hierarchies, in interaction.

10.7 Conclusions

A series of philosophical questions related to the idea of computation have been posed in different setups: Given a physical system, what can it compute? In which ways is digital computation different from other types of computation? Are there other types of computation? Why living cells compute? Can a rock compute as well? Can we compute with evolving systems? Is it advantageous to compute with such? What is a number? How to we represent it?

Many of the these questions are rather complex. Further, it has been argued that even seemingly practical questions in the list above have a surprising conceptual depth. For all these questions any attempt to formalize a rigorous answer (e.g. in pure mathematical terms) is bound to end in paradoxes. Some of the paradoxes have been addressed, and resolved to some extent. This has been done by discussion a few rigorous mathematical frameworks that can be used to address them.

Perhaps it is fair to say that, in relative terms, when compared to other types of computation, digital computation is well-understood. However, as soon as one leaves the comfort provided by the abundance of mathematical machinery used to describe digital computation, the world seems to be packed with paradoxes.

For example, loosely speaking, it is possible to argue that every rock can compute anything, which is clearly not the case. Two related solutions to this paradox have been suggested which, very briefly can be stated as: (1) there is no simple interface that can turn a rock into a computer; (2) for the rock, the representation is everything. Admittedly, from the dynamical point of view, as a system, the rock is hardly an interesting object. Why bother with philosophical constructs that explain why rocks do not compute? However, the situation changes rapidly when other systems are considered such as amorphous materials or self-organized amorphous materials that multiply and die, e.g. as living cells. Without a theory that can explain why rocks do not compute, there can hardly be a theory that explains why living cells do, for example.

Note that it is known that such an elementary concept of an integer number becomes hard to describe when thinking in rigorous philosophical and mathematical terms. In here we tried to address the issue from the information processing point of view too.

Living systems can be seen as powerful information processing devices, already at the single cell level, and, in particular, at the level of cell colonies or cell ensembles. Cells multiply, change types, aggregate and arrange themselves in space, all while being exposed to external influences. Perhaps out of the systems considered in this chapter, such systems are by far the hardest ones to address in this philosophical context. The key reason is that the structure of the configuration space of such systems evolves in time, as new cells are added and removed from the ensemble.

Why should one bother with such broad questions? There are several reasons. The first major reason is that we still do not have a mathematical machinery that could be used to argue why living cells compute. Such a mathematical approach should feature the following concepts: Abstract model versus implementation in terms of computational power, what are we throwing away, and what do the results of the previous subsection imply or mean for in-principle and in-practice (im)possibilities to compute/execute/problem solving.

The second reason is entirely practical, and equally, if not more important. The good fortune provided by Moore's Law is likely to end very soon. Moore's Law is not a natural law, but it has become a target, and it has been part of the roadmaps to lead the research and industrial developments in digital circuitry, and it has therefore had a great impact on industry and society. In somewhat simplistic terms, the law guarantees that we can continue building ever faster computers. There are many drives for this trend, both scientific and societal. For example, this state of affairs is one of the main reasons why unconventional computation is gaining in the number of followers. As a society we are facing many challenges if this trend of being able to perform fast computations cannot continue. It is possible that one can advance the field further by developing the engineering side. However, given the complexity of the task ahead, it is likely that an access to a systematic way of thinking might be a great aid in finding new information processing solutions in nature and adjusting the ones from nature. The discussion presented in this chapter should be seen as an illustration of what might be done to reach these goals.

References

Adamatzky, A. (2010). *Physarum Machines: Computers from Slime Mould.* World Scientific.

Ashby, William Ross (1956). *An introduction to cybernetics.* Champman & Hall.

Bar-Yam, Yaneer (2004). "Multiscale variety in complex systems". *Complexity* 9(4):37–45.

Beer, Stafford (1984). "The viable system model: Its provenance, development, methodology and pathology". *Journal of the Operational Research Society* 35:7–25.

Bennett, C. H. (1988). "Logical Depth and Physical Complexity". *The Universal Turing Machine: A Half-Century Survey.* Ed. by R. Herken. Oxford University Press, pp. 227–257.

Bremermann, H. J. (1962). "Optimization through evolution and recombination". *Self-Organizing Systems.* Ed. by Marshall C. Yovitis and George T. Jacobi. Spartan, pp. 93–106.

Brown, C. (2012). "Combinatorial-State Automata and Models of Computation". *Journal of Cognitive Science* 13:51–73.

Chalmers, D. J. (1996). "Does a rock implement every finite-state automaton?" *Synthese* 108:309–333.

Chrisley, R. L. (1994). "Why everything doesn't realize every computation". *Minds and Machines* 4:403–420.

Copeland, B. J. (1996). "What is computation?" *Synthese* 108:335–359.

Dini, P., C. L. Nehaniv, A. Egri-Nagy, and M. J. Schilstra (2013). "Exploring the Concept of Interaction Computing through the Discrete Algebraic Analysis of the Belousov-Zhabotinsky Reaction". *BioSystems* 112(2):145–162.

Dodig-Crnkovic, Gordana and Mark Burgin (2011). *Information and computation: Essays on scientific and philosophical understanding of foundations of information and computation.* Vol. 2. World Scientific.

Egri-Nagy, A., C. L. Nehaniv, and J. D. Mitchell (2014). *SgpDec – Hierarchical Decompositions and Coordinate Systems, Version 0.7.29.* URL: sgpdec.sf.net.

Foerster, Heinz von (2007). *Understanding understanding: Essays on cybernetics and cognition.* Springer.

GAP Group (2014). *GAP – Groups, Algorithms, and Programming, V 4.7.5.* URL: www.gap-system.org.

Glanville, Ranulph (2004). "A (cybernetic) musing: Control, variety and addiction". *Cybernetics & Human Knowing* 11(4):85–92.

Glanville, Ranulph, Hugh Dubberly, and Paul Pangaro (2007). "Cybernetics and service-craft: Language for behavior-focused design". *Kybernetes* 36(9/10):1301–1317.

Godfrey-Smith, P. (2009). "Triviality arguments against functionalism". *Philosophical Studies* 145:273–295.

Horsman, C., Susan Stepney, Rob C. Wagner, and Viv Kendon (2014). "When does a physical system compute?" *Proceedings of the Royal Society A* 470(2169):20140182.

Horsman, D. C. (2015). "Abstraction/Representation Theory for heterotic physical computing". *Phil. Trans. Roy. Soc. A* 373:20140224.

Horsman, Dominic, Viv Kendon, and Susan Stepney (2018). "Abstraction/Representation Theory and the Natural Science of Computation". *Physical Perspectives on Computation, Computational Perspectives on Physics.* Ed. by Michael E. Cuffaro and Samuel C. Fletcher. Cambridge University Press, pp. 127–149.

Horsman, Dominic, Susan Stepney, and Viv Kendon (2017a). "The Natural Science of Computation". *Communications of ACM* 60(8):31–34.

Horsman, Dominic, Susan Stepney, Viv Kendon, and J. P. W. Young (2017b). "Abstraction and representation in living organisms: when does a biological system compute?" *Representation and Reality in Humans, Other Living Organisms and Intelligent Machines.* Ed. by Gordana Dodig-Crnkovic and Raffaela Giovagnoli. Springer, pp. 91–116.

Joslin, D. (2006). "Real realization: Dennett's real patterns versus Putnam's ubiquitous automata". *Minds and Machines* 16:29–41.

Kauffman, S. (1993). *The Origins of Order: Self-Organisation and Selection in Evolution*. Oxford University Press.

Kendon, Viv, Angelika Sebald, and Susan Stepney (2015). "Heterotic computing: past, present, and future". *Phil. Trans. Roy. Soc. A* 373:20140225.

Kirby, K. (2009). "Putnamizing the Liquid State (extended abstract)". *NACAP 2009*.

Konkoli, Zoran (2015). "A Perspective on Putnam's Realizability Theorem in the Context of Unconventional Computation". *International Journal of Unconventional Computing* 11:83–102.

Krohn, K. and J. Rhodes (1965). "Algebraic Theory of Machines. I. Prime Decomposition Theorem for Finite Semigroups and Machines". *Transactions of the American Mathematical Society* 116:450–464.

Ladyman, J. (2009). "What does it mean to say that a physical system implements a computation?" *Theoretical Computer Science* 410:376–383.

Maler, O. (2010). "On the Krohn-Rhodes Cascaded Decomposition Theorem". *Time for Verification: Essays in Memory of Amir Pnueli*. Ed. by Z. Manna and D. Peled. Vol. 6200. LNCS. Springer.

Maruyama, Magoroh (1963). "The second cybernetics: Deviation-amplifying mutual causal processes". *American Scientist* 51:164–179.

Nehaniv, Chrystopher L. (2005). "Self-replication, Evolvability and Asynchronicity in Stochastic Worlds". *Stochastic Algorithms: Foundations and Applications*. Vol. 3777. LNCS. Springer, pp. 126–169.

Nehaniv, Chrystopher L, Frank Förster, Joe Saunders, Frank Broz, Elena Antonova, Hatice Kose, Caroline Lyon, Hagen Lehmann, Yo Sato, and Kerstin Dautenhahn (2013). "Interaction and experience in enactive intelligence and humanoid robotics". *IEEE Symposium on Artificial Life (IEEE ALIFE 2013)*. IEEE, pp. 148–155.

Nehaniv, Chrystopher L., John Rhodes, Attila Egri-Nagy, Paolo Dini, Eric Rothstein Morris, Gábor Horváth, Fariba Karimi, Daniel Schreckling, and Maria J. Schilstra (2015). "Symmetry structure in discrete models of biochemical systems: natural subsystems and the weak control hierarchy in a new model of computation driven by interactions". *Philosophical Transactions of the Royal Society A* 373:2040223.

Pepper, John W. (2003). "The evolution of evolvability in genetic linkage patterns". *BioSystems* 69(2):115–126.

Putnam, H. (1988). *Representation and Reality*. MIT Press.

Rhodes, J. (2010). *Applications of Automata Theory and Algebra via the Mathematical Theory of Complexity to Biology, Physics, Psychology, Philosophy, and Games*. World Scientific Press.

Robinson, Michael (1979). "Classroom control: Some cybernetic comments on the possible and the impossible". *Instructional Science* 8(4):369–392.

Scheutz, M. (1999). "When Physical Systems Realize Functions". *Minds and Machines* 9:161–196.

Searle, J. R. (1992). *The Rediscovery of the Mind.* MIT Press.

Shagrir, O. (2012). "Computation, Implementation, Cognition". *Minds and Machines* 22:137–148.

Shannon, C. E. (1948). "A mathematical theory of communication". *Bell System Technical Journal* 27(3):379–423.

Turing, A. (1936). "On Computable Numbers, with an Application to the Entscheidungsproblem". *Proceedings of the London Mathematical Society (2)* 42:A correction, ibid, 43, 1937, pp. 544-546, 230–265.

Varela, Francisco J. (1979). *Principles of Biological Autonomy.* North Holland.

Varela, Francisco J., Evan Thompson, and Eleanor Rosch (1991). *The Embodied Mind.* MIT Press.

Von Eckardt, B. (1995). *What is cognitive science?* MIT Press.

Wegner, P. (1997). "Why Interaction Is More Powerful than Algorithms". *Communications of the ACM* 40(5):80–91.

West-Eberhard, Mary Jane (1989). "Phenotypic plasticity and the origins of diversity". *Annual Review of Ecology and Systematics*:249–278.

Wiener, Norbert (1961). *Cybernetics or Control and Communication in the Animal and the Machine.* MIT Press.

Zeiger, H. P. (1967). "Cascade synthesis of finite-state machines". *Information and Control* 10(4):plus erratum, 419–433.

Chapter 11
Computability and Complexity of Unconventional Computing Devices

Hajo Broersma, Susan Stepney, and Göran Wendin

Abstract We discuss some claims that certain UCOMP devices can perform hypercomputation (compute Turing-uncomputable functions) or perform super-Turing computation (solve $\mathcal{NP}$-complete problems in polynomial time). We discover that all these claims rely on the provision of one or more unphysical resources.

11.1 Introduction

For many decades, Moore's Law (Moore, 1965) gave us exponentially increasing classical (digital) computing (CCOMP) power, with a doubling time of around 18 months. This cannot continue indefinitely, due to ultimate physical limits (Lloyd, 2000). Well before then, more practical limits will slow this increase. One such limit is power consumption. With present efforts toward exascale computing, the cost of raw electrical power may eventually be the limit to the computational power of digital machines: Information is physical, and electrical power scales linearly with computational power (electrical power = number of bit flips per second times bit energy). Reducing the switching energy of a bit will alleviate the problem and push the limits to higher processing power, but the exponential scaling in time will win in the end. Programs that need exponential time will consequently need exponential electrical energy. Furthermore, there are problems that are worse than being hard for CCOMP: they are (classically at least) *undecidable* or *uncomputable*, that is, impossible to solve.

CCOMP distinguishes three classes of problems of increasing difficulty (Garey and Johnson, 1979):

1. Easy (tractable, feasible) problems: can be solved by a CCOMP machine, in polynomial time, $O(n^k)$, or better.

© Springer International Publishing AG, part of Springer Nature 2018
S. Stepney et al. (eds.), *Computational Matter*, Natural Computing Series,
https://doi.org/10.1007/978-3-319-65826-1_11

2. Hard (intractable, infeasible) problems: take at least exponential time, $O(e^n)$, or exponential resources like memory, on a CCOMP machine.
3. Impossible (undecidable, uncomputable) problems: cannot be solved by a CCOMP machine with any (finite) amount of time or memory resource.

Unconventional Computing (UCOMP) (European Commission, 2009) is a diverse field including a wealth of topics: hypercomputation, quantum computing (QCOMP), optical computing, analogue computing, chemical computing, reaction-diffusion systems, molecular computing, biocomputing, embodied computing, Avogadro-scale and amorphous computing, memcomputing, self-organising computers, and more.

One often hears that UCOMP paradigms can provide solutions that go beyond the capabilities of CCOMP (Konkoli and Wendin, 2014). There is a long-held notion that some forms of UCOMP can provide tractable solutions to $\mathcal{NP}$-hard problems that take exponential resources (time and/or memory) for CCOMP machines to solve (Adleman, 1994; Copeland, 2004; Lipton, 1995; Ouyang et al., 1997; Siegelmann, 1995), and the challenge to solve $\mathcal{NP}$-hard problems in polynomial time with finite resources is still actively explored (Manea and Mitrana, 2007; Traversa and Di Ventra, 2017; Traversa et al., 2015). Some go further, to propose UCOMP systems that can handle classically undecidable or uncomputable problems (Cabessa and Siegelmann, 2011; Copeland and Shagrir, 2011; Hogarth, 1992).

Many of these analyses may be *theoretically* sound, in that, if it were possible to implement the schemes, they would behave as claimed. But, *is* it possible to implement such schemes, to build such a computer in the material world, under the constraints of the laws of physics? Or are the hypothesised physical processes simply too hard, or impossible, to implement?

Key questions we discuss in this chapter are:

1. Can UCOMP provide solutions to classically undecidable problems?
2. Can UCOMP provide more effective solutions to $\mathcal{NP}$-complete and $\mathcal{NP}$-hard problems?
3. Are classical complexity classes and measures appropriate to any forms of UCOMP?
4. Which forms of UCOMP are clearly and easily amenable to characterisation and analysis by these? And why?
5. Are there forms of UCOMP where traditional complexity classes and measures are not appropriate, and what alternatives are then available?

The idea that Nature is physical and does not effectively solve $\mathcal{NP}$-hard problems does not seem to be generally recognised or accepted by the UCOMP community. However, there is most likely no free lunch with UCOMP systems providing shortcuts, actually solving $\mathcal{NP}$-hard problems (Aaronson, 2005). The question is then, what is the real computational power of UCOMP machines: are there UCOMP solutions providing significant polynomial speed-up and energy savings, or more cost-effective solutions beyond the practical capability of CCOMP high performance computing, or different kinds of solutions for embodied problems, or something else? This is the subject of the discussion in this chapter.

In Sect. 11.2 we discuss what it means to be a computational problem. In Sect. 11.4 we discuss UCOMP and hypercomputation (computability) claims. In Sect. 11.5 we recap the classical definitions of computational complexity. In Sect. 11.6 we discuss the power of various quantum computing approaches. In Sect. 11.7 we discuss UCOMP and super-Turing computation (complexity) claims, and the actual computational power of a variety of UCOMP paradigms.

11.2 Computational problems and problem solving

In the context of problem solving, the term complexity of a problem is used to indicate the difficulty of solving that particular problem, in many cases relative to the difficulty of solving other problems. Two questions that need to be answered first are: what do we mean in this context by *problem* and by *problem solving*?

11.2.1 Difficulty

Within the area of CCOMP, solving a particular problem means developing an algorithmic procedure that is able to produce a solution to that problem. This assumes that the problem consists of a set of instances, each of which can be encoded as an input to the algorithmic procedure, and that the algorithmic procedure then produces an output that can be decoded into a solution for that instance of the problem. This implies that being able to solve such types of problems means being able to write and install a computer program on a digital device that, executed on an input representing any instance of the problem produces an output that serves as a solution to that particular instance.

This leads to two natural questions:

- Does an algorithm exist for solving a particular problem? This is a question of *decidability* or *computability*.
- If such an algorithm does exist, how efficient is it at solving the problem? This is a question of *complexity*.

If such a computer program is available, it is natural to measure the difficulty of solving the problem by the *time* it takes the computer program to come up with the solution. There are many issues with this measure. For example, the execution time depends on the type and speed of the computer (processor), the type and size of the (encoding of the) instance, and on how smart the designed algorithmic procedure and its implementation were chosen.

In order to tackle some of these issues, the theory usually involves just the number of basic computational steps in the algorithmic procedure, and relates this to a function in the size of the instances. Upper bounds on the value of this function for the worst case instances are taken to indicate the relative complexity of the problem when compared to other problems.

Another natural question to ask is how much *space* (memory) does the program need to use to solve the problem. Again, the analyses abstract away from the complexities of actual computer memory (caches, RAM, discs, and so on), to an abstract concept of a unit of space.

This approach does not immediately say whether a more complex problem is intrinsically *difficult*, nor whether the algorithmic procedure used is optimal or not in terms of the complexity. Identification of the least complex algorithm for problems is at the heart of the theory of computational complexity.

11.2.2 Decision, optimisation, and counting problems

There are different types of problems. One distinction is based on the type of solutions.

The main focus in the area of computational complexity is on *decision problems*, where the solution for each problem instance is YES or NO. The task is, given an arbitrary instance and a certain fixed property, to answer whether the given instance has that property.

Consider the travelling salesman problem (TSP). An instance of TSP comprises a set of cities, together with the mutual distances between all pairs of cities. A route is a permutation of the city list, corresponding to travelling through each city precisely once, returning to the starting city. The length of the route is the sum of the distances between the cities as travelled. Given some value x representing the length of the route, TSP can be cast as a decision problem: is there a route that does not exceed x? For a nice exposition on the many facets of TSP we refer the reader to Lawler et al. (1985).

Consider the k-SAT (satisfiability) problem (Garey and Johnson, 1979). A formula (instance) in this problem involves any number m of conjoined clauses, each comprising the disjunction of k terms. Each clause's k terms are drawn from a total of n Boolean literals, $b_1 \ldots b_n$, and their negations. For example, a 3-SAT problem instance could be the formula $(b_1 \vee b_2 \vee b_3) \wedge (\neg b_2 \vee b_3 \vee b_5) \wedge (b_1 \vee \neg b_3 \vee b_4) \wedge (\neg b_1 \vee b_3 \vee \neg b_5)$, which has $n = 5$ and $m = 4$. k-SAT is a decision problem: is there an assignment of truth values to the b_i that satisfies (makes true) the formula?

Decision problems differ from problems for which the solution is other than just YES or NO. A large class of problems for which this is the case, is the class of so-called *optimisation problems*. For these problems, it is not sufficient to come up with solutions, but the solutions are required to satisfy certain additional optimisation criteria. TSP can be cast as an optimisation problem: what is (the length of) a shortest route?

Another large class of problems that are not decision problems, is the class of *counting problems*. For these problems, the solutions are numbers rather than YES or NO. For TSP, one could, e.g., ask for the number of routes that are shorter than x, or for the number of different shortest routes.

Most optimisation and counting problems have decision counterparts (as is clear in the case of TSP above). Such optimisation and counting problems are obviously at least as difficult to solve as their decision counterparts.

11.2.3 Terminology

We use the term *hypercomputation* to refer to UCOMP models that can compute classically uncomputable functions (such as the Halting function, a total function that decides whether an arbitrary computer program halts on an arbitrary input). This is sometimes referred to as computation that "breaks the Turing barrier" or is "above the Turing limit" (that is, the barrier to, or limit on, computability).

We use the term *super-Turing computation* to refer to UCOMP models that can compute more efficiently (using exponentially fewer resources) than a Deterministic Turing Machine (DTM).

The UCOMP literature is not consistent in its use of these terms. Careful reading may be needed to determine if a particular claim is about computability or about complexity.

11.3 A brief review of CCOMP computability

11.3.1 Undecidable problems, uncomputable functions

Not all problems can be solved by an algorithmic procedure using a classical computer. It has been known since Turing (1937) that there are *undecidable* problems: those for which there is provably no algorithmic procedure to produce the correct YES/NO answer.

The earliest example of such a problem is the *Halting Problem*. In this problem, one has to write a computer program H that takes as its input any computer program P and input I, and outputs YES if P would eventually halt (terminate) when run on I, and outputs NO otherwise. There is provably no such H. Since then, many other examples of such undecidable problems have been established.

For problems not cast as decision problems, but in terms of computing the value of a function defined in a finite number of well-defined steps, there are *uncomputable* functions. Well-known examples include Kolmogorov complexity (Li and Vitányi, 1997), the Busy Beaver function (Rado, 1962), and Chaitin's omega halting probability (Chaitin, 1975; Chaitin, 2012). Note that by function in the above we mean a function on the natural numbers; such a function F is *(Turing) computable* if there is a Turing Machine that, on input n, halts and returns output $F(n)$. The use of Turing Machines here is not essential; there are many other models of computation that have the same computing power as Turing Machines.

The existence of (many) uncomputable functions of the above type follows from the fact that there are only *countably* many Turing Machines, and thus only countably many computable functions, but there are uncountably many functions on the natural numbers. Similarly, a set of natural numbers is said to be a *computable set* if there is a Turing Machine that, given a number n, halts with output 1 if n is in the set and halts with output 0 if n is not in the set. So for any set with an uncountable number of elements, most of its elements will be uncomputable. Hence most subsets of the natural numbers are uncomputable.

Decision problems can be encoded as subset problems: encode the problem instance as a unique natural number; the YES answers form a subset of these numbers; the decision problem becomes: is the number corresponding to the problem instance an element of the YES set? Hence most decision problems are uncomputable, that is, undecidable.

These undecidable problems and uncomputable functions are hard to solve or compute in a very strong sense: within the context of CCOMP it is simply impossible to solve or compute them.

11.3.2 Oracles and advice

Computability is an all or nothing property (although whether a problem class is computable may itself be an uncomputable problem). *Oracles* can be used to add nuance to this property: how much (uncomputable) help would be needed to make a problem computable? Less powerful oracles can also be considered when investigating complexity: how much oracular help is required to reduce the complexity of a problem class?

An oracle is an *abstract* black box that can take an input question from a DTM and output the answer. Oracles can be posited that provide answers to certain classes of problems, such as halting-problem oracles and $\mathcal{NP}$-problem oracles. An oracle is usually deemed to provide its answer in one step. (See Sect. 11.5.4 for a definition of classes $\mathcal{P}$ and $\mathcal{NP}$.)

Oracles can be posited, and their consequent abilities investigated theoretically, but they cannot be implemented on a classical computer, since they provide computational power above that of a DTM.

More recently introduced complexity classes try to capture additional computational power provided by allowing *advice* strings. An advice string is an extra input to a DTM that is allowed to depend on the length of the original input to the DTM, but not on the value of that input. A decision problem is in the complexity class $\mathcal{P}/f(n)$ if there is a DTM that solves the decision problem in polynomial time for any instance x of size n given an advice string of length $f(n)$ (not depending on x).

Trivially, any decision problem is in complexity class $\mathcal{P}/\exp$. If the input is of size n, then there are $O(2^n)$ possible input values x of size n. An exponentially large advice string can enumerate the $O(2^n)$ YES/NO answers to the decision problem as an exponentially large lookup table.

Advice strings can be posited, and their consequent abilities investigated theoretically. Given an advice string, it can be implemented along with the DTM using its advice, since the string could be provided as an input to the DTM. However, classically, the advice on that string would itself have to be computed somehow; if the string contains uncomputable advice, then classically it cannot exist to be provided to the DTM.

11.3.3 Church–Turing thesis

The *Church–Turing Thesis* (CTT) states that "every number or function that 'would naturally be regarded as computable' can be calculated by a Turing Machine" (Copeland, 2015). This is a statement about computability, in terms of a (digital) classical computer.

Vergis et al. (1986) reformulate this thesis in terms of analogue computers as: "any analogue computer with finite resources can be simulated by a digital computer". This is a statement about computability: (finite) analogue computers do not increase what is computable over classical digital computers.

Hypercomputation seeks to discover approaches that can expand the range of computable functions beyond those computable by Turing Machines; it seeks to invalidate the CTT.

11.4 Hypercomputation

11.4.1 Undecidable problems determined physically?

Hypercomputation is a diverse field with many ideas on how to compute classically uncomputable functions using physical and non-physical approaches. One of the major proponents of hypercomputation is Jack Copeland (Copeland, 2004; Copeland, 2015; Copeland and Shagrir, 2011). Arkoudas (2008) states:

> Copeland and others have argued that the CTT has been widely misunderstood by philosophers and cognitive scientists. In particular, they have claimed that the CTT is in principle compatible with the existence of machines that compute functions above the "Turing limit", and that empirical investigation is needed to determine the "exact membership" of the set of functions that are physically computable.

Arkoudas (2008) disputes this argument, and claims that it is a category error to suggest that what is computable can be studied empirically as a branch of physics, because computation involves an *interpretation* or *representation* component, which is not a concept of the physical sciences. (See also Horsman et al. (2014).)

11.4.2 Accelerated Turing Machines

An example of a theoretical hypercomputer is the Zeno Machine (Potgieter, 2006). A Zeno Machine is an Accelerated Turing Machine that takes $1/2^n$ units of time to perform its n-th step; thus, the first step takes $1/2$ units of time, the second takes $1/4$, the third $1/8$, and so on, so that after one unit of time, a countably infinite number of steps will have been performed. In this way, this machine formally solves the Halting Problem: is it halted at $t = 1$?.

Such a machine needs an exponentially growing bandwidth (energy spectrum) for operation, which is not a physically achievable resource.

Any physical component of such a machine would either run up against relativistic limits, and be moving too fast, or quantum limits, as it becomes very small, or both. The model implicitly relies on Newtonian physics.

11.4.3 General relativistic machines

There are various models that use General Relativistic effects to allow the computer to experience a different (and infinite) proper time from the (finite) time that the observer experiences. The best known of these is the Malament–Hogarth spacetime model (Etesi and Németi, 2002; Hogarth, 1992). The underlying concept is that the computer is thrown into one of these spacetimes, where it can be observed externally. If a computation does not halt, this can be determined in a finite time by the observer in the external reference frame, and so the set-up solves the Halting Problem.

This is an interesting branch of work, as it demonstrates clearly how the underlying laws of physics in the computer's material world can affect the reasoning used about possible computations.

However, there are several *practical* issues with this set-up. The computer has to be capable of running for an infinite time in its own reference frame. Also, the "tape" (memory) of the computer needs to have the potential to be actually infinite, not merely unbounded. It is not clear that such infinite time and infinite space can be physically realised.

11.4.4 Real number computation

A model of computation beyond the Turing limit has been formulated by Siegelmann (1995), involving neural networks with real-valued weights. Douglas (2003) and Douglas (2013) provides a critical analysis. The problem is the usual one for analogue systems: ultimate lack of precision; *in the end one needs exponential resources*. Analogue precision can be converted (by an ADC, Analogue-Digital Converter) into a corresponding digital range, which is effectively a memory requirement. $\mathcal{NP}$-problems (see later) require exponentially growing analogue precision, corresponding to a need for exponentially growing memory. Hypercomputational problems (computability) correspond to a need for infinite precision.

Real number hypercomputation (Blum, 2004) relies on physical systems being measurable to infinite precision. The underlying argument appears to be: physicists model the physical world using real numbers; real numbers have infinite precision and so contain infinite information; hence physical systems have infinite information; this information can be exploited to give hypercomputation. There are two problems with this argument.

The first problem is that the argument confuses the model and the modelled physical reality. Just because a quantity is modelled using a real number does not mean that the physical quantity faithfully implements those real numbers. The real-number model is in some sense 'richer' than the modelled reality; it is this extra richness that is being exploited in the theoretical models of hypercomputation. For example, consider Lotka–Volterra-style population models (Wangersky, 1978), where a real-valued variable is used to model the population number, which is in reality a discrete quantity: such models break down when the continuum approximation is no longer valid. Fluid dynamics has a continuous model, but in the physical world the fluid is made of particles, not a continuum, and so the model breaks down. The Banach–Tarski paradox (Wagon, 1985; Wapner, 2005) proves that it is possi-

ble to take a sphere, partition it into a finite number of pieces, and reassemble
those pieces into two spheres each the same size as the original; the proof relies on properties of the reals that cannot be exploited to double a physical
ball of material.

Secondly, even if some physical quantity were to contain arbitrary precision, there is strong evidence that it takes an exponentially increasing time
to extract each further digit of information (see Sect. 11.5.11).

11.4.5 Using oracles, taking advice

Cabessa and Siegelmann (2011) state:

> The computational power of recurrent neural networks is intimately related to the
> nature of their synaptic weights. In particular, neural networks with static rational
> weights are known to be Turing equivalent, and recurrent networks with static real
> weights were proved to be [hypercomputational]. Here, we study the computational
> power of a more biologically-oriented model where the synaptic weights can evolve
> rather than stay static. We prove that such evolving networks gain a [hypercom-
> putational] power, equivalent to that of static real-weighted networks, regardless of
> whether their synaptic weights are rational or real. These results suggest that evolu-
> tion might play a crucial role in the computational capabilities of neural networks.

A proposed rational-number hypercomputer avoids the issue of infinite
precision. The set-up described by Cabessa and Siegelmann (2011) is a neural network with rational, but changing ('evolving'), weights. However, the
changing weights are not computed by the network itself, nor are they provided by any kind of evolutionary feedback with a complex environment.
They are provided directly as input in the form of a sequence of increasing-
precision rational numbers: that is, an advice string.

Any claim of hypercomputation achieved through the use of an oracle or
advice needs to address the feasibility of implementing said oracle or advice.
These can provide hypercomputational power only if they are themselves
Turing-uncomputable,

11.4.6 Conclusion

Hypercomputation models tend to rely on one or more of:

- known incorrect models of physics (usually Newtonian, ignoring relativistic and/or quantum effects)
- physically-instantiated infinities (in time and/or space and/or some other
  physical resource)
- physically accessible infinite precision from real numbers
- Turing-uncomputable oracles or advice

There is currently no evidence that any of these essentially *mathematical* hypercomputation models are physically realisable. Their study is interesting, however, because they illuminate the various relationships between computability and physical (as opposed to mathematical) constraints. For example, they bring into focus an unconventional computational resource: precision.

Other facets of hypercomputation, of moving beyond computational paradigms other than Turing, are discussed in Stepney (2009).

11.5 A brief review of CCOMP complexity

We now move on to discussing super-Turing UCOMP models, which deal with computational complexity. First we briefly review some concepts of classical complexity theory. Further information can be found in any good textbook on computational complexity, such as Garey and Johnson (1979) and Sipser (1997).

11.5.1 Measuring complexity

Complexity in the classical setting of digital computing is typically a mathematically calculated or proven property, rather than an empirically measured property, for two main reasons.

Firstly, complexity refers to asymptotic properties, as the problem sizes grow. It would have to be measurable over arbitrarily large problem sizes to determine its asymptotic behaviour. This is particularly challenging for many UCOMP devices (including quantum computers) that to date only exist as small prototypes that can handle only small problem instances.

Secondly, complexity is a worst case property: the complexity of a problem (or class) is the complexity of the hardest problem instance (or hardest problem in that class). Some instances can be easy, other instances hard. If there are very few hard instances, these "pathological" instances may not be encountered during empirical sampling.

11.5.2 Easy, polynomial time problems

Edmonds (1965) was the first to distinguish good and bad algorithmic procedures for solving decidable problems. He coined the term *good algorithm* for an algorithmic procedure that produces the correct solution using a number of basic computational steps that is bounded from above by a polynomial function in the instance size. He also conjectured that there are decidable problems for which such good algorithms cannot be designed. This conjecture is still open, although there is a lot of evidence for its validity. We come back to this later.

The algorithms that Edmonds called good, are nowadays usually referred to as *polynomial* (time) algorithms, or algorithms with a polynomial (time) complexity. The corresponding problems are usually called polynomial(ly solvable) problems, but also referred to as easy, tractable, or feasible problems.

Define the function $f(n)$ to be the bound on an algorithm's number of basic computational steps in the worst case, for an instance of size n. Then for a polynomial (time) algorithm, $f(n)$ is $O(n^k)$, meaning that there exists a positive integer k and positive constants c and n_0 such that $f(n) \leq c \cdot n^k$ for all $n \geq n_0$. The n_0 is included in the definition because small problem instances do not determine the complexity: the complexity is characterised by what happens for *large* problem instances.

11.5.3 Hard, exponential time problems

Decidable decision problems for which no tractable (polynomial time) algorithm exists are called hard, intractable, or infeasible problems. These usually allow straightforward exponential algorithms: algorithmic procedures for solving them have worst case instances that take an exponential number of computational steps. The function $f(n)$ that bounds the number of computational steps, in the worst case for an instance of size n, is $O(c^n)$, for some positive constant c.

Similar to the conjecture of Edmonds (1965), it is nowadays widely believed that there are decision problems for which the only possible algorithmic procedures for solving them have an exponential complexity.

11.5.4 Complexity classes $\mathcal{P}$ and $\mathcal{NP}$

Based on the above distinction between easy and hard problems, the formally defined complexity class $\mathcal{P}$ consists of all decision problems that are tractable, that admit polynomial algorithms for solving them by a *classical Deterministic Turing Machine (DTM)*. A decision problem in $\mathcal{P}$ is also referred to as a problem with a polynomial complexity, or simply as a polynomial problem. The decision version of TSP described above has no known polynomial time algorithm to solve it.

Many textbooks, such as Garey and Johnson (1979) and Sipser (1997), provide a fundamental treatment of complexity class $\mathcal{P}$ in terms of Turing

Machines. There, it is argued that the problems in $\mathcal{P}$ are precisely those problems that can be encoded and decided on a DTM within a number of transitions between states that is bounded by a polynomial function in the size of the encoding (number of symbols) of the input.

The class $\mathcal{NP}$ can be defined in terms of Turing Machines as consisting of those problems that can be decided on a *Non-deterministic Turing Machine (NTM)* in polynomial time. A DTM has only one possible move at each step, determined by its state transition function along with its internal and tape state. In contrast, an NTM has potentially several alternative moves available at each step, and chooses one of these non-deterministically. The computation succeeds if at least one sequence of possible choices succeeds.

There are alternative ways to consider the working of an NTM: (i) it uses *angelic non-determinism* and always makes the correct choice; (ii) at each choice point, it 'branches' into parallel machines, taking all possible paths (hence using exponential space). An NTM can be implemented by serialising this branching approach (Floyd, 1967): if it has chosen a path and discovers it is the wrong path, it 'backtracks' and makes a different choice (hence potentially using exponential time). Hence a DTM can compute anything an NTM can compute, although potentially exponentially slower.

An NTM can also be considered as an *oracle machine*, a black box that provides candidate solutions for a specific class of problems (see Sect. 11.3.2). In the terminology used in textbooks like Garey and Johnson (1979) and Sipser (1997), a decision problem is in the class $\mathcal{NP}$ if, for any YES-instance of the problem there is a candidate solution that can be checked by an algorithmic procedure in polynomial time. So, instead of finding the correct answer for any instance in polynomial time, it is only required to be able to verify the correctness of a candidate solution for the YES-answer for any YES-instance in polynomial time.

The decision version of TSP described above is in $\mathcal{NP}$: the relevant candidate solution is a suitable short route, and the length of that given route can be calculated in polynomial time and checked to be at most x. Interpretation (i) of the NTM above has it 'angelically' making the correct choice at each city; interpretation (ii) has it exploring all exponential number of possible paths in parallel.

It is clear that $\mathcal{P} \subseteq \mathcal{NP}$: if a problem can be solved in polynomial time, it can certainly be checked in polynomial time.

It is widely believed that $\mathcal{P} \neq \mathcal{NP}$ (and that is the position we take in this chapter). Its proof (or disproof) is a fundamental open problem within mathematics and theoretical computer science (Aaronson, 2017). Many decision problems have been shown to be in $\mathcal{P}$, but for even more, such as TSP, it is not known whether they are in $\mathcal{P}$ or not.

11.5.5 $\mathcal{NP}$-complete problems

There are many decision problems for which the complexity status is currently unknown. To say at least something about their relative complexity, Cook (1971) and Levin (1973) developed useful machinery, which has led to the definition of the class of $\mathcal{NP}$-complete problems.

A problem in $\mathcal{NP}$ is called $\mathcal{NP}$-*complete* if it is the hardest of all problems in $\mathcal{NP}$, in the following sense. Consider two problems P and Q that are both in $\mathcal{NP}$. Suppose that there exists a polynomial reduction from P to Q, that is, a polynomial algorithm to transform any instance I of P into an instance J (of size bounded by a polynomial function in the size of I) of Q in such a way that I is a YES-instance of P if and only if J is a YES-instance of Q. Then any polynomial algorithm for solving Q can be transformed into a polynomial algorithm for solving P. In the sense of polynomial complexity, in such a case Q is at least as hard to solve as P. If the same holds for Q and any other problem instead of P in $\mathcal{NP}$, then Q is the hardest of all problems in $\mathcal{NP}$, in the above sense. Such a problem Q in $\mathcal{NP}$ is an $\mathcal{NP}$-complete problem.

Cook (1971) and Levin (1973) independently showed that there are $\mathcal{NP}$-complete problems. They each proved that the unrestricted Boolean satisfiability problem (SAT) is $\mathcal{NP}$-complete. This was a major breakthrough, because it allowed many other problems to be shown to be $\mathcal{NP}$-complete, by using a polynomial reduction from a known $\mathcal{NP}$-complete problem (starting with SAT) to the newly considered problem in $\mathcal{NP}$ (Karp, 1972). The TSP and k-SAT (with $k \geq 3$) decision problems (Sect. 11.2.2) are both $\mathcal{NP}$-complete; the 2-SAT problem is in $\mathcal{P}$.

If a polynomial algorithm exists for any of these $\mathcal{NP}$-complete problems, then a polynomial algorithm would exist for each of them, by using the reduction process used in their proofs of $\mathcal{NP}$-completeness. The existence of an ever growing number of $\mathcal{NP}$-complete problems for which nobody to date has been able to develop a polynomial algorithm provides significant evidence (although not proof) supporting the conjecture $\mathcal{P} \neq \mathcal{NP}$.

11.5.6 $\mathcal{NP}$-hard problems

For problems other than decision problems, such as the optimisation and counting problems mentioned earlier, their computational complexity is usually defined only if they are in $\mathcal{NP}$ and contain decision problems in $\mathcal{NP}$ as special cases, and hence are at least as difficult to solve as their decision counterparts. Such problems are called $\mathcal{NP}$-*hard* if they are at least as hard as an $\mathcal{NP}$-complete problem, that is, if a polynomial time algorithm for solving them would imply a polynomial algorithm for solving an $\mathcal{NP}$-complete (decision) problem. For a compendium of $\mathcal{NP}$-hard optimisation problems, see Crescenzi and Kann (2005).

11.5.7 Other classic complexity classes: $\mathcal{PSPACE}$ and $\mathcal{BPP}$

Since the introduction of the $\mathcal{P}$ and $\mathcal{NP}$ complexity classes, a whole zoo of further complexity classes has been defined and studied. Most of these classes are beyond the scope of this chapter, but we mention a few here that are relevant in the context of this chapter.

The complexity class $\mathcal{PSPACE}$ consists of decisions problems that can be solved using polynomial space on a DTM, meaning that the number of cells on the tape of the DTM that are needed to encode and solve a given instance is bounded by a polynomial function in the length of the input size. Note that no constraint is put on the time allowed for the solution (other than being finite). For this class, using an NTM does not add any extra computational power in terms of space use, because an NTM that uses polynomial space can be simulated by a DTM that uses (more but still) polynomial space (but it may use substantially more time).

We clearly have $\mathcal{NP} \subseteq \mathcal{PSPACE}$: if a problem can be checked in polynomial time, it cannot use more than polynomial space, since it has to visit all of that space. It is widely believed that $\mathcal{NP} \neq \mathcal{PSPACE}$, but again, there is no proof.

The complexity class $\mathcal{BPP}$ (Bounded-error Probabilistic Polynomial) consists of decision problems that can be solved in polynomial time by a *probabilistic* Turing Machine (PTM), i.e., a DTM that can make random choices between different transitions according to some probability distribution. (This is distinct from an NTM: a probabilistic TM makes a *random* choice; an NTM makes the 'correct' choice, or all choices, depending on the interpretation.) The probability that any run of the algorithm gives the wrong answer to a YES-NO question must be less than 1/3.

It is obvious that $\mathcal{P} \subseteq \mathcal{BPP}$: if a problem can be solved in polynomial time, it can be probabilistically solved in polynomial time. In this case, it is widely believed that $\mathcal{P} = \mathcal{BPP}$, but yet again, there is no proof. There is no known subset relation between $\mathcal{BPP}$ and $\mathcal{NP}$, in either direction.

11.5.8 Quantum complexity classes

A *quantum* TM (QTM), with a quantum processor and quantum tape (memory) is a model for a quantum computer, computing directly in memory (Deutsch, 1985).

Problems that can be solved by a QTM in polynomial time belong to the complexity class $\mathcal{BQP}$ (Fig. 11.1) (*Complexity Zoo website* n.d.; Montanaro, 2016; Watrous, n.d.). $\mathcal{BQP}$ is in some sense the quantum analogue of the classical $\mathcal{BPP}$, but there is a fundamental difference: the PTM proceeds via

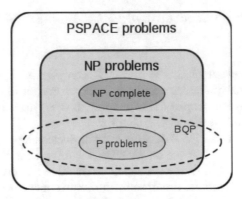

Fig. 11.1 Summary of relationships between computational complexity classes (https://en.wikipedia.org/wiki/BQP). See text for details.

random choices of unique states of the Finite State Machine reading and writing on the tape, while the QTM proceeds via quantum simultaneous superposition and entanglement of all the states. Therefore, the QTM proceeds through the Hilbert state space in a *deterministic* way via the time evolution operator defined by the Hamiltonian. The probabilistic aspects emerge when reading out the results; in some cases this can be done deterministically, in other cases one has to collect statistics.

Fig. 11.1 shows that $\mathcal{BQP}$ is a limited region of the complexity map, and (probably) does not include the $\mathcal{NP}$-complete class. There, in $\mathcal{BQP}$ and (probably) outside $\mathcal{P}$, we find problems like Shor's factorisation algorithm (Shor, 1997), providing exponential speed-up over the best known classical factorisation algorithm. Classic factorisation is believed to be neither $\mathcal{NP}$-complete, nor in $\mathcal{P}$. Another example is unstructured database search, which is classically "easy" (polynomial), but which shows quadratic speed-up with the Grover quantum search algorithm (Grover, 1996). See Montanaro (2016) for a recent overview of progress in the field, focusing on algorithms with clear applications and rigorous performance bounds.

There are further quantum complexity classes. In particular, $\mathcal{QMA}$ is the class where problems proposed by a quantum oracle can be verified in polynomial time by a quantum computer in $\mathcal{BQP}$ (*Complexity Zoo website* n.d.; Montanaro, 2016; Watrous, n.d.).

11.5.9 Complexity with advice: $\mathcal{P}/poly$ and $\mathcal{P}/log$

The most common complexity class involving advice is $\mathcal{P}/poly$, where the advice length $f(n)$ can be any polynomial in n. This class $\mathcal{P}/poly$ is equal to the class consisting of decision problems for which there exists a polynomial size Boolean circuit correctly deciding the problem for all inputs of length

n, for every n. This is true because a DTM can be designed that interprets the advice string as a description of the Boolean circuit, and conversely, a (polynomial) DTM can be simulated by a (polynomial) Boolean circuit.

Interestingly, $\mathcal{P}/\text{poly}$ contains both $\mathcal{P}$ and $\mathcal{BPP}$ and it also contains some undecidable problems (including the *unary* version of the Halting Problem). It is widely believed that $\mathcal{NP}$ is not contained in $\mathcal{P}/\text{poly}$, but again there is no proof for this. If has been shown that $\mathcal{NP} \not\subset \mathcal{P}/\text{poly}$ implies $\mathcal{P} \neq \mathcal{NP}$. Much of the efforts towards proving that $\mathcal{P} \neq \mathcal{NP}$ are based on this implication.

The class $\mathcal{P}/\log$ is similar to $\mathcal{P}/\text{poly}$, except that the advice string for inputs of size n is restricted to have length at most logarithmic in n, rather than polynomial in n. It is known that $\mathcal{NP} \subseteq \mathcal{P}/\log$ implies $\mathcal{P} = \mathcal{NP}$.

Restricting the advice length to at most a logarithmic function of the input size implies that polynomial reductions cannot be used to show that a decision problem belongs to the class $\mathcal{P}/\log$. To circumvent this drawback the prefix advice class Full-$\mathcal{P}/\log$ has been introduced (Balcázar and Hermo, 1998). The difference with $\mathcal{P}/\log$ is that in Full-$\mathcal{P}/\log$ each advice string for inputs of size n can also be used for inputs of a smaller size. Full-$\mathcal{P}/\log$ is also known as $\mathcal{P}/\log^*$ in the literature.

11.5.10 Extended Church–Turing thesis

The CTT (Sect. 11.3.3) is a statement about *computability*. The *Extended Church–Turing Thesis* (ECT) is a statement about *complexity*: any function naturally to be regarded as *efficiently* computable is efficiently computable by a DTM (Dershowitz and Falkovich, 2012). Here "efficiently" means computable by a DTM in polynomial time and space. A DTM is a basic model for ordinary *classical* digital computers solving problems tractable in polynomial time.

Consider the NTM (Sect. 11.5.4). If backtracking is the most efficient way to implement an NTM with a DTM (that is, if $\mathcal{P} \neq \mathcal{NP}$), then the ECT claims that a 'true' NTM cannot be implemented.

Vergis et al. (1986) reformulate the ECT in terms of analogue computers as: "any finite analogue computer can be simulated *efficiently* by a digital computer, in the sense that the time required by the digital computer to simulate the analogue computer is bounded by a polynomial function of the resources used by the analogue computer". That is, finite analogue computers do not make infeasible problems feasible. Thus, finite analogue computers cannot tractably solve $\mathcal{NP}$-complete problems.

Super-Turing computation seeks to discover approaches that can expand the range of efficiently computable functions beyond those efficiently computable by DTMs; it seeks to invalidate the ECT.

Quantum computing (QCOMP) can provide exponential speed-up for a few classes of problems (see Sect. 11.5.8), so the ECT is believed to have been invalidated in this case (Aaronson, 2013a; Aaronson, 2013b): quantum computing can provide certain classes of super-Turing power (unless $\mathcal{P} = \mathcal{NP}$). We can extend the ECT to: "any function naturally to be regarded as *efficiently* computable is efficiently computable by a Quantum Turing Machine (QTM)", and then ask if any *other* form of UCOMP can invalidate either the original ECT, or this quantum form of the ECT.

11.5.11 Physical oracles and advice

An interesting question in UCOMP is whether a *physical* system can be implemented that acts as some specific oracle or advice, that is, whether it is possible to build a physical add-on to a classical computer that can change the computability or complexity classes of problems.

A range of analogue devices have been posited as potential physical oracles. Their analogue physical values may be (theoretically) read with infinite, unbounded, or fixed precision, resulting in different (theoretical) oracular power.

Beggs and coauthors (see Ambaram et al. (2017) and references therein) have made a careful analysis of using a range of idealised physical experiments as oracles, in particular, studying the time it takes to interact with the physical device, as a function of the precision of its output. More precision takes more time. In each system they analyse, they find that the time needed to extract the measured value of the analogue system increases exponentially with the number of bits of precision of the measurement. They conjecture that

> for all "reasonable" physical theories and for all measurements based on them, the physical time of the experiment is at least exponential, i.e., the time needed to access the n-th bit of the parameter being measured is at least exponential in n.

The kind of physical analogue devices that Ambaram et al. (2017) analyse tend to use a *unary* encoding of the relevant value being accessed via physical measurement, for example, position, or mass, or concentration. So each extra digit of precision has to access an exponentially smaller range of the system being measured. See Fig. 11.2.

Similar points apply when discussing the input size n when analysing such devices: if the UCOMP device uses a unary encoding of the relevant parameter values, as many do, the input size n is exponentially larger than if a binary encoding were used.

Beggs et al. (2014) use such arguments to derive an *upper bound* on the power of such hybrid analogue-digital machines, and conjecture an associated "Analogue-digital Church–Turing Thesis":

> No possible abstract analogue-digital device can have more computational capabilities in polynomial time than $\mathcal{BPP}//\log^*$.

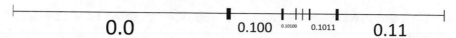

Fig. 11.2 Encoding a real number value as a position on a line. Extraction of each extra digit of precision requires access to an exponentially smaller region of the line.

Note that this conjecture refers to abstract (or idealised) physical devices, analogous to the way a DTM is also an abstract idealised device. Physical issues such as thermodynamic jitter and quantum uncertainty have still to be considered. Note also that the logarithmic advice has to be encoded somehow into the analogue device.

Blakey (2014) and Blakey (2017) has made a careful analysis of "unconventional resources" such as precision (measurement and manufacturing), energy, and construction material, and has developed a form of "model-independent" complexity analysis, that considers such unconventional resources in addition to the classical ones of space and time. Indeed, Blakey's analysis shows that the exponential cost of measurement precision is itself outweighed by the *infinite* manufacturing precision required for certain devices. Blakey's approach to analysing unconventional resources enables a formalisation of "the intuition that the purported [hypercomputational] power of these computers in fact vanishes once precision is properly considered".

11.5.12 Complexity as a worst case property

$\mathcal{NP}$-completeness is a worst case analysis: a problem is $\mathcal{NP}$-complete if it has at least *one* instance that requires exponential, rather than polynomial, computation time, even if all the remaining instances can be solved in polynomial time.

Cheeseman et al. (1991) note that for many $\mathcal{NP}$-complete problems, typical cases are often easy to solve, and hard cases are rare. They show that such problems have an "order parameter", and that the hard problems occur at the critical value of this parameter. Consider 3-SAT (Sect. 11.2.2); the order parameter is the average number of constraints (clauses) per Boolean literal, m/n. For low values the problem is underconstrained (not many clauses compared to literals, so easily shown to be satisfiable) and for high values it is overconstrained (many clauses compared to literals, so easily shown to be unsatisfiable). Only near a critical value do the problems become exponentially hard to determine.

Such arguments demonstrate that we cannot 'sample' the problem space to demonstrate problem hardness; complexity is not an experimental property. In particular, demonstrating that a device or process, engineered or natural, can solve some (or even many) $\mathcal{NP}$-complete problem instances tractably is not sufficient to conclude that it can solve all $\mathcal{NP}$-complete problem instances tractably.

The limitations that $\mathcal{NP}$-completeness imposes on computation probably hold for all natural analogue systems, such as protein folding, the human brain, etc. (Bryngelson et al., 1995). As noted above, just because Nature can efficiently solve *some* instances of problems that are $\mathcal{NP}$-complete does not mean that it can solve *all* $\mathcal{NP}$-complete problem instances (Bryngelson et al., 1995). To find the lowest free energy state of a general macromolecule has been shown to be $\mathcal{NP}$-complete (Unger and Moult, 1993). In the case of proteins there are amino acid sequences that cannot be folded to their global free energy minimum in polynomial time either by computers or by Nature. Proteins selected by Nature and evolution will represent a *tractable subset* of all possible amino acid sequences.

11.5.13 Solving hard problems in practice

Apart from trying to show that $\mathcal{P} = \mathcal{NP}$, there are other seemingly more practical ways to try to cope with $\mathcal{NP}$-complete or $\mathcal{NP}$-hard problems.

If large instances have to be solved, one approach is to look for fast algorithms, called *heuristics*, that give reasonable solutions in many cases. In some cases there are approximation algorithms for optimisation problems with provable approximation guarantees. This holds for the optimisation variant of the TSP restricted to instances for which the triangle equality holds (the weight of edge uv is at most the sum of the weights of the edges uw and wv, for all distinct triples of vertices u, v, w), and where one asks for (the length of) a shortest tour. This variant is known to be $\mathcal{NP}$-hard, but simple polynomial time heuristics have been developed that yield solutions within a factor of 1.5 of the optimal tour length (Lawler et al., 1985).

For many optimisation problems even guaranteeing certain approximation bounds is an $\mathcal{NP}$-hard problem in itself. This also holds for the general TSP (without the triangle inequality constraints) if one wants to find a solution within a fixed constant factor of the optimal tour length (Lawler et al., 1985).

A more recent approach tries to capture the exponential growth of solution algorithms in terms of a function of a certain fixed parameter that is not the size of the input. The aim is to develop a solution algorithm that is polynomial in the size of the input but maybe exponential in the other parameter. For small values of the fixed parameter the problem instances are tractable, hence the term fixed parameter tractability (the class $\mathcal{FPT}$) for such problems (Downey and Fellows, 1999).

An example is k-SAT (Sect. 11.2.2), parameterised by the number n of Boolean literals. A given formula of size N with n literals can be checked by brute force in time $O(2^n N)$, so linear in the size of the instance.

A related concept is that of preprocessing (data reduction or kernelisation). Preprocessing in this context means reducing the input size of the problem instances to something smaller, usually by applying reduction rules that take care of easy parts of the instances. Within parameterised complexity theory, the smaller inputs are referred to as the kernel. The goal is to prove that small kernels for certain $\mathcal{NP}$-complete or $\mathcal{NP}$-hard problems exist, and can be found in polynomial time. If small here means bounded by a function that only depends on some fixed parameter associated with the problem, then this implies that the problem is fixed parameter tractable.

The above definitions focus on worst case instances of the (decision) problems. It is not clear whether this is always a practical focus. There is a famous example of a class of problems in $\mathcal{P}$ – Linear Programming – for which empirical evidence shows that an exponential algorithm (the Simplex Method) for solving these problems very often yields faster solutions in practice than the polynomial algorithm (the Ellipsoid Method) developed subsequently (Papadimitriou, 1994).

For many algorithms, a worst case analysis gives limited insight into their performance, and can be far too pessimistic to reflect the actual performance on realistic instances. Recent approaches to develop a more realistic and robust model for the analysis of the performance of algorithms include average case analysis, smoothed analysis, and semi-random input models. All of these approaches are based on considering instances that are to a certain extent randomly chosen.

11.5.14 No Free Lunch theorem

Wolpert and Macready (1997) prove "no free lunch" (NFL) theorems related to the efficiency of search algorithms. They show that when the performance of any given search algorithm is averaged over all possible search landscapes, it performs no better than random search. This is because, whatever algorithm is chosen, if it exploits the structure of the landscape, there are always deceptive search landscapes that lead it astray. The only way not to be deceived is to search randomly. A problem of size n has a search space of size $O(2^n)$, and so the best classical search algorithm, where the performance is averaged over all the $O(2^{2^n})$ possible landscapes, is $O(2^n)$.

This does not mean that there are no search algorithms better than random search over certain subsets of search landscapes: algorithms that exploit any structure common across the subset can perform better than random. More generally, if some search landscapes are more likely than others, algorithms that can exploit that information can do better (Wolpert, 2012).

Natural processes such as Darwinian evolution, which may be interpreted as a form of search algorithm, are almost certainly exploiting the structure of their search landscapes. This has consequences for nature-inspired search algorithms, such as evolutionary algorithms, if they are to be exploited on 'unnatural' landscapes. See also the comments on protein folding in Sect. 11.5.12.

11.6 Quantum information processing

Quantum computers are able to solve some problems much faster than classical computers (*Complexity Zoo website* n.d.; Montanaro, 2016; Shor, 1997; Watrous, n.d.). However, this does not say much about solving computational problems that are hard for classical computers. If one looks at the map of computational complexity (Fig. 11.1), classifying the hardness of computational (decision) problems, one finds that the $\mathcal{BQP}$ class of quantum computation covers a rather limited space, not containing really hard problems. One may then ask what is the fundamental difference between CCOMP and QCOMP, and what kind of problems are hard even for a quantum computer (Aaronson, 2005; Aaronson, 2008; Aaronson, 2009; Aaronson, 2013b)?

11.6.1 Digital quantum computation

The obvious difference between CCOMP and QCOMP is that CCOMP is based on classical Newtonian physics and special and general relativity, while QCOMP is based on quantum physics, as illustrated in Figs. 11.3a,b. Digital CCOMP progresses by gate-driven transitions between specific classical memory configurations of an N-bit register $R(t_k)$, each representing one out of 2^N instantaneous configurations.

QCOMP, on the other hand, progresses by gate-driven transitions between specific quantum memory states $|\Psi(t_k)\rangle$, each representing instantaneous superposition of 2^N configurations. The quantum memory states are coherent amplitudes with well-defined phase relations. Moreover, the states of the qubits can be entangled, i.e., not possible to write as a product of states. In the case of two qubits, the canonical example of entanglement is that of Bell states: non-entangled product states are $|00\rangle$ or $|11\rangle$ or $(|0\rangle+|1\rangle)(|0\rangle+|1\rangle) = |00\rangle+|01\rangle+|10\rangle+|11\rangle$. The Bell states $|00\rangle\pm|11\rangle$ and $|0\rangle\pm|10\rangle$ are clearly not product states, and represent in fact maximum entanglement of two qubits. This can be generalised to more qubits, e.g., the Greenberger–Horne–Zeilinger (GHZ) "cat state": $|000\rangle+|111\rangle$. This entanglement represents non-classical correlations, at the heart of the exponential power of QCOMP. Entanglement allows us to construct maximally entangled superpositions with only a linear amount of physical resources, e.g., a large cat state: $\frac{1}{\sqrt{2}}(|0......00\rangle+|1.....11\rangle)$. This is what allows us to perform non-classical tasks and provide quantum speed-up (Horodecki et al., 2009; Jozsa and Linden, 2003).

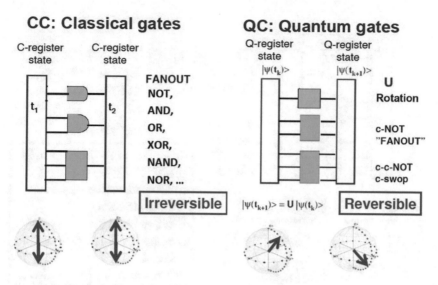

Fig. 11.3 a. Comparison of CCOMP and QCOMP. (left) CCOMP: irreversible gates with arithmetic-logic unit (ALU) and memory separated. The memory is the storage, with classical bits 0,1 representing the poles on the Bloch unit sphere. Classical gates are basically hardwired, irreversible and performed in the ALU. Gates are clocked. (right) QCOMP: Computing in memory – the memory is the computer. Quantum bits (qubits) $\alpha|0\rangle + \beta|1\rangle$ span the entire Bloch sphere. Quantum gates are reversible and performed on the "memory" qubits by software-controlled external devices. Gates are not clocked.

QCOMP is basically performed directly in memory. One can regard the qubit memory register as an array of 2-level quantum transistors, memory cells, where the gates driving and coupling the transistors are external *classical* fields controlled by classical software run on a CCOMP. This emphasises that a quantum computer can only implement a polynomial number of gates, and that the name of the game is to devise *efficient* decompositions of the time-evolution operator in terms of universal gates. The goal is of course to construct single-shot multi-qubit gates implementing long sequences of canonical elementary gates to synthesise the full time-evolution operator $U = exp(-iHt)$ (Fig. 11.3).

QCOMP depends, just like CCOMP, on encoding/decoding, error correction, and precision of measurement and control. To go beyond $\mathcal{BQP}$ essentially takes non-physical oracle resources, or unlimited precision, requiring exponential resources and ending up in $\mathcal{QMA}$ or beyond.

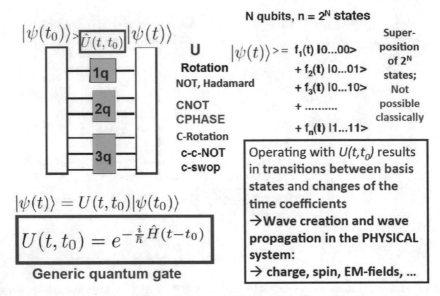

Generic quantum gate

$$|\psi(t)\rangle = U(t, t_0)|\psi(t_0)\rangle$$

$$U(t, t_0) = e^{-\frac{i}{\hbar}\hat{H}(t-t_0)}$$

N qubits, n = 2^N states

| U | $|\psi(t)\rangle \geq = f_1(t)\,|0...00\rangle$ | Super-position of 2^N states; Not possible classically |

Rotation
NOT, Hadamard

CNOT
CPHASE
C-Rotation
c-c-NOT
c-swop

$$|\psi(t)\rangle \geq = f_1(t)\,|0...00\rangle$$
$$+ f_2(t)\,|0...01\rangle$$
$$+ f_3(t)\,|0...10\rangle$$
$$+ ....$$
$$+ f_n(t)\,|1...11\rangle$$

Operating with $U(t,t_0)$ results in **transitions between basis states and changes of the time coefficients**
→**Wave creation and wave propagation in the PHYSICAL system:**
→ **charge, spin, EM-fields, ...**

Fig. 11.3 b. Comparison of CCOMP and QCOMP (ctd). (left) The time evolution of the state of the quantum computer is implemented by the unitary time evolution operator U, which can be broken down into elementary gates (like NOT, Hadamard, CNOT, C-Rotation). (right) The quantum state is, in general, an entangled superposition of all configurations of the memory register. Entanglement implies that the state is not a product state, containing non-classical correlations that provide polytime solution of certain problems that take exponential time for classical computers. The quantum gates are operated by a classical computer, which means that a quantum computer can only solve problems that take at most a polynomial number of gates to solve. A universal set of quantum gates (Hadamard (square-root of bit flip), X (bit flip), CNOT, and T (general rotation)) guarantees the existence of a universal QCOMP, like a UTM, but may likewise need exponential resources.

11.6.2 Quantum simulation

Feynman (1982) was among the first to point out that quantum systems need to be described by quantum systems. Electronic structure calculation with full account of many-body interactions is $\mathcal{QMA}$-hard (Aaronson, 2009; Schuch and Verstraete, 2009; Whitfield et al., 2013). Therefore, taking an example from biochemistry, to efficiently compute the properties of a catalysing enzyme or the workings of a ribosome will require a quantum simulator to achieve the precision needed in reasonable time.

A QCOMP emulator/simulator is basically an analogue machine: an engineered qubit-array where the interactions between qubits (memory cells) are implemented by substrate-defined or externally induced local and global couplings. The static or quasi-static (adiabatic) interactions can be tuned to implement specific Hamiltonians describing physical models or systems (or even something unphysical), and time-dependent driving will implement dynamic response. All the interactions provide together an effective time-dependent Hamiltonian and a corresponding time-evolution operator $U = exp[-iH_{eff}(t)\ t\ ]$. The induced time-evolution will be characteristic for the system and can be analysed (measured) to provide deterministic or statistical answers to various questions. Note that there is no fundamental difference between digital and analogue QCOMP: if we drive the qubits by, e.g., fast external microwave pulse trains, we can design the time-evolution operator U to generate the specific elementary universal 1q and 2q gates of the quantum circuit model.

Quantum simulation of physical systems (Brown et al., 2010; Georgescu et al., 2014; Wendin, 2017) is now at the focus of intense engineering and experimental efforts (Barends et al., 2015; Barends et al., 2016; Barreiro et al., 2011; Blatt and Roos, 2012; Boixo et al., 2016b; Cirac and Zoller, 2010; Lanyon et al., 2010; O'Malley et al., 2016; Peruzzo et al., 2014; Salathe et al., 2015; Wang et al., 2015) and software development (Bauer et al., 2016; Bravyi and Gosset, 2016; Häner et al., 2016; Häner et al., 2018; Reiher et al., 2017; Valiron et al., 2015; Wecker and Svore, 2014). Materials science and chemistry will present testing grounds for the performance of quantum simulation and computing in the coming years.

11.6.3 Adiabatic quantum optimisation (AQO)

AQO is the analogue version of quantum computing and simulation. It starts from the ground state of a simple known Hamiltonian and slowly (adiabatically) changes the substrate parameters into describing a target Hamiltonian, manoeuvring through the energy landscape, all the time staying in the ground state. The final state and the global minimum then present the solution to the target problem (Farhi et al., 2014; Farhi and Harrow, 2014). AQO is potentially an efficient approach to quantum simulation but has so far been limited to theoretical investigations, e.g., with applications to quantum phase transitions and speed limits for computing. Possibly there is a Quantum No-Free-Lunch theorem stating that digital quantum gate circuits need quantum error correction and AQO needs to manoeuvre adiabatically through a complicated energy landscape, and in the end the computational power is the same.

11.6.4 Quantum annealing (QA)

QA is a version of quantum optimisation where the target Hamiltonian (often a transverse Ising Hamiltonian) is approached while simultaneously lowering the temperature. This is the scheme upon which D-Wave Systems have developed their QA processors, the most recent one built on a chip with a 2000 qubit array and a special cross-bar structure. Despite indications of quantum entanglement and tunnelling within qubit clusters (Boixo et al., 2016a; Denchev et al., 2016), there is no evidence for quantum speed-up (Rønnow et al., 2014; Zintchenko et al., 2015) – so far optimised classical algorithms running on modest classical computers can simulate the quantum annealer.

11.6.5 Quantum machine learning (QML)

QML is an emerging field, introducing adaptive methods from machine language (ML) classical optimisation and neural networks to quantum networks (Aaronson, 2015b; Biamonte et al., 2016; Schuld et al., 2015; Wiebe et al., 2014; Wiebe et al., 2015; Wittek, 2016). One aspect is using ML for optimising classical control of quantum systems. Another, revolutionary, aspect is to apply ML methods to quantum networks for quantum enhanced learning algorithms. The field is rapidly evolving, and we refer to a recent review (Biamonte et al., 2016) for an overview of progress and for references.

11.7 Computational power of classical physical systems and unconventional paradigms

As already mentioned in the Introduction, and discussed to some extent, there is a veritable zoo of UCOMP paradigms (European Commission, 2009). Here we claim that the only decisive borderline is the one that separates classical problems (Newtonian Physics and Relativity) from problems governed by Quantum Physics, which includes some combinatorial problems profiting from the Quantum Fourier Transform (QFT). Quantum information processing and class $\mathcal{BQP}$ is discussed in Sect. 11.6. In this section we focus on a few classical problems of great current interest, representative for the polynomial class $\mathcal{P}$.

There are further issues of measuring the complexity of problems running on UCOMP devices. The actions of the device might not map well to the parameters of time, space, and problem size needed for classical complexity analysis. And the computation may use resources not considered in classical complexity analysis, for example, the time needed to read out a result.

11.7.1 DNA computing

Computing with DNA or RNA strands was first investigated theoretically. Bennett (1982) imagines a DTM built from RNA reactions:

> The tape might be a linear informational macromolecule analogous to RNA, with an additional chemical group attached at one site to encode the head state [...] and location. Several hypothetical enzymes (one for each of the Turing Machine's transition rules) would catalyse reactions of the macromolecule with small molecules in the surrounding solution, transforming the macromolecule into its logical successor.

Shapiro (2012) proposes a more detailed design for a general purpose polymer-based DTM. Qian et al. (2010) describe a DNA-based design for a stack machine. These designs demonstrate that general purpose polymer-based computing is possible, at least in principle. None of these designs challenge the ECT: they are all for DTMs or equivalent power machines.

Adleman (1994) was the first to implement a form of DNA computing in the wetlab, with his seminal paper describing the solution to a 7-node instance of the Hamiltonian path problem. This is an $\mathcal{NP}$-complete decision problem on a graph: is there a path through a graph that visits each node exactly once? Adleman's approach encodes the graph nodes and edges using small single strands of DNA, designed so that the edges can stick to the corresponding vertices by complementary matching. Sufficient strands are put into a well mixed system, and allowed to stick together. A series of chemical processes are used to extract the resulting DNA, and to search for a piece that has encoded a solution to the problem. The time taken by these processes is linear in the number of nodes, but the number of strands needed to ensure the relevant ones meet and stick with high enough probability grows exponentially with the number of nodes (Adleman, 1994). Essentially, this set-up needs enough DNA to construct all possible paths, to ensure that the desired solution path is constructed. So this algorithm solves the problem in polynomial time, by using massive parallelism, at the cost of exponential DNA resources (and hence exponential space). Hartmanis (1995) calculates that this form of computation of the Hamiltonian path on a graph with 200 nodes would need a mass of DNA greater than that of the earth.

Lipton (1995) critiques Adleman's algorithm, because it is "brute force" in trying all possible paths. He describes a (theoretical) DNA algorithm to solve the $\mathcal{NP}$-complete SAT problem (Sect. 11.2.2). For a problem of n Boolean variables and m clauses, the algorithm requires a number of chemical processing steps linear in m. However, it also requires enough DNA to encode "all possible n-bit numbers" (that is, all possible assignments of the n Boolean variables), so it also requires exponential DNA resources.

So these special-purpose forms of DNA computing, focussed on $\mathcal{NP}$-complete problems, trade off exponential time for exponential space (massively parallel use of DNA resources). Additionally, it is by no means clear that the chemical processing and other engineering facilities would remain polynomial in time once the exponential physical size of the reactants kicks into effect.

Other authors consider using the informational and constructive properties of DNA for a wide range of computational purposes. For example, implementations of tiling models often use DNA to construct the tiles and program their connections.

The Wang tile model (Wang, 1961) has been used to show theorem proving and computational capabilities within, e.g., DNA computing. It was introduced by Wang, who posed several conjectures and problems related to the question whether a given finite set of Wang tiles can tile the plane. Wang's student Robert Berger showed how to emulate any DTM by a finite set of Wang tiles (Berger, 1966). Using this, he proved that the undecidability of the Halting Problem implies the undecidability of Wang's tiling problem.

Later applications demonstrate the (computational) power of tiles; see, e.g., Yang (2013, Chap. 6). In particular, $\mathcal{NP}$-complete problems like k-SAT have been solved in linear time in the size of the input using a finite number of different tiles (Brun, 2008). The hidden complexity lies in the exponentially many parallel tile assemblies (the computation is nondeterministic and each parallel assembly executes in time linear in the input size).

As for the latter example, in each of these models the complexity properties need to be carefully established. Properties established in one implementation approach may not carry over to a different implementation. For example, Seelig and Soloveichik (2009) consider molecular logic circuits with many components arranged in multiple layers built using DNA strand displacement; they show that the time-complexity does not necessarily scale linearly with the circuit depth, but rather can be quadratic, and that catalysis can alter the asymptotic time-complexity.

11.7.2 Networks of evolutionary processors

An "Accepting Hybrid Network of Evolutionary Processors" (AHNEP) is a theoretical device for exploring language-accepting processes. Castellanos et al. (2001) describe the design. It comprises a fully connected graph. Each graph node contains: (i) a simple evolutionary processor that can perform certain point mutations (insertion, deletion, substitution) on data, expressed as rewrite rules; (ii) data in the form of a multiset of strings, which are processed in parallel such that all possible mutations that can take place do so. In particular, if a specified substitution may act on different occurrences of a symbol in a string, each occurrence is substituted in a different copy of the string. For this to be possible, there is an arbitrarily large number of copies of each string in the multiset. The data moves through the network; it must pass a filtering process that depends on conditions of both the sender and receiver.

Castellanos et al. (2001) demonstrate that such networks of linear size (number of nodes) can solve $\mathcal{NP}$-complete problems in linear time. Much subsequent work has gone into variants (Margenstern et al., 2005), and determining bounds on the size of such networks. For example, Manea and Mitrana (2007) find a constant size network of 24 nodes that can solve $\mathcal{NP}$ problems in polynomial time; Loos et al. (2009) reduce that bound to 16 nodes. Alhazov et al. (2014) prove that a 5 node AHNEP is computationally complete.

Note that some of the papers referenced demonstrate that AHNEPs can solve $\mathcal{NP}$-complete problems in polynomial time. They manage to do so in the same way the DNA computers of the previous section do: by exploiting exponential space resources. The set-up exploits use of an exponentially large data set at each node, by requiring an arbitrarily large number of each string be present, so that all possible substitutions can occur in parallel.

11.7.3 Evolution in materio

Evolution *in materio* (EiM) is a term coined by Miller and Downing (2002) to refer to material systems that can be used for computation by manipulating the state of the material through external stimuli, e.g., voltages, currents, optical signals and the like, and using some fixed input and output channels to the material for defining the wanted functionality. In EiM, the material is treated as a black box, and computer-controlled evolution (by applying genetic algorithms or other optimisation techniques, using a digital computer) is used to change the external stimuli (the configuration signals) in such a way that the black box converges to the target functionality, i.e., the material system produces the correct output combinations, representing solutions to the problem when certain input combinations, representing problem instances of the problem, are applied. Experimental results show that this approach has successfully been applied to different types of problems, with different types of materials (Broersma et al., 2016), but mainly for either small instances of problems or for rather simple functionalities like Boolean logic gates. Interestingly, using EiM, reconfigurable logic has been evolved in a stable and reproducible way on disordered nanoparticle networks of very small size, comparable to the size that would be required by arrangements of current transistors to show the same functionality (Bose et al., 2015).

It is impossible and it would not be fair to compare the complexity of the solution concept of EiM to that of classical computation. First of all, apart from the (digital) genetic algorithms or other optimisation techniques that are used to manipulate the system, there is no algorithmic procedure involved in the actual computation. The material is not executing a program to solve any particular problem instance; instead, a set of problem instances and their target outputs are used in the evolutionary process of configuring the material. In that sense, the material is more or less forced to produce the correct (or an approximate solution that can be translated into a correct) solution for that set of problem instances. If this is not the whole set of possible instances, there is no guarantee that the material outputs the correct solution for any of the other problem instances. In fact, since fitness functions are used to judge the quality of the configurations according to the input-output combinations they produce, even the correctness of the output for individual instances that are used during the evolutionary process is questionable, unless they are checked one by one at the end of this process. In a way, for problems with an unbounded number of possible instances, the EiM approach can be regarded as a heuristic without any performance guarantees for the general problem. So, it is not an alternative to exact solution concepts from classical computation, and hence it cannot claim any particular relevance for (exactly) solving $\mathcal{NP}$-hard or $\mathcal{NP}$-complete problems, let alone undecidable problems.

Secondly, in EiM the time it takes for the evolutionary process to converge to a satisfactory configuration of the material for solving a particular problem is the crucial measure in terms of time complexity. After that, the material system does, in principle, produce solutions to instances almost instantaneously. In a sense, this evolutionary process can be regarded as a kind of preprocessing, but different from the preprocessing that is used in classical computation to decrease the size of the instances, an important concept in the domain of FPT. Clearly, there are issues with scalability involved in EiM. It is likely that a limited amount of material, together with a limited amount of input and output channels, and a limited amount of configuration signals, has a bounded capability of solving instances of a problem with an unbounded number of possible instances. It seems difficult to take all of these aspects into account in order to define a good measure for the capability of EiM to tackle hard problems. Such problems are perhaps not the best candidates for the EIM approach. Instead, it might be better to focus future research on computational tasks that are difficult to accomplish with classical computational devices; not difficult in the sense of computational complexity but in the sense of developing and implementing the necessary computer programs to perform the tasks. One might think of classification tasks like speech, face and pattern recognition.

11.7.4 Optical computing

It is possible to use optical systems to compute with photons rather than electrons. Although this is a somewhat unconventional computational substrate, the computation performed is purely classical.

Some authors suggest more unconventional applications of optical components. Woods and Naughton (2005) and Woods and Naughton (2009) discuss a form of spatial optical computing that encodes data as images, and computes by transforming the images through optical operations. These include both analogue and digital encodings of data.

Reif et al. (1994) describe a particular idealised ray tracing problem cast as a decision problem, and show that it is Turing-uncomputable. They also note that the idealisations do not hold in the physical world:

> Theoretically, these optical systems can be viewed as general optical computing machines, if our constructions could be carried out with infinite precision, or perfect accuracy. However, these systems are not practical, since the above assumptions do not hold in the physical world. Specifically, since the wavelength of light is finite, the wave property of light, namely diffraction, makes the theory of geometrical optics fail at the wavelength level of distances.

Blakey (2014) has furthermore formalised the intuition that the claimed hypercomputational power of even such idealised computers in fact vanishes once precision is properly considered.

Wu et al. (2014) construct an optical network than can act as an oracle for the Hamiltonian path decision problem. Their encoding approach addresses the usual precision issue by having exponentially large delays; hence, as they say, it does not reduce the complexity of the problem, still requiring exponential time. They do however claim that it can provide a substantial speed-up factor over traditional algorithms, and demonstrate this on a small example network. However, since the approach explores all possible paths in parallel, this implies an exponential power requirement, too.

11.7.5 MEM-computing

MEM-computing has been introduced by Traversa and Di Ventra (2015), Traversa and Di Ventra (2017), and Traversa et al. (2015) as a novel non-Turing model of computation that uses interacting computational memory cells – memprocessors – to store and process information in parallel on the same physical platform, using the topology of the interaction network to form the specific computation.

Traversa and Di Ventra (2015) introduce the Universal Memcomputing Machine (UMM), and make a strong claim:

> We also demonstrate that a UMM has the same computational power as a non-deterministic Turing machine, namely it can solve $\mathcal{NP}$-complete problems in polynomial time. However, by virtue of its information overhead, a UMM needs only an amount of memory cells (memprocessors) that grows polynomially with the problem size. ... Even though these results do not prove the statement $\mathcal{NP} = \mathcal{P}$ within the Turing paradigm, the practical realization of these UMMs would represent a paradigm shift from present von Neumann architectures bringing us closer to brain-like neural computation.

The UMM is essentially an analogue device. Traversa and Di Ventra (2015) state:

> a UMM can operate, in principle, on an infinite number of continuous states, even
> if the number of memprocessors is finite. The reason being that each memprocessor
> is essentially an analog device with a continuous set of state values

then in a footnote acknowledge:

> Of course, the actual implementation of a UMM will limit this continuous range to
> a discrete set of states whose density depends on the experimental resolution of the
> writing and reading operations.

Traversa et al. (2015) present an experimental demonstration with 6 memprocessors solving a small instance of the NP-complete version of the subset sum problem in only one step. The number of memprocessors in the given design scales linearly with the size of the problem. The authors state:

> the particular machine presented here is eventually limited by noise—and will thus
> require error-correcting codes to scale to an arbitrary number of memprocessors

Again, the issue is an analogue encoding, here requiring a Fourier transform of an exponential number of frequencies, and accompanying exponential requirements on precision, and possibly power. As we have emphasised earlier (Sect. 11.5.1), complexity is an asymptotic property, and small problem instances do not provide evidence of asymptotic behaviour. See also Saunders (2016) for a further critique of this issue. Traversa et al. (2015) state that this demonstration experiment "represents the first proof of concept of a machine capable of working with the collective state of interacting memory cells", exploring the exponentially large solution space in parallel using waves of different frequencies. Traversa et al. (2015) suggest that this is similar to what quantum computing does when solving difficult problems such as factorisation. However, although quantum computing is a powerful and physical model, there is no evidence that it can efficiently solve $\mathcal{NP}$-hard problems. The power of quantum computing is quantum superposition and entanglement in Hilbert space, not merely classical wave computing using collective coherent classical states. The oracles needed for a quantum computer to solve problems in $\mathcal{QMA}$ most likely do not exist in the physical world. Aaronson (2005) examines and refutes many claims to solving $\mathcal{NP}$-hard problems, demonstrating the different kinds of smuggling that are used, sweeping the eventual need for exponential resources under (very large) carpets. This is also underlined in Aaronson (2015a), a blog post providing an extended critique of the claims in Traversa et al. (2015).

In order to address these scaling limitations of the analogue UMM, Traversa and Di Ventra (2017) present their *Digital* Memcomputing Machine (DMM). They claim that DMMs also have the computational power of nondeterministic Turing machines, able to solve $\mathcal{NP}$-complete problems in polynomial time with resources that scale polynomially with the input size. They define a dynamical systems model of the DMM, and prove several properties of the model. They provide the results of several numerical simulations of a DMM circuit solving small instances of an $\mathcal{NP}$-complete problem, and include a discussion of how their results suggest, though do not prove, that $\mathcal{P} = \mathcal{NP}$. The computational power of the DMM is claimed to arise from its "intrinsic parallelism" of operation. This intrinsic parallelism is a consequence of the DMM components communicating with each other in an analogue manner during a computational state transition step. The DMM is digital insofar as it has a digital state at the beginning and end of a computational step. However, its operation has the same fundamentally analogue nature as the UMM during the intrinsically parallel execution of a computational step, and so all the issues of precision and noise will still need to be addressed before any super-Turing properties can be established.

11.7.6 Brain computing

The brain is generally considered to be a natural physical adaptive information processor subject to physical law; see, e.g., Bassett and Gazzaniga (2011), Chesi and Moro (2014), Juba (2016), and Schaul et al. (2011). As such it must essentially be a classical analogue "machine", and then the ECT states that it can, in principle, be simulated efficiently by a digital classical computer.

This "limitation" of the brain is not always accepted, however, especially by philosophers. Leaving aside far-fetched quantum-inspired models, brain-inspired models sometimes assume that the brain is able to efficiently solve $\mathcal{NP}$-hard problems, see e.g. Traversa et al. (2015), and therefore can serve as a model for super-Turing computing beyond classical digital DTMs. The underlying idea is likely that (human) intelligence and consciousness are so dependent on processing power that classical digital computers cannot efficiently model an intelligent self-conscious brain – such problems must necessarily be $\mathcal{NP}$-hard.

The view of this chapter's authors is that our brain (actually any animal brain) is a powerful but classical information processor, and that its workings remain to be found out. The fact that we have no real understanding of the difference between a conscious and unconscious brain is most likely not to be linked to the lack of processing capacity.

One side of the problem-solving capacity of the brain is demonstrated in game playing, as illustrated by the performance of the AlphaGo adaptive program of Google DeepMind (Silver et al., 2016), run on a digital computer and winning over both the European and the world champions (Metz, 2016), beating the human world champion 4–1 in a series of Go games. AlphaGo is adaptive, based on deep neural networks (machine learning) and tree search, probably representing a significant step toward powerful artificial intelligence (AI). Since the human champion no doubt can be called intelligent, there is some foundation for ascribing some intelligence to the AlphaGo adaptive program. The problem of characterising artificial intelligence can be investigated via game playing (Schaul et al., 2011).

Games present $\mathcal{NP}$-hard problems when scaled up (Viglietta, 2012). Aloupis et al. (2015) have proved the $\mathcal{NP}$-hardness of five of Nintendo's largest video game franchises. In addition, they prove $\mathcal{PSPACE}$-completeness of the Donkey Kong Country games and several Legend of Zelda games.

For AlphaGo not only to show some intelligence, but also be aware of it, i.e., aware of itself, is of course quite a different thing. This does not necessarily mean that consciousness presents a dramatically harder computational task. But it then needs mechanisms for self-observation and at least short-term memory for storing those observations. When AlphaGo then starts describing why it is making the various moves, thinking about them (!), and even recognising its errors, then one may perhaps grant it some consciousness, and perhaps even intuition.

The argument that the brain violates the ECT appears to rest on the fact that brains can solve certain problems that are uncomputable or $\mathcal{NP}$-hard. However, this argument confuses the *class* of problems that have these properties with the individual instances that we can solve. So, for example, despite our being able to prove whether *certain* programs terminate, there is no evidence that we can prove whether *any* program terminates.

We hold that the brain is a natural, physical, basically analogue information processor that *cannot* solve difficult instances of $\mathcal{NP}$-hard problems. Therefore intelligence, consciousness, intuition, etc. must be the result of natural computation processes that, in principle, can be *efficiently* simulated by a classical digital computer, given some models for the relevant brain circuitry. The question of polynomial overhead is a different issue. Perhaps it will be advantageous, or even necessary, to emulate some brain circuits in hardware in order to get reasonable response times of artificial brain models. Such energy-efficient neuromorphic hardware is already emerging (Esser et al., 2016; Merolla et al., 2014) and may soon match human recognition capabilities (Maass, 2016).

11.7.7 Conclusion

These discussed forms of unconventional physically realisable computing are unable to solve $\mathcal{NP}$-hard problems in polynomial time, unless given access to an uncomputable oracle or some "smuggled" exponential resource, such as precision, material, or power. So, hard instances of $\mathcal{NP}$ problems cannot be solved efficiently. Various approaches to solving $\mathcal{NP}$-hard problems result in at best polynomial speed-up. The quantum class $\mathcal{BQP}$ does indicate that quantum computers can offer efficiency improvements for some problems outside the $\mathcal{NP}$-complete class (always assuming $\mathcal{P} \neq \mathcal{NP}$).

11.8 Overall conclusions and perspectives

We have provided an overview of certain claims of hypercomputation and super-Turing computation in a range of unconventional computing devices. Our overview covers many specific proposals, but is not comprehensive. Nevertheless, a common theme emerges: all the devices seem to rely on one or another *unphysical* property to work: infinite times or speeds, or infinite precision, or uncomputable advice, or some unconsidered exponential physical resource.

There is value in examining a wide range of unconventional theoretical models of computation, even if those models turn out to be unphysical. After all, even the theoretical model that is the DTM is unphysical: its unbounded memory tape, necessary for its theoretical power, cannot be implemented in our finite bounded universe. Our physical digital computers are all finite state machines. Claims about *physical* implementability of models more powerful than the DTM, when the DTM itself is unphysical, need to be scrutinised carefully, and not in the realm of mathematics (their theoretical power), but rather in that of physics (their implementable power).

One issue that UCOMP helps foreground is this existence of *physical* constraints on *computational* power (Aaronson, 2005; Aaronson, 2009; Aaronson, 2013b; Aaronson, 2015a; Denef and Douglas, 2007; Potgieter, 2006). That there might be such physical limits to computational power may be difficult to accept, judging from a wealth of publications discussing and describing how to efficiently solve $\mathcal{NP}$-hard problems with physical computers. However, as we have argued in this chapter, there is no convincing evidence that classical (non-quantum) computational devices (whether analogue or digital, engineered or evolved) can be built to *efficiently* solve problems outside classical complexity class $\mathcal{P}$.

The Laws of Thermodynamics, which address energy conservation and entropy increase, express bounds on what is physically possible. A consequence of these laws is that perpetual motion machines are physically *impossible*, and any purported design will have a flaw somewhere. These are laws of physics, not provable mathematical theorems, but are well-evidenced. The laws are flexible enough that newly discovered phenomena (such as the convertibility of mass and energy) can be accommodated.

The CTT and ECT appear to play an analogous role in computation. They express bounds on what computation is *physically* possible. A consequence of these bounds, if they are true, is that hypercomputing and super-Turing computing are *physically* impossible. And they are similarly flexible that newly discovered phenomena (such as quantum computing) can be accommodated. This demonstrates a fundamental and deep connection between computation and the laws of physics: computation can be considered as a natural science, constrained by reality, not as an abstract branch of mathematics (Horsman et al., 2017).

The CTT and ECT can be expressed in a, slightly tongue-in-cheek, form echoing the laws of thermodynamics:

1st Law of Computing: You cannot solve uncomputable or $\mathcal{NP}$-hard problems efficiently unless you have a physical infinity or an efficient oracle.
2nd Law of Computing: There are no physical infinities or efficient oracles.
3rd Law of Computing: Nature is physical and does not solve uncomputable or $\mathcal{NP}$-hard problems efficiently.
Corollary: Nature necessarily solves uncomputable or $\mathcal{NP}$-hard problems only approximately.

This raises the question: what can UCOMP do? Given that UCOMP does not solve uncomputable or even $\mathcal{NP}$-hard problems (and this also applies to quantum computing), what is the future for UCOMP? Instead of simply trying to do conventional things faster, UCOMP can focus on novel applications, and novel insights into computation, including:

- Insight into the relationship between physics and computation
- New means for analogue simulation/optimisation
- Huge parallelisation
- Significant polynomial speed-up
- Novel forms of approximate solutions
- Cost-effective solutions
- Solutions beyond the practical capability of digital HPC
- Solutions in novel physical devices, for example, programmed synthetic biological cells

UCOMP offers many things. But it does not offer hypercomputing or super-Turing computing realisable in the physical world.

Acknowledgements

H.B. acknowledges funding from the European Community's Seventh Framework Programme (FP7/2007-2013) under grant agreement number 317662 (the FP7 FET NASCENCE project). S.S. acknowledges partial funding by the EU FP7 FET Coordination Activity TRUCE (Training and Research in Unconventional Computation in Europe), project reference number 318235. G.W. acknowledges support by the European Commission through the FP7 SYMONE and Horizon 2020 RECORD-IT projects, and by Chalmers University of Technology.

References

Aaronson, Scott (2005). "NP-complete problems and physical reality". *ACM SIGACT News* 36(1):30–52.

Aaronson, Scott (2008). "The Limits of Quantum Computers". *Scientific American* 298(3):62–69.

Aaronson, Scott (2009). "Computational complexity: Why quantum chemistry is hard". *Nature Physics* 5(10):707–708.

Aaronson, Scott (2013a). *Quantum Computing Since Democritus*. Cambridge University Press.

Aaronson, Scott (2013b). "Why Philosophers Should Care About Computational Complexity". *Computability: Gödel, Turing, Church, and Beyond*. Ed. by B. J. Copeland, C. J. Posy, and O. Shagrir. MIT Press.

Aaronson, Scott (2015a). *Memrefuting*. www.scottaaronson.com/blog/?p= 2212.

Aaronson, Scott (2015b). "Read the fine print". *Nature Physics* 11:291–293.

Aaronson, Scott (2017). "P =? NP". www.scottaaronson.com/papers/pnp.pdf.

Adamatzky, Andrew, ed. (2017). *Advances in Unconventional Computing, vol 1*. Springer.

Adleman, Leonard M. (1994). "Molecular computation of solutions to combinatorial problems". *Science* 266:1021–1024.

Alhazov, A., R. Freund, and Y. Rogozhin (2014). "Five nodes are sufficient for hybrid networks of evolutionary processors to be computationally complete". *UCNC 2014*. Vol. 8553. LNCS. Springer, pp. 1–13.

Aloupis, G., E. D. Demaine, A. Guo, and G. Viglietta (2015). "Classic Nintendo games are (computationally) hard". *Theoretical Computer Science* 586:135–160.

Ambaram, Tânia, Edwin Beggs, José Félix Costa, Diogo Poças, and John V. Tucker (2017). "An Analogue-Digital Model of Computation: Turing Machines with Physical Oracles". *Advances in Unconventional Computing, vol 1*. Ed. by Andrew Adamatzky. Springer, pp. 73–115.

Arkoudas, K. (2008). "Computation, hypercomputation, and physical science". *Journal of Applied Logic* 6(4):461–475.

Balcázar, José and Montserrat Hermo (1998). "The Structure of Logarithmic Advice Complexity Classes". *Theoretical Computer Science* 207:217–244.

Barends, R., L. Lamata, J. Kelly, L. García-Álvarez, A. G. Fowler, A. Megrant, E. Jeffrey, T. C. White, D. Sank, J. Y. Mutus, B. Campbell, Yu Chen, Z. Chen, B. Chiaro, A. Dunsworth, I.-C. Hoi, C. Neill, P. J. J. O'Malley, C. Quintana, P. Roushan, A. Vainsencher, J. Wenner, E. Solano, and John M. Martinis (2015). "Digital quantum simulation of fermionic models with a superconducting circuit". *Nature Commun.* 6:7654.

Barends, R., A. Shabani, L. Lamata, J. Kelly, A. Mezzacapo, U. Las Heras, R. Babbush, A. G. Fowler, B. Campbell, Y. Chen, Z. Chen, B. Chiaro, A.

Dunsworth, E. Jeffrey, E. Lucero, A. Megrant, J. Y. Mutus, M. Neeley, C. Neill, P. J. J. O'Malley, C. Quintana, P. Roushan, D. Sank, A. Vainsencher, J. Wenner, T. C. White, E. Solano, H. Neven, and John M. Martinis (2016). "Digitized adiabatic quantum computing with a superconducting circuit". *Nature* 534:222–226.

Barreiro, J. T., M. Müller, P. Schindler, D. Nigg, T. Monz, M. Chwalla, M. Hennrich, C. F. Roos, P. Zoller, and R. Blatt (2011). "An open-system quantum simulator with trapped ions". *Nature* 470:486–491.

Bassett, D. S. and M. S. Gazzaniga (2011). "Understanding complexity in the human brain". *Trends in Cognitive Sciences* 15(5):200–209.

Bauer, Bela, Dave Wecker, Andrew J. Millis, Matthew B. Hastings, and Matthias Troyer (2016). "Hybrid Quantum-Classical Approach to Correlated Materials". *Phys. Rev. X* 6(3):031045.

Beggs, Edwin, José Félix Costa, Diogo Poças, and John V. Tucker (2014). "An Analogue-Digital Church-Turing Thesis". *International Journal of Foundations of Computer Science* 25(4):373–389.

Bennett, Charles H. (1982). "The thermodynamics of computation—a review". *International Journal of Theoretical Physics* 21(12):905–940.

Berger, Robert (1966). "The undecidability of the domino problem". *Memoirs of the American Mathematical Society* 66:1–72.

Biamonte, Jacob, Peter Wittek, Nicola Pancotti, Patrick Rebentrost, Nathan Wiebe, and Seth Lloyd (2016). *Quantum Machine Learning.* eprint: arXiv: 1611.09347[quant-ph].

Blakey, Ed (2014). "Ray tracing – computing the incomputable?" *Proc DCM 2012.* Ed. by B. Löwe and G. Winskel. Vol. 143. EPTCS, pp. 32–40.

Blakey, Ed (2017). "Unconventional Computers and Unconventional Complexity Measures". *Advances in Unconventional Computing, vol 1.* Ed. by Andrew Adamatzky. Springer, pp. 165–182.

Blatt, R. and C. F. Roos (2012). "Quantum simulations with trapped ions". *Nature Physics* 8:277–284.

Blum, L. (2004). "Computing over the reals: Where Turing Meets Newton". *Notices of the AMS* 51(9):1024–1034.

Boixo, S., V. N. Smelyanskiy, A. Shabani, S. V. Isakov, M. Dykman, V. S. Denchev, M. Amin, A. Smirnov, M. Mohseni, and H. Neven (2016a). "Computational Role of Multiqubit Tunneling in a Quantum Annealer". *Nature Commun.* 7:10327.

Boixo, Sergio, Sergei V. Isakov, Vadim N. Smelyanskiy, Ryan Babbush, Nan Ding, Zhang Jiang, John M. Martinis, and Hartmut Neven (2016b). *Characterizing Quantum Supremacy in Near-Term Devices.* eprint: arXiv:1608. 00263[quant-ph].

Bose, S. K., C. P. Lawrence, Z. Liu, K. S. Makarenko, R. M. J. van Damme, H. J. Broersma, and W. G. van der Wiel (2015). "Evolution of a designless nanoparticle network into reconfigurable Boolean logic". *Nature Nanotechnology* 10:1048–1052.

Bravyi, S. and D. Gosset (2016). "Improved Classical Simulation of Quantum Circuits Dominated by Clifford Gates". *Phys. Rev. Lett.* 116:250501.

Broersma, H . J., J. F. Miller, and S. Nichele (2016). "Computational Matter: Evolving Computational Functions in Nanoscale Materials". *Advances in Unconventional Computing Volume 2: Prototypes, Models and Algorithms.* Ed. by A. Adamatzky, pp. 397–428.

Brown, K. L., W. J. Munro, and V. M. Kendon (2010). "Using Quantum Computers for Quantum Simulation". *Entropy* 12:2268–2307.

Brun, Yuriy (2008). "Solving satisfiability in the tile assembly model with a constant-size tileset". *Journal of Algorithms* 63(4):151–166.

Bryngelson, J. D., J. Nelson Onuchic, N. D. Socci, and P. G. Wolynes (1995). "Funnels, pathways, and the energy landscape of protein folding: A synthesis". *Proteins: Structure, Function and Bioinformatics* 21(3):167–195.

Cabessa, J. and H. T. Siegelmann (2011). "Evolving recurrent neural networks are super-Turing". *Proc. IJCNN 2011.* IEEE, pp. 3200–3206.

Castellanos, Juan, Carlos Martín-Vide, Victor Mitrana, and José M. Sempere (2001). "Solving NP-complete problems with networks of evolutionary processors". *IWANN 2001.* Vol. 2084. LNCS. Springer, pp. 621–628.

Chaitin, Gregory J. (1975). "A Theory of Program Size Formally Identical to Information Theory". *Journal of the ACM* 22(3):329–340.

Chaitin, Gregory J. (2012). "How Much Information Can There Be in a Real Number?" *Computation, Physics and Beyond.* Springer, pp. 247–251.

Cheeseman, Peter, Bob Kanefsky, and William M Taylor (1991). "Where the Really Hard Problems Are". *Proc. IJCAI 1991.* Morgan Kaufmann, pp. 331–337.

Chesi, C. and A. Moro (2014). "Computational complexity in the brain". *Measuring Grammatical Complexity.* Ed. by F. J. Newmeyer and L. B. Preston. Oxford University Press, pp. 264–280.

Cirac, J. I. and P. Zoller (2010). "Goals and opportunities in quantum simulation". *Nature Phys.* 8:264–266.

Complexity Zoo website (n.d.). complexityzoo.uwaterloo.ca/Complexity_Zoo.

Cook, Stephen (1971). "The complexity of theorem proving procedures". *Proceedings of the Third Annual ACM Symposium on Theory of Computing* :151–158.

Copeland, B. J. (2004). "Hypercomputation: philosophical issues". *Theoretical Computer Science* 317(1–3):251–267.

Copeland, B. J. (2015). "The Church-Turing Thesis". *The Stanford Encyclopedia of Philosophy.* Ed. by Edward N. Zalta. Summer 2015.

Copeland, B. J. and O. Shagrir (2011). "Do accelerating Turing machines compute the uncomputable?" *Minds and Machines* 21(2):221–239.

Crescenzi, P. and V. Kann (2005). *A compendium of NP optimization problems.* www.nada.kth.se/~viggo/problemlist/compendium.html.

Denchev, V. S., S. Boixo, S. V. Isakov, N. Ding, R. Babbush, J. Martinis V. Smelyanskiy and, and H. Neven (2016). "What is the Computational Value of Finite Range Tunneling?" *Phys. Rev. X* 6:031015.

Denef, F. and M. R. Douglas (2007). "Computational complexity of the landscape: Part I". *Annals of Physics* 322(5):1096–1142.

Dershowitz, N. and E. Falkovich (2012). "A Formalization and Proof of the Extended Church-Turing Thesis". *EPTCS* 88:72–78.

Deutsch, David (1985). "Quantum Theory, the Church-Turing Principle and the Universal Quantum Computer". *Proceedings of the Royal Society A* 400(1818):97–117.

Douglas, Keith (2003). "Super-Turing Computation: A Case Study Analysis". www.philosopher-animal.com/papers/take6c.pdf. MA thesis. Carnegie Mellon University.

Douglas, Keith (2013). "Learning to Hypercompute? An Analysis of Siegelmann Networks". *Computing Nature: Turing Centenary Perspective*. Ed. by G. Dogic-Crnkovic and R. Giovagnoli. Springer, pp. 201–211.

Downey, Rod G. and Michael R. Fellows (1999). *Parameterized Complexity*. Springer.

Edmonds, Jack (1965). "Paths, trees and flowers". *Canadian J. of Math.* 17 :449–467.

Esser, S. K., P. A. Merolla, A. S. Cassidy J. V. Arthur and, R. Appuswamy, A. Andreopoulos, D. J. Berg, J. L. McKinstry, T. Melano, D. R. Barch, C. di Nolfo, P. Datta, A. Amir, B. Taba, M. D. Flickner, and D. S. Modha (2016). "Convolutional networks for fast, energy-efficient neuromorphic computing". *PNAS* 41(113):668–673.

Etesi, Gábor and István Németi (2002). "Non-Turing Computations Via Malament–Hogarth Space-Times". *International Journal of Theoretical Physics* 41(2):341–370.

European Commission (2009). "Unconventional Formalisms for Computation". *Expert Consultation Workshop*.

Farhi, Edward, Jeffrey Goldstone, and Sam Gutmann (2014). *A Quantum Approximate Optimization Algorithm*. eprint: arXiv:1411.4028[quant-ph].

Farhi, Edward and Aram W. Harrow (2014). *Quantum Supremacy through the Quantum Approximate Optimization Algorithm*. eprint: arXiv:1602.07674[quant-ph].

Feynman, R. P. (1982). "Simulating Physics with Computers". *Int. J. Theor. Phys.* 21(6/7):467–488.

Floyd, Robert W. (1967). "Nondeterministic Algorithms". *Journal of the ACM* 14(4):636–644.

Garey, M. R. and D. S. Johnson (1979). *Computers and Intractability: A Guide to the Theory of NP-Completeness*. W. H. Freeman.

Georgescu, I. M., S. Ashhab, and Franco Nori (2014). "Quantum simulation". *Rev. Mod. Phys.* 86:153–185.

Grover, L. K. (1996). "A fast quantum mechanical algorithm for database search". *Proc. 28th Annual ACM Symposium on the Theory of Computing*. ACM Press, pp. 212–219.

Häner, Thomas, Damian S. Steiger, Mikhail Smelyanskiy, and Matthias Troyer (2016). "High Performance Emulation of Quantum Circuits". *Proc. SC 2016*. eprint: arXiv:1604.06460[quant-ph].

Häner, Thomas, Damian S Steiger, Krysta Svore, and Matthias Troyer (2018). "A software methodology for compiling quantum programs". *Quantum Science and Technology* 3(2):020501.

Hartmanis, Juris (1995). "The structural complexity column: On the Weight of Computations". *Bulletin of the European Association for Theoretical Computer Science. EATCS* 55:136–138.

Hogarth, Mark L. (1992). "Does General Relativity Allow an Observer to View an Eternity in a Finite Time?" *Foundations of Physics Letters* 5:173–181.

Horodecki, R., P. Horodecki, M. Horodecki, and K. Horodecki (2009). "Quantum entanglement". *Rev. Mod. Phys* 81(2):865–942.

Horsman, C., Susan Stepney, Rob C. Wagner, and Viv Kendon (2014). "When does a physical system compute?" *Proceedings of the Royal Society A* 470(2169):20140182.

Horsman, Dominic, Susan Stepney, and Viv Kendon (2017). "The Natural Science of Computation". *Communications of ACM* 60(8):31–34.

Jozsa, R. and N. Linden (2003). "On the role of entanglement in quantum-computational speed-up". *Proc. R. Soc. Lond. A* 459:2011–2032.

Juba, B. (2016). "Computational complexity and the Function-Structure-Environment Loop of the Brain". *Closed-Loop Neuroscience*. Ed. by A. El Hady. Academic Press, pp. 131–144.

Karp, Richard M. (1972). "Reducibility Among Combinatorial Problems". *Complexity of Computer Computations*. Ed. by R. E. Miller and J. W. Thatcher. Plenum, pp. 85–103.

Konkoli, Z. and G. Wendin (2014). "On information processing with networks of nano-scale switching elements". *Int. Journal of Unconventional Computing* 10(5–6):405–428.

Lanyon, B. P., J. D. Whitfield, G. G. Gillett, M. E. Goggin, M. P. Almeida, I. Kassal, J. D. Biamonte, M. Mohseni, B. J. Powell, M. Barbieri, A. Aspuru-Guzik, and A. G. White (2010). "Towards quantum chemistry on a quantum computer". *Nature Chemistry* 2:106–111.

Lawler, Eugene L., Jan Karel Lenstra, A. H. G. Rinnooy Kan, and D. B. Shmoys (1985). *The Traveling Salesman Problem: A Guided Tour of Combinatorial Optimization*. Wiley.

Levin, Leonid (1973). "Universal search problems". *Problems of Information Transmission* 9(3):(in Russian), 115–116.

Li, Ming and Paul Vitányi (1997). *An Introduction to Kolmogorov Complexity and Its Applications*. 2nd edn. Springer.

Lipton, Richard J. (1995). "DNA solution of hard computational problems". *Science* 268(5210):542–545.

Lloyd, Seth (2000). "Ultimate physical limits to computation". *Nature* 406(6799):1047–1054.

Loos, Remco, Florin Manea, and Victor Mitrana (2009). "Small universal accepting networks of evolutionary processors with filtered connections". *11th International Workshop on Descriptional Complexity of Formal Systems*. Ed. by J. Dassow, G. Pighizzini, and B. Truthe. EPTCS 3, pp. 173–182. eprint: arXiv:0907.5130[cs.FL].

Maass, Wolfgang (2016). "Energy-efficient neural network chips approach human recognition capabilities". *PNAS* 113(41):11387–11389.

Manea, F. and V. Mitrana (2007). "All NP-problems can be solved in polynomial time by accepting hybrid networks of evolutionary processors of constant size". *Information Processing Letters* 103(3):112–118.

Margenstern, Maurice, Victor Mitrana, and Mario J Pérez-Jiménez (2005). "Accepting Hybrid Networks of Evolutionary Processors". *Proc. DNA 2004*. Vol. 3384. LNCS. Springer, pp. 235–246.

Merolla, P. A., J. V. Arthur, A. S. Cassidy R. Alvarez-Icaza and, J. Sawada, F. Akopyan, B. L. Jackson, N. Imam, C. Guo, Y. Nakamura, B. Brezzo, I. Vo, S. K. Esser, R. Appuswamy, B. Taba, A. Amir, M. D. Flickner, W. P. Risk, R. Manohar, and D. S. Modha (2014). "A million spiking-neuron integrated circuit with a scalable communication network and interface". *Science* (345):668–673.

Metz, C. (2016). *Google's AI Wins Fifth And Final Game Against Go Genius Lee Sedol.* www.wired.com/2016/03/googles-ai-wins-fifth-final-game-go-genius-lee-sedol/.

Miller, Julian F. and Keith Downing (2002). "Evolution in materio: Looking beyond the silicon box". *Proc. NASA/DoD Evolvable Hardware Workshop*, pp. 167–176.

Montanaro, A. (2016). "Quantum algorithms: an overview". *npj Quantum Information* 2:15023.

Moore, Gordon (1965). "Cramming More Components onto Integrated Circuits". *Electronics Magazine* 38(8):114–117.

O'Malley, P. J. J., R. Babbush, I. D. Kivlichan, J. Romero, J. R. McClean, R. Barends, J. Kelly, P. Roushan, A. Tranter, N. Ding, B. Campbell, Y. Chen, Z. Chen, B. Chiaro, A. Dunsworth, A. G. Fowler, E. Jeffrey, A. Megrant, J. Y. Mutus, C. Neill, C. Quintana, D. Sank, A. Vainsencher, J. Wenner, T. C. White, P. V. Coveney, P. J. Love, H. Neven, A. Aspuru-Guzik, and J. M. Martinis (2016). "Scalable Quantum Simulation of Molecular Energies". *Phys. Rev. X* 6:031007.

Ouyang, Q., P. D. Kaplan, S. Liu, and A. Libchaber (1997). "DNA solution of the maximal clique problem". *Science* 278:446–449.

Papadimitriou, C. H. (1994). *Computational Complexity*. Addison-Wesley.

Peruzzo, A., J. McClean, P. Shadbolt, M-H Yung, X-Q Zhou, P.J. Love, A. Aspuru-Guzik, and J.L. O'Brien (2014). "A variational eigenvalue solver on a photonic quantum processor". *Nature Comm.* 5:4213.

Potgieter, P. H. (2006). "Zeno machines and hypercomputation". *Theoretical Computer Science* 358(1):23–33.

Qian, Lulu, David Soloveichik, and Erik Winfree (2010). "Efficient Turing-Universal Computation with DNA Polymers". *DNA Computing and Molecular Programming*. Vol. 6518. LNCS. Springer, pp. 123–140.

Rado, Tibor (1962). "On non-computable functions". *The Bell System Technical Journal* 41(3):877–884.

Reif, J., J. Tygar, and Y. Akitoshi (1994). "Computability and complexity of ray tracing". *Discrete and Computational Geometry* 11(3):265–288.

Reiher, Markus, Nathan Wiebe, Krysta M. Svore, Dave Wecker, and Matthias Troyer (2017). "Elucidating Reaction Mechanisms on Quantum Computers". 114(29):7555–7560.

Rønnow, T. F., Z. Wang, J. Job, S. Boixo, S. V. Isakov, D. Wecker, J. M. Martinis, D. A. Lidar, and M. Troyer (2014). "Defining and detecting quantum speedup". *Science* 334(6195):420–424.

Salathe, Y., M. Mondal, M. Oppliger, J. Heinsoo, P. Kurpiers, A. Potocnik, A. Mezzacapo, U. Las Heras, L. Lamata, E. Solano, S. Filipp, and A. Wallraff (2015). "Digital quantum simulation of fermionic models with a superconducting circuit". *Phys. Rev. X* 5:021027.

Saunders, Daniel (2016). "A Survey and Discussion of Memcomputing Machines". djsaunde.github.io/survey-discussion-memcomputing.pdf.

Schaul, Tom, Julian Togelius, and Jürgen Schmidhuber (2011). *Measuring intelligence through games*. eprint: arXiv:1109.1314[cs.AI].

Schuch, N. and F. Verstraete (2009). "Computational complexity of interacting electrons and fundamental limitations of density functional theory". *Nature Physics* 5:732–735.

Schuld, M., I. Sinayskiy, and F. Petruccione (2015). "An introduction to quantum machine learning". *Contemporary Physics* 56(2):172–185.

Seelig, G. and D. Soloveichik (2009). "Time-complexity of multilayered DNA strand displacement circuits". *DNA Computing and Molecular Programming*. Ed. by R. Deaton and A. Suyama. Vol. 5877. LNCS. Springer, pp. 144–153.

Shapiro, Ehud (2012). "A mechanical Turing machine: blueprint for a bio-molecular computer". *Interface focus* 2:497–503.

Shor, P. W. (1997). "Polynomial-time algorithms for prime factorization and discrete logarithms on a quantum computer". *SIAM Journal of Computing* 26:1484–1509.

Siegelmann, H. (1995). "Computation beyond the Turing limit". *Science* 268(5210):545–548.

Silver, David, Aja Huang, Chris J. Maddison, Arthur Guez, Laurent Sifre, George van den Driessche, Julian Schrittwieser, Ioannis Antonoglou, Veda Panneershelvam, Marc Lanctot, Sander Dieleman, Dominik Grewe, John Nham, Nal Kalchbrenner, Ilya Sutskever, Timothy Lillicrap, Madeleine Leach, Koray Kavukcuoglu, Thore Graepel, and Demis Hassabis (2016). "Mastering the game of Go with deep neural networks and tree search". *Nature* 529(7587):484–489.

Sipser, Michael (1997). *Introduction to the Theory of Computation.* PWS Publishing.

Stepney, Susan (2009). "Non-Classical Hypercomputation". *International Journal of Unconventional Computing* 5(3–4):267–276.

Traversa, Fabio L. and Massimiliano Di Ventra (2015). "Universal Memcomputing Machines". *IEEE transactions on neural networks and learning systems* 26(11):2702–2715.

Traversa, Fabio L. and Massimiliano Di Ventra (2017). "Polynomial-time solution of prime factorization and NP-complete problems with digital memcomputing machines". *Chaos* 27(2):023107.

Traversa, Fabio L., C. Ramella, F. Bonani, and Massimiliano Di Ventra (2015). "Memcomputing NP-complete problems in polynomial time using polynomial resources and collective states". *Science Advances* 1(6):e1500031.

Turing, Alan M. (1937). "On Computable Numbers, with an Application to the Entscheidungsproblem". *Proc. London Mathematical Society* s2-42(1):230–265.

Unger, R. and J. Moult (1993). "Finding the lowest free energy conformation of a protein is an NP-hard problem: Proof and implications". *Bulletin of Mathematical Biology* 55(6):1183–1198.

Valiron, B., N. J. Ross, P. Selinger, D. S. Alexander, and J. M. Smith (2015). "Programming the Quantum Future". *Communications of the ACM* 58(8):52–61.

Vergis, A., K. Steiglitz, and B. Dickinson (1986). "The complexity of analog computation". *Mathematics and Computers in Simulation* 28(2):91–113.

Viglietta, G. (2012). "Gaming Is a Hard Job, But Someone Has to Do It!" *Fun with Algorithms.* Ed. by E. Kranakis, D. Krizanc, and F. Luccio. Vol. 7288. LNCS. Springer, pp. 357–367.

Wagon, Stan (1985). *The Banach–Tarski Paradox.* Cambridge University Press.

Wang, Hao (1961). "Proving theorems by pattern recognition–II". *Bell System Technical Journal* 40(1):1–41.

Wang, Y., F. Dolde, J. Biamonte, R. Babbush, V. Bergholm, S. Yang, I. Jakobi, P. Neumann, A. Aspuru-Guzik, J.D. Whitfield, and J. Wrachtrup (2015). "Quantum simulation of helium hydride cation in a solid-state spin register". *ACS Nano* 9:7769.

Wangersky, Peter J. (1978). "Lotka-Volterra Population Models". *Annual Review of Ecology and Systematics* 9:189–218.

Wapner, Leonard M. (2005). *The Pea and the Sun: a mathematical paradox.* A K Peters.

Watrous, J. (n.d.). "Quantum computational complexity". *Encyclopedia of Complexity and Systems Science.* Ed. by R. A. Meyers. Springer, pp. 7174–7201.

Wecker, Dave and Krysta M. Svore (2014). *LIQUi| >: A Software Design Architecture and Domain-Specific Language for Quantum Computing*. eprint: arXiv:1402.4467[quant-ph].

Wendin, G. (2017). "Quantum information processing with superconducting circuits: a review". *Reports on Progress in Physics* 80:106001.

Whitfield, J. D., P. J. Love, and A. Aspuru-Guzik (2013). "Computational complexity in electronic structure". *Physical Chemistry Chemical Physics* 15:397–411.

Wiebe, Nathan, Ashish Kapoor, and Krysta M. Svore (2014). *Quantum Deep Learning*. eprint: arXiv:1412.3489[quant-ph].

Wiebe, Nathan, Ashish Kapoor, and Krysta M. Svore (2015). "Quantum algorithms for nearest-neighbor methods for supervised and unsupervised learning". *Quantum Information and Computation* 15(3-4):316–356.

Wittek, Peter (2016). *Quantum Machine Learning: What Quantum Computing Means to Data Mining*. Academic Press.

Wolpert, David H. (2012). *What the no free lunch theorems really mean; how to improve search algorithms*. Working Paper 2012-10-017. SFI.

Wolpert, David H. and William G. Macready (1997). "No Free Lunch Theorems for Optimization". *IEEE Trans. Evol. Comp* 1(1):67–82.

Woods, Damien and Thomas J. Naughton (2005). "An optical model of computation". *Theoretical Computer Science* 334:227–258.

Woods, Damien and Thomas J. Naughton (2009). "Optical computing". *Applied Mathematics and Computation* 215(4):1417–1430.

Wu, Kan, Javier García de Abajo, Cesare Soci, Perry Ping Shum, and Nikolay I Zheludev (2014). "An optical fiber network oracle for NP-complete problems". *Light: Science & Applications* 3(2):e147.

Yang, J. C.-C. (2013). "Computational complexity and decidability of tileability". PhD thesis. UCLA. URL: www-users.math.umn.edu/~jedyang/papers/yang-thesis.pdf.

Zintchenko, I., E. Brown, and M. Troyer (2015). "Recent developments in quantum annealing". www.scottaaronson.com/troyer.pdf.

Chapter 12
Encoding and Representation of Information Processing in Irregular Computational Matter

John S. McCaskill, Julian F. Miller, Susan Stepney, and Peter R. Wills

Abstract Representation is a crucial concept in classical computing. Unconventional computational devices pose a series of challenges to representational issues, including unary analogue encodings, the representation of inputs and outputs, and sometimes the inaccessibility of internal states. Of particular interest are successive representational adaptation and refinement in relation to natural information processes, both during biological evolution and in evolving material and smart microparticle systems. Some examples are discussed in this chapter.

12.1 Introduction

There are three important questions for the usability of unconventional computing (UCOMP): how to represent data and information in unconventional computational material; how to encode specific values and programs in that representation; for autonomous systems, how to decide on which information needs to be resolved. The first two are related: representations need to be implementable, and encodings targeting those representations need to be feasible.

In this chapter, we discuss some potential issues with encoding values in UCOMP devices, and then discuss three particular systems highlighting the third issue: evolution *in materio*; biological encoding; and encoding in microscopic electro-chemical systems.

© Springer International Publishing AG, part of Springer Nature 2018
S. Stepney et al. (eds.), *Computational Matter*, Natural Computing Series,
https://doi.org/10.1007/978-3-319-65826-1_12

12.2 Digital and analogue encodings

One primary data type that needs to be represented in a computational system is the *number*, be it integer- or real-valued. The same number (say, four), can be logically represented in many ways: decimal digits ('4'), binary digits ('100'), Gray coded ('110'), unary encoding ('1111'), even Roman numerals ('IV'). The logical representation needs a corresponding physical representation. Indeed, the logical representation in the previous sentence is described by means of the physical representation of symbols on paper or screen.

A classical *digital* computer is so called because its basic representation is of the binary *digits* 0 and 1, typically represented by two distinct physical voltages. Larger values are represented by combinations of these physical 0's and 1's, with intervening levels of abstraction ('4' represented abstractly as '100', in turn represented as three physical voltages).

This is a based representation. In everyday life, we use base ten. Most digital computers use base two. Some unconventional digital devices use other bases, such as three (either as $-1, 0, 1$, or as $0, 1, 2$). An important feature of a based representation is that the length of the represented number (number of digits needed) is *logarithmic* in the size of the value of the number. It exploits the combinatoric possibilities of strings of symbols to achieve this compression.

Single stranded unmodified unfolded DNA could be considered to be a degenerate form of base four representation, with symbols (rather than digits) A, C, G, T, encoding $4^3 = 64$ possible values per triplet, with the genetic code then mapping each value to one of twenty amino acids. These triplet codons have a 'most significant' and 'least significant' base within the genetic code, with the value of the least significant base having a restricted effect on the represented amino acid.

Many analogue computers instead represent numerical values by some continuous quantity (say, voltage). So the value '4' would be represented by $4k$ volts (or metres, or kilograms, or...), where k is some problem-dependent scaling factor; the value 'x' would be represented by xk volts. This is a *unary* encoding: the size of the encoded value is proportional to the size of the encoding value. Hence such an analogue representation is *exponentially larger* than a corresponding digital representation.

This feature of unary representation can be an issue for some forms of UCOMP. Values have to be scaled to ensure they are representable. And in particular, there is a precision issue. To add one more place of (binary) precision to a binary-encoded value, a single extra digit is needed. To add one place to a unary-encoded (analogue) value, that value must be set or measured with double the precision (Fig. 12.1), and there is a (typically quite small) limit to the precision with which physical values can be set or measured.

In the systems discussed below, typical continuous signals include voltages, field strengths and chemical concentrations. In the presence of thermal

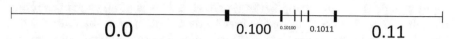

0.1   0.10   0.101   0.1010   0.10100   ...

$\vdash$———————————■——————├─┼┼┤——■—————————┤

0.0   0.100   0.10100   0.1011   0.11

Fig. 12.1 Increasing precision (top) encoding a real number value as a binary number. Doubling precision involves adding one extra binary digit to encode the number; (bottom) encoding a real number value as a position on a line. Doubling precision requires halving the region of the line used to encode the number.

fluctuations, the precision of analogue quantities is limited by the amplitude of fluctuations, e.g. 25.4 mV corresponds to kT for a single (electron) charge. Number fluctuations in equilibrium for molecules limit counting resolution to the square root of the number of molecules in many circumstances.

12.3 Encoding information in evolving material systems

To encode information in a material system requires a way of placing the material in a particular state. For example, while this article is being written this document is being viewed on a liquid crystal display (LCD) device. In a LCD there is a thin layer of liquid crystal held between two sheets of glass each of which is covered with a grid of transparent electrodes. In addition, the electrode-liquid crystal sandwich is placed between two polarizing light filters that are orientated at right angles to each other. The liquid crystal molecules are electrically polarized so they are sensitive to electric fields. Thus when voltages are applied to the electrode arrays, the orientation of the molecules can be changed and this affects the light transmitted.

In LCDs the voltages merely configure (i.e. twist) the molecules to allow us to view text (or images) on a screen. Thus, in general we supply a vector of real-valued voltages and we read (literally) the output from the LCD visually. In many computational problems we would like to obtain a function that can transform a vector of inputs to a vector of outputs. For example in machine learning classification problems one seeks a function that can assign a class to a vector of input values. The idea is that we might learn a function that can predict what class previously unknown instances of input data belong to. Such functions can be extremely useful in many application domains. For instance, the input vector could be a set of medical measurements taken from a patient. One might be trying to diagnose which of a number of medical conditions a patient is suffering. In machine learning many techniques have been devised to attempt to solve such problems. Such techniques represent a solution (one that predicts successfully new instances) in many ways, however most if not all, reduce to a set of mathematical equations that act on the input data to produce an output vector that predicts the class.

In principle, it is possible for physical materials to provide such functions. To do this one needs a way of transforming input information into a set of input signals that can be applied to a material. This is often called the input-mapping. One also needs to decide how to read signals from the material and how these can be transformed into information that represents a solution to a computational problem. This is called the output-mapping. Finally, one needs a set of configuration signals that can also be applied to the material that affects the behaviour of the material. If the material is to be useful in solving a computational problem we need a method that can allow us to find a good configuration. This is akin to the set of mathematical equations that machine learning techniques devise. The technique known as evolution *in materio* (EiM) (Harding et al., 2008; Miller and Downing, 2002; Miller et al., 2014) uses evolutionary algorithms (Holland, 1975) to search for configurations of a material that allow it to solve computational problems. A schematic showing how EiM can be used to configure materials for computation is shown in Figure 12.2.

One of the first materials investigated in this regard was liquid crystal where Harding and Miller (2004), Harding and Miller (2005), and Harding and Miller (2007) showed that configurations of a LCD could be evolved to allow it to distinguish between different frequency square-waves, control a simulated-robot navigating a simple maze and carry-out logical functions.

Materials have many physical properties and it is not obvious what are the most appropriate and useful ways of presenting and encoding information supplied to a material (binary or floating point representation, encoded in voltages, different frequency waves, light, and so on). Let us consider evolution *in materio*, of carbon nanotube systems (Miller et al., 2014; Mohid and Miller, 2015; Mohid et al., 2016), to give a specific example. Here, inputs, outputs, and configurations are supplied as voltages to an array of electrodes embedded in the computational material. Such voltages can encode analogue values, or, by thresholding, digital values. Figure 12.3 shows an electrode array connecting to a sample of carbon nanotubes embedded in an insulating polymer.

Another material system used for EiM was gold nanoparticles on an electrode array (see Figure 12.4). It was found that configurations of voltages could be found that made the system compute any two-input Boolean function.

If some problem is being tackled by 'analogue' computation, in the original sense of the computational process being 'by analogy' to the original problem, then the input and output values can themselves be the direct analogues of the problem values: the main issues are scaling and precision. If the computation is not analogous, however, more thought must be put into how inputs and outputs are represented.

For example, consider using an EiM system to compute a solution to the classic Travelling Salesman Problem (TSP). The desired output is a permutation of 'city' indices, indicating the shortest route (see, for example, Lawler

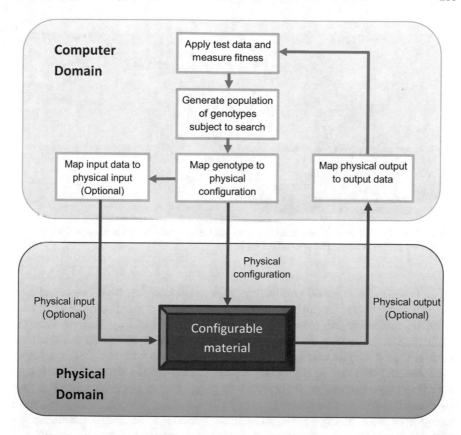

Fig. 12.2 Evolution *in materio* uses an evolutionary algorithm on conventional computer to search for configurations of materials that can carry out desired input-output mappings that solve computational problems.

Fig. 12.3 An electrode array interfaced to a material sample of carbon nanotubes embedded in PMMA (polymer).

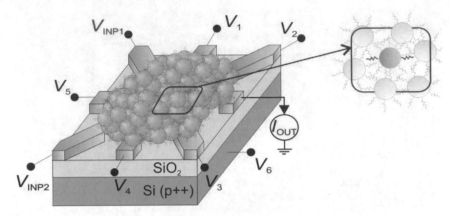

Fig. 12.4 An electrode array interfaced to gold nanoparticles with attached separating molecules (octanethiols) (Bose et al., 2015)

et al. (1985)). In classical computing, a permutation can be represented as a list of integers, and evolutionary operators defined to maintain the list as a valid permutation (no missing cities, no duplicated cities). But we have no such high level representations or operators available to us *in materio*; we have a list of output voltages. We need to use these to form a permutation. One method of doing so it to take the list of real-valued voltage outputs and sort them into increasing order: the sort permutation required to do this can be considered to be the desired output permutation (see Fig. 12.5). We have many decades of using high level representations in classical computing; we will have to develop novel approaches to representation in unconventional devices.

In classical computing one considers the internal representation, occurring inside the computer during the computation, as well as the external representation of the input/output values. This is not possible with basic EiM, as there is no computational model of the internals of the material: evolution treats the material as a 'black box'. It is possible to apply a computational model onto such systems. For example, Reservoir Computing (RC) has been used as an 'unconventional virtual machine' for computation with carbon nanotubes (Dale et al., 2017a; Dale et al., 2016a; Dale et al., 2016b; Dale et al., 2017b). This could provide a potential route for analysing the internal computational representations in the material in terms of the underlying RC model.

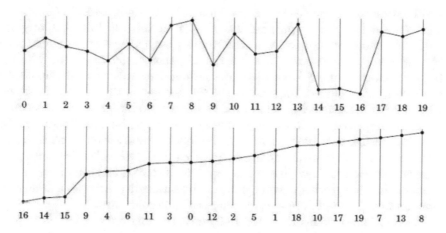

Fig. 12.5 (Top) the output, a list of 20 real numbers, represented as a 20-D point drawn in parallel coordinates (Inselberg, 1985); (bottom) the same values, with the parallel axes ordered so that the components are in increasing order: the sorted axis indexes are the permutation represented by the 20-D point

12.4 Biological information encoding and the evolution of a translation apparatus

Biological computational matter is encoded in DNA, allowing arbitrary changes in DNA sequences to have an impact on functionality. Additionally, the boot-block for the operating system, the code for constructing the map from sequence to function, is also materially encoded in DNA, in terms of the phase equilibria that underlie the "ecology" of interacting amino acid side chains inside folded proteins (Carter, Jr and Wills, 2018; Wolfenden et al., 2015), in particular, those proteins (aaRS enzymes) that operate the genetic code by simultaneously recognizing and matching specific amino acids and their cognate tRNAs. This provides a second level of abstraction of information from physical and chemical constraints, giving biological systems a remarkable ability to evolve new functionality. How could such a strongly evolvable and abstract system arise and what are its implications and potential for other forms of computational matter?

The clearest demonstration of the encoding of biological information in DNA is the efficacy of cloning with an artificially synthesized genome. Gibson et al. (2010) copied the DNA nucleotide base sequence information from the complete genome of *Mycoplasma mycoides* cells and then synthesized, from scratch, a very similar sequence which they then introduced into a system capable of interpreting the information – a DNA-voided cell of the closely related species *M. capricolum*. The interpreter system was able to maintain its integrity while transforming itself into the progenitor cell of a new species, which corresponded to the engineered genome, was designated JVCI-syn1.0, and displayed a phenotype practically indistinguishable from the original native *M. mycoides*. Messages in the English language were encrypted into otherwise superfluous parts of the artificial genome, demonstrating the arbitrary character of DNA-encoded information. However, what distinguishes the biologically relevant information in the genome is the manner in which its semantic content relies on a process of interpretation that is executed by machinery that can only be maintained through its own operation. In chemical terms, the interpretation of biological information is obligatorily autocatalytic. The self-reinforcing effect of autocatalysis offers the only possible explanation for how an arbitrary system of (biological) semantics could, short of the intervention of some external intentionality, arise spontaneously from an initial state of apparently complete molecular disorder.

In evolutionary terms the advent of genetic coding represented an important transition, perhaps the definitive transition, in the origin of life. If there existed, prior to the evolution of the protein synthetic translation apparatus, an autocatalytic "RNA World", a system comprising a restricted self-sustaining set of ribozymes (RNA catalysts) that mutually catalysed their own formation, then the mapping from those molecules' sequences onto their catalytic properties would have been "given in advance" so to say, governed by the outcome of spontaneous folding processes and the like that were essentially unregulated by the system as a whole. On the other hand, all biological systems operate a genetic code that defines a genotype-to-phenotype mapping from nucleic acid sequences to the catalytic properties of proteins. This mapping from information to chemical reaction enhancement is arbitrary with respect to the laws of physics and chemistry but is for all intents and purposes universal across the entire tree of life because it is the single surviving outcome of a process of stepwise self-organisation in which molecular biological operations progressively developed ever tighter, integrated, system-wide computational control of the chemical reaction processes involved in biochemical construction, maintenance and energy consumption.

There is a very interesting link between the computational control of physico-chemical processes afforded by genetically coded protein synthesis and the exquisitely detailed molecular composition and heterogeneous self-organized structure of systems in which translation of genetic information occurs. The genealogy of every living system can be traced back to a common origin through discrete generations involving the inheritance of both a library of genetic information and a material system existing in a privileged thermodynamic state and with a corresponding molecular composition that allows it to interpret the genetic information it contains as a blueprint for its own construction. Encoded protein synthesis is a cooperative process that cannot evolve in systems in which there is pure competition for survival among different replicating polymer sequences. Furthermore, the requisite evolutionary cooperation in the network of reactions needed for translation can neither spontaneously appear nor be sustained in a well-mixed (homogeneous) chemical system. Thus, some sort of spatially resolved structure, the result of either compartmentalization or Turing-type reaction-diffusion coupling, is required at the very first stage of genetic coding, when the first bits of truly "genetic" information were autocatalytically coupled to their interpretation through a nascent system of primitive computation: apparently a one-bit code sustained by two enzymes with distinct coding assignment functions, mutually encoded in the complementary sequences of the separate strands of the same DNA double helix (Wills, 2016).

12.5 Information encoding and translation in electronic-chemical systems

We propose that the facilely mutable information of electronics be coupled with the synthetically and functionally diverse and powerful information processing in chemical computational matter to enable humanly engineered computational matter to expand its potential.

Electronics is the dominant form of human-synthesized information processing, and hence largely defines our technical interfaces to the material world, residing in the machines and systems that we employ in our homes, factories, transportation, sensors, tools, and communication. It has enabled a remarkable transition in our society's ability to program material world processes and events. Electronic processing is also fundamental to chemical matter, in as much as the chemical bond is electronic in nature and chemical reactions reflect intricate quantum rearrangements of electronic states. In both contexts, electronic programming can operate extremely fast, allowing long sequences of transitions, compounding information from many different sources, to control processes on human-relevant timescales. For these reasons, it is both interesting and important to understand (i) the potential for interfacing electronic systems with chemical information processing systems; and (ii) the limitations and potential in encoding chemical and higher order computational matter functionality in electronics. Following the insights of the previous section on biological information coding and translation, we are curious about the process of bootstrapping an encoded translation system between electronic and chemical information.

12.5.1 Key concept: electronic genomes

A close analogy can be drawn between the processing of genetic information to construct enzyme catalysts and the use of electronic information interfaced with microscopic chemical processors (Fig. 3 of McCaskill et al., 2012). Because it is so easily and densely stored in a form that is essentially decoupled from the immediate effects of other processes, as well as being used to control events at the molecular level, electronically accessible information is eminently suitable as a mode of "genetic book-keeping" in systems that employ chemical computation. As in DNA, information stored in electronic bits can be copied and edited facilely, in contrast with the complex processes of fabrication required to copy the most material structures including molecules. The encoding of hard to copy structures and processes in generically copyable forms of information is the key digital abstraction enabling both biology and the current information age.

12.5.2 Interfacing electronic and chemical systems: micro/nano electrodes and alternatives (e.g. light)

Electronic information is highly amenable to the control of molecular processes, down to the level of individual polymer chains being ratcheted through nanopores in steps of a single monomer unit. It can also be used for the ultraprecise control of electrode processes, including the runtime modification of the distinctive functional specifications of micro- or nano-electrodes and their immediate fluid, active-surface or quasi-membrane environments. Thus, the development of interfaces between chemical and electronic information offers a vast range of possibilities for computation, molecular construction and process control in nanotechnologies. Not only can different voltage levels electrochemically turn on different reactions, and these reactions provide the conditions e.g. as catalysts for further reactions, but different reaction products at spatially orchestrated electrodes can interact and react to form further products and structures. Furthermore, electrodes can interact electrokinetically with ionic solutions to direct the transport, concentration and separation of chemicals. The control of complex chemical processes through spatio-temporal electronic control of microelectrodes is an area that we are only beginning to unravel. Apart from acting in direct control, such electronic signals can also modulate and direct purely chemical pattern formation as in reaction-diffusion systems. Electrochemical sensors have demonstrated an impressive diversity of target molecules and sensitivities in recent years, underscoring the two-way nature of this interface to digital information, especially when analog electronic as well as chemical signal amplification are employed prior to analog digital conversion.

Optical and opto-electronic interfacing to chemical systems provides a wireless and surface-independent technique for interfacing to bulk chemical systems. Imaging systems for both structured illumination and imaging of chemical systems have been perfected at macroscopic scales and now support nanoscale super-resolution beneath the wavelength of the light employed. Parallel spatial structuring with spatial light modulators, digital mirror devices and masks are complemented by fast scanning serial techniques for directly writing spatial patterns in 2D or 3D to chemical systems, inducing for example polymerization and changes in phase in the media involved.

12.5.3 The advantage of autonomous particles

The siting of a variety of electronic-chemical interfaces on autonomously powered microscopic devices, rather than on a large cabled surface, adds dimensions of completely new possibilities to the type of molecular-level computation that can be constructively instantiated in electro-chemical devices, in the same way as the advents of both genetic coding and multicellularity each marked a transition to previously inconceivable opportunities for biological evolution. The analogies are striking. Just as the genetic code originated in the obligatory cooperation of two autonomous units with dual versions of the same general function with distinguishable specificities (the Class I and II amino acyl-tRNA synthetases – aaRSs), so too could a "gas" of initially identical devices suspended in a suitable fluid bifurcate into subpopulations of units that performed complementary, separately controllable chemical functions of a kind simultaneously demanded by some shared electronic program able to fulfill a defined goal. Likewise, the association of individual units to form diverse conglomerates offers further possibilities, not only for the efficient execution of multistep tasks but also for the selection of "morphogenic stages" in the development of systems with extraordinary levels of computational specificity.

12.5.4 Lablets: electrochemically functional autonomous microscopic reaction walls made of silicon electronic chiplets

Lablets (tiny labs) have been designed to be used for autonomous experimentation and share some of the essential features of both cells and chemical labs (McCaskill et al., 2017). Both chemical labs and cells need to have a restricted reaction vessel, separating the place where reactions may occur from the rest of the world/system. They both require a source of energy and a means of converting this into useful work and/or chemical synthesis. Most importantly they need an information platform to control the opening and closing of the reaction vessel, the selection, input and output of chemicals, including reagents and catalysts. In addition, they both require a chemical separation mechanism allowing only selective products to be enriched and maintained, while waste is removed, and mechanisms for sensing progress in chemical reactions. Of course, in standard chemical labs the information platform controlling chemical processing is either played directly by a chemist or indirectly with the help of computer controlled machines (such lab automats). In cells, the key functions are mostly played by membranes for compartmentation and selective transport, metabolism for energy and construction chemistry and information control by genes encoding proteins to direct the choice of processes and to allow sensing and separations. In lablets, a reaction vessel can be reversibly formed by one of them docking on a flat surface or two of them docking together, to provide restricted diffusional access to the contents retained in the relief profile. Since diffusional interchange is typically on the timescale of 10s or more for such lablets, there is significant potential for advancing local chemical concentrations and processes. Energy stems from electric fields and is accumulated and stored as separated charge in an encapsulated supercapacitor (Sharma, McCaskill, et al., 2017), currently occupying about half the area of the lablet. Information is saved in the silicon substrate electronically and directs electrochemical and/or electrokinetic actuators and sensors.

Lablets were first proposed by McCaskill et al. (2012) and constructed in the MICREAgents project (www.micreagents.eu) at the scale of 100–140 µm. Partners in the project focused on the separate functions of lablets such as reversible association, internal logic, electronic control of chemical concentrations and supercapacitor power. They have been further developed in the EON Seed Grant Project (2016–2017); see also Chapter 6.

12.5.5 Two-way interfacing electronic genomes on lablets with chemical control and sensing

Information in replicable and editable form is a vital resource to both biology and society. Functionally deployed information in biology is generally "folded" or "deployed" in a condensed or convoluted form, as in proteins, that precludes copying. Instead, the genes realized using DNA act like design blueprints or CAD programs that can be readily copied. Digital electronic information is also in a form that can readily be copied, in contrast with the material and chemical artefacts resulting from processes directed by this information. Electronic genomes have been proposed by McCaskill (Wagler et al., 2012) as a useful encoding of information for microscopic chemistry. McCaskill and Wills have developed the idea of an electronic to chemical translation code as analogous to the protein translation code in biology. The flow of information is in both directions in biology, with signal sensing changing protein concentrations which can change the RNA-mediated expression of other proteins from their genes. Independently of the many significant complications of this picture, unraveled by modern biochemistry and molecular biology, most information in the DNA remains constant during the lifetime of a cell while the RNA expression patterns may change significantly. Likewise, the electronic operation of lablets involves a program, the code for which is not being rewritten during normal operation, and various information state bits of information, which change in response to certain sensor, timer, or succession events. As with the genome, lablet programs can be communicated from a functional lablet to a new lablet in a process mirroring cellular reproduction (mitosis, but meiosis and sexual recombination of genomes may also be realized).

The range of phenomena induced by or sensed by microelectrode potentials in aqueous chemical solutions is extraordinarily diverse, context dependent and linkable to both selected chemical reactions and overall mechanical events (such as docking). The modulation of ionic distributions is already richly nonlinear in the Nernst Planck level of description, especially when the geometric scale is commensurate with the Debye length (for low concentrations and/or nanoscale dimensions), so that there is firstly a non-trivial encoding between electronics and ionics. Certain ions, like H+, modulate a wealth of reactions and structural equilibria for instance through the biasing of protonation and hence the charge state of molecules. Other ions can be involved in specific reactions, redox or otherwise, electrochemical or in solution, and their concentration changes influence the rates of reactions. Specific threshold potentials on electrodes (compared with the solution potential) can switch on specific electrochemical reactions (following Butler–Volmer threshold kinetics which turn on like the diode current law). Furthermore, potentials can release specific ions reversibly from porous structures on electrodes that have been imprinted to hold them, and these electrodes can so act as reversible reservoirs for specific chemicals (Frasconi et al., 2010). Of course, encoding specificity of response is not straightforward, given the multitude of possible effects. However, hysteresis effects can be employed to bootstrap specificity: for example, electrode potentials can be first designed to perform specific coatings on electrodes and then the repertoire of specific signals further diversified by these coating. Here we can only hint at the range of the possibilities, noting that many other physical effects, including electrowetting and electroosmotic phenomena will play a role. As in the complexity of protein folding, it is not necessary for all these effects to be separable and modular for an effective encoding of functionality to be possible.

12.5.6 Stepwise evolution of a translation system between microelectrode signals and chemical functionalities

We envisage the possibility of designing and building electronic-chemical systems in which constructive functionalities can spontaneously progress to more finely differentiated, information-rich states through a series of transitions analogous to what is seen in the development of the genetic code. A realistic mechanism for the stepwise self-organization of genetic coding has already been demonstrated in a system that was set up to have functionalities embedded in a hierarchical fashion, allowing an initial "easy" transition to a binary code and then a "harder" transition to a four-letter code (Wills, 2009). We first observe that the actual genetic code created its own quasi-hierarchical "design", writing step by step into the space of nucleotide triplet codons an ever more detailed map of the diverse roles of amino acids in folded proteins. What facilitated this remarkable evolution of computational complexity in nature was autocatalytic feedback: the coded placement of amino acids at specified positions in protein sequences was dependent on the functional effects of amino acids being placed at certain positions in the sequences of the enzymes (aaRSs) that defined the coding relationships. However, coding self-organization alone is not enough: it is also necessary for local success in coding to give selective advantage to the encoded information on which it relies. An extremely simple way of meeting this requirement has been implemented in studies of gene-replicase-translatase systems (Füchslin and McCaskill, 2001), demonstrating a plausible mechanism for the simultaneous corralling of a code and the rare information needed for its autocatalytic maintenance.

12.5.7 Bootstrapping up to cell-like functionality using smart particles carrying electronic genomes

We see no ultimate impediment to the recapitulation of this deep evolutionary process in electronic-chemical devices. The key features of the implementation environment are: (i) electronically stored "genomic" programs and local chemical environments should both exert influence over the functionality of electrodes in contact with the fluid milieu/interface; (ii) entities that have specific functional effects at and near electrodes should be constructed through parametrically controlled sequences of chemical events within near the fluid milieu/interface; (iii) a feedback mechanism for the local, selective preservation of electronic programs that sustain autocatalysis of functionalities in the chemical environment; and (iv) the embedding of functional effects in the space of sequence-wise constructible entities should be sufficiently diverse, differentiated and complex to cater for the emergence of autocatalytic sets of functional molecules/conglomerates. The third requirement captures the ubiquitous biological phenomenon of the genotype-phenotype mapping being defined by an operational physico-chemical system that is under the immediate influence of the local information that it interprets. The fourth requirement is rather abstract but can be understood by analogy with the rich variation of ribozymal or enzymatic functionality across nucleotide or amino acid sequence space. We envisage self-creating devices whose emergence in electronic-chemical systems is driven by the constrained channeling of dissipative processes for the achievement of materially defined goals, especially the directed synthesis of special organic compounds, polymers or nano-architectures.

12.5.8 Connection with reservoir computing

Unlike the digital electronic system, with its precisely programmed deterministic switching, both the electrical and the chemical system response to the temporal voltage control signals on sets of microelectrodes is complex, involving significant hysteresis and dependence on environmental factors (such as the concentration of various chemicals in the medium). For systems involving NPs and CNTs it has been demonstrated that the electrical properties of various nanoscale structured media have the echo state property and hence (Jaeger, 2001) can be employed as a bulk learning medium (as a simpler and powerful substitute for neural networks) with only surface connections needing to be learnt. No doubt, certain aqueous chemical systems, coupling physical and chemical reaction effects will share this property and hence allow, from an electronic perspective, complex learning and memory. From the chemical perspective, long term memory responses will generally involve the synthesis of specific substances and structures in the aqueous coupled system. This coupling of interface controlled reservoir computing with chemical system self-organization should open a powerful approach to computational matter in the future.

12.6 Conclusions

Unconventional computing devices need new techniques for representing and encoding their inputs, outputs, and programs.

Most unconventional devices have non-existent, or still rather primitive, computational models; they are often treated as black boxes. This makes it difficult to think about and apply internal programming representations to them. As the discipline progresses, higher level models should become available, allowing more sophisticated representations to be employed. Reservoir Computing appears to be an interesting model applicable to many systems.

Currently, much of the focus on representation is on inputs and outputs. These can be digital or analogue. Analogue representations can have scaling and precision issues.

The construction of copyable technical information systems that must communicate with complex physical or chemical systems shares many of the encoding issues faced by biological systems in genetic encoding, and it is fruitful to understand how effective coupling between such systems can be established and encoded as a single problem.

References

Bose, S. K., C. P. Lawrence, Z. Liu, K. S. Makarenko, R. M. J. van Damme, H. J. Broersma, and W. G. van der Wiel (2015). "Evolution of a designless nanoparticle network into reconfigurable Boolean logic". *Nature Nanotechnology* 10:1048–1052.

Carter, Jr, Charles W. and Peter R. Wills (2018). "Interdependence, Reflexivity, Fidelity, Impedance Matching, and the Evolution of Genetic Coding". *Molecular Biology and Evolution* 35(2):269–286.

Dale, Matthew, Julian F. Miller, and Susan Stepney (2017a). "Reservoir Computing as a Model for *In Materio* Computing". *Advances in Unconventional Computing, vol 1*. Ed. by Andrew Adamatzky. Springer, pp. 533–571.

Dale, Matthew, Julian F. Miller, Susan Stepney, and Martin A. Trefzer (2016a). "Evolving Carbon Nanotube Reservoir Computers". *UCNC 2016*. Vol. 9726. LNCS. Springer, pp. 49–61.

Dale, Matthew, Julian F. Miller, Susan Stepney, and Martin A. Trefzer (2016b). "Reservoir Computing *in Materio*: An Evaluation of Configuration through Evolution". *ICES 2016 at SSCI 2016*. IEEE.

Dale, Matthew, Susan Stepney, Julian F. Miller, and Martin Trefzer (2017b). "Reservoir Computing *in Materio*: a computational framework for evolution in Materio". *Proc. IJCNN 2017*. IEEE, pp. 2178–2185.

Frasconi, Marco, Ran Tel-Vered, Michael Riskin, and Itamar Willner (2010). "Electrified selective 'sponges' made of Au nanoparticles". *J. Am. Chem. Soc.* 132(27):9373–9382.

Füchslin, Rudolf M. and John S. McCaskill (2001). "Evolutionary self-organization of cell-free genetic coding". *PNAS* 98(16):9185–90.

Gibson, Daniel G., John I. Glass, Carole Lartigue, Vladimir N. Noskov, Ray-Yuan Chuang, Mikkel A. Algire, Gwynedd A. Benders, Michael G. Montague, Li Ma, Monzia M. Moodie, Chuck Merryman, Sanjay Vashee, Radha Krishnakumar, Nacyra Assad-Garcia, Cynthia Andrews-Pfannkoch, Evgeniya A. Denisova, Lei Young, Zhi-Qing Qi, Thomas H. Segall-Shapiro, Christopher H. Calvey, Prashanth P. Parmar, Clyde A. Hutchison, Hamilton O. Smith, and J. Craig Venter (2010). "Creation of a bacterial cell controlled by a chemically synthesized genome". *Science* 329:52–56.

Harding, Simon L. and Julian F. Miller (2004). "Evolution in materio: a tone discriminator in liquid crystal". *Proc. CEC 2004*. Vol. 2, pp. 1800–1807.

Harding, Simon L. and Julian F. Miller (2005). "Evolution in materio : A real time robot controller in liquid crystal". *Proc. NASA/DoD Conference on Evolvable Hardware*, pp. 229–238.

Harding, Simon L. and Julian F. Miller (2007). "Evolution In Materio: Evolving Logic Gates in Liquid Crystal". *International Journal of Unconventional Computing* 3(4):243–257.

Harding, Simon L., Julian F. Miller, and Edward A. Rietman (2008). "Evolution in Materio: Exploiting the Physics of Materials for Computation." *International Journal of Unconventional Computing* 4(2):155–194.

Holland, John H. (1975). *Adaptation in Natural and Artificial Systems*. University of Michigan Press.

Inselberg, Alfred (1985). "The plane with parallel coordinates". *The Visual Computer* 1(2):69–91.

Jaeger, Herbert (2001). *The "echo state" approach to analysing and training recurrent neural networks*. Tech. rep. GMD Report 148. German National Research Center for Information Technology.

Lawler, Eugene L., Jan Karel Lenstra, A. H. G. Rinnooy Kan, and D. B. Shmoys (1985). *The Traveling Salesman Problem: A Guided Tour of Combinatorial Optimization*. Wiley.

McCaskill, John S. et al. (2017). "CMOS2 lablet design and synthesis". preprint.

McCaskill, John S., Günter von Kiedrowski, Jürgen Öhm, Pierre Mayr, Lee Cronin, Itamar Willner, Andreas Herrmann, Steen Rasmussen, Frantisek Stepanek, Norman H. Packard, and Peter R. Wills (2012). "Microscale Chemically Reactive Electronic Agents". *International Journal of Unconventional Computing* 8:289–299.

Miller, Julian F. and Keith Downing (2002). "Evolution in Materio: Looking Beyond the Silicon Box". *The 2002 NASA/DoD Conference on Evolvable Hardware*. Ed. by Adrian Stoica, Jason Lohn, Rich Katz, Didier Keymeulen, and Ricardo Salem Zebulum. IEEE, pp. 167–176.

Miller, Julian F., Simon L. Harding, and Gunnar Tufte (2014). "Evolution-in-materio: evolving computation in materials". *Evolutionary Intelligence* 7:49–67.

Mohid, Maktuba and Julian F. Miller (2015). "Evolving Solutions to Computational Problems Using Carbon Nanotubes". *International Journal of Unconventional Computing* 11(3–4):245–281.

Mohid, Maktuba, Julian F. Miller, Simon L. Harding, Gunnar Tufte, Mark K. Massey, and Michael C. Petty (2016). "Evolution-in-materio: solving computational problems using carbon nanotube–polymer composites". *Soft Computing* 20(8):3007–3022.

Sharma, A., John S. McCaskill, et al. (2017). "Lablet Supercapacitor". preprint.

Wagler, Patrick F., Uwe Tangen, Thomas Maeke, and John S. McCaskill (2012). "Field programmable chemistry: Integrated chemical and electronic processing of informational molecules towards electronic chemical cells". *Biosystems* 109:1–16.

Wills, Peter R. (2009). "Informed Generation: physical origin and biological evolution of genetic codescript interpreters". *J. Theor. Biol* 257:345–358.

Wills, Peter R. (2016). "The generation of meaningful information in molecular systems". *Philosophical Transactions of the Royal Society A* 374 :20150066.

Wolfenden, Richard, Charles A. Lewis, Yang Yuan, and Charles W. Carter (2015). "Temperature dependence of amino acid hydrophobicities". *PNAS* 112(24):7484–7488.

Chapter 13
BIOMICS: a Theory of Interaction Computing

Paolo Dini, Chrystopher L. Nehaniv, Eric Rothstein, Daniel Schreckling, and Gábor Horváth

Abstract This chapter provides a summary of the results of the BIOMICS project[1], specifically from the point of view of the development of a mathematical framework that can support a productive collaboration between cell biochemistry, dynamical systems, algebraic automata theory, and specification languages, leading to a theory of Interaction Computing (IC).

The main objective of the BIOMICS project was to map the spontaneous order-construction ability of cellular biochemistry to computer science in the form of a new model of computation that we call Interaction Computing. The project did not achieve this objective, but it lay the groundwork for developing a mathematical theory of IC, it developed a computational framework that can support IC based on an extension of Abstract State Machines (ASMs) (Börger and Stärk, 2003) to Abstract State Interaction Machines (ASIMs), and reached a number of intermediate objectives.

13.1 Introduction

The perspective of BIOMICS is different from most of the other UCOMP cluster projects funded by the 2011 FET Proactive UCOMP call, in a manner that is best explained by relying on the Abstraction/Representation theory of computation (Horsman et al., 2014). In this theory a duality is assumed between mathematical models of computation and corresponding physical substrates. The intention is to allow a wide variety of possible substrates which, through appropriate representations, can enact a wide range of possible computations. This framework is consistent with the various kinds of substrates that the UCOMP projects utilize, which are different from the standard von Neumann architecture. As shown in Figure 13.1, as a substrate

---

[1] http://www.biomicsproject.eu

© Springer International Publishing AG, part of Springer Nature 2018
S. Stepney et al. (eds.), *Computational Matter*, Natural Computing Series,
https://doi.org/10.1007/978-3-319-65826-1_13

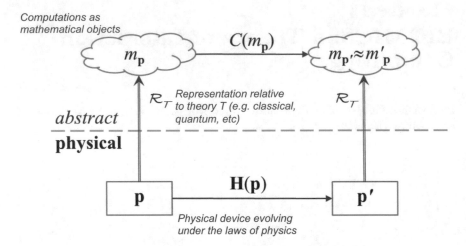

Fig. 13.1 An almost commuting diagram (based on Horsman et al. (2014))

evolves according to the laws of physics from an initial state p to a new state p', a computation is said to occur if the representation of p' is sufficiently close to the result of evolving the mathematical representation of p from the same initial state.

As shown in Figure 13.2, computations are seen as changes of states of a physical substrate. However, in this figure a further refinement step distinguishes the abstract mathematical model from a computational or machine model which closely resembles the physical substrate. For example, the machine model of von Neumann computers involves a mathematical problem that is compiled into machine code expressed in terms of the binary number system, which corresponds to two voltage levels in the silicon substrate and is implemented with (Boolean) logic gates.

In BIOMICS we introduced an additional layer between the computational model and the physical substrate. This is shown in Figure 13.3, in the column labelled 'Abstract View'. The idea is to rely on conventional von Neumann machines for the substrate, and to emulate different kinds of biological systems to achieve different kinds of unconventional computation. In BIOMICS we focus exclusively on the biochemistry of the cell as the substrate to be emulated, and we call such an object an Interaction Machine (IM). Note that by 'emulation' we do not mean that we are trying to develop a system biology model of a particular pathway or set of pathways. Rather, we mean that we are trying to capture some structural and dynamical aspects of biochemical systems and specifying the computational system (i.e., the IM) in such a way that the execution of a given computation will involve similar structural and architectural properties, and similar dynamical properties. 'Similar' here can mean anything from 'isomorphic' to 'analogous'.

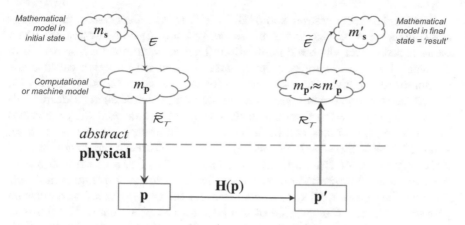

Fig. 13.2 A computation (based on Horsman et al. (2014))

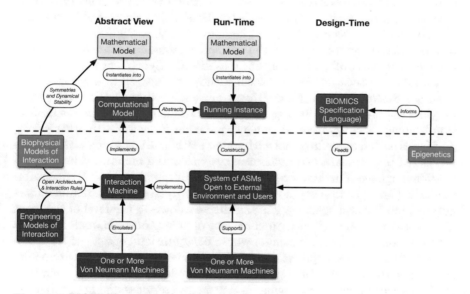

Fig. 13.3 BIOMICS computational framework

As shown on the left of the figure, the properties of the IM are to be derived from continuous and discrete biophysical models of interaction, for example systems of ordinary differential equations (ODEs) and interacting automata. In addition, since it is to be expected that engineering practice leads mathematical theorization by several years, the research also relies on systems and models from distributed engineering systems and architectures. The rest of the figure provides more details of the run-time and design-time aspects of the framework.

The fundamental assumption of BIOMICS is that a successful mapping of the behaviour of biology to the behaviour of computational systems is likely to be based on an algebraic foundation. This map cannot be isomorphic in the sense that, for example, a spring-mass system with friction can provide an isomorphic model of an LRC circuit (or vice versa). Ultimately the reason is that there is no common global minimization principle such as Hamilton's principle of least action from which the dynamics of biochemical systems and of interacting automata can both be derived. However, one of the main results of BIOMICS research has been to realize that, on the one hand, Richard Bellman's Dynamic Programming (Bellman, 1957) offers a theoretical framework for general optimization problems that is more general than Hamilton's and that has been applied to a wide number of computational and decision processes. On the biology side of the gap, on the other hand, Hamiltonian dynamics has been suitably generalized to dissipative systems through Freidlin and Wentzell's (Freidlin and Wentzell, 1998) stochastic theory of large deviations, which ultimately also relies on Bellman's Principle of Optimality.

The bridge between biology and computation that BIOMICS has begun to formalize, therefore, relies on the stochastic modelling of meta-stable biochemical systems and on treating them as discrete dynamical systems, which in turn can be seen as mathematical models of finite-state automata. The Abstract State Machines (ASMs) software engineering methodology, then, provides the final step to an algebraically and coalgebraically sound specification language and iterative refinement modelling framework. In other words, ASMs are both a modelling tool with sound mathematical properties that can be related to automata and dynamical systems and a human-readable specification language. Furthermore, by iterative refinement the initial executable model and specification can be expressed in progressively more detailed (executable) models and specifications, all the way down to the level of the code. The object that is envisaged to come out of this process is analogous to a compiler compiler,[2] i.e. a machine whose computation consists of the fulfilment of dynamically expressed requirements coming from the environment. In other words, the abstract and run-time equivalent to cellular biochemistry (IM) that synthesizes the enzymes and proteins (services and apps) that are required to fulfill specific requirements and tasks, in real time, in response to transduction pathway signals from outside the cell.

13.2 Problem as originally posed

As shown in Figure 13.4, the starting and fundamentally algebraic assumptions were that (1) knowledge of the invariants of biological behaviour might help understand self-organization, construction of order, and dynamical sta-

---

[2] A compiler compiler is a compiler whose compiled output is a compiler.

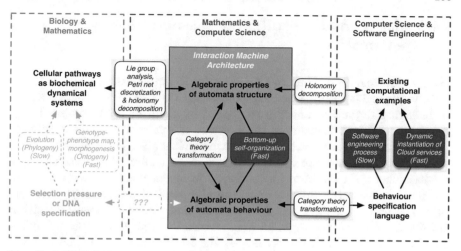

Fig. 13.4 BIOMICS research framework

bility as possible forms of such invariance; and that (2) suitable mathematical mappings would relate such invariant structures to the corresponding invariant computational structures in the discrete models of the *same* biochemical systems. More precisely, we postulated that the Lie symmetries of systems of ordinary differential equations (ODEs) modelling metabolic pathways might be related by the Chevalley construction to the simple non-abelian groups (SNAGs) found in the Krohn-Rhodes (Krohn and Rhodes, 1965) or holonomy Zeiger, 1967 decomposition of finite-state automata derived as discretized models of the *same* biochemical systems. A category theory adjunction would then relate the algebraic properties of automata structure to the algebraic properties of automata behaviour, and other category theory functors would in turn relate the behaviour to a specification language.

It is important to realize that in moving downwards in the IM Architecture box in the centre of Figure 13.4 one is essentially solving a direct or analysis problem, whose solution is unique: given a structure, it is relatively easy to find the corresponding behaviour. On the other hand, moving upwards in the same diagram is analogous to the 'inverse' or design problem, which is very hard since the solution is not unique: in general, given a specification of behaviour, more than one structure will satisfy it. BIOMICS attempted to solve the latter problem by taking inspiration from biology and, where possible, by utilizing isomorphic models based on functorial relationships (which preserve symmetries and morphisms) between the different domains: continuous dynamical systems, discrete automata, and language specification.

13.3 Intermediate results: physics and biology perspective

By spontaneous order construction we refer to ontogenetic processes rather than to phylogenetic, evolutionary processes.[3] The order construction ability of biological organisms appears to depend on their ability to maintain 'dynamically stable' behaviour in the presence of external inputs and internal propagation of signals and materials at multiple scales. The ability of biological organisms to react to external signals in a meaningful and useful way is a consequence of coevolution with the environment itself, implying that not just *any* environment will do. From the viewpoint of statistical physics self-organization can be understood as the minimization of free energy, which is consistent with the open-system architecture the above description implies. The 'self' in self-organization is merely the fall towards equilibrium of a system that is continually kept *away* from equilibrium by a flow of high-free energy 'nutrients' or 'inputs'. Therefore, self-organization depends on open systems interacting with a compatible environment in such a way that the inputs keep them away from thermodynamic equilibrium, but also that they remain within a dynamically stable range of possible behaviours. Furthermore, the interactions relate also to the components internal to the system, whose number can change at run-time depending on the needs of the moment.

If the system were allowed to reach equilibrium, dynamical stability could be regarded as a set of possible equilibria, generally called 'meta-stable states' in the literature. If, on the other hand, the system is always kept away from equilibrium even while it falls towards it, then dynamical stability must be associated with the sets of pre-images of the equilibria, i.e. orbits which fall in their basins of attraction. The crucial point, made by Prigogine long ago, is that in open systems what we perceive as ordered structure and behaviour does *not* correspond to equilibria, but occurs 'far from equilibrium'. In fact, Prigogine seems to imply that being far from equilibrium is a *condition* for such structures to form.

This puts a different complexion on the research problem definition, and reflects the BIOMICS assumption that self-organization depends on the continual and 'dynamical' interaction of the component parts of a system. The challenge is that knowledge of such orbits of pre-images seems to require knowledge of the closed-form analytical solution of the dynamical systems in question. The concern here was not the solution itself, since after all it can be obtained numerically, but the constants of the "motion" and the integrals of the "motion". Even if we restrict the problem to low-dimensional non-linear systems of ODEs for the species concentrations, the problem re-

---

[3] We should distinguish between 'time evolution', a concept which predates Darwin and refers to time-dependent state changes of dynamical systems, and 'biological evolution' with the familiar Darwinian meaning. In this discussion, when talking about evolution we are referring to time evolution.

mains formidable. In fact, the concept of 'integrability' of differential equations means different things in applied disciplines from what it means in pure mathematics. In applied disciplines, 'integrability' tends to mean that the solution to a particular differential problem can be expressed in terms of elementary, transcendental, or special functions – or at least in terms of quadratures. In pure mathematics, finding a symmetry is tantamount to solving a problem, even though no elementary function exists to express such a solution, or the solution is in a non-invertible implicit (and therefore unusable) form.

A turning point in the project took place when we found a very interesting paper on the concept of the 'quasi-potential' (Zhou et al., 2012), which connected ideas and results from Hamiltonian and Lagrangian dynamics to dissipative biochemical systems and to global stability properties through a stochasticity perspective. While studying the derivation of the Master equation in Van Kampen's text on stochastic processes we realized that stochastic models should be seen as extensions of the mathematical concept of "number" in a rather similar way to how negative numbers, first, and imaginary numbers, subsequently, also generally came to be accepted as valid and "legitimate" by Medieval and Renaissance mathematicians. Stochastic methods based on probability theory, in other words, go well beyond the reduction of complex phenomena to statistical averages, and are able to capture properties of systems that are otherwise beyond the reach of current analytical methods. BIOMICS deliverable (Dini et al., 2016) documents and explains the theories and the mathematics behind the quasi-potential with the aim to advance the analytical and mathematical understanding of dynamical stability.

13.4 Intermediate results: mathematical perspective

13.4.1 Lie group analysis of biochemical systems

The mapping from Lie groups to the SNAGs found in the cascade decomposition of automata turned out to be unworkable. This finding is not based on new mathematical theorems but, rather, on studying and understanding some of the very advanced mathematical theorems developed as part of the monumental effort known as the classification of the finite simple groups. BIOMICS wrote two reports (Figula et al., 2014; Halasi et al., 2013) to explain some parts of this theory, make it accessible to a wider audience of less advanced mathematicians and mathematics students, and to instantiate it within the specific problems addressed by the project. Very briefly, a part of the findings is as follows.

Systems involving more than a single, 1st-order ODE admit, and require for their integration, a Lie group whose Lie algebra is *solvable* with dimension at least equal to the number of ODEs in the system. However, by the Chevalley construction a finite SNAG is obtained from a *simple* Lie algebra, i.e. a Lie algebra tangent to a *simple* Lie group, which by definition does not have nontrivial normal subgroups (is not 'solvable'). In spite of this set-back, we still think there ought to be a connection between the invariant properties of biological (dynamical) systems and the invariant properties of computations of the corresponding finite-state automata, as follows.

Further analysis of the correspondence between finite and continuous groups highlights that the current problem as posed runs into a "level mismatch", in the sense that in the case of ODEs the invariant under the action of a Lie group is the ODE itself (or system thereof), whereas the invariant we wish to capture is associated with the *solution* of the ODE. Whereas the former invariant is visualizable as the 'hull' in the jet-space (Ibragimov, 1992), the latter is associated with the first integral, the level sets of which are the solution curves. As explained in (Bluman and Cole, 1974), the symmetry vector field of a given ODE *does* preserve the family of solution curves (this can in fact be regarded as the condition by which the Lie symmetries are found) but not necessarily the first integral surface.

Although it is well-known that first integrals are not unique, when looked at in this manner this result is highly counter-intuitive – but nevertheless true. It can be explained intuitively by noting that the symmetry condition by which Lie symmetries are derived is a condition on a *differential* structure, the functional form of the system of ODEs whose visualization is the hull, whereas since the solution curves involve an integration step they will satisfy the system up to some constant. Therefore, the Lie transformation that maps the system of ODEs to itself (equivalently, whose jet-space prolongation maps the hull to itself) cannot affect that constant. Since the constant is the value of the level set (i.e. the height) of the first integral surface, and therefore determines which specific solution we are referring to, if these constants for a given family of curves are permuted it follows that the shape of the corresponding surface will change even though the family itself is still the same set of curves as before. This is one way to see why the first integral surface of a given problem is not unique. The only kind of vector field that maps the first integral surface to itself is (necessarily) tangent to the level sets, and for this reason it is known as the 'solution flow'. Put otherwise, a given first integral is an 'absolute invariant' (Bluman and Cole, 1974) of the solution flow vector field, but not of the infinitesimal Lie symmetries that help us arrive at the solution.

In light of the above, a potentially fruitful point of view is to focus on the fundamental properties of groups, i.e. their association with symmetries. Paraphrasing Ian Stewart (Stewart, 1989), (a) a symmetry is an invertible transformation that preserves some aspect of the structure of a mathematical object; and (b) it is easily proven that the set of all such symmetries always forms a group. The converse is that the presence of a group always implies that something is being conserved. Thus, it appears that we need to focus on the computational properties that are conserved by the groups acting on subsets of states in the holonomy decomposition of a biological automaton, and that we need to compare them to the first integrals of the ODEs modelling the same systems in the continuous domain. The (continuous) groups for which the first integrals are absolute invariants correspond to the solution flow rather than to the Lie groups. Clearly, therefore, a necessary condition to make progress in this direction is to work with problems whose complete analytical solution we have achieved. We can report some small but potentially significant progress here, achieved by our University of Debrecen (UD) partner.

Namely, UD has been able to find two linearly independent infinitesimal Lie symmetries (defining a two-dimensional solvable Lie algebra) that solve a large class of systems of two 1st-order ODEs. It is important to clarify that most if not all biochemical systems are obtained from chemical equations as so-called 'rate equations', which is why they are 1st- rather than higher-order. More importantly, these systems of 1st-order ODEs are autonomous, because time does not figure explicitly in chemical reaction equations but only through the rate constants. Therefore, *all* such autonomous systems of ODEs are characterized by a hull that is flat along the time axis. Therefore, any translation along time maps the hull to itself (maps the ODE to itself). Therefore, all such systems admit so-called time-translation symmetries (Dini et al., 2013). These symmetries are trivially found (Dini et al., 2013) and only lead to the solution of the problem for a simple ODE but not for a system. What UD have found in Year 3 of BIOMICS is another Lie symmetry which, together with the time-translation symmetry, form a 2-dimensional Lie group that solves a large class of 2-ODE, 1st-order systems.

13.4.2 Framework for interaction computing

Finite discrete automata models of biological systems such as the lac operon, the Krebs cycle and p53-mdm2 genetic regulation constructed from systems biology models have canonically associated algebraic structures (their transformation semigroups). These contain permutation groups (local substructures exhibiting symmetry) that correspond to 'pools of reversibility'. These natural subsystems are related to one another in a hierarchical manner by the notion of 'weak control'. In (Nehaniv et al., 2015b) we present natural subsystems arising from several biological examples and their weak control hierarchies in detail.

We have shown that SNAGs can occur as the symmetry groups acting in the natural subsystems. BIOMICS explained how SNAGs can work as a basis for computation as they are functionally complete (like the two-element Boolean algebra in logic), reviewed the background and recently demonstrated bounds on the realization of arbitrary finitary functions, and proved new results showing how discrete systems with SNAGs such as the p53-mdm2 genetic regulatory system or ensembles of such systems could exploit this to achieve finitary universal computation.

In Nehaniv et al. (2015b) we introduced interaction machines as ensemble structures that dynamically grow or change their topologies based on internal and external interaction, and outlined how these discrete dynamical systems can implement novel dynamic computational structures (e.g. dynamic cascades for positional number systems). We also applied the interaction machine framework to show how it can naturally model biological systems that change their own structure (e.g. multicellular differentiation with cell division), discussed the interpretation of permutation groups in temporally changing interacting ensembles, and proved that ensembles of the natural subsystems can be arranged according to the weak control hierarchy to emulate a given discrete finite automaton. Moreover, we proved that the last can be achieved with a dynamic cascade, generalizing the holonomy method in algebraic automata theory for finite automata to decomposition using interaction machines. This gives one of the foundational blocks upon which further work on interaction computing can be built.

13.4.3 Category theory and coalgebraic framework

BIOMICS D2.1 (Nehaniv et al., 2014a) explains the functorial constructions and adjoint relations within the categories arising in the study of algebraic structure of continuous and discrete models of cellular pathways and targeting the mathematical models of Interaction Computing, providing mathematical tools to transfer results and constructions between these domains while preserving dynamical stability structure. We have documented the results of our investigation of categories arising in considering dynamical and algebraic aspects of widely used systems biology models. In order to relate discrete and continuous symmetries, this has required the deeper development of understanding the functorial and adjoint relations between these categories as well as various mathematically abstract categories including several categories of labelled directed multigraphs and automata. This investigation has allowed us to characterize categorical constructions in various graph categories and to use these results to understand the analogous constructions in automata-theoretic and sometimes in algebraic categories. Investigations also treat fundamental constructions in transformation representations categories closely related to automata such as partial transformation semigroups and pointed transformation semigroups. New results on the functoriality of the Krohn-Rhodes algebraic automata-theoretic invariants of primes, irreducibles, and complexity of finite dynamical systems are also obtained (as well as on their skeleton orderings).

Moreover, the following are included as new and original mathematical results formulating as categories: systems of ODEs, systems of biochemical reactions and their relationship to categories of automata, transformation semigroups, and Petri nets. The first two categories are likely to have importance in mathematics and systems biology that transcends this project. We rigorously showed that generally the constructions of the automorphism group are not functorial for many important categories. Nevertheless, theorems were proved that show that symmetries can be mapped functorially between various discrete and continuous formulations of models of biochemical and biological systems. Functorial relations established between the mathematical realms studied here were reviewed in a section on Functorial Systems Biology and Symmetries, giving details of the structure-preserving mappings (functors) between interdisciplinary realms, and documenting the homomorphisms between symmetries (automorphism groups) and between endomorphism monoids of these various mathematical realms needed for the understanding of discrete and continuous models of dynamical systems. We also showed a new result that 'internal' automorphism groups of finite dynamical systems yield hierarchical (Krohn-Rhodes) decompositions of these systems using only simpler components already present in the system. Relations between behaviours and their realizations, and coalgebras and monads, and their applications as foundational mathematics for the biological and mathematical basis of interaction computing were also described.

Interaction machines are formulated category-theoretically and coalgebraically in BIOMICS D2.2 (Nehaniv et al., 2015a). We have produced a category theory framework relating the categories arising in the study of cellular metabolic and regulatory pathways/networks as dynamical systems. This is intended to create rigorous functorial formal tools for translating algebraic expressions of dynamical stability to logical specifications, and conversely to functorially generate dynamically stable automata and interaction machines realizing specified behaviour. Moreover BIOMICS has defined various categories of interaction machines algebraically and coalgebraically. The latter is particularly important for the understanding and specification of their behaviours. We formulated morphisms for these objects (interaction machines) for the first time. Even the notion of morphism for automata networks introduced in BIOMICS work as a special case is new. We have explored functorial and adjunction relations between these categories and other domains already mathematically described earlier, as well as describing the existence and structure of finite limits and colimits which allow for the synthesis of new systems from old in a universal manner.

This groundwork allows us to employ the power and conceptual clarification of a category-theoretic approach for which we laid the foundations in BIOMICS deliverables D2.1 and D2.2 for further work in Interaction Computing. We examined the notion of dynamical stability, developing the example of the calcium cycle in cardiac cells. Further formal work carried out in D2.2 establishes methods and tools for the constrained realization of interaction machines and methods of specification that will be useful in the creation of dynamically stable Interaction Computing environments.

13.5 Intermediate results: computer science perspective

During the development of the BIOMICS project, the idea of what or how Interaction Machines should look like was constantly changing. The Interaction Computing Framework presented in Deliverable 3.1.1 (Nehaniv et al., 2014b) described Interaction Machines as dynamically changing cascades of networks of deterministic finite state machines, equipped with feedback functions that enable the transformation of inputs from global inputs to local inputs based on interactions with the environment and local conditions in the dynamic topology. In Deliverable 4.1 (Rothstein and Schreckling, 2015), we modelled Interaction Machines using coalgebras capable of describing the behaviour of black-box Mealy machines with a recursive structure, i.e., inside the coalgebras, we would see a network of other black-box Mealy machines (in coalgebraic representation). Finally, in Deliverable 4.2, we opted to empower Abstract State Machines (ASM) (Börger and Stärk, 2003) so that they could satisfy the requirements of Interaction Computing. This latter model has been iteratively refined to obtain *Abstract State Interaction Machines* (ASIMs), the machine model that we explain in this section.

Adopting ASIMs as the underlying machine model for Interaction Computing has several advantages over other machine models. Most notably is that ASIMs do not require users to anticipate all possible states during specification, unlike deterministic finite automata; instead, ASIMs have a notion of initial state(s) and a program that allows them to update their set of current states. Both the initial state(s) and the program can be conveniently described using ASM rules.

ASIMs, like biological systems, have the capacity to dynamically grow, and to deploy or retract structures and resources in response to ongoing interactions, like the dynamically growing machines described in Deliverable D3.1.1 (Nehaniv et al., 2014b) (published in final form as Nehaniv et al. (2015b)). ASIMs also inherit the notion of *abstract states* from ASMs; *i.e.*, the state of an ASIM is not given just by a name or label, but by a first-order algebraic structure – a Σ-algebra for a signature Σ – which assigns concrete values to the ground terms of functions of the signature Σ. Finally, a practical advantage is that we find open source executions frameworks for ASMs that can be adapted and modified; most notably *CoreASM* (Farahbod and Glaesser, 2011), which supports the design and execution of ASMs.

In this section, we formally introduce Abstract State Interaction Machines (ASIMs) and their components. Using CoreASM's architecture (Farahbod and Glaesser, 2011) as inspiration, we take a modular approach and define a set of internal components for ASIMs, following the requirements set by the new Interaction Computing paradigm. Ultimately, these components are in charge of handling different aspects of the behaviour of ASIMs, and provide support to operations that allow ASIMs to handle algebraic structures, process expressions, and communicate. These components of ASIMs are: the *parser*, the *interpreter*, the *scheduler*, the *mailbox* and the *abstract storage*.

We emphasize that from a computer science point of view the level of innovation achieved is limited, and that the discussion that follows is meant for a broad interdisciplinary audience, in line with the spirit of the project. Thus, the liberal use of analogies and metaphors from biology is meant more to help non-computer scientists understand the functional properties of the components described than to impress a computer science audience. However, the architecture and components described can be seen as starting points for further UCOMP research that builds on the significant interdisciplinary effort already expended by BIOMICS and that has resulted in these new capabilities of ASIMs relative to ASMs:

- Creation and deletion of ASIMs
- Rules (policies) that control the interaction between ASIMs (and help build hierarchies)
- The exchange of rules which can change (rewrite) the behaviour of one or a set of ASIMs

13.5.1 Parser

The parser of an ASIM is the component in charge of categorising pieces of information and determining whether they can be processed and used by the ASIM. The role of the parser is then similar to that of cell membranes: they work as a filter to determine what is useful and what not to the cell, and they allow useful information inside the cell. The parser is also in charge of determining the type of an information element; for instance, the parser determines that the expression {1,2,3} constructs a set, and that the expression [1,2,3] constructs a list, but it also determines that both {1,2,3} and [1,2,3] construct collections.

The parser is the component that enables ASIMs to handle algebraic structures. Extending the parser of an ASIM empowers it with the ability to recognise new structures, ultimately extending its ability to react to and modify these new structures. Parsers are configured by a set of *grammar rules*, which usually refer to the construction formulas of the elements they describe. This implies that is is possible for ASIMs to treat non-well founded structures, like streams of elements (sequences of infinite length), if these streams are represented as pairs $\langle head, tail \rangle$, where *head* is an element and *tail* is another stream (i.e., another head-tail pair).

The job of the parser is complemented by the job of the interpreter, which breaks down the structures recognized by the parser into simpler elements.

13.5.2 Interpreter

Food can be seen as structures that combine simpler, more elementary structures, including fats, carbohydrates, and proteins. The cells in our body need our digestive system to break down food into these elementary structures so that they can be useful. The interpreter of an ASIM is the component that "digests" the algebraic structures recognised by the parser, and returns a set of simpler structures that the ASIM understands and can use to continue its execution. For instance, the interpretation of a rule yields sets of updates to the current state should the rule be executed, the interpretation a policy yields sets of agents that satisfy the policy, and the interpretation of a term yields the value of the term in the algebra described by the state of the ASIM.

Interpreters empower programming languages with the ability to add layers of abstraction, positively affecting their expressivity. Without interpreters, we would have to program computers using low level code. Similarly, without the ASIM interpreter, we would have to define the rules of ASIMs in terms of sets of updates, losing one of the key properties of ASMs: the ability to describe algorithms at the right level of abstraction.

13.5.3 Scheduler

An ASIM may want to modularise its functionalities so that specialised local agents are individually responsible for them. If this is the case, then the ASIM now has the responsibility to coordinate these local agents so that they act appropriately. To fulfil this task, the ASIM uses its *scheduler*.

At a very high level, the scheduler of an ASIM works very similarly to the scheduler of CoreASM: at the beginning of each step, the scheduler evaluates the *scheduling policy* of the ASIM to determine a set of its agents, and then sends a signal to them so that they run their program. For example, the *free-for-all policy*

```
forall a in Agents do schedule a
```

tells the scheduler that all local agents have to run at this step, and the *choose-one policy*

```
choose a in Agents with cond(a) do schedule a
```

tells the scheduler to randomly select only one local agent among those that satisfy the condition `cond`. A detailed explanation of scheduling policies can be found in Morris and Schreckling, 2015, Section 2.3.4. A step for these local agents should be understood as a single execution of their programs; thus, we see that there are two notions of step: a high-level for the ASIM where scheduling and message passing happens, and a low-level for each of the local agents where they run their program.

13.5.4 Mailbox

The mailbox component is one of the new additions to the ASM formalism, which aims to describe ASMs with communication capabilities, i.e., communicating ASMs (see Börger and Schewe (n.d.)). ASIMs naturally inherit the communication capabilities of communicating ASMs. The mailbox of an ASIM empowers the ASIM so that it can send and receive messages to and from other ASIMs, and we think of the mailbox as the interface between the ASIM and its communication environment.

The mailbox manifests in the abstract storage (explained below) as two primitive locations: the monitored *inbox* location and the output *outbox* location. The inbox location updates at each step, and it evaluates to the set of message elements that the ASIM received since it last checked its mailbox. Messages can be placed in the output location for delivery by means of the *send message* rule

$$\text{send } \underbrace{\texttt{Element}}_{\text{body}} \text{ to } \underbrace{\texttt{"asim}_2\texttt{"}}_{\text{receiver}} \text{ with subject } \underbrace{\texttt{String}}_{\text{subject}}.$$

At the moment, we abstract entirely from the process of transporting messages, and we assume reliable and fast communication between ASIMs; however, it is an interesting line of research to consider transport of messages in unreliable communication environments.

13.5.5 Abstract storage

The abstract storage of an ASIM is the component in charge of managing the memory and knowledge, and it inherits its semantics from ASM states and locations (see Börger and Stärk, 2003, Section 2.4). The abstract storage plays a fundamental role in the interpretation of terms, because they usually refer to the value of locations in the abstract storage, which can change over time. For instance, if an ASIM A stored values 2 and 3 in the locations x and y, respectively, and an ASIM B stored values 1 and 1 in x and y, then the interpretation of the term x+y by A is the value 5, while the interpretation of x+y by B is the value 2. Different interpretations not only apply to terms, but also to rules and policies: depending on the state of an ASIM, a rule produces different updates; e.g., a conditional rule yields different updates depending on the truth value of the branching condition. Similarly, a conditional policy may schedule different local agents depending on the truth value of the branching condition.

The *primitive locations* of ASIMs are locations that are always present in the signature of ASIMs. Figure 13.5 shows how the primitive locations *initial, program, policy, inbox* and *outbox* are part of the abstract storage. We use

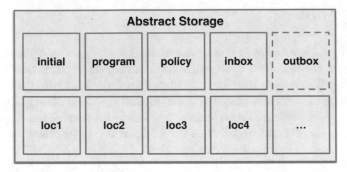

Fig. 13.5 Abstract storage of ASIMs. The primitive locations are *initial, program, policy, inbox* and *outbox*.

these locations to configure ASIMs and affect their behaviour during runtime. For example, during each step of the ASIM, the program is interpreted and evaluated, yielding a set of updates that are applied to the abstract storage, and changing the program location is a way to alter the set of updates to the storage. Similarly, if we change the policy in the policy location, the ASIM will trigger its local agents differently. We now briefly describe the primitive locations.

13.5.5.1 initial

The *initial* location – *initial(self)* – contains a rule that initialises the ASIM. This rule is only executed once, when the ASIM is created. The execution of this rule does not count towards the number of steps that the ASIM has executed. Changing the contents of the initial location does not directly affect the execution of the ASIM.

13.5.5.2 program

The *program* location contains the rule that the ASIM executes every step. We can change the behaviour of an ASIM by changing the contents of its program location; however, this change has to be explicitly carried out by the current program of the ASIM. For example, the programs

```
rule R1 = par x:=x+1 program := R2 endpar
rule R2 = par x:=x−1 program := R1 endpar
```

alter the program location by assigning the other rule when executed. An ASIM "dies" if its program sets the value of its program location to the no-op rule **skip** or to an undefined value.

13.5.5.3 policy

The *policy* location contains the policy that the scheduler of the ASIM uses to select which local agents execute during the current step. Using the program, an ASIM can change its scheduling policy by updating the policy location. Changing the scheduling policy results in the different components being triggered in a different pattern, ultimately affecting the overall behaviour of the ASIM.

13.5.5.4 inbox

The *inbox* location is a monitored (i.e. read-only) location that contains the messages that were received between the previous step and the current step of the ASIM. The mailbox component is the entity responsible for putting the incoming messages in the inbox location so that they are available to the ASIM during execution.

13.5.5.5 outbox

The *outbox* location contains the messages generated by the ASIM during the current step. This location is an output location, so the ASIM cannot read it, but can write to it instead. To write in the outbox location, we use a *send message* rule. This location is accessed by the mailbox, which takes the messages out of it and passes them to the communication environment.

13.6 Conclusions and recommendations

From the point of view of interdisciplinary collaboration, the BIOMICS project made significant progress, but areas were identified where interdisciplinary communication remained limited. **Future research should invest more focused effort at the biology-mathematics and physics-computer science interfaces.** The importance of the roles of physics and of stochastic processes was underestimated. The project would have fared better if there had been more team members in these two areas from the beginning.

In reference to Figure 13.4, while category theory was clearly important in its ability to provide structural-algebraic "maps" of different domains – and structure-preserving functors between them – the construction of adjunctions between structure and behaviour was very difficult in the absence of a full understanding from physics and biology of desirable algebraic properties of automata structure. Furthermore, **an area that would have benefited**

from more focused interdisciplinary collaboration is the coalgebraic perspective and formalism.

The interface between pure mathematics and physics was very fertile. The applied scientists in the project, especially those with a physics background, benefited greatly from the collaboration with algebraists and geometers, both in the discrete algebraic automata and graph theory topics as well as in differential geometry of Lie groups. The applied problems the project was concerned with were of smaller relevance to the pure mathematicians, but in any case the meetings were always interesting and productive for all participants and **a foundation was laid upon which further collaborative projects in the general UCOMP area could be built, especially with the analysts and their work on SDEs.**

Another project activity that was very successful was the collaboration between mathematics and computer science, in particular around the development of extensions to the ASMs in the form of the ASIMs. The most significant and impressive aspect of this collaboration was that the topics of collaboration spanned from the most abstract category theory and coalgebraic formalizations to the most applied software engineering tools and techniques, specification languages, and architectural considerations. **Future UCOMP research should extend this extremely successful interaction, because the solid basis upon which ASIMs have been built provides a mathematically rigorous specification and software engineering environment that can accept any mathematically formalizable models and specifications from other disciplines such as biology and physics.**

The problem that remained most impervious to analysis, formalization, and understanding was dynamical stability as a mathematically formalizable foundation of self-organizing behaviour of open systems composed of a variable number of interacting components. However, the quasi-potential of meta-stable biochemical systems associated with a variational formulation of their SDE models did open new perspectives on dynamical systems that we had not expected. **An area of future UCOMP research that deserves more attention is the strengthening of the formal and theoretical connections between the quasi-potential, the control theory of the Hamilton-Jacobi-Bellman equation, and the symmetry analysis of dynamical systems, in particular as they relate to Noether's theorem and the search for conserved quantities.** Our hunch remains that it should be possible to express dynamical stability as some kind of generalization of such conserved quantities, probably within a stochastic formulation.

References

Bellman, R. E. (1957). *Dynamic Programming*. Princeton University Press.

Bluman, G. W. and J. D. Cole (1974). *Similarity Methods for Differential Equations*. Springer.

Börger, E. and R. Stärk (2003). *Abstract State Machines: A Method for High-Level System Design and Analysis*. Springer.

Börger, Egon and Klaus-Dieter Schewe (n.d.). *Communication in Abstract State Machines*. (in preparation).

Dini, P., F. Karimi, C. Nehaniv, Á. Bonivárt, G. Horváth, Z. Muzsnay, Á. Figula, T. Milkovszki, A. J. Munro, and F. Ruzsnavszky (2016). *D3.2: Further Analysis of Cellular Pathways*. BIOMICS Deliverable, European Commission. URL: biomicsproject.eu/file-repository/category/11-public-files-deliverables.

Dini, P., C. L. Nehaniv, M. J. Schilstra, F. Karimi, G. Horváth, Z. Muzsnay, K. Christodoulides, Á. Bonivárt, N. Y. den Breems, A. J. Munro, and A. Egri-Nagy (2013). *D1.1.1: Tractable Dynamical and Biological Systems for Numerical Discrete, and Lie Group Analysis*. BIOMICS Deliverable, European Commission. URL: biomicsproject.eu/file-repository/category/11-public-files-deliverables.

Farahbod, Roozbeh and Uwe Glaesser (2011). "The CoreASM Modeling Framework". *Softw. Pract. Exper.* 41(2):167–178.

Figula, Á., Z. Halasi, G. Horváth, and K. Podoski (2014). *D1.3.2: Examples Based on the Chevalley Correspondence between Lie Groups and SNAGs*. BIOMICS. URL: www.biomicsproject.eu.

Freidlin, M. I. and A. D. Wentzell (1998). *Random Perturbations of Dynamical Systems*. Springer.

Halasi, Z., G. Horváth, and K. Podoski (2013). *D1.3.1: Introduction to the Chevalley Correspondence between Lie Groups and SNAGs*. BIOMICS. URL: www.biomicsproject.eu.

Horsman, C., Susan Stepney, R. Wagner, and Viv Kendon (2014). "When does a physical system compute?" *Proceedings of the Royal Society A* 470(2169):20140182.

Ibragimov, N. K. (1992). "Group analysis of ordinary differential equations and the invariance principle in mathematical physics (for the 150th anniversary of Sophus Lie)". *Russian Mathematical Surveys* 47(4):89–156.

Krohn, K. and J. Rhodes (1965). "Algebraic Theory of Machines. I. Prime Decomposition Theorem for Finite Semigroups and Machines". *Transactions of the American Mathematical Society* 116:450–464.

Morris, Eric Rothstein and Daniel Schreckling (2015). *D4.2: Human-readable, Behaviour-based Interaction Computing Specification Language*. BIOMICS deliverable, European Commission. URL: www.biomicsproject.eu.

Nehaniv, C. L., F. Karimi, E. Rothstein, and P. Dini (2015a). *D2.2: Constrained Realization of Stable Dynamical Organizations, Logic, and Interaction Machines.* BIOMICS Deliverable, European Commission. URL: biomicsproject.eu/file-repository/category/11-public-files-deliverables.

Nehaniv, C. L., J. Rhodes, A. Egri-Nagy, P. Dini, E. Rothstein Morris, G. Horváth, F. Karimi, D. Schreckling, and M. J. Schilstra (2015b). "Symmetry structure in discrete models of biochemical systems: natural subsystems and the weak control hierarchy in a new model of computation driven by interactions". *Philosophical Transactions of the Royal Society A* 373:20140223.

Nehaniv, C., F. Karimi, and D. Schreckling (2014a). *D2.1: Functors and Adjoints for Discrete and Continuous Dynamical Cellular Systems Symmetries.* BIOMICS. URL: www.biomicsproject.eu.

Nehaniv, Chrystopher L., John Rhodes, Attila Egri-Nagy, Paolo Dini, Eric Rothstein Morris, Gábor Horváth, Fariba Karimi, Daniel Schreckling, and Maria J. Schilstra (2014b). *D3.1.1: Mathematical Framework for Interaction Computing.* BIOMICS deliverable, European Commission. URL: www.biomicsproject.eu.

Rothstein, E. and D. Schreckling (2015). *D4.1: Candidate for a (Co)algebraic Interaction Computing Specification Language.* BIOMICS Deliverable, European Commission. URL: biomicsproject.eu/file-repository/category/11-public-files-deliverables.

Stewart, I. (1989). *Galois Theory.* London: Chapman and Hall.

Zeiger, H. P. (1967). "Cascade synthesis of finite-state machines". *Information and Control* 10(4):plus erratum, 419–433.

Zhou, X. J., M. D. S. Aliyu, E. Aurell, and S. Huang (2012). "Quasi-potential landscape in complex multi-stable systems". *Journal of the Royal Society Interface* 9:3539–3553.

Chapter 14
Reservoir Computing with Computational Matter

Zoran Konkoli, Stefano Nichele, Matthew Dale, and Susan Stepney

Abstract The reservoir computing paradigm of information processing has emerged as a natural response to the problem of training recurrent neural networks. It has been realized that the training phase can be avoided provided a network has some well-defined properties, e.g. the echo state property. This idea has been generalized to arbitrary artificial dynamical systems. In principle, any dynamical system could be used for advanced information processing applications provided that such a system has the separation and the approximation property. To carry out this idea in practice, the only auxiliary equipment that is needed is a simple read-out layer that can be used to access the internal states of the system. In the following, several applications scenarios of this generic idea are discussed, together with some related engineering aspects. We cover both practical problems one might meet when trying to implement the idea, and discuss several strategies of solving such problems.

14.1 Introduction

What is reservoir computing? The term is not easy to define as this paradigm of computation features several concepts that originate from various scientific disciplines, physics, mathematics, computer science, philosophy, and information processing engineering. The term 'reservoir computing' servers as a global tag that marks several related but still somewhat different points of view. Just to illustrate the point, the question, what is a reservoir? probably has many answers depending on whom one asks.

Perhaps the easiest way to gain a deeper understanding of what reservoir computing is, is to look back and analyse how it all started. Reservoir computing was suggested independently by two groups, both focusing on a distinct information processing feature of recurrent neural networks, namely the neural network training issue. In the first instance, reservoir computing

© Springer International Publishing AG, part of Springer Nature 2018
S. Stepney et al. (eds.), *Computational Matter*, Natural Computing Series,
https://doi.org/10.1007/978-3-319-65826-1_14

emerged as a practical training procedure for recurrent neural networks: Echo state networks, ESN (Jaeger and Haas, 2004; Jaeger, 2001b). In the second instance, it emerged as a model of computation: Liquid State Machines, LSM (Maass et al., 2002; Natschläger et al., 2002), suggested to describe how a recurrent neural network can process a multi-modal input from a changing environment in real time. Both studies emphasised, either implicitly or explicitly, the concept of the reservoir as a high dimensional dynamical system with an extremely rich space of internal states.

The LSM is a model of computation with, in principle, universal expressive power. The model can be used to describe a class of machines that operate on continuous time series data. The model has been formalised in rigorous mathematical terms, e.g. on the same footing as the Turing machine concept. The LSM model has universal expressive power provided the space of time series signals is restricted (e.g. to continuous and bounded signals), and provided the machines have some special properties (e.g. the fading memory property).

Taken together, the simplest possible answer to the original question might be that reservoir computing is a particular model of computation, where the reservoir component is realized by a very high dimensional non-autonomous (open) dynamical system (Strogatz, 1994) with a rich space of internal states. Such dynamical systems can process information and perform computations (Dambre et al., 2012; Stepney, 2012). The computation being performed can be observed as a projection of the trajectory the system takes through its state space. However, one should keep in mind that there are numerous issues that need to be addressed given the rather broad scope of the definition. These issues are discussed in the following. For anybody interested in reservoir computing, the material presented in this chapter should provide sufficient information to further investigate these issues in detail.

Thus the chapter is organised as follows. First a brief description of reservoir computing is provided in Sect. 14.2, where the ESN concept and LSM are introduced. LSM is discussed very briefly. The main purpose behind this section is to introduce the main building blocks of reservoir computing. Sect. 14.3 contains a discussion regarding the question: what is a good reservoir? This is an important conceptual question. Various physical reservoirs are discussed in Sect. 14.4, which contains an overview of several up-to-date hardware realisations of the reservoir computing concept. Sect. 14.5 discusses an example of a meta-reservoir, where the reservoir is realised not by a physical system, but as an abstraction of a physical system (using cellular automata). This is followed by a discussion on using arbitrary materials in the reservoir computing context, in Sect. 14.6. The concluding Sect. 14.7 contains some important highlights.

14.2 Reservoir computing essentials

14.2.1 Echo state networks: the dynamics

Echo state networks is a term that describes a supervised learning principle for recurrent neural networks (Jaeger, 2007; Jaeger and Haas, 2004; Jaeger, 2001b; Lukoševičius and Jaeger, 2009; Lukoševičius et al., 2012; Yildiz et al., 2012). The network dynamics is usually modelled as follows. Assume that the internal state of the system can be described by a vector variable $x \in \mathbb{R}^n$ where $\mathbb{R}$ is the set of real numbers. Assume that time is discrete $t = \hat{t}\tau$ with $\hat{t} \in \mathbb{Z}$ where $\mathbb{Z}$ is the set of integers, $\mathbb{Z} \equiv \{\cdots, -2, -1, 0, 1, 2, \cdots\}$.

Conceptually, the fact that time extends infinitely in the past is important. τ denotes an arbitrary but fixed time scale. In the following, to simplify the notation the hat symbol is omitted, and t is used instead of $\hat{t}$. The state of the system is updated at every time step as

$$x_t = f(W x_{t-1} + V u_t) \equiv F(x_{t-1}, u_t) \tag{14.1}$$

where: $u_t \in \mathbb{R}^m$ are inputs at each time step; matrices W and V have dimensions $n \times n$ and $n \times m$ respectively.

The above mapping implicitly defines a reservoir F. The reservoir is also equipped with a read-out layer y. In mathematical terms this read-out layer is represented as

$$y_t = \psi(x_t) \tag{14.2}$$

where $y_t \in \mathbb{R}^l$ denotes the output vector and ψ denotes a suitably chosen "wrapper" function.

14.2.2 Echo state networks: the key experimental insight

The key idea that motivated the idea of the reservoir was the realisation that if the structure of a recurrent neural network is rich enough then there is no need to train the full network. There is no need to adjust matrix W. Instead, it is sufficient to train *only* the read-out layer ψ.

This insight has important practical implications since, in general, recurrent neural networks are not easy to train. The question is whether the approach can be generalised to other dynamical systems. It can; however, it cannot be used to train just any network, or just any dynamical system. Only systems that posses some well-defined properties can be trained in such a way. One of the key properties that such a system must have is the *echo state property*.

Intuitively, systems with the echo state property behave in a special way under arbitrary input. If the dynamics of the system is highly non-linear then an arbitrary input will 'excite' the system in the sense that different regions of the configuration space will be populated on different inputs. Thus the internal state of the system can be seen as a *unique* transform of the input. In this sense the system has a finite memory of the input it has experienced up to a certain point in time. This is an intuitive definition of the echo state property. Earlier inputs 'echo' in the system for a finite amount of time. The functionality of the read-out layer is simply to 'pick' the result of the computation by inspecting whether a particular region of the configuration space is populated. In technical terms this can be done by using simple linear regression.

In this construction the recurrent neural network acts as a reservoir of states. It is clear from the construction that in principle any dynamical system might be used for computation. It is intuitively clear that the complexity of the function computed depends on the properties of a reservoir used to implement the setup. In this context, a question of great practical importance is which systems are good reservoirs? This key question, alas, is not easy to answer. There are some generic guidelines but it is very hard for a given system to judge whether it has the echo state property or not. For example, as an illustration, consider the following.

Every dynamical system should have something that resembles the echo state. After all, majority of dynamical system can be driven by an external input. When exposed to an external influence, a system will change its state depending on what it has 'experienced'. This motivates the following key question:

> In what way is the echo state property special and why   (14.3)
> would it guarantee information processing abilities?

Perhaps the easiest way to understand the issue is to look back to the original mathematical formulation.

14.2.3 The echo state property

Since the original publication (Jaeger, 2001b) that discusses the echo state property and its importance in detail, refinements of the original mathematical theorem have occurred, e.g. Yildiz et al. (2012), where constantly new insights are being added. It seems that the echo state property is not easy to formalise mathematically.

The definition of the echo state property:

The reservoir has the echo state property iff there exists a function $\mathcal{E}$ such that

$$x_t = \mathcal{E}(u_t, u_{t-1}, u_{t-2}, \cdots, u_{-\infty}) \qquad (14.4)$$

Once the explicit definition of the echo state property has been given, it is timely to re-visit the key question posed in (14.3). For example, assume that x describes the internal degrees of freedom of a brick and that the aim is, against all odds, to turn the brick into a reservoir computer. While it is hard to engineer an input that might affect the brick, let us, for the sake of the discussion, assume that the brick has been placed into an oven. Then an input can consist of heating it up according to arbitrary temperature variations, $u_t \in \mathbb{R}^1$. Assume that the read-out interface measures the amount of internal energy stored in the brick, $y_t \in \mathbb{R}^1$. This device converts a time series consisting of arbitrary temperature values to a single real number (the internal energy of the system expressed in arbitrary units). Does the system just defined has the echo state property or not? More specifically, can one define $\mathcal{E}$ for such a system?

Alas, such questions do not have an easy or a straight forward answer. There is no generic recipe that one can use to answer such questions. For example, the question has been addressed when the reservoir consist of a recurrent neural networks (Jaeger, 2007; Jaeger and Haas, 2004; Jaeger, 2001b; Lukoševičius and Jaeger, 2009; Lukoševičius et al., 2012; Yildiz et al., 2012). Some conditions are known but in general the issue is still open for further analysis.

14.2.4 Why is the echo state property not realised trivially?

The present state of the network is an echo of all previous inputs, as suggested by Jaeger (2001b). Note that x is not present in the list of arguments. There is an immediate objection to this formula. The number of arguments is infinite, what good is it? Another question one can ask is: The formula follows more or less automatically from the construction, what is so special about it? For example, one could apply iteratively Eq. 14.1 and conclude that iterating a finite number number of times gives

$$x_t = H^{(h)}(u_t, u_{t-1}, u_{t-2}, \cdots, u_{t-h+1}; x_{t-h}) \qquad (14.5)$$

where $H^{(h)}$ is always known and can be easily found. For example after two iterations

$$H^{(2)} = F(F(x_{t-2}, u_{t-1}), u_t) \qquad (14.6)$$

or after three iterations

$$H^{(3)} = F(F(F(x_{t-3}, u_{t-2}), u_{t-1}), u_t) \qquad (14.7)$$

Provided the limit $h \to \infty$ can be safely taken it follows that

$$\mathcal{E} = \lim_{h \to \infty} H^{(h)} \qquad (14.8)$$

Such limits cannot be taken *a priori* and accordingly the existence of Eq. 14.4 cannot be guaranteed. However, this limit can be taken for systems with echo state property.

There is a way of stating the echo state property in a less intuitive way with more mathematical rigour, as detailed by Jaeger (2001b). One simply introduces the notion of equivalent reservoir state and input sequences, which avoids the infinity argument. However, this is not discussed here. The main point is that this rather abstract echo state property guarantees that other features that are more important from the practical point are satisfied. For example, if the system has the echo state property then in some approximative sense the infinite sequence in Eq. 14.4 can be truncated and

$$x_t \approx \tilde{\mathcal{E}}(u_t, u_{t-1}, u_{t-2}, \cdots, u_{t-h+1}) \qquad (14.9)$$

which is the property that is more important from a practical information processing point of view. The internal state of the system depends on the immediate history, but not too distant history. Further, note that there is no dependence on the "initial" condition in the past x_{t-h}. This implies that such systems can be used for real-time (on-line) computation.

14.3 Metrics of reservoir quality

In the Reservoir Computing literature a few principle quantitative measures for examining the computational characteristics of a reservoir exist, building on Bertschinger and Natschläger (2004)'s work with recurrent neural networks and Legenstein and Maass (2007b)'s investigations into computational power in dynamical systems and neural circuits. These, what we have labelled "reservoir metrics", can be divided into: (a) measuring reservoir dynamics; and (b) estimating the diversity of the projected feature space, and therefore the efficiency of the kernel-style readout process. Another informative measurement is the short-term Memory Capacity of a reservoir introduced by Jaeger (2001a).

An intriguing aspect of these metrics is that they tend to strongly correlate, implying that no metric is mutually exclusive of the other. This suggest that general reservoir performance could increase if the metrics were used to reduce the overall search space for finding suitable reservoirs.

Reservoir dynamics are typically focused on measures of criticality, or chaotic behaviour, linking directly to the theory that being near/at the "edge of chaos" can produce advantageous and computationally expressive properties (Langton, 1990). For simulated reservoirs this is typically done through the empirical estimation of the Lyapunov exponents (LE) for a dynamical system (Bertschinger and Natschläger, 2004; Chrol-Cannon and Jin, 2014; Legenstein and Maass, 2007b; Verstraeten and Schrauwen, 2009).

To calculate the Lyapunov Exponents, and quantify a systems criticality, one can measure the divergence between two close trajectories due to some small perturbation.

Many investigations commonly evaluate the largest (maximal) Lyapunov exponent as the largest tends to dominate (Gibbons, 2010; Rosenstein et al., 1993). In general, a system with a maximal Lyapunov exponent $\lambda \approx 0$ is somewhere near the *edge of chaos*. A system with $\lambda > 0$ features largely chaotic behaviour and an ordered, or sub-critical, system has an LE of $\lambda < 0$.

Other interpretations and methods also exist, such as Verstraeten and Schrauwen (2009)'s examination of the local Lyapunov spectrum and the Jacobian of the reservoir around a particular point in the phase space – rather than the global predictability of the system. Other more recent dynamic measures include the use of mean-field theory to create a "self-consistent statistical description of the reservoir dynamics" based on Lyapunov stability analysis (Massar and Massar, 2013; Wainrib and Galtier, 2016).

The property known as the "Kernel quality" evaluates a reservoir's ability to produce diverse and complex mappings of the driving input stream that can consequently increase the classification performance of a linear decision-hyperplane (Legenstein and Maass, 2007a).

Kernel quality, also known as the *linear separation property*, as stated in Sect. 14.6.1, has an accompanying metric referred to as the *generalisation capability* of a reservoir. The two properties are closely coupled and can be measured using a similar ranking mechanism. The first, kernel quality, measures a reservoir's ability to produce diverse reservoir states given significantly different input streams. The second measures the reservoir's capability to generalise given similar input streams with respect to a target function.

Both measurements can be carried out using the method in Büsing et al. (2010), by computing the rank r of an $n \times m$ matrix M, with the two methods differing only in the selection of m input streams $u_i, ..., u_m$, i.e. input streams being largely different or of similar type/class. Büsing et al. (2010) explain that a good reservoir should possess a high kernel quality and a low generalisation rank. Both Chrol-Cannon and Jin (2014) and Büsing et al. (2010) show that the maximal Lyapunov exponent and the kernel quality frequently correlate.

Class separation is another metric directly linked to phase space diversity. Separation, as a result of different classes of input stimuli, is measured as the average distance between resulting states, given the assumption that significantly different inputs should generate significantly different reservoir

states (Chrol-Cannon and Jin, 2014; Norton and Ventura, 2010). Konkoli and
Wendin (2014) offer another method for identifying reservoir quality by measuring the dissimilarity between output states and a linear combination of
the inputs, i.e. determining if the non-linear frequency response of a network
cannot be approximated by a linear mixture of delayed inputs.

Measuring the short-term memory capacity of a reservoir was first outlined
by Jaeger (2001a) as a quantitative measurement to observe the echo state
property.

To determine the memory capacity of a reservoir one should measure how
many delayed versions of the input $u(n-k)$ the outputs can recall or recover
with precision. As Jaeger describes, using the equation in 14.10, memory
capacity can be measured by how much variance of the delayed input can
be recovered, summed over all delays (Jaeger, 2001a). This is carried out
by training individual output units to recall the input at time k with the
maximum capacity MC of an N node reservoir typically bounded by its size,
i.e. $MC \leq N$, although this may not hold true for a physical reservoir.

$$MC = \sum_{k=1}^{\infty} MC_k = \sum_{k=1}^{\infty} \frac{cov^2(u(n-k), y(n))}{\sigma^2(u(n))\sigma^2(y(n))} \qquad (14.10)$$

The MC measurement is typically in harmony with the dynamic behaviour
of the system. The short-term capacity can be helpful in identifying the
boundaries between static structure that provides memory, and the point
of complex dynamics that gives us processing. As such, one might expect a
chaotic system to lose information regarding previous inputs at a faster rate
and a more ordered regime to increase input retention.

14.4 Physical reservoirs

14.4.1 Reservoirs in hardware

Any type of high-dimensional dynamical system with the right dynamic properties could potentially be used for reservoir computing. Fernando and Sojakka (2003) demonstrate that waves produced on the surface of a bucket of
water can be used to solve nonlinear problems, e.g. XOR and speech recognition, and a simple readout layer is be enough to accomplish correct classification. Jones et al. (2007) succeed in using the Gene Regulatory Network of an
Escherichia coli bacterium as an LSM and successfully solve the XOR problem and the signal phase discrimination problem. Another implementation of
an ESN in a Gene Regulatory System is presented by Dai (2004). The work
of Jones et al. (2007) and Dai (2004) indicates that RC may be implemented
within gene regulatory networks in a cell.

Another unconventional system recently applied to reservoir computing is the *Atomic Switch Network*. This approach focuses on the electrical and chemical properties of a physical memristive material, in an attempt to mimic the vast complexity, emergent dynamics, and connectivity of the brain. To create the highly-interconnected networks of silver nanowires a reaction is induced, generating a bottom-up, self-assembly process. Through the triggered electrochemical reaction, coated copper seed nucleation sites spawn large quantities of silver nanowires of various lengths. Large random networks form, creating crossbar junctions between nanowires. When exposed to gaseous sulphur these turn to $Ag|Ag_2S|Ag$ nanoscale metal-insulator-metal (MIM) junctions. To establish the functional memristive junctions (Atomic Switches) an external activation (a bias voltage) is supplied, generating a temporary resistance drop.

The emergent behaviour and dynamics of ASNs can be observed through fluctuations in network conductivity, a result of spontaneous switching between discrete metastable resistance states. These locally excited regions cause cascading changes in resistance throughout the network, providing its heterogeneous behaviour. Moreover, the non-linear responses to resistive switching are reported to result in higher harmonic generation (HHG), which is also suggested as a useful measure for quantitatively evaluating reservoir dynamics (Sillin et al., 2013).

A clear advantage of the ASN technique is that it allows some degree of regulation in fabrication, a scalable methodology and further control through "resistance control" training (Stieg et al., 2014). For example, varying the parameters of the nucleation sites (copper seeds) can alter the network structure and therefore the substrates dynamics. The relative size, numbers and pitch of copper seeds can determine the length of wires, forming distant connections or confining spatial regions to dendrite-like structures, thus ultimately defining the density of connections (Sillin et al., 2013).

ASNs appear to be natural candidates for reservoir computing as they form high-dimensional recurrent networks with many controllable parameters. So far, they have been used in the context of reservoir computing on only one task, as far as we are aware. A new scaled-up ASN system proposed by Aguilera et al. (2015) should provide more clarification on the advantages of using ASNs as reservoirs. The new system features 128 input/outputs compared to the original 16 used by Sillin et al. (2013) and Stieg et al. (2014), increasing the number of possible points to extract electrical measurements.

Arguably the most competitive physical reservoirs currently available are the optoelectronic and photonic reservoirs (Appeltant et al., 2011; Larger et al., 2012; Vandoorne et al., 2011; Vandoorne et al., 2014). In the Appeltant et al. (2011) approach, shown in Figure 14.1, a new methodology is used, replacing a physical network of nodes with a *single* non-linear node and a delay line. By implementing the network as a delay system, only one node is needed to mimic a much larger network. This is done by creating *virtual* nodes (separated by time) within the delay line using time-multiplexing at the input; a combination of sample and hold operations mixed with an additional input mask.

The new methodology is simple and extremely fast in implementation, but inevitably restricts the system to serial processing (via the delay loop), removing the traditional parallelism of reservoir networks. The limit to computational speed therefore depends on the state update given by the length of the delay line. Another issue is that the real-valued networks created in these fibre-based systems lack the use of phase information, and therefore, restrict themselves to a much smaller possible state space when using light (Vandoorne et al., 2014).

The *nanophotonic* chip represents an alternative method, exploiting the propagation of light through silicon and more closely resembling the classical neural network structure.

This technique uses coherent light, instead of incoherent in the fibre-based example, applying both amplitude and phase of light to provide a state space that can feature both real and complex numbers. Vandoorne et al. (2011) combine active components such as optical amplifiers to create the reservoir dynamics on chip, requiring an undesirable amount of power given the scale of the system.

A new passive chip proposed by Vandoorne et al. (2014) significantly overcomes many of these drawbacks. The passive chip comprises of photonic crystals with a periodic nanostructure that restricts the propagation of certain frequencies of light known as the band gap. Adding a line defect to the crystal produces a photonic crystal waveguide, effectively a process by which light is forced between the defect. Cavities are then created along the line defect to create optical "resonators" by trapping light. The resonators are combined together in a matrix-style network (e.g. 4×4) to form a reservoir open to various training and readout mechanisms. For example, Vandoorne et al. (2014) uses a linear passive photonic reservoir, and the non-linearity is added at the readout through the inherent non-linearity of the measuring photo-detectors.

This new photonic architecture provides a very power efficient alternative, using only the power provided at the input. It can also easily integrate into traditional CMOS architectures.

14.4.2 Searching for material reservoirs

Evolution *in materio* (EiM) aims to 'program' matter by using a heuristic search to find configurations of physical signals that cause a material to carry out desired transformations of inputs to outputs (Miller et al., 2014). As yet, the field of EiM has not emphasised or intentionally exploited temporal or memory-related phenomena in the materials used. It tends to use highly specific mappings from input data to applied material inputs. In addition, it

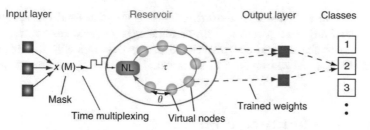

Fig. 14.1 A single non-linear node with delayed feedback (Appeltant et al., 2011). A new system derived from delay systems theory where virtual nodes are created in the delay loop τ to represent the hidden layer. The number of virtual nodes N is separated by time θ given by $\theta = \tau/N$.

uses specific mappings from measured outputs (sampled and held in buffers) to the desired outputs specified in the computational problem.

Recent work has used EiM to evolve task-specific reservoirs for a variety of computational tasks (Dale et al., 2016a; Dale et al., 2016b; Dale et al., 2017). Reservoir computing appears to offer a standard methodology for extracting computation which can be applied to materials directly, thus avoiding the requirement for new mapping definitions for different tasks. This provides a universal way to obtain a specific response from a material using little more than gradient descent.

Matter can feature enormous complexity, and compared to deterministic simulated networks can arguably exhibit a much larger and diverse state space.

As all conceptual reservoirs try to harness richness, some material systems may appear to be natural candidates (e.g, an ASN or a bucket of water, Sect. 14.4.1). However, a material system under no *additional* external influence may struggle to create any desirable reservoir behaviour. An adaptation of the evolution-in-materio methodology could be used to manipulate many diverse material systems into being good reservoirs. Therefore, an evolutionary search would aim to discover natural reservoir characteristics that may only be observable under unique material stimuli.

The metrics discussed in Sect. 14.3 offer a unique opportunity to discover specific types of reservoirs (both in materials and beyond), or form the basis of a *generic* reservoir favourable across all metrics. Therefore, particularly in the context of evolved material reservoirs, instead of using the metrics to understand why certain reservoirs are more computationally significant than others we can use the measures as evolutionary incentives.

A *generic* reservoir could contain many beneficial information processing characteristics, suggesting a somewhat generalisable system is plausible. However, many of the metrics require some level of compromise, such as wanting the contradicting properties of both highly nonlinear dynamics and a large memory capacity. For this reason, one might instead use metric-*guided* reservoirs in a practical sense as evolvable 'signposts' used to reduce the *con-*

figuration search space of a material. This is hypothesised on the principle that an evolved configuration – implementing a generic reservoir – will exhibit much of the wanted computational properties, but will possibly require an additional local search to find an optimal reservoir for different tasks.

14.4.3 The brain as a reservoir

The conjecture that a simple linear classifier can extract complex computation from distributed neuronal activity is clearly poignant to physical processes that occur within the brain. The brain encompasses a mass of highly complex architectures with specialised regions undergoing different tasks. Ultimately, one might perhaps ask: Is RC a suitable metaphor for brain-like computing, or is it just another way of utilizing neural networks and make them more trainable?

It has been shown that regions such as the primary visual and auditory cortex can operate in a similar fashion to a reservoir when an additional readout is applied. Nikolic et al. (2006) use the primary visual cortex of a cat to test whether a simple linear classier can extract information related to visual stimuli. Under anesthesia, probes are placed into multiple architectural levels within the cortex to simultaneously record different neuronal activity. The visual stimuli used come in the form of different alphabetical letters to induce spike train activity. It was discovered that:

> the system's memory for the past stimulation is not necessarily erased by the presentation of a new stimulus, but it is instead possible to extract information about multiple stimuli simultaneously.

This implies that multiple sources of information, including that of previous states (i.e. memory) are superimposed upon the network. This reportedly allows XOR classification on the input through linear classifier extraction, directly showing that this region by itself is performing nonlinear computation. Klampfl et al. (2009) show similar behaviour within the primary auditory cortex in response to tone sequences.

If we think about regions of the brain acting as reservoirs from an evolutionary standpoint, how do these specialised parts evolve if they are not simply learned? Is the proposed methodology discussed in Sect. 14.4.2 utilising a similar mechanism, evolving physical states through electro-chemical stimulation, or network structure, to create an abundance of computationally expressive activity to which other decoding/readout neurons can extract computation?

A clear advantage the brain has compared to the current hardware-based reservoirs is its increased dimensionality. Both fractal-networks (Atomic Switches Networks) and the materials explored in evolution-in-materio are currently restricted to both a 2-dimensional substrate and observation method, i.e. electrode recordings typically on one planar surface. Increasing dimensionality (both in structure and measurement) allows greater communication between non-neighboring elements and allows access to more spatial points within the network where interesting behaviour may occur.

Hierarchical and modular reservoirs more closely resemble architectures of the brain and are briefly discussed and summarised by Lukoševičius and Jaeger (2009). Creating a hierarchical/modular reservoir could possibly lessen the dimensionality problem in a physical system. Having layers of networks, or multiple material sub-systems, should provide a more exploitable and expressive state space where layers/modules can contain different usable features, such as varying internal timescales and memory properties.

14.5 Cellular automata as reservoir

In this section we briefly introduce cellular automata (CA) and show that certain types of CA can be used for reservoir computing. Inputs are mapped into the CA initial state and nonlinear computation is performed by the CA while evolved for a certain number of time steps. A discussion of potential uses and advantaged of reservoir computing using cellular automata is given.

14.5.1 Cellular automata

Cellular automata, originally studied by von Neumann in the 1940s (von Neumann, 1966), are idealised versions of parallel and decentralised computing systems, based on a myriad of small and unreliable components called cells. Even if a single cell itself can do very little, the emergent behavior of the whole system is capable to obtain complex dynamics. In CA each cell can only communicate with a few other cells, most or all of which are physically close (neighbours). One implication of this principle is that there is no central controller; no one cell has a global view of the entire system.

Formally, a cellular automaton is a countable discrete array of cells i with a discrete-time update rule Φ that executes in parallel on local neighbourhoods of a specified radius r. In every time step the cells allow values in a finite alphabet A of symbols: $\sigma_t^i \in \{0, 1, \ldots, k-1\} \equiv A$. The local update rule is $\sigma_{t+1}^i = \Phi\left(\sigma_t^{i-r}, \ldots, \sigma_t^{i+r}\right)$. At time t, the state s_t of the cellular automaton is the configuration of the finite or infinite spatial array: $s_t \in A^N$, where A^N is the set of all possible cell value permutations on a lattice of size N. The CA global update rule $\Phi : A^N \to A^N$ executes Φ in parallel to all sites in the lattice: $s_t = \Phi(s_{t-1})$. For finite N, the boundary cells are usually dealt with by having the whole lattice wrap around into a torus, thus boundary cells are connected to "adjacent" cells on the opposite boundary.

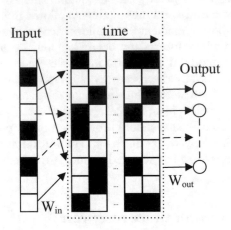

Fig. 14.2 Elementary cellular automaton space-time used as reservoir. Adapted from Yilmaz (2015).

Some cellular automata rules are proven to be Turing complete, i.e. computationally universal. Examples are the elementary rule 110 (Cook, 2004), Conway's Game of Life (Berlekamp et al., 1982), and the X-rule (Soto and Wuensche, 2015). Wolfram (1984) classifies rules into four classes: homogeneous, oscillating, chaotic, and complex. The rules in this last class produce long-lived complex localized structures. Langton (1990) coins the term "edge of chaos" to identify a region in the CA rule space where there is a phase transition between ordered and chaotic dynamics. Turing-complete rules are found in this area.

14.5.2 CA as reservoir

It has been proposed that cellular automata may be used as reservoir of dynamical systems (Yilmaz, 2014; Yilmaz, 2015). The input layer is mapped to cellular automata cells and projected into an expressive and discriminating space. The cellular automata evolution produces a space-time set of the CA state space that can be used as reservoir. The CA size should reflect the size of the input features. Yilmaz (2014) propose two possible inputs schemes, one where each cell in the cellular automaton receives a weighted sum of the input dimensions, and one where each dimension is mapped randomly to one automaton cell. The only design effort is the choice of the CA rule. In Figure 14.2, a possible implementation of CA space-time used as reservoir is shown.

Cellular automata time evolution intrinsically possesses a very rich computational representation, in particular for rules that produce dynamics at the edge-of-chaos. If only the final converged CA-state is used, such a rich computational representation is not fully exploited. For this reason, the entire time evolution of the CA is typically used as the reservoir of nonlinear computation. In Yilmaz (2015), 5-bit and 20-bit memory problems are solved with the Game of Life rule and with elementary one-dimensional binary rules.

There are several advantages on using CA over classical RNN reservoir, both theoretical and practical. CA possess long-short term memory and their reservoir design is trivial, it reduces to the selection of the right rule. If edge-of-chaos rules are selected, Turing complete computational power is present in the reservoir. This is not always easily proven in traditional reservoir models. Moreover, CA are easily implemented in hardware, e.g. FPGA or GPU, their theoretical analysis is easier, they allow Boolean logic and Galois fields algebra (Yilmaz, 2015).

14.6 Reservoir computing as a computational model for unconventional material computing

The previous sections list several implementations of the reservoir computing concept either by using a concrete reservoir or by using a meta-reservoir. One of the possibilities that has not be investigated extensively so far, is to use materials with sufficiently rich properties as a reservoir. For example, amorphous materials are a typical candidate, but there are other numerous possibilities. Here we consider the suitability of reservoir computing as a (mathematical) model for particular classes of computing with matter. To do this, Liquid State Machines are re-visited, from a somewhat specific angle that favors material computation. This naturally leads to the heart of the topic as discussed in the second sub-section. Some engineering challenges are discussed thereafter, together with possible advantages of reservoir computing.

14.6.1 Liquid state machines

Let us consider the Liquid State Machine model of reservoir computing, as described in Natschläger et al. (2002). We have a time series of vector inputs $\mathbf{u}(t)$. We have a time series of vector "liquid states" $\mathbf{x}(t)$, observable states of the liquid machine. These states are some function of all the prior inputs: $\mathbf{x}(t) = \mathcal{E}(\mathbf{u}(t' < t))$. This observed liquid state $\mathbf{x}(t)$ is filtered, to get a time series of vector outputs $\mathbf{v}(t) = \psi(\mathbf{x}(t))$.

There are three components to this model that can be engineered:

1. The function $\mathcal{E}$: this captures the material properties of the system, relative to the observation states
2. The choice of observed state $\mathbf{x}(t)$: for a physical device, $\mathbf{x}$ might be a pattern of ripples on a liquid surface, or a set of voltages measured on the surface of a solid material, say, but would not be an unobservable detailed microstate.
3. The choice of output filter ψ

Natschläger et al. (2002) introduce the *separation property*. This important property to some extent guarantees that the model has broad expressive power, in some sense equivalent to the expressive power of the Turing machine. For systems with the separation property, "all output-relevant differences ... of two time series $\mathbf{u}_1(.)$ and $\mathbf{u}_2(.)$ ... are reflected in the corresponding liquid states $\mathbf{x}_1(t)$ and $\mathbf{x}_2(t)$", and hence in the corresponding material microstates $\boldsymbol{\mu}_1(t)$ and $\boldsymbol{\mu}_2(t)$. That is, whenever we wish to distinguish $\mathbf{u}_1(.)$ from $\mathbf{u}_2(.)$, through $\mathbf{v}_1(t) \neq \mathbf{v}_2(t)$, then we require a material with sufficiently rich dynamics such that $\mathcal{E}_0(\mathbf{u}_1(.)) \neq \mathcal{E}_0(\mathbf{u}_2(.))$, since neither Ω nor ψ is a function of $\mathbf{u}$.

14.6.2 Reservoir computing as a theory of material computing

The first key component of the theory of material computing is the theory of the material itself. To be used for reservoir computing that material must have a sufficiently good associated theory.

There are several reasons why such a theory is needed. To begin with, the theory is needed to be able to use bottom up strategies which are necessary for systematic investigations. Even a simple system such as an automaton with input and output cannot be realised without a description of the system's dynamics. As an example, consider the generic constructions presented in Horsman et al. (2014) and Konkoli (2015). Any form of information processing requires that a physical states of the system (the configuration space) are identified as information processing states. In such a way, the physical transitions in the configuration space perform computation. Without an understanding of how the transitions in the configuration space occur, it would be impossible to envision how they should be used form information processing.

Further, without such a theory the material cannot be used to compute, that is, cannot be used *to predict the outcome of an abstract evolution* (see Horsman et al. (2014) and Sect. 10.3.2 here); its behaviour can merely be compared to the results of computations performed elsewhere. Such a theory may be based on the underlying physics of the material, it may be an abstract mathematical or computational model, or it may be a descriptive model discovered by, for example, an evolutionary algorithm (Kendon et al., 2015).

Commonly, in the discussion of reservoir computing the material properties captured in $\mathcal{E}$ and the observed state $\mathbf{x}$ are not separated out as done above, but are merged into a single given property of the reservoir. However, when using this model for material computing, it is important to separate them: $\mathcal{E}$ is a property of the material, and $\mathbf{x}$ is a property of how we observe the material, which we may have control over at the time of programming. We can capture this by including the (unobservable) microstates $\boldsymbol{\mu}$ explicitly, thus:

$$\boldsymbol{\mu}(t) = \mathcal{E}_0(\mathbf{u}(t' < t)) \tag{14.11}$$

$$\mathbf{x}(t) - \Omega(\boldsymbol{\mu}(t)) = \Omega(\mathcal{E}_0(\mathbf{u}(t' < t))) = \mathcal{E}(\mathbf{u}(t' < t)) \tag{14.12}$$

$$\mathbf{v}(t) = \psi(\mathbf{x}(t)) \tag{14.13}$$

where $\mathcal{E}_0$ is the microscopic material function and Ω is the function that projects this onto the observable macrostate $\mathbf{x}$. Now we see that the three parameters of the computation are the material $\mathcal{E}_0$, the macrosate projection Ω, and the output filter ψ. If we wish to use material to compute under this model, these are the three parameters we need to engineer.

14.6.3 Some strategies for engineering material properties: towards a material machine

The key idea is that the material should do most of the computation, i.e. function as a reservoir. Any other auxiliary equipment used to realise other components should not perform significant computation. Taken together, the reservoir prepared in conjunction with the auxiliary equipment is referred as a "material machine".

Both Ω and ψ are filters that potentially lose information about the inputs and observed state. In order to perform a particular computation, i.e. to design a *special purpose material machine*, we therefore need an $\mathcal{E}_0$ that is rich enough to provide the required spread of outputs. This is exactly the separation property introduced by Natschläger et al. (2002).

The computational burden is shared amongst these three parameters, that is, between the reservoir $\mathcal{E}_0$, the observation Ω, and the output filter ψ. Natschläger et al. (2002) point out this tradeoff: the reservoir can be very simple (although still rich enough to support the separation property: it cannot be a brick), requiring a computationally powerful filter; or the material can be very rich, requiring a much simpler filter. In the case where both the reservoir and the filter are implemented *in silico*, this tradeoff is benign. However, for material computation, the reservoir is implemented in a physical substance, the observation mediates between this material and further computation, and the filter is typically a conventional computation. Now the tradeoff becomes more important: we (presumably) wish the bulk of the computation to be performed by the material, followed by a relatively simple observation (voltage readouts from a few electrodes, rather than complex pattern recognition of surface ripples, say), and completed by a relatively simple filter computation. This argues for dynamically rich materials.

One programs the reservoir through the choice of ψ, and possibly Ω (for example, the positioning or number of readout electrodes). This is performed via some training or search algorithm: one provides the system with a set of "training" inputs $\mathbf{u}^i(.)$ and their corresponding desired outputs $\mathbf{v}^i(t)$, and adjusts ψ (and possibly Ω) via some algorithm until the observed outputs $\mathbf{v}_0^i(t)$ sufficiently approximate the desired outputs. *In materio* computing traditionally uses an evolutionary algorithm for this task. The assumption is that the resulting Ω/ψ have sufficiently generalised the problem that previously unseen inputs $\mathbf{u}'(.)$ produce the desired outputs $\mathbf{v}'(t)$. If the reservoir has insufficiently rich dynamics, if $\mathcal{E}_0$ is too constrained, it will not be possible to find an Ω/ψ that reproduce the desired $\mathbf{v}^i(t)$. This training process, along with the generalisation assumption, provides the underlying theory needed to exploit the reservoir as a computer.

14.6.4 Possible advantages of material computing

The advantage of the reservoir model for analysing material computation is its "black box" nature: the "programming" chooses Ω and ψ given particular material properties $\mathcal{E}_0$. This fits well with how much current material computing works: we have a material, and we can change how we observe it (where we place the electrodes, say), and how we post-process the outputs, but we cannot program the material properties (other than by throwing away the substrate and replacing it with a different one).

Exploiting the reservoir model for material computing provides a framework within which we can:

- choose appropriate training/search algorithms to program the physical reservoir
- choose appropriate classes of observation functions Ω, for example, determining the minimum number of electrode readouts needed
- use the reservoir model to understand the material, for example, to characterise the material's computational power and memory capacity via reservoir analysis
- use the reservoir model to design novel computational materials, by providing a specification of, and constraints on, the underlying $\mathcal{E}_0$

The reservoir model as it stands is not sufficient for all computational materials. The reservoir's $\mathcal{E}_0$ is assumed fixed, but if a material reconfigures or assembles, this would become dynamic: $\mathcal{E}_0(t)$. Such systems would require more sophisticated models than ones based on open dynamical systems; in such cases the system has a further meta-dynamics: it is a dynamical system with a dynamical structure.

14.7 Conclusions

The main ambition was to provide an up to date overview of reservoir computing and the key concepts that define it: the reservoir, and the read-out layer. A reservoir is a very high dimensional non-autonomous (open) dynamical system with a rich space of internal states. The reservoir transforms input sequences into internal states, changing one representation for the other. They key idea behind the reservoir computing concept is that this transformation is so sensitive to the features of the input signal so that each feature will have a unique representation in the internal state space of the reservoir (however, too much sensitivity is not good either). Thus the computation is performed automatically, almost for free. To extract the result of the computation (stored in the internal states of the system), one only needs a read-out layer. This has profound implications for information processing engineering: to achieve some specific information processing functionality, it should be sufficient to optimise (train) the read-out layer, in principle without ever touching the reservoir.

This insight originated independently from several studies. In this chapter the Echo state network and the Liquid state machine paradigms have been heavily emphasised. However, it has also been realized independently by others that during the training of the neural network, the dominant changes occur in the output weights (Schiller and Steil, 2005). Again, this points to the fact that only the outer read-out layer needs to be trained, not the full network.

Our goal has been to review the reservoir computing paradigm from a rather broad engineering perspective, with an emphasis on material computation, cellular automata, and the human brain. For example, both the reservoir and the read-out layer components can be engineered in many ways, the questions are, given that the goal is to exploit reservoir computing in practice, what should one do? are there any strategies one should follow?

Several up-to-date realisations of the reservoir have been discussed. Apart from the standard example of the reservoir as a bucket of water (Fernando and Sojakka, 2003), we have covered computing with opto-electronic components and atomic switch networks), and reservoir computing in *E. coli* bacteria (Jones et al., 2007). There are many other realizations that have not been discussed.

A special section has been dedicated to discussing the use of various materials as reservoirs. For example, within the SYMONE project an attempt has been made to investigated the use of amorphous memristor networks for such purposes, both experimentally and theoretically (Bennett, 2014; Bennett et al., 2016; Konkoli and Wendin, 2014). In the literature there is no broader focused effort to address this possibility of exploiting materials in this way. This is somewhat surprising, given the obvious technological importance of such amorphous reservoirs in general, and the revival of *in materio* computation ideas in the recent past. Should the idea turn feasible, very likely a range of materials could be exploited that way. It was timely to provide a systematic expose of, what we believe, are the key ideas and concepts, which we summarized in one term: the material machine.

In Konkoli (2015) the concept of the functional information processing invariance (or a degree of freedom) has been suggested to emphasise the fact that not all degrees of freedom can be useful for computation, for various reasons. For example, due to engineering difficulties, microscopic degrees of freedom cannot be "reached" (addressed) directly. Further, even if they could be reached directly, truly microscopic degrees of freedom usually fluctuate. A typical text-book example are the position and the velocity of a molecule in a liquid, or in a gas. Microscopic degrees of freedom are better described by stochastic equations of motion than by deterministic laws. On the other hand, by definition, macroscopic degrees of freedom capture regular features of the microscopic (highly fluctuating) variables and, as a result, can and are exploited for computation. As an illustration, consider the voltage difference at the transistor pins. This degree of freedom (observable) is weakly dependent on the individual position of electrons in the material. A systematic discussion regarding the role of information processing degrees of freedom in reservoir computing can be found in Konkoli (2016).

This distinction between microscopic degrees of freedom is of paramount importance in the context of material computation engineering. Without thorough understanding of the related engineering concepts it will likely be hard to design reliable information processing devices. It is possible that the lack of understanding of how to describe such systems will negatively affect our ability to engineer them.

For example, consider the case of amorphous materials. To begin with, for amorphous materials it is hard to make a clear separation between microscopic and macroscopic degrees of freedom. Even for macroscopic degrees or freedom, the equations of motion are stochastic (e.g. polymer gels, or spin glasses). Such systems exhibit multi scale dynamics and are never really at rest. It is clear that this state of affairs challenges our understanding of what can be done with such systems in terms of information processing. In technical terms, these difficulties can be expressed by simply stating that the information processing degrees of freedom exhibit a dynamics in a rugged energy landscape (*cf.* Konkoli (2015) and references therein). We are suggesting reservoir computing as a way to address these conceptual challenges, as a first step towards constructing a theory of information processing with such systems. For a more generic construction regarding the issue of constructing a reservoir computer from an arbitrary dynamical system, see Konkoli (2016). A separate chapter on the philosophy of computation partially address a similar problem: how to use a generic systems for any type of computation.

Here we have not covered one important aspect of reservoir computing in depth: its mathematical foundation, the Stone-Weierstrass approximation theorem. To guarantee universal expressive power of the reservoir computing model, it is implicit the construction that there is a class (collection) of reservoirs to choose from that can be combined in various ways (an algebra of reservoirs) to achieve particular functionality.[1] This fact is not obvious and has not be addressed extensively in the literature. A study (Konkoli, 2016) covers this particular aspect of reservoir computing, where the term *reservoir machine* (as a Liquid State Machine) is coined to emphasise the goal of constructing a programmable (multi-purpose) information processing device, but by using a fixed reservoir. This is possible since sufficiently complex reservoirs can act as the required collection of smaller reservoirs (mini-reservoirs).[2]

In brief, in this chapter we have focused on some specific aspects of computing with materials, thus the emphasis on the term *material machine*, and perhaps implicitly also on a "cellular machine" or a "brain machine". We suggest an embryo of a generic theory of reservoir computing with materials.

References

Aguilera, Renato, Eleanor Demis, Kelsey Scharnhorst, Adam Z. Stieg, Masakazu Aono, and James K. Gimzewski (2015). "Morphic atomic switch networks for beyond-Moore computing architectures". *Interconnect Technology Conference and 2015 IEEE Materials for Advanced Metallization Conference (IITC/MAM), 2015*. IEEE, pp. 165–168.

Appeltant, Lennert, Miguel Cornelles Soriano, Guy Van der Sande, Jan Danckaert, Serge Massar, Joni Dambre, Benjamin Schrauwen, Claudio R. Mirasso, and Ingo Fischer (2011). "Information processing using a single dynamical node as complex system". *Nature Communications* 2:468.

Bennett, Christopher H. (2014). "Computing with Memristor Networks". Master thesis. URL: publications . lib . chalmers . se / publication / 218659 - computing-with-memristor-networks.

---

[1] For example, this requirement is what the Liquid State Machine model builds on (Maass et al., 2002; Natschläger et al., 2002).

[2] This paradigm is also emphasized in the original Echo State Network formulation. (Jaeger and Haas, 2004; Jaeger, 2001b)

Bennett, Christopher, Aldo Jesorka, Göran Wendin, and Zoran Konkoli (2016). "On the inverse pattern recognition problem in the context of the time-series data processing with memristor networks". *Advances in Unconventional Computation.* Ed. by Andrew Adamatzky. Vol. 2. Prototypes and algorithms. Springer.

Berlekamp, E. R., J. H. Conway, and R. K. Guy (1982). *Winning Ways for Your Mathematical Plays.* Academic Press.

Bertschinger, N. and T. Natschläger (2004). "Real-time computation at the edge of chaos in recurrent neural networks". *Neural Computation* 16(7) :1413–1436.

Büsing, L., B. Schrauwen, and R. Legenstein (2010). "Connectivity, dynamics, and memory in reservoir computing with binary and analog neurons". *Neural Computation* 22(5):1272–1311.

Chrol-Cannon, J. and Y. Jin (2014). "On the Correlation between Reservoir Metrics and Performance for Time Series Classification under the Influence of Synaptic Plasticity". *PLoS One* 9(7):e101792.

Cook, Matthew (2004). "Universality in elementary cellular automata". *Complex Systems* 15(1):1–40.

Dai, Xianhua (2004). "Genetic Regulatory Systems Modeled by Recurrent Neural Network". *Advances in Neural Networks (ISNN 2004).* Ed. by Fu-Liang Yin, Jun Wang, and Chengan Guo. Vol. 3174. LNCS. Springer, pp. 519–524.

Dale, Matthew, Julian F. Miller, Susan Stepney, and Martin A. Trefzer (2016a). "Evolving Carbon Nanotube Reservoir Computers". *UCNC 2016.* Vol. 9726. LNCS. Springer, pp. 49–61.

Dale, Matthew, Julian F. Miller, Susan Stepney, and Martin A. Trefzer (2016b). "Reservoir Computing *in Materio*: An Evaluation of Configuration through Evolution". *ICES 2016 at SSCI 2016.* IEEE.

Dale, Matthew, Julian F. Miller, Susan Stepney, and Martin A. Trefzer (2017). "Reservoir Computing *in Materio*: a computational framework for evolution *in Materio*". *Proc. IJCNN 2017.* IEEE, pp. 2178–2185.

Dambre, Joni, David Verstraeten, Benjamin Schrauwen, and Serge Massar (2012). "Information Processing Capacity of Dynamical Systems". *Sci. Rep.* 2:514.

Fernando, Chrisantha and Sampsa Sojakka (2003). "Pattern Recognition in a Bucket". *Advances in Artificial Life.* Vol. 2801. LNCS. Springer, pp. 588–597.

Gibbons, T. E. (2010). "Unifying quality metrics for reservoir networks". *Proc. IJCNN 2010.* IEEE, pp. 1–7.

Horsman, C., Susan Stepney, Rob C. Wagner, and Viv Kendon (2014). "When does a physical system compute?" *Proceedings of the Royal Society A* 470(2169):20140182.

Jaeger, H. (2001a). *Short term memory in echo state networks.* GMD-Forschungszentrum Informationstechnik.

Jaeger, H. (2007). "Echo state network". *Scholarpedia* 2:2330.

Jaeger, H. and H. Haas (2004). "Harnessing nonlinearity: Predicting chaotic systems and saving energy in wireless communication". *Science* 304:78–80.

Jaeger, Herbert (2001b). *The "echo state" approach to analysing and training recurrent neural networks*. Tech. rep. GMD Report 148. German National Research Center for Information Technology.

Jones, Ben, Dov Stekel, Jon Rowe, and Chrisantha Fernando (2007). "Is there a liquid state machine in the bacterium *Escherichia coli*?" *IEEE Symposium on Artificial Life, 2007.* IEEE, pp. 187–191.

Kendon, Viv, Angelika Sebald, and Susan Stepney (2015). "Heterotic computing: past, present, and future". *Phil. Trans. Roy. Soc. A* 373:20140225.

Klampfl, S., S.V. David, P. Yin, S.A. Shamma, and W. Maass (2009). "Integration of stimulus history in information conveyed by neurons in primary auditory cortex in response to tone sequences". *39th Annual Conference of the Society for Neuroscience, Program.* Vol. 163.

Konkoli, Zoran (2015). "A Perspective on Putnam's Realizability Theorem in the Context of Unconventional Computation". *International Journal of Unconventional Computing* 11:83–102.

Konkoli, Zoran (2016). "On reservoir computing: from mathematical foundations to unconventional applications". *Advances in Unconventional Computation.* Ed. by Andrew Adamatzky. Vol. 1. Theory. Springer.

Konkoli, Zoran and Göran Wendin (2014). "On information processing with networks of nano-scale switching elements". *International Journal of Unconventional Computing* 10:405–428.

Langton, Chris G (1990). "Computation at the edge of chaos: phase transitions and emergent computation". *Physica D: Nonlinear Phenomena* 42(1):12–37.

Larger, Laurent, Miguel C. Soriano, Daniel Brunner, Lennert Appeltant, Jose M. Gutiérrez, Luis Pesquera, Claudio R. Mirasso, and Ingo Fischer (2012). "Photonic information processing beyond Turing: an optoelectronic implementation of reservoir computing". *Optics express* 20(3):3241–3249.

Legenstein, Robert and Wolfgang Maass (2007a). "Edge of chaos and prediction of computational performance for neural circuit models". *Neural Networks* 20(3):323–334.

Legenstein, Robert and Wolfgang Maass (2007b). "What makes a dynamical system computationally powerful?" *New directions in statistical signal processing: From systems to brain.* Ed. by Simon Haykin, José C. Principe, Terrence J. Sejnowski, and John McWhirter. MIT Press, pp. 127–154.

Lukoševičius, M. and H. Jaeger (2009). "Reservoir computing approaches to recurrent neural network training". *Computer Science Review* 3:127–149.

Lukoševičius, M., H. Jaeger, and B. Schrauwen (2012). "Reservoir Computing Trends". *KI - Künstliche Intelligenz* 26:365–371.

Maass, Wolfgang, Thomas Natschläger, and Henry Markram (2002). "Real-time computing without stable states: A new framework for neural computation based on perturbations". *Neural Computation* 14(11):2531–2560.

Massar, Marc and Serge Massar (2013). "Mean-field theory of echo state networks". *Physical Review E* 87(4):042809.

Miller, J. F., S. Harding, and G. Tufte (2014). "Evolution-in-materio: evolving computation in materials". *Evolutionary Intelligence* 7(1):49–67.

Natschläger, T., W. Maass, and H. Markram (2002). "The "Liquid Computer": A Novel Strategy for Real-Time Computing on Time Series (Special Issue on Foundations of Information Processing)". *TELEMATIK* 8 :39–43.

Nikolic, Danko, Stefan Haeusler, Wolf Singer, and Wolfgang Maass (2006). "Temporal dynamics of information content carried by neurons in the primary visual cortex". *Advances in neural information processing systems*, pp. 1041–1048.

Norton, D. and D. Ventura (2010). "Improving liquid state machines through iterative refinement of the reservoir". *Neurocomputing* 73(16):2893–2904.

Rosenstein, M. T., J. J. Collins, and C. J. De Luca (1993). "A practical method for calculating largest Lyapunov exponents from small data sets". *Physica D: Nonlinear Phenomena* 65(1):117–134.

Schiller, U. D. and J. J. Steil (2005). "Analyzing the weight dynamics of recurrent learning algorithms". *Neurocomputing* 63:5–23.

Sillin, H. O., R. Aguilera, H. Shieh, A. V. Avizienis, M. Aono, A. Z. Stieg, and J. K. Gimzewski (2013). "A theoretical and experimental study of neuromorphic atomic switch networks for reservoir computing". *Nanotechnology* 24(38):384004.

Soto, José Manuel Gómez and Andrew Wuensche (2015). *The X-rule: universal computation in a non-isotropic Life-like Cellular Automaton*. eprint: arXiv:1504.01434[nlin.CG].

Stepney, Susan (2012). "Nonclassical Computation: a dynamical systems perspective". *Handbook of Natural Computing, volume 4*. Ed. by Grzegorz Rozenberg, Thomas Bäck, and Joost N. Kok. Springer. Chap. 59, pp. 1979–2025.

Stieg, A. Z., A. V. Avizienis, H. O. Sillin, R. Aguilera, H. Shieh, C. Martin-Olmos, E. J. Sandouk, M. Aono, and J. K. Gimzewski (2014). "Self-organization and Emergence of Dynamical Structures in Neuromorphic Atomic Switch Networks". *Memristor Networks*. Springer, pp. 173–209.

Strogatz, S. H. (1994). *Nonlinear dynamics and chaos*. Westview Press.

Vandoorne, K., J. Dambre, D. Verstraeten, B. Schrauwen, and P. Bienstman (2011). "Parallel reservoir computing using optical amplifiers". *IEEE Transactions on Neural Networks* 22(9):1469–1481.

Vandoorne, K., P. Mechet, T. Van Vaerenbergh, M. Fiers, G. Morthier, D. Verstraeten, B. Schrauwen, J. Dambre, and P. Bienstman (2014). "Experimental demonstration of reservoir computing on a silicon photonics chip". *Nature Communications* 5:3541.

Verstraeten, D. and B. Schrauwen (2009). "On the quantification of dynamics in reservoir computing". *Artificial Neural Networks–ICANN 2009*. Springer, pp. 985–994.

von Neumann, John (1966). *Theory of Self-Reproducing Automata.* Ed. by Arthur W. Burks. Champaign, IL, USA: University of Illinois Press.

Wainrib, Gilles and Mathieu N Galtier (2016). "A local Echo State Property through the largest Lyapunov exponent". *Neural Networks* 76:39–45.

Wolfram, Stephen (1984). "Universality and complexity in cellular automata". *Physica D: Nonlinear Phenomena* 10(1):1–35.

Yildiz, I. B., H. Jaeger, and S. J. Kiebel (2012). "Re-visiting the echo state property". *Neural Networks* 35:1–9.

Yilmaz, Ozgur (2014). "Reservoir Computing using Cellular Automata". *CoRR*:eprint: arXiv:1410.0162[cs.NE].

Yilmaz, Ozgur (2015). "Connectionist-Symbolic Machine Intelligence using Cellular Automata based Reservoir-Hyperdimensional Computing". *CoRR*:eprint: arXiv:1503.00851[cs.ET].

Chapter 15
Multivalued Logic at the Nanoscale

Barbara Fresch, M. V. Klymenko, Raphael D. Levine, and
Françoise Remacle

Abstract Molecular and nanostructured systems for logic processing are
typically characterized by more than two internal states. The implementation of multivalued logic is thus a natural strategy to minimize storing space,
to reduce the burden of interconnections and to enhance the complexity of
the logic processing. We discuss the application of multivalued logic at the
nanoscale by considering different physical implementations of multivalued
processing. Unconventional hardware such as molecular electronic states have
been used to implement multivalued decision trees and decomposition of logic
functions in base five. We discuss an all-optical set-up where the dynamics
of molecular states excited by a sequence of laser pulses realizes an unprecedented density of logic processing through the parallelism inherent in the
quantum dynamical evolution. Moreover, the search for low energy computing devices that can be interfaced with the conventional CMOS technology
led to the design of several multivalued logic schemes in solid state nanostructures. We report in detail a possible implementation of a ternary full-addition
in quantum dots embedded in a solid state matrix.

15.1 Introduction

Logic processing in nanoscale devices requires the introduction of logic designs that are alternatives to the switching theory that implements Boolean
functions in the transistors. Within Boolean logic (named after the work by
George J. Boole 1847 (Boole, 2009)), logic variables take two values, true
and false, usually denoted 1 and 0 respectively. Logic operations are realized as switching functions, referring to their early physical realizations by
two-position relay networks or, alternatively, by two-states contact networks.
However, new computing systems like solid state nanostructures (Amlani et
al., 1999; Chen et al., 1996; Fresch et al., 2012; Fresch et al., 2017a; Fresch

© Springer International Publishing AG, part of Springer Nature 2018
S. Stepney et al. (eds.), *Computational Matter*, Natural Computing Series,
https://doi.org/10.1007/978-3-319-65826-1_15

et al., 2017b; Klein et al., 2010; Klein et al., 2007; Mol et al., 2011; Ziegler et al., 2012) and molecular devices (Elbaz et al., 2010; Elbaz et al., 2012; Fresch et al., 2013; Fresch et al., 2017c; Margulies et al., 2007; Orbach et al., 2014; Raymo and Giordani, 2002; Remacle and Levine, 2001; Remacle et al., 2001) are typically characterized by far more than two internal states. Due to quantisation in confined systems, nanostructures like quantum dots (QDs) have many discrete charge and energy states; and, at the molecular level, every charge state is characterized by several discrete electronic and vibrational states. Moreover, the response of these systems to external stimuli is not binary: electronic transport, optical absorption/emission, chemical concentrations are continuous physical quantities that provide a many-value output depending on the resolution of the experimental detection.

Multivalued logic (MVL) appears as a promising route to exploit the information processing capabilities of unconventional hardware like nanostructured and molecular systems. An essential advantage of a multivalued encoding is that less space is required to store information, for example, the number nine is denoted as 1001 in binary, as 100 in ternary and as 9 in decimal notation. The complementary aspect is that one needs to resolve as many physical states of the device as the number of values that the logical variable can assume. In MVL, more information is processed at each operation reducing the burden of interconnections that is one of the major drawbacks in binary switching networks and the primary source of energy dissipation. The richness of MVL over the traditional binary design is reflected in the exponentially increasing number of possible logic functions: there are 2^{2^n} Boolean logic functions of n variables while this number is p^{p^n} in the p-valued case. Among various types of MVL, ternary logic receives more attention than others. If one defines a cost function which is proportional to the space of storage (length of word $\propto 1/\log(p)$) and to the number of states (p) than the most efficient base for the implementation of a logic system is the natural base ($e = 2.71828$) (Hurst, 1984). From this argument the best integer base for logic encoding is three rather than two. However, when dealing with hardware implementations the choice of the MVL system to employ is also driven by the physics of the logic device.

In this chapter, we do not provide a review of the theory of multivalued logic (Bolc and Borowik, 1992; Fitting and Orlowska, 2013; Miller and Thornton, 2008; Rescher, 1969) but we rather present selected implementations of multivalued logic at the nanoscale. It is often the physics of the system and the capabilities/limitations of our macroscopic measurement apparatus that determine the logic design that is implemented.

In Sect. 15.2 we introduce some basic concepts of MVL that are used in the subsequent sections focused on two different physical implementations.

In Sect. 15.3 we present the theory and the implementation of parallel logic processing in a molecular system excited by laser pulses (Fresch et al., 2015; Fresch et al., 2013; Yan et al., 2015). The optical set-up is ultrafast and we discuss how parallel processing stems from the quantum dynamical evolution of the molecular electronic states. This dynamics can be mapped into the branches of a logic decision tree, so that the optical response carries the multivalued outputs corresponding to all possible combinations of multivalued inputs. The spatial decomposition of the non-linear optical response also allows reading in parallel several macroscopic outputs in different directions; in this context we discuss the spectral decomposition of a five-valued logic function.

In Sect. 15.4 we deal with quantum dots embedded in a solid state matrix gated by electrodes in a transistor-like geometry. Such a system, even if presenting unconventional transport characteristics due to the quantisation of charge, has the advantage of being fully compatible with the CMOS technology. Due to quantum confinement, electrons are transferred one at a time implying low dissipation compared to macroscopic current. The charging characteristics of gated nanostructures allowed the implementation of a complete set of ternary gates (Klein et al., 2007) and of ternary operations like multiplication (Klein et al., 2010) and addition (Klymenko and Remacle, 2014; Mol et al., 2011). Here, we discuss in details the realisation of addition modulo three in a quantum-dot integrated together with a charge sensor based on a single-electron transistor (Klymenko and Remacle, 2014). In the concluding section we outline the significant features of the different MVL implementations and discuss future directions for logic on molecular and nanostructured devices.

15.2 Basic concepts in multivalued logic

A multivalued discrete logic variable takes values from a finite set of integers (Miller and Thornton, 2008). The cardinality of this set defines the radix of the logic, p, and corresponds to the number of logic values used in a multiple-valued numbering system. A p-valued numbering system which has a continuous monotonic set of integers, given as $(0, 1, ..., p-1)$, is called an unbalanced system (or unsigned system). The binary numbering system $(0, 1)$ is a subset of this continuous set of integers. A balanced numbering system uses odd radices and includes negative numbers, which gives a monotonic set of integers $(-(p-1)/2, ..., 0, ..., (p-1)/2)$. For example, the unbalanced ternary notation uses the set of logic values $(0, 1, 2)$ while the balanced ternary system is specified by the triad $(-1, 0, +1)$. The use of balanced versus unbalanced encoding depends both on the intended application and on the physical system that realizes the logic operations. We use both notations in the following sections. Table 15.1 reports the ternary addition and multiplication for the two kinds of encoding. Notice that the multiplication in balanced ternary has no carry. This allows for the multiplication of a long number made of several digits by a constant, where each digit multiplication can be treated by a separate unit, without any need of transfer of information from one unit to the

Addition

	-1	0	1
-1	$1(-1)$	-1	0
0	-1	0	1
1	0	1	$-1(1)$

	0	1	2
0	0	1	2
1	1	2	$0(1)$
2	2	$0(1)$	$1(1)$

Multiplication

	-1	0	1
-1	1	0	-1
0	0	0	0
1	-1	0	$-1(1)$

	0	1	2
0	0	0	0
1	0	1	2
2	0	2	$1(1)$

Table 15.1 Truth tables for addition and multiplication of two ternary digits in balanced $(-1, 0, 1)$ and unbalanced (0,1,2) encoding. The digit in parenthesis is the carry.

next. The balanced ternary multiplier has been implemented experimentally both in chemical systems (Orbach et al., 2015) and solid state devices (Klein et al., 2010). The design of a complete set of ternary gates in unbalanced encoding has been implemented on three tunnel coupled QD (Klein et al., 2007). Designs for ternary addition have been proposed in single electron devices both in balanced (Mol et al., 2011) and in unbalanced (Klymenko and Remacle, 2014) notation. In Sect. 15.4 the latter case is discussed in detail.

Multivalued encoding has the evident advantage of requiring less space to store information. The use of a multivalued numbering system allows the reduction of the number of inputs and outputs. A function of four binary variables $(0, 1)$ can be viewed as a function of two variables in base four $(0, 1, 2, 3)$. Figure 15.1a illustrates this correspondence for the function *exor4*, that is the addition modulo 2 of four bits. The same compact representation can be applied to operations with several outputs: a multiple-output Boolean function $(f_0, f_1, ..., f_{m-1})$ can be represented by a unique integer-valued function whose values at $x = (x_1, .., x_n)$ are given by

$$f_Z(x) = \sum_{i=0}^{m-1} f_i(x_1, ..., x_n) \, 2^i \tag{15.1}$$

For example, the half addition of two Boolean variables is a two-input/two-output function, see Figure 15.1b: one output, f_0, is the sum modulo two of the input variables corresponding to an EXOR operation, the other output, f_1, is the carry to be transmitted for the addition of the next digit and it is realized by an AND gate on the two input variables. By using the integer representation given in Eq. 15.1, also called word representation at the computer level (Remacle et al., 2005), the two outputs can be expressed as a single function taking values on the finite set $(0, 1, 2)$.

In Sect. 15.3.2 we show the implementation of the Boolean half addition read as a three-valued function on the non-linear optical response of a molecular system (Fresch et al., 2015). Beyond obtaining a more compact representation, the use of multivalued logic also enhances the complexity of the possible logic operations. Indeed, as the radix of the logic increases, the number of possible functions that can be implemented grows exponentially. Only a small subset of the functions accepting two four-valued inputs can be interpreted as Boolean functions of four binary inputs as *exor4* of Figure 15.1a. Most of the functions of multivalued variables do not correspond to any Boolean operation, as an example we report the addition modulo 4 in the last column of Figure 15.1a. Generally, an n-variable logic function maps n multivalued inputs to a multivalued output within the same radix. The corresponding multivalued algebra provides the framework for expressing and manipulating multivalued logic functions. Because of the exponential increase in the number of possible functions (there are p^p possible functions of a single variable and p^{p^2} functions of two variables for the p-valued logic) the choice of the set of functions to implement is important. In many cases the used functions are chosen in analogy of the corresponding Boolean operations. The binary AND is translated as the minimum *min*-function in multivalued operation, the binary OR as the maximum *max*-function, while EXOR is replaced by the addition modulo p. However, the choice is not unique. Here, and in particular in Sect. 15.3, we make extensive use of the multivalued generalisation of a specific algebraic expression known as Sum of Product (SOP) form (Mano et al., 2015; Stankovic and Astola, 2006; Stanković et al., 2012). In the SOP expression, variables are organised into product terms while the product terms are connected by the addition operation. The SOP form of a logic function represents its spectral decomposition in a given set of logic basis function. Such decomposition can be represented graphically by a logic decision tree. Let us explain these concepts by first considering the simpler case of a two-input Boolean function. In Boolean logic the basis functions for the SOP decomposition are the MIN-terms. A MIN-term is a product (AND) of all variables in the function, in direct or complemented form, with the property of being equal to 1 only for a specific sequence of inputs (e.g. $\bar{x}_1\bar{x}_2$ is 1 for (00)). For two variables we have four MIN-terms. For example, the SOP form of the EXOR function reads $0\,(\bar{x}_1\bar{x}_2) + 1\,(\bar{x}_1x_2) + 1\,(x_1\bar{x}_2) + 0\,(x_1x_2) = \bar{x}_1x_2 + x_1\bar{x}_2$. Binary decision trees are the graphical representation of this function decomposition with respect to the set of MIN-terms (Stankovic and Astola, 2006; Stanković et al., 2012). Figure 15.1c shows the binary decision tree representing the EXOR function. In the tree structure, the basis functions are expressed through the labels at the edges: the product of the literals from the root node to a terminal node along a specific path represents a MIN-term. For example, the leftmost path of Figure 15.1c represents the MIN-term $\bar{x}_1\bar{x}_2$. A function decomposition rule is applied at each non-terminal node of the decision tree. In the case of the binary decision tree showed in Figure 15.1c the function is expanded at the nodes of the i-th level according to the Shannon decomposition rule (S)

$$f\left(x_1, ..., x_n\right) = \bar{x}_i f_0\left(x_1, ..., x_{i-1}, 0, x_{i+1}, ..., x_n\right) +$$
$$x_i f_1\left(x_1, ..., x_{i-1}, 1, x_{i+1}, ..., x_n\right) \qquad (15.2)$$

where f_0, f_1 are the cofactors of f with respect to x_i. The values at the terminal nodes are the spectral coefficients of the MIN-term decomposition; these coefficients are the values of the function for the input sequence represented by the corresponding MIN-term (Mano et al., 2015). Therefore, by reading the decision tree of figure 15.1c one can derive the SOP expression for the EXOR function $\bar{x}_1 x_2 + x_1 \bar{x}_2$. In general, for a Boolean function of n inputs we obtain 2^n terminal nodes containing the coefficients of each MIN-term. For logic functions of Boolean variables, $x_1, ..., x_n$, computing its MIN term decomposition amounts to determine the output for all possible inputs (Stanković et al., 2012).

a)

$X_1X_2X_3X_4$	f	X_1X_2	f	exor4	$X_1 \oplus X_2$
0000	f(0000)	00	f(00)	0	0
0001	f(0001)	01	f(01)	1	1
0010	f(0010)	02	f(02)	1	2
0011	f(0011)	03	f(03)	0	3
0100	f(0100)	10	f(10)	1	1
0101	f(0101)	11	f(11)	0	2
0110	f(0110)	12	f(12)	0	3
0111	f(0111)	13	f(13)	1	0
1000	f(1000)	20	f(20)	1	2
1001	f(1001)	21	f(21)	0	3
1010	f(1010)	22	f(22)	0	0
1011	f(1011)	23	f(23)	1	1
1100	f(1100)	30	f(30)	0	3
1101	f(1101)	31	f(31)	1	0
1110	f(1110)	32	f(32)	1	1
1111	f(1111)	33	f(33)	0	2

b)

x1 x2	f_1 (AND)	f_0 (EXOR)	f_2
00	0	0	0
01	0	1	1
10	0	1	1
11	1	0	2

c)

$$\text{SOP}: \ 0\left(\bar{x}_1 \bar{x}_2\right) + 1\left(\bar{x}_1 x_2\right) + 1\left(x_1 \bar{x}_2\right) + 0\left(x_1 x_2\right)$$

Fig. 15.1 (a) Tabular representation of the 4-binary input function *exor4* as a 2-quaternary input function and of the quaternary function addition modulo 4. (b) Truth table of the 2 outputs of a binary half adder written as a single-output ternary function. (c) Binary decision tree generating the Sum of Product decomposition of the EXOR logic function

One can generalize the spectral decomposition for a logic function of n variables of radix r in terms of sum of (Hadamard) products of characteristic functions (Stanković et al., 2012). Characteristic functions can be seen as the multivalued generalization of the binary literals x_i and $\bar{x}_i$. For a multivalued variable x_j of radix p the characteristic functions $J_i(x_j)$ is defined as

Input x_1x_2	$J_0(x_1)$	$J_{-1}(x_1)$	$J_1(x_1)$	$J_0(x_2)$	$J_{-1}(x_2)$	$J_1(x_2)$
0 0	1	0	0	1	0	0
0 −1	1	0	0	0	1	0
0 1	1	0	0	0	0	1
−1 0	0	1	0	1	0	0
−1 −1	0	1	0	0	1	0
−1 1	0	1	0	0	0	1
1 0	0	0	1	1	0	0
1 −1	0	0	1	0	1	0
1 1	0	0	1	0	0	1

Table 15.2 Vector representation of the 6 characteristic functions for 2 ternary variables input x_1x_2

$$J_i(x_j) = \begin{cases} 1, & \text{if } x_j = i; \\ 0, & \text{otherwise.} \end{cases} \qquad (15.3)$$

In matrix notation, the functions $J_i(x_j)$ can be represented as vectors of dimensions p^n and they can be multiplied by the Hadamard product to generate the basis for the spectral decomposition of an n-input multivalued function. Technically, the SOP expression is given by

$$f(x_1, ..., x_n) = \sum_{j=1}^{r^n} a_j \left(J_{i_1}(x_1), J_{i_2}(x_2), ..., J_{i_n}(x_n) \right)_j$$

where the product $\left(J_{i_1}(x_1), J_{i_2}(x_2), ..., J_{i_n}(x_n) \right)_j$ is the analog of a MIN term in Boolean logic and a_j is the multivalued coefficient. To see this, let us consider explicitly a function of 2 ternary variables, x_1 and x_2 in balanced notation $(-1, 0, 1)$. In this case we have 6 characteristic functions of dimension 3^2, explicitly reported in Table 15.2, and we can generate 9 different Hadamard products $J_i(x_1), J_j(x_2)$.

An example of a Hadamard product is $J_0(x_1)J_{-1}(x_2) = [01000000]^T$. The SOP of a ternary function $f(x_1, x_2)$ is its spectral decomposition in the basis given by Hadamard products:

$$\begin{aligned} f(x_1, x_2) = \ & f(00)J_0(x_1)J_0(x_2) \oplus f(0{-}1)J_0(x_1)J_{-1}(x_2) \oplus \\ & f(10)J_1(x_1)J_0(x_2) \oplus f(-10)J_{-1}(x_1)J_0(x_2) \oplus \\ & f(-1{-}1)J_{-1}(x_1)J_{-1}(x_2) \oplus f(-11)J_{-1}(x_1)J_1(x_2) \oplus \\ & f(10)J_1(x_1)J_0(x_2) \oplus f(1{-}1)J_1(x_1)J_{-1}(x_2) \oplus \qquad (15.4) \\ & f(11)J_1(x_1)J_1(x_2) \end{aligned}$$

where $\oplus$ is addition modulo 3. In the order of the inputs given in Table 15.2, the output of the ternary multiplier shown in Table 15.1 is the vector $[00001-10-11]^T$. The SOP of the ternary multiplier takes the form:

$$
\begin{aligned}
f(x_1, x_2) = \ & 1J_{-1}(x_1)J_{-1}(x_2) \oplus (-1)J_{-1}(x_1)J_1(x_2) \oplus \\
& (-1)J_1(x_1)J_{-1}(x_2) \oplus 1J_1(x_1)J_1(x_2)
\end{aligned}
\tag{15.5}
$$

In Sect. 15.3.3 we show how the spectral decomposition of a multivalued function can be performed in parallel by taking advantage of the multi-directional optical emission of a molecular system excited by ultrafast laser pulses (Yan et al., 2015). We use three variables and a radix of $r = 5$, i.e., the variables take the integer values 0, ± 1 and ± 2 in balanced notation. The Hadamard product, e.g., $J_{-2}(x_1)J_1(x_2)J_0(x_3)$, is an element of the basis set that identifies the input sequence $(-2, 1, 0)$. The corresponding coefficient for the function decomposition is the output of the function for the same sequence of inputs (Stanković et al., 2012).

15.3 Multivalued Logic performed by laser excited molecular system

Molecular systems are versatile platforms for the implementation of logic at the nanoscale since they respond to external stimuli of different nature (chemical, electrical, optical, ...) and they are characterized by discrete (quantized) internal states. The logic designs we discuss in the following are based on the quantum dynamics of electronic states excited by the interaction with laser pulses. The inputs are supplied in parallel through a broad-band excitation of different molecular transitions. The logic output is carried by the molecular response that is measured by stimulated emission.

15.3.1 Non-linear optical response

Chromophoric molecules absorbing and emitting in the UV-visible range can be excited by a train of femtosecond laser pulses. Non-linear optical spectroscopies measure the molecular response for different excitation conditions (Cho, 2009; Mukamel, 1995). In particular, two-dimensional photon-echo spectroscopy (2D-PE) pumps and probes the electronic dynamics through the interactions of the molecular states with three short laser pulses (Collini, 2013). The laser pulses induce transitions between the molecular energy levels. The time evolution of the system is described by the density matrix, $\rho(t)$, whose diagonal and off-diagonal elements represent the populations and the coherences of the molecular energy levels. In the experimental scheme shown in Figure 15.2a, the three wave-vectors of the laser pulses exciting the sample at times τ_1, τ_2 and τ_3 are denoted as $\mathbf{k}_1$, $\mathbf{k}_2$ and $\mathbf{k}_3$ respectively. The signal is observed after the 3rd laser-matter interaction and depends on the three positive delay times between successive laser pulses, conventionally denoted as the coherence time, $\tau = \tau_2 - \tau_1$, the population time, $T = \tau_3 - \tau_2$ and the detection time, t. The macroscopic full polarization of the system at the time t, $P(t) = Tr\left[\hat{\mu}\rho(t)\right]$, is the expectation value of the transition dipole operator $\hat{\mu}$ in the density matrix $\rho(t)$ of the ensemble of molecules. The third laser stimulates emission that can be detected in different particular directions in space that is denoted $\mathbf{k}_l$. The molecular polarization at position $\mathbf{r}$ created by the sequence of light-matter interactions can be written in terms of its directional components

$$P(t, \mathbf{r}) = \sum_l P_l(t)\, e^{i\mathbf{k}_l \mathbf{r}} \tag{15.6}$$

where $P_l(t)$ is the partial polarization of the ensemble in the spatial direction l. The macroscopic direction vectors, $\mathbf{k}_l$, are defined by the so-called phase matching conditions

$$\mathbf{k}_l = \sum_i l_i \mathbf{k}_i \tag{15.7}$$

where $\mathbf{k}_i$ is the propagation direction of the i-th pulse (Brüggemann et al., 2007; Kato and Tanimura, 2001; Seidner et al., 1995) and l_i are integer coefficients. The signal in each such direction corresponds to the value of a specific component of the macroscopic polarization, Eq. 15.6. The experimental set-up for photon-echo spectroscopy is such that the particular phase-matching direction $\mathbf{k}_{PE} = -\mathbf{k}_1 + \mathbf{k}_2 + \mathbf{k}_3$, called the echo direction, is measured. A two dimensional spectrum is obtained as the double Fourier Transform (FT) of the PE signal with respect to the coherence time ($\tau \to \omega_1$) and the detection time ($t \to \omega_2$). The 2D spectrum resolves the dynamics of the system along the excitation (ω_1) and the emission (ω_2) frequencies for each population time T. Different evolution pathways contribute to the spectral intensity in specific regions of the 2D map. Such pathways can be analysed for weak pulses, within the limits of third order time dependent perturbation theory. To illustrate this concept let us consider a three level system as depicted in Figure 15.2b: an electronic transition between the ground (g) end the excited state in the ground vibrational state (e_0) and in an excited vibrational state (e_1). The coherences created by the first pulse evolve with their characteristic frequency during the time τ, these frequencies are observed after Fourier transforming along the ω_1 axis. The second pulse acts on these coherences bringing the system in a population state (i.e. gg, e_0e_0, e_1e_1) or in a coherent superposition of the excited state vibrational levels (i.e. e_1e_0, e_0e_1) that in turn evolves during the population time T. The third pulse brings the system

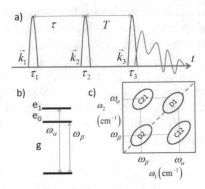

Fig. 15.2 (a) Laser pulse sequence in 2D photon-echo spectroscopy. (b) Three energy-level system: an electronic transition where two vibrational levels of the excited state are populated. (c) Schematic representation of a 2D-PE spectrum.

in the coherences that is detected during the time t and appears along ω_2 in the 2D spectra. Each interaction with the laser connects different elements of the density matrix; an evolution pathway where the system evolves in the coherence ge_0 during τ and during t contributes in the diagonal region D2 of the 2D spectrum, see Figure 15.2c. If the coherence ge_0 excited during τ is transferred to the coherence e_1g detected during t, this pathway appears in the off-diagonal region C21, and so on. The number and the nature of the possible pathways are defined by the level structure, the structure of the transition dipole operator and the mechanisms of energy transfer active in a specific system and a specific environment.

15.3.2 Multi-terminal decision tree of a half adder

The several dynamical pathways promoted by the interaction with the laser pulses are a physical implementation of the branches of logic decision trees (Fresch et al., 2015; Fresch et al., 2013). Each laser-matter interaction assigns the value of a logic variable, while the output is read on the frequency resolved 2D-PE map. An important aspect of this implementation is that all the transitions within the spectral bandwidth of the laser are simultaneously excited and all the dynamical pathways contribute to the measured 2D spectrum. From the logical point of view, the capability of exciting and reading simultaneously different pathways allows the computation of the logic function for all the possible input strings *in parallel*. Both binary and multivalued logic trees have been implemented (Fresch et al., 2013). Here we discuss in detail the realisation of a multi-terminal decision tree, which is a binary tree admitting multivalued outputs at the terminal nodes. Multi-terminal trees represent multi-output binary function at the integer level, see Eq. 15.1. In

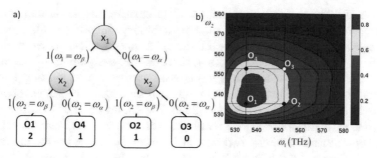

Fig. 15.3 (a) Multi-terminal logic tree representing the half addition as an integer function, see Figure 15.1b. The terminal nodes (leafs) report the spectral positions for reading the integer output. (b) Experimental 2D-PE spectra of the chromophore Tamra for $T = 435$ fs, the colour-code shows the three-valued reading of the output

particular we show the implementation of the half addition, whose truth table is shown in Figure 15.1b, by means of the 2D-PE optical response of the chromophore molecule TAMRA (5'-carboxy-tetramethylrhodamine) (Fresch et al., 2015). The two input variables to be added are provided by the first and the third laser pulses of the 2D-PE sequence of Figure 15.2a. To first approximation, the dynamics of Tamra involves two vibrational levels of the excited state as shown in Figure 15.2b. The first laser-matter interaction assigns the value of the first logic proposition, x_1 = *the excited state is in its ground vibrational state upon the interaction with the first laser pulse*. For x_1 = *true* the ge_0 coherence is created, evolving with frequency ω_β, while for $not(x_1)$ = *true* the system is described by the ge_1 coherence characterized by ω_α. Therefore, on the logical plane, the first laser matter interaction implements the Shannon decomposition Eq. 15.2 of the computed function with respect to x_1 and it corresponds to the first node of the corresponding multi-terminal decision tree shown in Figure 15.3a. The decomposition with respect x_1 appears along the excitation frequency ω_1 of the 2D response map, see Figure 15.3b: in the $\omega_1 = \omega_\beta$ slice of the spectrum we find the cofactor $f(1, x_2)$ defined in the spectral position O_1 and O_2 while for $\omega_1 = \omega_\alpha$ we can read the other cofactor $f(0, x_2)$ defined in O_3 and O_4. The second laser acts on the created coherences, this interaction brings the system either in a population state (gg, e_0e_0, e_1e_1) or a vibrational coherence (e_0e_1, e_1e_0). The third laser assigns the value of the second logic variable defined as the proposition x_2 = *the interaction with the laser leaves the system in the vibrational ground state coherence*. The branches of the tree ending with x_2 = TRUE represent dynamical pathways evolving with ω_β during the detection time t, position O_1 and O_4 in the spectrum, while x_2 = FALSE corresponds to $\omega_2 = \omega_\alpha$, which is spectral positions O_2 and O_3.

At the leaves (terminal nodes) of the logic tree shown in Figure 15.3a we have 0, 1 or 2, which is the integer output of the half adder function for the inputs that constitute the path from the root to the leaf, see truth table of

Figure 15.1b. The reading of the spectral intensities has to be mapped into the ternary set (0, 1, 2) rather than to a binary output (0, 1). Since the experimental error in the reading of the relative intensities is estimated to be 1% from repeated measurements, a three-valued assignment of the output is reliable. The three-valued output is read in the corresponding spectral positions showed in Figure 15.3b in the experimental 2D-PE spectrum of the sample at a population time T=435fs. The colour-code of the 2D spectra shows that we achieve a 3-valued reading of the output in agreement with the integer representation of the two-output functions of the addition operation. The main diagonal peak is assigned to the highest logic value 2, the two cross-peaks reads as 1 and the high frequency diagonal peak corresponds to the logical zero. Notice that the function is implemented in parallel by the quantum dynamics of the chromophore.

15.3.3 Spectral decomposition of multivalued logic function by spatially resolved emission

The parallelism achieved by the frequency resolved PE signal discussed in Sect. 15.3.2 stems from the quantum dynamical evolution. However, a further level of parallel processing (Yan et al., 2015) by coherent spectroscopy is achieved by considering as logic output the signal emitted in different spatial direction as given by eqns.(15.6)–(15.7). In principle, the sum defining the molecular polarization in terms of its directional components, Eq. 15.6 should contain an infinite number of terms to be an exact decomposition. In practice, the sum can be truncated either by retaining those transitions that are allowed up to a given order in perturbation theory, or, in a non-perturbative approach, by fitting the intensity of the experimental signal (Brüggemann et al., 2007; Kato and Tanimura, 2001; Seidner et al., 1995). Therefore in practice, the total polarization can be described exactly by a finite number of directional components. The number of directions, $\mathbf{k}_l$, that contribute to the sum is determined by the number and the strength of the pulses. The 2D-PE signals used in Sect. 15.3.2, defined by the phase matching conditions $-\mathbf{k}_1 + \mathbf{k}_2 + \mathbf{k}_3$, is only one out of the 44 phase matching directions that can be measured for weak fields, when a 3-rd order description is valid. Other directions involving 3 photons are for example $2\mathbf{k}_1 - \mathbf{k}_2$ and $2\mathbf{k}_2 - \mathbf{k}_1$, while the transmittance of the pump and the probe pulses due to stimulated emission and resonance Raman processes are observed in the $\mathbf{k}_1$ and $\mathbf{k}_2$ directions respectively. For stronger pulses, up to 146 signals (1st, 3rd and 5th orders) could be detected. In summary, even for lasers of the intensity as commonly used in photon echo experiments there are many observable directional components of the total polarization.

As demonstrated in Yan et al. (2015), the spatial decomposition of the non-linear optical response implements the SOP decomposition of multivalued logic functions, Eq. 15.5. The sets of inputs are given by the sets of integers $(l_1, ..., l_i, ...)$ that define the phase matching directions, $\mathbf{k}_l = \sum_i l_i \mathbf{k}_i$, Eq. 15.7. They are therefore inherently multivalued. The outputs are the binned values of the integrated values of the partial polarizations, $P_l(t)$. The logic function can be designed since the full polarization depends on the specificities of the molecular system and the characteristics of the sequence of pulses with which it interacts. The number of variables of the logic function is given by the number of pulses in the sequence. The radix of the multivalued logic variables is determined by the maximum absolute values of the integers $(l_1, ..., l_i, ...)$, physically governed by the strength of the pulses that dictates the order of the perturbation expansion needed to describe the partial polarization signals. In the example discussed below, we consider three laser pulses as in Figure 15.2a whose strengths lead to a radix of 5 for the logic variables. The vector defining the phase matching direction (l_1, l_2, l_3) with $l_i = \mp 2, \mp 1, 0$ selects a branch of the decomposition tree of the logic function, see Figure 15.4a. Therefore, the signal S_l measured in the direction $l = (l_1, l_2, l_3)$ is the coefficient of the term $J_{l_1}(x_1) J_{l_2}(x_2) J_{l_3}(x_3)$ in the Sum of Product expansion. All the values of the partial polarizations are processed in parallel and can be measured simultaneously directly at the macroscopic level using homodyne detection. The coefficients in all directions are the complete signature of the system dynamics. From a logic point of view, they fully determine the function that is computed since they correspond to its output values and to the coefficients of the expansion in a Sum of Products. In Figure 15.4 we report the calculated response (b) and the corresponding logic encoding (c) obtained for a five-level model system.

The level structure and transition dipole patterns of the molecular system, the characteristics of the pulse sequence (the polarization and carrier frequencies of the pulses, delay between the different pulses) and the interaction with the environment (dephasing rates leading to homogeneous and inhomogeneous broadening) determine which function of 3 five-valued variable is computed. Since we consider logic functions of three five-valued variables, there are $5^3 = 125$ sets of possible inputs which leads to a total number of possible functions of 5^{125}. Of the 5^{125} functions, only a very restricted number can be computed.

The first limitation comes from the number of spatial directions in which a non-negligible signal can be detected. A perturbation analysis can be performed to analyse the magnitude of the signal in the different phase matching directions $\mathbf{k}_l$ defined by the triad (l_1, l_2, l_3). The contributions to the partial polarization, $P_l(t)$, in the direction $\mathbf{k}_l$ that satisfies $\sum_{i=1}^{3} |l_i| = n$ are dominated by the n-th order processes of the perturbation expansion. For three pulses, the corresponding first order, third order and fifth order lead to six directions $\mathbf{k}_l$ for first order (corresponding to the sets of three integers $\{l\}_1$), 38 for third order (corresponding to the sets of three integers $\{l\}_3$) and 102 for fifth order (corresponding to the sets of three integers $\{l\}_5$), see, e.g., Yan et al. (2015, Table 1) for enumeration of the first order and third or-

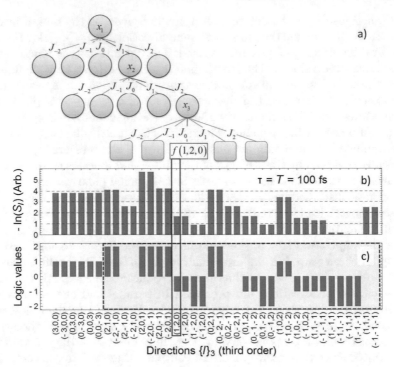

Fig. 15.4 (a) Multi-valued decision tree representing the Sum of Product decomposition of a multivalued function. (b) Computed homodyne signals S_l in different phase-matching directions for a five-level model system, and (c) their logic encoding. To obtain the logic outputs, the ln of S_l is binned into radix 5 values.

der directions. These directions correspond to all detectable signals for field strengths that allow reaching fifth order processes. We have computed 146 partial polarizations up to fifth order for a five-level model system. Including the fifth order guarantees that the first and third order signals are numerically accurate but we only use the first and third order signals in the logic implementation. Limiting the logic implementation to third order signals leads to non zero values in a maximum of 44 directions, 6 at first order and 38 at third order. These sets of inputs are the x axis labels in Figure 15.4b–c. If one does not encode outputs in the first order signals and if one eliminates the 6 signals $(\pm 3, 0, 0)$, $(0, \pm 3, 0)$, and $(0, 0, \pm 3)$ which correspond to a radix of 7, the signal is not zero in 32 directions. This means one can compute the functions which have a non zero output for a set of 32 triads of 5 valued inputs at most and are zero for all the other possible sets of inputs (125-32). This leads a maximum number of 5^{32} different functions. Within this subset of directions at a given order n, $\left\{ P_l^{(j)}(t) \right\}$ in half of the directions are linearly independent and the other half, $\left\{ P_{-l}^{(j)}(t) \right\}$ are the complex conjugates of the former, $P^{(j)}_{-l}(t) \equiv P^{(j)}_{-l_1,-l_2,-l_3}(t) = \left[P^{(j)}_{l_1,l_2,l_3}(t) \right]^*$. This relation further reduced to the number of function that can be implemented.

Even considering these limitations, the number of functions that can be computed remains remarkable. The spatial decomposition of the non-linear optical response generated by interference effects within the ensemble of molecules defines simultaneously all possible sets of input in parallel and computes the corresponding outputs that can be read simultaneously in the phase matching directions. The multivalued logic function that is computed can be designed by controlling the molecular system and the laser pulse sequence, see Yan et al. (2015) for more examples.

15.4 Ternary logic in solid state nanostructures

Recent progress in single-electron nano-electronics has stimulated designing logic gates on quantum dots (QDs) and single-electron transistors (SETs) for high-performance low-energy computations (Hoekstra, 2009). Early proposals were based on circuits with single electron transistors (Chen et al., 1996) operating in switching mode similar to conventional CMOS electronics. However, these devices can operate beyond the switching paradigm which leads to increasing the complexity of the logic operations implemented on a single device (Klein et al., 2010; Klein et al., 2007; Lee et al., 2008; Mol et al., 2011). In this context single-electron devices can be used for implementing MVL.

15.4.1 Physics of single-electron devices

A single-electron device can be defined as a device that "provides a means to precisely control the charging of a small conducting region at the level of one electron. These devices operate using Coulomb blockade or single-electron charging effect" (Durrani, 2009; Grabert and Devoret, 2013). The simplest circuits which exhibit single-electron charging effects are the single-electron box and the single electron transistor (see Figure 15.5). The single-electron box is a metallic island, often a quantum dot, connected by a tunnel junction with an electron reservoir and electrostatically coupled with the gate V_g. The single-electron transistor consists of two electrodes, the drain and the source, connected through tunnel junctions to the island. The electrical potential of the island can be tuned by a third electrode, known as the gate, which is electrostatically coupled to the island.

To transfer one electron into the island, the Coulomb energy $E_c = e^2/2C$ (Wasshuber, 2012) has to be supplied. Neglecting thermal effects, the energy is supplied by the bias voltage V_g. As long as the bias voltage is small enough, smaller than a threshold, no electron can tunnel because not enough energy

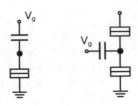

Fig. 15.5   Schematic representation of a single-electron box (left) and a single-electron transistor (right)

is available to charge the island. This effect arising from the quantization of charge is called the Coulomb blockade. Raising the bias voltage will populate the island with one, then two and more electrons, leading to a staircase-like characteristic charging curve. The Coulomb blockade effect is significant only if the Coulomb energy is larger than the thermal energy. Otherwise thermal fluctuations smear out the quantization effects. The necessary condition is $E_c = e^2/2C > k_B T$, where k_B is Boltzmann's constant and T is the absolute temperature. This means that the capacitance C has to be smaller than 12 aF for the observation of charging effects at the temperature of liquid nitrogen (77 K) and smaller than 3 aF for charging effects to appear at room temperature (300 K). This requires island with a diameter smaller than 15 nm and 5 nm respectively.

Using single-electron devices to perform logic operations faces several problems. One of them is an extremely low operational temperature. Recently, this problem has been solved by designing extremely small quantum dots in the channels of nanowire transistors (Lavieville et al., 2015). As a result, logic gates based on the single-electron transistor operating at room temperature has been fabricated (Lavieville et al., 2016). Another problem is a high sensitivity of the drain current to source-drain voltage fluctuations. To overcome this issue, the operating point can be stabilized including the conventional field-effect transistor operating in the saturation regime in the drain circuit as has been proposed by Inokawa et al. (2003). This technique has allowed the design of several successful multivalued logic circuits (Inokawa et al., 2003; Kim et al., 2012).

15.4.2 Quantum dot ternary-valued full-adder

We consider an example of a ternary full-adder implemented on a quantum-dot integrated together with a charge sensor based on a single-electron transistor (Klymenko and Remacle, 2014). The device operates at the temperature of 4 K. The full adder processes three inputs, a pair of ternary-valued digits, A and B to be added and a carry-in, C_{in}, resulting from the addition

Sum ($C_{in}=0$)	0	1	2
0	0	1	2
1	1	2	0
2	2	0	1

Sum ($C_{in}=1$)	0	1	2
0	1	2	0
1	2	0	1
2	0	1	2

Table 15.3 The truth tables for computing the sum of two ternary inputs for two possible values of the carry-in bit

C_{out} ($C_{in}=0$)	0	1	2
0	0	0	0
1	0	0	1
2	0	1	1

C_{out} ($C_{in}=1$)	0	1	2
0	0	0	1
1	0	1	1
2	1	1	1

Table 15.4 The truth tables for computing the carry-out of two ternary inputs for two possible values of the carry-in bit

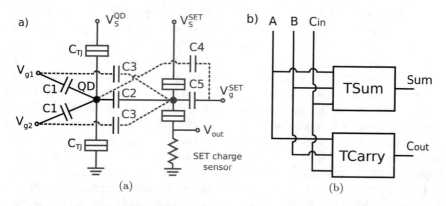

Fig. 15.6 (a) The equivalent circuit for QD-SET device. (b) Decomposing the ternary-valued full-adder into two logic units computing directly sum and carry-out, Cout. The logic units TSum and TCarry are represented by the same equivalent circuit

of the previous digit. It yields two outputs, the sum output, S, and carry-out, C_{out}. We operate with unbalanced ternary variables, represented by $(0, 1, 2)$. The carry out takes only two values, 0 and 1. The truth tables of the sum and the carry outputs are given in Tables 15.3 and 15.4, respectively. Tables 15.3 and 15.4 have a diagonal structure in the sense that all the elements standing on diagonals perpendicular to the main diagonal are equal.

For implementing the logic operations shown in Tables 15.3 and 15.4 we use a dual-gate single quantum-dot integrated with a charge sensor based on a single-electron transistor (QD-SET), see Figure 15.6a.

The QD-SET devices have three ternary inputs. Two input signals, V_{g1} and V_{g2}, are supplied by the voltage levels on the two gate electrodes attached to QD. The third input is the voltage level at the gate electrode of the single-electron transistor, V_g^{SET}. The output signals are determined by the electric current passing through the SET charge sensor while the QD operates in the Coulomb blockade regime storing a fixed number of electrons. Electric current flows through the QD only during transient processes caused by switching from one electron number to another. The QD-SET devices can be realized experimentally using lateral electrostatically defined quantum dots (Gonzalez-Zalba et al., 2012; Horibe et al., 2012). They are characterized by small sizes and low-energy consumption compared to other computational devices based on SETs. Conventional logic synthesis is usually carried out on a set of elementary logic gates. In contrast to conventional electronics, we do not use a set of binary gates for implementing more complex multivalued logic. We also do not decompose the full addition into two half additions. Rather, we propose a global method for the logic synthesis in QD devices. Taking advantage of the complex current-voltage characteristics of QD-SET, the ternary-valued full adder is implemented with two units schematically shown in Figure 15.6b, the TSum and the TCarry, directly processing the three ternary inputs. Each of these units is composed of a QD-SET device with a specific set of capacitances. Finding the value of these capacitances to implement the ternary addition is not an easy task in view of the number of parameters and the complexity of the targeted output. In order to overcome these difficulties, a multi-objective optimization design technique using a genetic algorithm has been developed (Klymenko and Remacle, 2014). The searching space is determined by elements of the capacitance matrix describing electrostatic couplings in the QD-SET and the objective functions of the full adder are defined as the maximal absolute error over the actual device logic outputs relative to the ideal truth tables of the sum and the carry-out in base 3. To compute the objective function, one needs to know the dependence of the SET electrical current on the voltage levels applied on the gate electrodes. To do that, we use the capacitance model together with a linear transport theory leading to a simple analytical expression for the dependence of the electric current on the chemical potentials of the electrodes and quantum dots (Beenakker, 1991). In Figure 15.7, the dependence of the electric current on the gate voltages V_{g1} and V_{g2} is shown for optimized parameters. The current flow exhibits peaks resulting from the Coulomb blockade effect in the SET. The peaks contain a number of abrupt jumps being a consequence of changing the charge configuration on the QD. This effect was experimentally observed in a similar setup in Lavieville et al. (2016). In the current maps shown in Figure 15.7, markers indicate the voltage levels used for encoding the inputs for the ternary addition. In the optimization procedure, we impose the values of voltages encoding the ternary variable $(0, 1, 2)$ to be equally spaced. To ensure a reliable operation of the device, the output signal should not fall into the instability regions of QD designated by areas with a fluctuating signal in Figure 15.7. The physical ability to perform complex logic operation on a QD-SET device results from the interplay of Coulomb blockade effects in the QD and SET, which is controlled by the electrostatic coupling between them and with the gate electrodes.

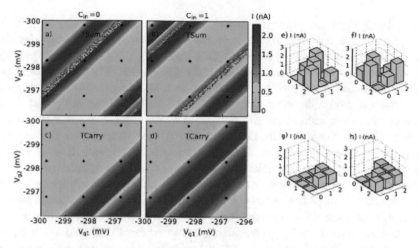

Fig. 15.7 Dependence of the electrical current in the charge sensor on the voltage levels on the gate electrodes, V_{g1} and V_{g2}, see Fig. 15.6(a). The panels (a) and (b) show the output current map for TSum unit for $C_{in} = 0$ and 1, respectively. The output current maps of TCarry are shown in (c) and (d). The values of the gate voltages V_{g1} and V_{g2} encoding the inputs are shown as filled dots. (e) and (f) show the histograms of the output current for S and C_{out} as a function of the inputs for $C_{in} = 0$ and panels (g) and (h) correspond to S and C_{out} for $C_{in} = 1$.

The proposed ternary-valued full adder is characterized by low energy consumption, since the device operates in a single-electron transport regime and consists of two elements only. The set up can be cascaded by adding an amplifier and is scalable. It is compatible with already experimentally realized devices based on QD-SET systems operating at low temperature.

15.5 Conclusion

Multivalued logic is the natural logic system for unconventional devices based on molecules and nanostructures. This is because quantisation offers several discrete states that can encode multi-valued variables. We have discussed two different physical systems that were used for multivalued computing: molecules and single electron solid state devices.

In molecular systems, discrete electronic and vibrational states can be addressed optically and their time evolution can be mapped to multivalued logic operations. The striking feature of using a molecular system for logic processing is parallelism. For the frequency resolved output reported in Sect. 15.3.2, parallel logic processing relies on the simultaneous excitation of several transitions and the subsequent quantum dynamics. The core idea for the parallel implementation of a molecular decision tree by the system dynamics is the branching between the states of the system due to their interaction with the pulses. Each time the pulse interacts with the molecule, another logic input of the function is resolved, which corresponds to a new subtree in the decision tree. The response of the system depends both on the value of the input and on its dynamical state when it interacts with the pulse. Therefore, the device operates as a finite state machine and not as a simple gate. Another layer of parallelism is available when the outputs are read in different spatial directions as in the implementation of Sect. 15.3.3. Here, parallelism is inherently implemented because all the partial polarizations that define the outputs are processed simultaneously. The outputs, which are read directly on the macroscopic level, can be multivalued because the high dynamical range of partial polarization measurements by nonlinear coherent spectroscopy allows for high resolution of the signals. A wider discussion of the perspectives and limitations of computing by non-linear optical molecular response, also with reference to the conventional computing paradigm, can be found in Chapter 4 of this volume. One of the main current limitation of implementing logic processing through the optical molecular response is the difficulty of interfacing the molecular units and the output signal to the existing Boolean computing technology. To integrate multivalued logic units with standard hardware, nanostructures embedded in a solid matrix are promising. We have shown that the quantisation of charge in quantum dots allows the implementation of a ternary full-adder in a solid state device that is fully compatible with the current CMOS technology. In this case, the multivalued encoding offers a more compact and energy-efficient design.

The logic implemented on molecular states is parallel, ultrafast and relies on the quantum dynamics induced by light-matter interactions. On the contrary, the ternary adder of Sect. 15.4 relies on the sensitivity of a SET device to the static charge state of a quantum dot. Nonetheless, for both implementations the quantisation of the state of the system typical of the sub-nanometric scale plays a key role. The physics of quantum systems is triggering the development of new logic processing paradigms. On the other hand several conceptual and technological challenges have to be addressed to fully exploit the potentialities of molecules and nanostructures for computing technology. The goal of using single molecules as tiny logic processors contrasts with our need of a macroscopic reading of the output. This problem is overcome by averaging procedures. We can average over many processes in a single device. This is the case when we read a macroscopic current that implies many electronic tunnelling events through the quantum dot. Alternatively, we can average over many systems as we do by measuring the optical response of a molecular ensemble. The exploitation of fluctuations and variability at the nanoscale is a promising avenue for future developments. Moreover, it is important to provide strategies for the integration of these new computing devices with existing technologies. This is not an easy task but it is an essential one in order to maximise the impact and the applicability of new logic paradigms. The design of organised molecular systems and solid state nanostructures is a step toward the integration of unconventional computing devices and current technology.

Acknowledgments

Most of the material presented in this chapter has been developed within the FP7 FET EC Project MULTI (317707) and the FP7 FET EC Project TOLOP (318397). We acknowledge the support of the H2020 FET Open project COPAC (766563). B.F. acknowledges the support of the Italian Ministero dell'Istruzione, Università e Ricerca through the grant Rita Levi Montalcini – 2013, and F.R. the support of Fonds National de la Recherche Scientifique, FRS-FNRS, Belgium.

References

Amlani, Islamshah, Alexei O. Orlov, Geza Toth, Gary H. Bernstein, Craig S. Lent, and Gregory L. Snider (1999). "Digital Logic Gate Using Quantum-Dot Cellular Automata". *Science* 284(5412):289–291.

Beenakker, C. W. J. (1991). "Theory of Coulomb-blockade oscillations in the conductance of a quantum dot". *Phys. Rev. B* 44(4):1646–1656.

Bolc, L. and P. Borowik (1992). *Many-Valued Logics 1: Volume 1: Theoretical Foundations*. Springer.

Boole, G. (2009). *The Mathematical Analysis of Logic: Being an Essay Towards a Calculus of Deductive Reasoning*. Cambridge University Press.

Brüggemann, Ben, Pär Kjellberg, and Tõnu Pullerits (2007). "Non-perturbative calculation of 2D spectra in heterogeneous systems: Exciton relaxation in the {FMO} complex". *Chemical Physics Letters* 444(1-3):192–196.

Chen, R. H., A. N. Korotkov, and K. K. Likharev (1996). "Single-electron transistor logic". *Applied Physics Letters* 68(14):1954–1956.

Cho, M. (2009). *Two-Dimensional Optical Spectroscopy*. CRC Press.

Collini, Elisabetta (2013). "Spectroscopic signatures of quantum-coherent energy transfer". *Chem. Soc. Rev.* 42(12):4932–4947.

Durrani, Z.A.K. (2009). *Single-Electron Devices and Circuits in Silicon*. Imperial College Press.

Elbaz, Johann, Oleg Lioubashevski, Fuan Wang, Françoise Remacle, Raphael D. Levine, and Itamar Willner (2010). "DNA computing circuits using libraries of DNAzyme subunits". *Nat Nano* 5(6):417–422.

Elbaz, Johann, Fuan Wang, Françoise Remacle, and Itamar Willner (2012).
    "pH-Programmable DNA Logic Arrays Powered by Modular DNAzyme
    Libraries". *Nano Letters* 12(12):6049–6054.

Fitting, M. and E. Orlowska (2013). *Beyond Two: Theory and Applications of
    Multiple-Valued Logic.* Studies in Fuzziness and Soft Computing. Physica-
    Verlag HD.

Fresch, B., J. Verduijn, J. A. Mol, S. Rogge, and F. Remacle (2012). "Query-
    ing a quasi-classical Oracle: One-bit function identification problem im-
    plemented in a single atom transistor". *EPL (Europhysics Letters)* 99(2)
    :28004.

Fresch, Barbara, Juanita Bocquel, Dawit Hiluf, Sven Rogge, Raphael D.
    Levine, and Françoise Remacle (2017a). "Multivariable Logic Functions
    in Parallel by Electrically Addressing a Molecule of Three Dopants in Sil-
    icon". *ChemPhysChem* 18:1790–1797.

Fresch, Barbara, Juanita Bocquel, Sven Rogge, Raphael D. Levine, and
    Françoise Remacle (2017b). "A Probabilistic Finite State Logic Machine
    Realized Experimentally on a Single Dopant Atom". *Nano Letters* 17(3)
    :1846–1852.

Fresch, Barbara, Marco Cipolloni, Tian-Min Yan, Elisabetta Collini, R. D.
    Levine, and F. Remacle (2015). "Parallel and Multivalued Logic by the
    Two-Dimensional Photon-Echo Response of a Rhodamine–DNA Com-
    plex". *The Journal of Physical Chemistry Letters* 6(9):1714–1718.

Fresch, Barbara, Dawit Hiluf, Elisabetta Collini, R. D. Levine, and F.
    Remacle (2013). "Molecular decision trees realized by ultrafast electronic
    spectroscopy". *Proceedings of the National Academy of Sciences* 110(43)
    :17183–17188.

Fresch, Barbara, Françoise Remacle, and Raphael D. Levine (2017c). "Imple-
    mentation of Probabilistic Algorithms by Multi-chromophoric Molecular
    Networks with Application to Multiple Travelling Pathways". *ChemPhys-
    Chem* 18:1782–1789.

Gonzalez-Zalba, M Fernando, Dominik Heiss, and Andrew J Ferguson (2012).
    "A hybrid double-dot in silicon". *New Journal of Physics* 14(2):023050.

Grabert, H. and M.H. Devoret (2013). *Single Charge Tunneling: Coulomb
    Blockade Phenomena In Nanostructures.* Springer.

Hoekstra, J. (2009). *Introduction to Nanoelectronic Single-Electron Circuit
    Design.* Pan Stanford Publishing.

Horibe, Kosuke, Tetsuo Kodera, Tomohiro Kambara, Ken Uchida, and Shunri
    Oda (2012). "Key capacitive parameters for designing single-electron tran-
    sistor charge sensors". *Journal of Applied Physics* 111(9):093715.

Hurst, S. L. (1984). "Multiple-Valued Logic: its Status and its Future". *IEEE
    Transactions on Computers* C-33(12):1160–1179.

Inokawa, H., A. Fujiwara, and Y. Takahashi (2003). "A multiple-valued logic
    and memory with combined single-electron and metal-oxide-semiconductor
    transistors". *IEEE Transactions on Electron Devices* 50(2):462–470.

Kato, Tsuyoshi and Yoshitaka Tanimura (2001). "Multi-dimensional vibrational spectroscopy measured from different phase-matching conditions". *Chemical Physics Letters* 341(3–4):329–337.

Kim, S. J., J. J. Lee, H. J. Kang, J. B. Choi, Y.-S. Yu, Y. Takahashi, and D. G. Hasko (2012). "One electron-based smallest flexible logic cell". *Applied Physics Letters* 101(18):183101.

Klein, M., J. A. Mol, J. Verduijn, G. P. Lansbergen, S. Rogge, R. D. Levine, and F. Remacle (2010). "Ternary logic implemented on a single dopant atom field effect silicon transistor". *Applied Physics Letters* 96(4):043107.

Klein, Michael, S. Rogge, F. Remacle, and R. D. Levine (2007). "Transcending Binary Logic by Gating Three Coupled Quantum Dots". *Nano Letters* 7(9):2795–2799.

Klymenko, M. V. and F. Remacle (2014). "Quantum dot ternary-valued full-adder: Logic synthesis by a multiobjective design optimization based on a genetic algorithm". *Journal of Applied Physics* 116(16):164316.

Lavieville, Romain, Sylvain Barraud, Christian Arvet, Christian Vizioz, Andrea Corna, Xavier Jehl, Marc Sanquer, and Maud Vinet (2016). "Demonstration of Single Hole Transistor and Hybrid Circuits for Multivalued Logic and Memory Applications up to 350 K Using CMOS Silicon Nanowires". *Advanced Electronic Materials* 2(4):1500244.

Lavieville, Romain, François Triozon, Sylvain Barraud, Andrea Corna, Xavier Jehl, Marc Sanquer, Jing Li, Antoine Abisset, Ivan Duchemin, and Yann-Michel Niquet (2015). "Quantum Dot Made in Metal Oxide Silicon-Nanowire Field Effect Transistor Working at Room Temperature." *Nano Letters* 15(5):2958–2964.

Lee, C. K., S. J. Kim, S. J. Shin, J. B. Choi, and Y. Takahashi (2008). "Single-electron-based flexible multivalued logic gates". *Applied Physics Letters* 92(9):093101.

Mano, M.M., C.R. Kime, and T. Martin (2015). *Logic and Computer Design Fundamentals*. Prentice Hall.

Margulies, David, Clifford E. Felder, Galina Melman, and Abraham Shanzer (2007). "A Molecular Keypad Lock: A Photochemical Device Capable of Authorizing Password Entries". *Journal of the American Chemical Society* 129(2):347–354.

Miller, D.M. and M.A. Thornton (2008). *Multiple Valued Logic: Concepts and Representations*. Morgan & Claypool.

Mol, J. A., J. van der Heijden, J. Verduijn, M. Klein, F. Remacle, and S. Rogge (2011). "Balanced ternary addition using a gated silicon nanowire". *Applied Physics Letters* 99(26):263109.

Mukamel, S. (1995). *Principles of nonlinear optical spectroscopy*. Oxford University Press.

Orbach, Ron, Sivan Lilienthal, Michael Klein, R. D. Levine, Françoise Remacle, and Itamar Willner (2015). "Ternary DNA computing using 3 × 3 multiplication matrices". *Chem. Sci.* 6(2):1288–1292.

Orbach, Ron, Fuan Wang, Oleg Lioubashevski, R. D. Levine, Françoise Remacle, and Itamar Willner (2014). "A full-adder based on reconfigurable DNA-hairpin inputs and DNAzyme computing modules". *Chem. Sci.* 5(9) :3381–3387.

Raymo, Françisco M. and Silvia Giordani (2002). "All-optical processing with molecular switches". *Proceedings of the National Academy of Sciences* 99(8):4941–4944.

Remacle, F., J. R. Heath, and R. D. Levine (2005). "Electrical addressing of confined quantum systems for quasiclassical computation and finite state logic machines". *Proceedings of the National Academy of Sciences of the United States of America* 102(16):5653–5658.

Remacle, F. and R. D. Levine (2001). "Towards a molecular logic machine". *The Journal of Chemical Physics* 114(23):10239–10246.

Remacle, F., Shammai Speiser, and R. D. Levine (2001). "Intermolecular and Intramolecular Logic Gates". *The Journal of Physical Chemistry B* 105(24):5589–5591.

Rescher, N. (1969). *Many-valued logic.* McGraw-Hill.

Seidner, Luis, Gerhard Stock, and Wolfgang Domcke (1995). "Nonperturbative approach to femtosecond spectroscopy: General theory and application to multidimensional nonadiabatic photoisomerization processes". *The Journal of Chemical Physics* 103(10):3998–4011.

Stankovic, R. and J.T. Astola (2006). *Spectral Interpretation of Decision Diagrams.* Springer.

Stanković, R.S., J.T. Astola, and C. Moraga (2012). *Representation of Multiple-Valued Logic Functions.* Morgan & Claypool.

Wasshuber, C. (2012). *Computational Single-Electronics.* Springer.

Yan, Tian-Min, Barbara Fresch, R. D. Levine, and F. Remacle (2015). "Information processing in parallel through directionally resolved molecular polarization components in coherent multidimensional spectroscopy". *The Journal of Chemical Physics* 143(6):064106.

Ziegler, Martin, Rohit Soni, Timo Patelczyk, Marina Ignatov, Thorsten Bartsch, Paul Meuffels, and Hermann Kohlstedt (2012). "An Electronic Version of Pavlov's Dog". *Advanced Functional Materials* 22(13):2744–2749.

Chapter 16
Nanoscale Molecular Automata: From Materials to Architectures

Ross Rinaldi, Rafael Gutierrez, Alejandro Santana Bonilla,
Gianaurelio Cuniberti, and Alessandro Bramanti

Abstract When investigating possible molecular forms for next-generation electronics, the architectures and computing paradigms – either resembling those of classical electronics, or being entirely new – are often established a priori. Research on materials is a subsequent step, which aims to find, in the vast world of molecular materials, those most closely resembling the needed properties. Sometimes, the opposite approach can be both necessary and fruitful. Looking at the characteristics of real-world molecules, and adapting the architecture to them where a tradeoff is possible, is likely a more effective approach than trying to find the right molecule, based on a long list of requirements, often very difficult to fulfil. Here, the problem of matching architecture and materials is introduced, using the promising Quantum-dot Cellular Automata (QCA) paradigm.

16.1 Introduction: from old to new: the traps

The development of QCA is an interesting case study because it lends itself to general remarks about the development of novel computational paradigms. First of all, QCA are Boolean systems. Although intrinsically quantum (as they are based on charge confinement and tunnelling) they can be viewed as classical at the macroscale. The cell polarization, measuring the charge density distribution among the diagonals, is a classical observable, so that the cells are bistable in a classical sense. Computation comes from their electrostatic interaction, in turn dependent on the cell topology. In fact, a complete set of logical gates has been demonstrated, so that Boolean QCA networks can be built, which are fully equivalent to their silicon-based counterparts. This is a boon for designers, who can reuse much of the digital known-how developed through the past decades, though with some adaptation. Moreover, apart from practical reasons, a sort of 'principle of continuity' is satisfied,

© Springer International Publishing AG, part of Springer Nature 2018
S. Stepney et al. (eds.), *Computational Matter*, Natural Computing Series,
https://doi.org/10.1007/978-3-319-65826-1_16

according to which, in developing new systems, our minds tends to recycle as much as possible of their ancestors – just like the earliest cars resembled horseless carriages, while only subsequent refinements began to optimise their design for the exigencies of engine-powered vehicles.

The other great merit of QCA is that, on the physical side, they did *not* exceed in such continuity, in this being one step ahead of mainstream research. In fact, much work in molecular electronics during the 1990s and later was devoted to searching molecular transistors. This was based on the implicit assumption that transistors are necessary for computation, However seemingly supported by the indisputable success of transistors, this assumption is not that straightforward. After so many years of (mostly fruitless) research along this line, two remarks are in order. In the first place, no real equivalent of silicon transistors has been found, and this is not so amazing. Silicon-based transistors emerge from the complex physics of semiconductors, with its highly nonlinear charge transport dynamics, Such concoction of physical phenomena does *not* lead to computational applications *per se*. The encoding of computation (analogue, thanks to approximately linear signal amplification, or Boolean, exploiting opposite saturation conditions to represent the two logical values) is a superposition, and partly an adaptation. An extremely succesful one, producing highly performing devices, which moreover have kept shrinking and improving for decades; and, yet, an adaptation. Just like any encoding of abstract computation into matter, it is somewhat arbitrary: an association of values and relationships to physical quantities and interactions. At the molecular scale, where the physics is different, there is no reason to think that trying to reproduce the same physical phenomena should be the only, or even the best way to encode digital logics, if ever possible. If the typical behaviour of matter changes, the best way to encode computation will change as well. In this respect, QCA fit the nanoscale scenario, exploiting quantum charge confinement and tunneling (along with electrostatic interaction) which are typical in nanostructure, rather than trying to mimick larger-scale devices.

On the other hand, QCA have been developed theoretically from highly idealized models, in which the cell dots are all the same as to size and state distribution, the cells are perfectly square and the cell spacing is uniform and fully controlled. These are tacit, but important assumptions. In fact, as QCA are based on electrostatics, little alteration of the mentioned parameters can lead to unpredictable imbalance in otherwise symmetric states, potentially jeopardizing the logical functionality. This is particularly critical since QCA should ultimately be implemented with molecular cells, in which ambient temperature operation is expected to be possible (Wang and Lieberman, 2004). At even moderately larger scales – such as metal nanoislands separated by tens of nanometers (Amlani et al., 1999) – the thermal enlargement of states limits the operation temperature to mK, definitely impractical for most electronic devices. However, molecules are not that controllable as to their geometry and shape distribution, if only because their synthesis and deposition chemistry often pose severe constraints. As a consequence, real-world QCA network may not (and, probably, will not) fulfil the implicit high symmetry requirements of classical QCA. This can be seen as a drawback, or as the starting point for further development of the QCA paradigm. Before we draw some conclusions in that respect, we shall evaluate the effect of molecular nonidealities on QCA operation in some simple, but very significant cases.

16.2 Modelling molecular-based QCA

Quantum Cellular Automata (QCA) have been proposed as a new and revolutionary paradigm for classical binary computing (Lent, 2000). The basic computational unit, the QCA cell, consists of quantum dots connected in such a way as to allow both charge confinement on the dots and charge exchange between pairs of dots. Few (usually two) mobile charges can move between strongly localized electronic states. Bits of information (0 and 1) are then encoded by different geometrical arrangements of the charges within the cell.

In molecular-based QCA, the role of the quantum dots is taken over by molecular complexes with localized electronic states, e.g. redox centers capable of accepting and donating electrons (Lambert et al., 2005). These charge centers are interconnected by bridging ligands, whose electronic properties determine the amount of charge localization on each quantum dot by acting as tunnel barriers (Van Voorhis et al., 2010).

First attempts to deal with the delicate interplay between charge transfer between redox centers and the "transparency" of the linking bridges were pioneered by C. Lent and coworkers and were mostly based on model-based approaches (Lu and Lent, 2008; Rahimi and Nejad, 2012). In such models the basic quantity is the so-called response function, which encodes features from the electronic structure – ET matrix element – information on the configuration of the system (Lu and Lent, 2008).

A major issue, which has not been thoroughly addressed is the problem of how real-world structural asymmetries can affect the m-QCA response, i.e. how deviations from ideal linear or square arrays influence the intra-cell charge transfer as well as the communication between cells and thus the computational properties of m-QCA (Arima et al., 2012b; Crocker et al., 2009; Crocker et al., 2008; Dysart, 2013; Huang et al., 2004; Macucci, 2010; Niemier and Kogge, 2001; Ottavi et al., 2011; Pulimeno et al., 2013; Rojas et al., 2002; Sturzu et al., 2005; Wasio et al., 2012).

In what follows, we illustrate this problem by addressing, within a minimal model-based approach, the influence of orientational distortions on the m-QCA response (Santana Bonilla et al., 2014). *We address first the problem at the level of a single model m-QCA cell, before proceeding afterwards to show results for a network model based on the Hubbard Hamiltonian.*

16.3 Minimal two-sites m-QCA cell

For the sake of simplicity, we consider a half-cell m-QCA, which consists of two redox centers separated by a featureless tunnel barrier, which can be implemented e.g. by using a conjugated chain linker. The goal is to compute the cell response in presence of a driver, which we assume to be a simple classical dipole, and whose main function is to start the switching process in the second molecule (target molecule), in analogy to the external voltage source needed to set in the switching process in semiconductor quantum-dot QCA implementations (Macucci, 2010).

Thus, we associate with the driver the quantities $q_{1,2}$, representing the excess in the charge population that can freely move between the driver redox centers. Assuming only one mobile charge, we have the condition $q_1 + q_2 = 1$. In the case of the target molecule, the net population is related to the associated occupation probabilities in the (ground state) wave function. We treat the problem within an diabatic-to-adiabatic transformation approach, within which the interplay between classical Coulombic interactions (driver-target) and quantum mechanical effects (ET process within the target) can be described.

16.3.1 Diabatic to adiabatic transformation

To describe intra-molecular ET processes, the simplest approach relies on a two-state approximation, taking as a reference point the localized diabatic states representing initial and final stages of the ET process (Van Voorhis et al., 2010). The corresponding Hamiltonian matrix is simply given by:

$$\begin{bmatrix} H_{aa} & H_{ab} \\ H_{ba} & H_{bb} \end{bmatrix} \begin{bmatrix} c_a \\ c_b \end{bmatrix} = E \begin{bmatrix} c_a \\ c_b \end{bmatrix} \qquad (16.1)$$

Here, $H_{aa} = \langle \phi_a | H | \phi_a \rangle$, $H_{bb} = \langle \phi_b | H | \phi_b \rangle$ and $H_{ab} = H_{ba}^* = \langle \phi_a | H | \phi_b \rangle$. The corresponding orthogonal eigenfunctions (diabatic states) for H_{aa} and H_{bb} are denoted by $|\phi_a\rangle$ and $|\phi_b\rangle$ with associated eigenvalues E_a and E_b, respectively. H_{aa} and H_{bb} correspond to the cases where the excess of charge is localized either at the upper or lower part of the target molecule, and can be considered as the initial and final stages of the ET process, respectively. Since the charge is fully localized in those states, both matrix elements can be analytically calculated using basic electrostatics. For the fully symmetrical case, where $d = L$, see the left panel of Fig.16.1, we get:

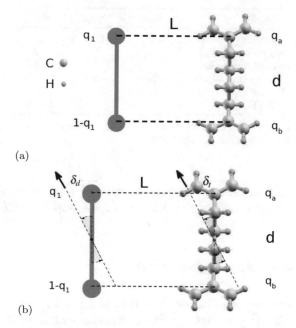

Fig. 16.1 Schematic representation for the driver-target configurations. The driver molecule is represented by two partial charges q_1, q_2 such that $q_1 + q_2 = 1$, and separated by a distance d. The electric field of the driver induces a switching process in the target. (a) Symmetrical situation where both components are static. (b) Coordinated rotations between the driver and the target. In the small angle approximation, the angular distortions can be related to the linear displacements δ_d and δ_t of the driver and target molecules, respectively. [Adapted from Santana Bonilla et al. (2014) with permission from the PCCP Owner Societies.]

$$H_{aa} = \frac{e^2}{4\pi\epsilon_0}\left[\frac{q_1}{L} + \frac{(1-q_1)}{2\sqrt{L}}\right] \qquad (16.2)$$

$$H_{bb} = \frac{e^2}{4\pi\epsilon_0}\left[\frac{q_1}{\sqrt{2}L} + \frac{(1-q_1)}{L}\right]$$

H_{ab} and H_{ba} matrix elements, on the other side, mix the diabatic states. Diagonalizing the Hamiltonian is straightforward and its eigenvalues are given by: $2E_{\pm} = H_{aa} + H_{bb} \pm \sqrt{(H_{aa} - H_{bb})^2 + 4H_{ab}^2}$. Using the adiabatic solution, the coupling between diabatic states at the degeneracy point ($H_{aa} = H_{bb}$) can be computed as: $\gamma = H_{ab} = \frac{E_+ - E_-}{2}$. Here, we consider only super-exchange mediated ET, where the donor-acceptor charge transfer takes place via a tunneling process, with no population of the bridge states. In this regime, γ can be written as an exponential function of the donor-acceptor separation R:

$$\gamma = \gamma_0 e^{-\alpha R} \qquad (16.3)$$

Complex	$\alpha(nm^{-1})$	$\gamma_0(eV)$	$\gamma(eV)$
1,4-diallyl butane	4.66	6.68	
allyl-$(CH_2)_3$-allyl			0.52
allyl-$(CH_2)_9$-allyl			0.0119
diferrocenylpolyenes	0.84	0.12	
FC-1-FC			0.061
FC-5-FC			0.028

Table 16.1 Typical reference parameters used in Eq. 16.3 for the two studied molecule types (Lu and Lent, 2008; Ribou et al., 1996)

where α is system-dependent. Reference values for the electronic coupling elements are displayed in Table 16.3.1, see also Lu and Lent (2008).

16.3.2 Cell response function

The cell response (or polarization) function is defined by $P_2 = \text{Tr}\{\rho_t\sigma_3\} = |c_a|^2 - |c_b|^2 = 2|c_a|^2 - 1$. Here, ρ_t is the density matrix of the target and $\sigma_3 = diag(1, -1)$ is a Pauli matrix. Within the two-state approximation, the $c_{a,b}$ are the coefficients of the expansion of the ground state wave function in the diabatic basis. The corresponding polarization for the (classical) driver is then simply $P_1 = q_1 - q_2 = 2q_1 - 1$.

Using the adiabatic energy eigenvalues $E_\pm$, we get $c_a^2 = \gamma^2/(\gamma^2 + (E_+ - H_{aa})^2)$, and the target polarization P_2 can be expressed as a function of the driver polarization P_1 as:

$$P_2 = \frac{2}{1 + \{\beta P_1 + \sqrt{(\beta P_1)^2 + 1}\}^2} - 1 \qquad (16.4)$$

with

$$\beta = \frac{e^2}{4\pi\epsilon_0}\left[\frac{2 - \sqrt{2}}{2}\right]\frac{1}{\gamma L} \qquad (16.5)$$

β encodes information on both the electronic properties of the target, γ, and geometrical features of the problem, L (Lu and Lent, 2008). How is this result, derived for an ideal half-cell modified, when angular distortions of the driver and the target are allowed?

16.3.2.1 Cell response: angular distortions

In the right panel of Fig. 16.1 we schematically illustrate a situation, where both, target and driver molecules with length d are allowed to rotate about their corresponding centers of mass. We limit our discussion to the linear regime of small angular distortions $\theta_{t,d}$ with $\sin\theta_{t,d} \approx \theta_{t,d} = 2\delta_{t,d}/d$, and t, d denoting the target and driver distortions, respectively. In this limit, the diabatic states are found to be:

$$H_{aa} = \frac{e^2}{4\pi\epsilon_0} \left[\frac{q_1}{(L - \delta_d - \delta_t)} \right.$$

$$\left. + \frac{(1 - q_1)}{\sqrt{(L + \delta_d + \delta_t)^2 + (d^2 - 4\delta_t^2)}} \right] \tag{16.6}$$

$$H_{bb} = \frac{e^2}{4\pi\epsilon_0} \left[\frac{q_1}{\sqrt{(L - \delta_d - \delta_t)^2 + (d^2 - 4\delta_d^2)}} \right.$$

$$\left. + \frac{(1 - q_1)}{(L + \delta_d - \delta_t)} \right]$$

The corresponding polarization function can then be written as follows:

$$P_2 = \frac{2}{1 + \{(\beta_1 P_1 + \beta_2) + \sqrt{(\beta_1 P_1 + \beta_2)^2 + 1}\}^2} - 1 \tag{16.7}$$

The parameters $\beta_{1,2}$ are given by:

$$\beta_1 = \frac{e^2}{4\pi\epsilon_0} \frac{1}{2\gamma} \left[\frac{1}{(L - \delta_d + \delta_t)} + \frac{1}{(L + \delta_d - \delta_t)} \right.$$

$$- \frac{1}{\sqrt{(L + \delta_d + \delta_t)^2 + (d^2 - 4\delta_t^2)}}$$

$$\left. - \frac{1}{\sqrt{(L - \delta_d - \delta_t)^2 + (d^2 - 4\delta_d^2)}} \right] \tag{16.8}$$

$$\beta_2 = \frac{e^2}{4\pi\epsilon_0} \frac{1}{2\gamma} \left[\frac{1}{(L - \delta_d + \delta_t)} - \frac{1}{(L + \delta_d - \delta_t)} \right.$$

$$+ \frac{1}{\sqrt{(L + \delta_d + \delta_t)^2 + (d^2 - 4\delta_t^2)}}$$

$$\left. - \frac{1}{\sqrt{(L - \delta_d - \delta_t)^2 + (d^2 - 4\delta_d^2)}} \right] \tag{16.9}$$

In the previous equations, we consider in general different distortions for the driver (δ_d) and the target (δ_t). However, to simplify the discussion in the following, we consider only symmetric cases where $|\delta_t| = |\delta_d| = \delta$. Based on this model, we can define two types of distortions: (i) in-phase displacements, where $sgn(\delta_t) = sgn(\delta_d)$, and (ii) out-of-phase displacements with $sgn(\delta_t) = -sgn(\delta_d)$.

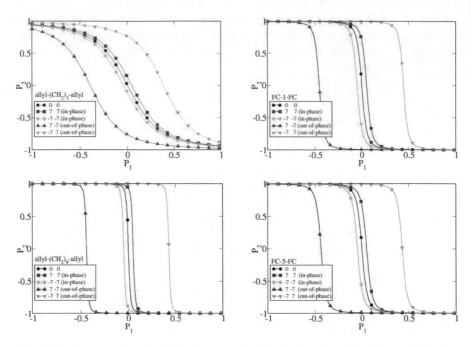

Fig. 16.2 Response function of the target molecule as a function of the driver polarization for the case of coupled angular distortions. Results for the alkyl-diene molecules with two different bridge lengths as well as for the diferrocenyl based systems are shown. The general notation θ_d, θ_t indicates the angular distortions (in degrees) of the driver (d) and target (t). As mentioned in the text, we assume for simplicity $|\theta_d| = |\theta_t| = \theta$. The differences in the signs correspond to two qualitative different situations: in-phase displacements of the target and the driver ($\theta(-\theta), \theta(-\theta)$), and (ii) out-of-phase displacements ($\theta(-\theta), -\theta(\theta)$). The main effect of the angular distortions is to induce a horizontal shift of the target's response function, so that a non-zero target polarization may appear even if the driver polarization is zero. Thus, even small angular displacements can dramatically destroy the required sstructure of the response function of the m-QCA. [Reproduced from Santana Bonilla et al. (2014) with permission from the PCCP Owner Societies.]

The polarization functions for these different cases are shown in Fig. 16.2 for the special case $L = d/2$. As we clearly see there, the main influence of angular distortions is to shift the target polarization along the P_1-axis in a way that sensitively depends on the type of the considered collective distortions (in- or out-of-phase). This clearly induces a strong perturbation of the QCA response function. The value of P_2 at zero driver polarization is related to the β_2 parameter as $P_2 = 2/(1 + \{\beta_2 + \sqrt{(\beta_2)^2 + 1}\}^2) - 1$, so that as long as β_2 does not vanish, a non-zero, topology-induced, residual polarization will exist and thus the target polarization displays a lag w.r.t. the driver. The strongest modifications of the polarization are found to occur for the out-of-phase distortions, which can induce a strong shift for angular displacements of the order of $\theta = \pm 7°$. In real molecular systems we may expect in general

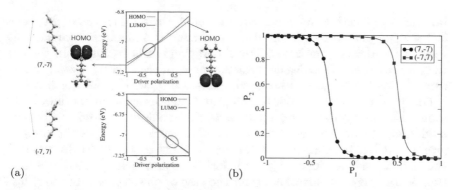

(a)　　　　　　　　　　　　　　　　　　(b)

Fig. 16.3 (a) Calculated HOMO and LUMO energy levels for the 1,4-diallyl butane radical cation where (out-of-phase) angular distortions of both target and driver are taken into account, see also Fig. 16.2. The angular distortions between driver and target are (i) $(7,-7)$ and (ii) $(-7,7)$. Notice the shift (encircled) of the anti-crossing point of the molecular states to the left or right of the zero driver polarization in dependence of the relative angular distortion of the driver and target. The shifts are not fully symmetric, which is only reflecting the fact that the real molecular system is not fully planar. Also shown in the figure are the charge density plots of the HOMO state for the two limiting driver polarizations $P_1 = -1$ and $P_1 = 1$. (b) Corresponding cell response function. [Reproduced from Santana Bonilla et al. (2014) with permission from the PCCP Owner Societies.]

smaller angular distortions; their influence should be most likely noticeable for situations where no strong covalent bonding to the substrate takes place or when the active molecular species are attached to the substrate via longer inert linkers, which might increase the mechanical flexibility of the system.

The sensitivity on the relative phase of the distortions can be qualitatively understood by looking at the behavior of the β_2 parameter in the limit of $|\delta/(d/2)| \ll 1$. For in-phase motions $(sgn(\delta_t) = sgn(\delta_d))$, we get $\beta_2 \sim -(1/\gamma L)(1 + (d/L)^2)^{-3/2}(\delta/L)$, while for the out-of-phase motion $(sgn(\delta_t) = -sgn(\delta_d))$, $\beta_2 \sim (1/\gamma L)(\delta/L)$. Hence, this correction has different signs depending on the type of distortion and it is easy to realize that the shift in P_2 (at $P_1 = 0$) will be stronger for the out-of-phase displacements.

16.3.3 Validating the minimal model: first-principle calculations

To show to which degree the previously discussed scenarios can be implemented in a real molecular system, we show here first-principle based calculations of the 1,4-diallyl butane radical cation using the density-functional tight binding code including self-consistent charge calculations (SCC-DFTB) (Aradi et al., 2007) as well as dispersion interactions (Elstner et al., 2001). As starting point, a dipole driver has been placed parallel to the 1,4-diallyl butane radical cation. As previously indicated, the total charge of the driver is 1 and we plot the variation of the molecular orbitals of the target while varying the driver polarization P_1. To provide a mobile charge in the system, we consider the molecular cation, where an electron has been removed from the lower allyl-group leading to a situation where the anti-bonding level is singly occupied in the upper group and non-occupied in the lower allyl group. Charge transfer is expected, since the localized electron at the lower allyl-group can occupy one of the non-bonding levels at the opposite allyl-end group as it has been already demonstrated (Lent et al., 2003). In Fig. 16.3, the HOMO and LUMO energy levels for the molecule are plotted as a function of the driver polarization P_1 for the case of out-of-phase rotations by 7 degrees.

The switching of the target polarization while adiabatically varying the driver polarization takes place around the anti-crossing region of the adiabatic states (or at the crossing point of the diabatic states). In a real molecule, these states can be related to the HOMO and LUMO frontier orbitals. This picture is similar to a Landau-Zener (Nitzan, 2006) interpretation of charge transfer: the effective (time-dependent) reaction parameters can be associated with the driver-target distance L and, once L is fixed, with the rate of change of the driver polarization. In the case of angular distortions, a shift in the anti-crossing point is found, whose sign depends on the relative orientation of driver and target, compare the top and bottom panels of Fig. 16.3. This means, the target polarization is non-vanishing at $P_1 = 0$, the target response shows a lag with respect to the driver, and this is just the effect found in the minimal model calculations for static angular distortions, see Fig. 16.2 for comparison.

16.4 Boolean networks in real-world QCA

Molecular QCA will require electrically bistable cells, that is, molecules including a mobile charge and a fixed, equal and opposite countercharge. Although systems of molecules can be immobilized and subsequently oxidized, zwitterionic complexes represent an interesting alternative, for they exhibit intrinsic charge separation. Whatever solution may be chosen in the future, the countercharge should remain immobile irrespective of the position of the mobile charge. In case of an externally added counterion, its own steric hindrance might be of help in this respect. Moreover, the possible asymmetry of the counterion should not cause excessive imbalance between the energy states of the cell. Ideally, the countercharge should remain in a symmetric position among the dots. The ideal QCA assumption that a countercharge is uniformly 'smeared' across the four corner dots (equivalently, half charge per dot) could only be mimicked by a double-charge counterion fixed exactly in the middle of the cell. Assuming that the cell is made of two paired molecular half cells, a somewhat easier solution, two one-charge counterions in the middle of each half-cell (that is, along two facing sides of the square cell) would no more exhibit central symmetry. The consequence would be different electrostatic interaction along the two cell alignment directions along the grid. The exact number and positions of the counterions are just the first nonideality considered in this model, and generally overlooked in QCA modeling.

Other nonidealities concern the geometry of the molecules. Here, molecular half cells comprising two dot-moieties are considered, but the conclusions can be readily extended to four-dot molecules. Real-world molecules may be characterized by two angles (polar and azymuthal, ϕ and θ). The first, measured on a plane parallel to the substrate with respect to the alignment directions, controls the squareness of the cell. The second is related to the planarity of the molecular system, and should be 90° with respect to a substrate-normal axis. Realistic molecules may show deviations in both respects (see Bramanti et al. (2015) for example) so that, measuring the influence of nonidealities in the value of these parameters is fundamental to evaluate the real usability of a molecule in QCA.

Again, the spacing between molecules along the grid axes x and y may not be uniform, nor are the axes themselves necessarily normal to each other – axis steps Δx and Δy and an angle α may be the related parameters.

All these nonidealities and related parameters are summarized in Fig. 16.4. In addition, an intrinsic energy imbalance ε between the two dots can be

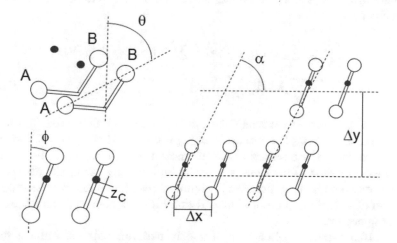

Fig. 16.4 Schematic geometry and relevant geometric parameters. The θ and ϕ angles (left) express the polar orientation (measured from the normal to the substrate) and azimuth orientation (measured from one of the two lattice axes) respectively. The lattice axes, in turn, form an angle α (right). Along them, the molecules are aligned with generally unequal steps Δx and Δy. The red dots represent the counterions, standing at some fixed distance from the dot-to-dot axis and displaced by z_C from the middle point.

considered. This often occurs in real-world molecules, in which the moieties implementing the Boolean dots, even if equal – and, so, with equal ground-state energies when insulated – interact with the substrate and surrounding molecules in different ways, as well as with each other, causing a constant additional energy split. As a result, one Boolean state is favored over the other.

Simulations were carried out to evalute the effect of all such nonidealities on the functionality of QCA. The results, summarized in the next section, were often surprising.

16.4.1 Modeling realistic molecular QCA

Few-cell systems can be modeled exactly. The ground-state configuration can be obtained solving the stationary Schrödinger equation:

$$H \left| \psi \right\rangle = E H \left| \psi \right\rangle \tag{16.10}$$

This picture obviously neglects the clocking signal, applied in QCA to synchronize the information flow through the network and make it directional. Or, in slightly different terms, it reproduces the final state of a molecular system, after a (quasi-)adiabatic clocking, which makes the dynamics of the system negligible. The second-quantization Hamiltonian for a single molecule, or half-cell,

$$H = \frac{1}{2}\varepsilon \sum_i (n_{i,B} - n_{i,A}) + \sum \gamma \left[a_{1,i}^\dagger a_{0,i} + a_{0,i}^\dagger a_{1,i} \right]$$
$$+ \sum i,j E_{i,j} \frac{n_i n_j}{|R_i - R_j|} \tag{16.11}$$

includes a first term expressing the intrinsic energy imbalance, then a coupling term expressing the interdot conjugation, and finally the electrostatic term, expressing the interaction of each molecule with its neighbors, as usual expressed in terms of kink energies – the kink energy being the energy cost of having two oppositely polarized neighbor cells. The a and n operators are, with usual notation, the creation and annihilation operators and the numbering operator.

Fig. 16.5 shows the behavior of a driver-driven pair vs. some nonideal parameter value. The results are expressed in terms of polarization which, considering a whole cell and denoting with $\rho_{b,i}$ the i-th dot in the diagonal encoding the Boolean value b, reads:

$$P = \frac{\rho_{1,1} + \rho_{1,2} - \rho_{0,1} - \rho_{0,2}}{\rho_{1,1} + \rho_{1,2} + \rho_{0,1} + \rho_{0,2}} \tag{16.12}$$

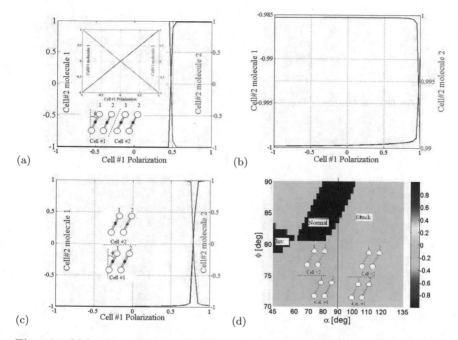

Fig. 16.5 Molecular polarizations within a driven cell (curves blue and green for the two molecules, respectively) coupled with a driver. The polarization inside the single molecules of the driver varies linearly (a, inset). The parameters $\theta = 90°$, $\alpha = 90°$, $\Delta x = 1$ and $\Delta x = 2$ nm are fixed at canonical values. The nonideality considered is ϕ, which equals 85° and 80° in (a) and (b) respectively, for two horizontally aligned cells. In (c), $\phi = 85°$ for vertically aligned cells. In (d), the reciprocal behaviour of the two cells is plotted versus ϕ and α – molecules aligned along y. In the red region the two-cell line operates correctly, in the blue region the behavior becomes inverting. Finally, in the largest green region, the driven cell is stuck at a logic value irrespective of the driver.

varying between -1 and $+1$ for Boolean 0 and 1, respectively. The polarization of a single molecule is easily obtained reducing Eq. 16.12 to a two-dot case and dropping off the Boolean labeling. In the driver, the polarization is imposed; in the driven molecule, it is calculated. In the classical, symmetrical case, the polarization of the driven cell shows a symmetric, sharp response vs. the polarization of the driver. The region around 0 features a steep variation (mostly linear, with good approximation) and, even for small magnitude driver polarizations, the curve reaches the pertinent asymptotic zone. The simulations in Fig. 16.5 show that the symmetry is altered even by small parametric variations, especially in ϕ. In the top-left figure, an angle $\phi = 85°$ (with barely a 5° variation with respect to the canonical value) introduces considerable asymmetry in the driven's response. A further, equally slight variation ($\phi = 80°$) definitely impairs the bistability of the cell (top-right figure). In the bottom-left figure, $\phi = 85°$ like in the top-left, but the two cells are aligned along y, not x. The distance is the same, but the electro-

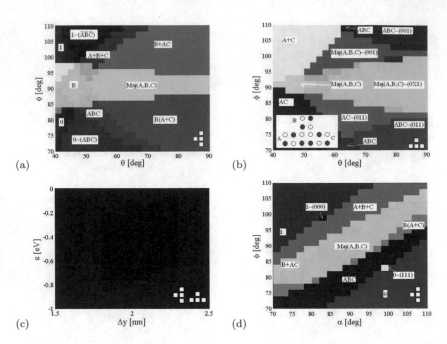

Fig. 16.6 (a) and (b) Majority-like configurations as sketched in the inset are explored as to their logical functionality vs. varying θ and ϕ. (c) Tweaking ε and Δy, both orientations may work fine. (d) The xy lattice angle α confirms a delicate parameter, though outside the majority region some other potentially useful functions are found.

static interaction of the electrons with the two counterions changes, and this is enough to affect the bistability of the cell in a much more severe way than in the previous case. Finally (bottom-right figure) a representation of the joint effect of varying ϕ and α (the latter being the angle between the grid's axes on the anchoring substrate) shows that the zone where the driver-driven pair acts as expected is comparatively small, and critically affected by both angles. An even smaller area shows an anti-aligning relationship between the cells, while in the remainder of the explored space, the driven cell is no longer bistable. Preliminary experiments on candidate molecules for QCA have already proven that variations in the geometric parameters as large as those probed here are all but rare.

The majority gate (or majority voter) is one of the two building blocks of QCA logic, along with the inverter. The output cell aligns its polarization to the majority of polarizations in the three input cells. With the classical, perfectly symmetric geometry, a majority gate works equally well however oriented. Here, due to the lack of symmetry, at least two configurations (rotated 90° with respect to each other) must be investigated.

In Figure 16.6, both were explored ((a) and (b) respectively) vs. varying θ and ϕ. For each point considered, the logic table of the resulting gate was computed. In the map, each colour corresponds to a different logic function, expressed in the usual Boolean notation in the label. The tilde followed by a logical configuration of inputs indicates that, for such particular input combination, the gate yields an undefined output value – one for which the molecules exhibit a polarization smaller than 0.5 in magnitude. An X in some combinations indicates that the indeterminacy is seen for both values of the corresponding input.

As seen, the region is extremely variegated, with different logical functions cropping out also against modest parametric variations. More interestingly, the maps look very different for the two orientations of the gate. It should be noted, however, that close to many apparently strange and useless logical functions, unexpected logic tables such as of three-input ANDs (or, dually and symmetrically, ORs) can be found, normally unavailable in classical QCA limiting to such simple cell sets.

Anyway, one would like both majority orientations to work properly, to make the circuit design better or, possibly, feasible. Supposing that the non-indealities, if not eliminated, can be modified to some extent, as if they were 'tuning knobs', one might for instance tweak the intrinsic energy imbalance ε (e.g. inserting different, or differently-linked moieties) along with the y step (e.g. with a different substrate or supramolecular mediators). This proves a potentially effective strategy – figure (c), where, in the red region, both configurations work.

Finally, one of the two majority-like configurations is tested vs. ϕ and α (bottom-right figure) which, again, prove delicate parameters, because of their influence on the electrostatic equilibrium underlying the intercellular interaction.

16.4.2 Materials design architectures design materials

The results presented – in particular those of Fig. 16.6 – lay the ground for some simple but fundamental remarks. First of all, slight differences in the geometry and energy structure of the molecules may produce dramatic changes in the functional outcome. Since the molecular parameters can be controlled up to an extent (especially when joint control is needed), this must be accepted, although, in some cases, the Boolean functionality may be severely affected. However, useful configurations may be unexpectedly found, as for instance in Fig. 16.6a. This might lead to material-driven, modified versions of the QCA paradigm. In a sense, this extends the QCA conception of computation adapted to matter, incorporating what are initially considered nonidealities of the matter itself.

On the other hand, tweaking one or few of the molecular parameters with different synthesis or anchoring can correct the nonidealities, at least partly, so limiting the extent of the modifications to the QCA paradigm. The pro-

R. Rinaldi, R. Gutierrez, A. Santana Bonilla, G. Cuniberti, A. Bramanti

cess towards this new technology is, then, one in which the materials and architectures 'design' each other, mutually adapting until acceptable functionality is implemented. Such matching of the physical and abstract layers of the computing machines cannot be further ignored, for any molecular electronic solution to get out of the lab and reach for the shelves of consumer electronics.

16.5 Conclusion and outlook

On the experimental side very few examples of working molecular QCA cells have been presented in the literature (Arima et al., 2012a; Joyce et al., 2009; Qi et al., 2003; Yan, 2008) the main limitations being the small size of the molecules and, inherently, the complex experimental techniques required. Qi et al. (2003) proposed a device composed by vertically oriented two dot cells, sandwiched between two electrodes. The molecular compound was trans-Ru-(dppm)2(C≡CFc)Cl(NCCH2CH2NH2, which was suitable to undergo to chemical oxidation upon exposure to [FcH][PF6]. Switching between the two active states (RuIIFeIII and RuIIIFeII) was proved by means of Capacitance-Voltage experiments, involving the reduced and oxidized molecular layer. The same group proposed a new device architecture (Joyce et al., 2009), in which QCA cells were immobilized onto two highly-doped windows of silicon, beside two polysilicon electrodes gating a single-electron transistor (SET). When the molecule charge switches upon the applied electric field, the local electrostatic potential of the SET is expected to change. Elsewhere, different QCA units were proposed (Arima et al., 2012a) consisting of ferrocene molecules containing carbazole. In particular, carbazole is relatively stable, quite easily functionalized, and well-known as electron-donor and hole-transporter. Electrochemical characterization showed among others that both ferrocenyl units undergo fast (Nernstian) electron transfer processes generating, in the positive potential region, either fully- (Fc+-Fc+) or partly-oxidized (Fc+ -Fc) species. Scanning Tunnelling Microscopy (STM) experiments showed switching in those units, immobilized onto gold surfaces. A possible implementation of a QCA clocking circuit was proposed by Yan (2008): the molecular cells were placed on an array of metallic micron-sized wires, which were positively or negatively polarized in order to shift the charges (electrons) down or up, respectively. Electrostatic force microscopy experiments were used to map the clocking circuit and show how to drive computation through QCA molecular gates.

In conclusion, although computation via QCA has been studied in detail from the theoretical point of view, implementation into a real molecular system is still lacking. This is due to: (i) the large number of properties, both at molecular and supra-molecular level, which have to be embedded into suitable molecular candidates; (ii) the small dimensions of molecular QCA cells, which require highly advanced and complex techniques to spatially locate and manipulate them in an ordered network. However, QCA still represent a remarkable examples of innovative thinking and perhaps the most prominent in the post-Moore processing technologies, exploiting intrinsic properties of matter at the nanoscale (quantum confinement and tunnelling) as well as electrostatic interaction to implement Boolean computation without the need of transistors. The way to their molecular implementation goes through the understanding of the relevant properties of real-world molecules and, possibly, their inclusion in future architectures.

Acknowledgments

A.S.B. and R.G. thank A. Dianat for very helpful discussions. This work was partly funded by the EU within the project *Molecular Architectures for QCA-inspired Boolean Networks* (MolArNet, project nr. 318516). A.S.B. thanks the Max Planck Institute for the Physics of Complex Systems for financial support. This work has also been partly supported by the German Research Foundation (DFG) within the Cluster of Excellence "Center for Advancing Electronics Dresden". Computational resources were provided by the ZIH at the Dresden University of Technology.

References

Amlani, I., A. O. Orlov, G. Toth, G. H. Bernstein, C. S. Lent, and G. L. Snider (1999). "Digital Logic Gate Using Quantum-dot Cellular Automata". *Science* 284:289–291.

Aradi, B., B. Hourahine, and Th. Frauenheim (2007). "DFTB+, a sparse matrix-based implementation of the DFTB method". *J. Phys. Chem. A* 26(26):5678–5684.

Arima, V., M. Iurlo, L. Zoli, S. Kumar, M. Piacenza, F. Della Sala, F. Matino, G. Maruccio, R. Rinaldi, F. Paolucci, M. Marcaccio, P.G. Cozzi, and A. Bramanti (2012a). "Toward Quantum-dot Cellular Automata units: thiolated-carbazole linked bisferrocenes". *Nanoscale* 4:813–823.

Arima, Valentina, Matteo Iurlo, Luca Zoli, Susmit Kumar, Manuel Piacenza, Fabio Della Sala, Francesca Matino, Giuseppe Maruccio, Ross Rinaldi, Francesco Paolucci, Massimo Marcaccio, Pier Giorgio Cozzi, and Alessandro Paolo Bramanti (2012b). "Toward quantum-dot cellular automata units: thiolated-carbazole linked bisferrocenes". *Nanoscale* 4(3):813–823.

Bramanti, A. P., A. Santana-Bonilla, and R. Rinaldi (2015). "Quantum-dot Cellular Automata: Computation with Real-world Molecules". *Int. Journ. of Unconventional Computing* 11:63–82.

Crocker, Michael, X. Sharon Hu, and Michael Niemier (2009). "Defects and faults in QCA-based PLAs". *J. Emerg. Technol. Comput. Syst.* 5(2):1–27.

Crocker, Michael, Michael Niemier, X. Sharon Hu, and Marya Lieberman (2008). "Molecular QCA design with chemically reasonable constraints". *J. Emerg. Technol. Comput. Syst.* 4(2):1–21.

Dysart, T. J. (2013). "Modeling of Electrostatic QCA Wires". *IEEE Transactions on Nanotechnology* 12(4):553–560.

Elstner, M., P. Hobza, T. Frauenheim, S. Suhai, and E. Kaxiras (2001). "Hydrogen bonding and stacking interactions of nucleic acid base pairs: a density-functional-theory based treatment". *J. Chem. Phys* 114(12):5149–5155.

Huang, Jing, M. Momenzadeh, M. B. Tahoori, and Fabrizio Lombardi (2004). "Defect characterization for scaling of QCA devices [quantum dot cellular automata]". *Proceedings, 19th IEEE International Symposium on Defect and Fault Tolerance in VLSI Systems, 2004. DFT 2004.* Pp. 30–38.

Joyce, R. A., H. Qi, T. P. Fehlner, C. S. Lent, A. O. Orlov, and G. L. Snider (2009). "A System to Demonstrate the Bistability in Molecules for Application in a Molecular QCA Cell". *2009 IEEE Nanotechnology Materials and Devices Conference*, pp. 46–49.

Lambert, Christoph, Chad Risko, Veaceslav Coropceanu, Jürgen Schelter, Stephan Amthor, Nadine E. Gruhn, Jason C. Durivage, and Jean-Luc Brédas (2005). "Electronic Coupling in Tetraanisylarylenediamine Mixed-Valence Systems: The Interplay between Bridge Energy and Geometric Factors". *Journal of the American Chemical Society* 127(23):8508–8516.

Lent, Craig S. (2000). "Bypassing the Transistor Paradigm". *Science* 288(5471):1597–1599.

Lent, Craig S., Beth Isaksen, and Marya Lieberman (2003). "Molecular Quantum-Dot Cellular Automata". *J. Am. Chem. Soc.* 125(4):1056–1063.

Lu, Yuhui and Craig S. Lent (2008). "A metric for characterizing the bistability of molecular quantum-dot cellular automata". *Nanotechnology* 19(15):155703.

Macucci, Massimo (2010). "Quantum Cellular Automata". *Nanotechnology*. Wiley.

Niemier, Michael T. and Peter M. Kogge (2001). "Problems in designing with QCAs: Layout = Timing". *International Journal of Circuit Theory and Applications* 29(1):49–62.

Nitzan, Abraham (2006). *Chemical Dynamics in Condensed Phases: Relaxation, Transfer, and Reactions in Condensed Molecular Systems. Quantum Dynamics using time-dependent Schroedinger equation.* Oxford University Press.

Ottavi, M., S. Pontarelli, E. P. DeBenedictis, A. Salsano, S. Frost-Murphy, P. M. Kogge, and Fabrizio Lombardi (2011). "Partially Reversible Pipelined

QCA Circuits: Combining Low Power With High Throughput". *IEEE Transactions on Nanotechnology* 10(6):1383–1393.

Pulimeno, A., M. Graziano, A. Sanginario, V. Cauda, D. Demarchi, and G. Piccinini (2013). "Bis-Ferrocene Molecular QCA Wire: Ab Initio Simulations of Fabrication Driven Fault Tolerance". *IEEE Transactions on Nanotechnology* 12(4):498–507.

Qi, H., S. Sharma, Z. Li, G. L. Snider, A. O. Orlov, C. S. Lent, and T. P. Fehlner (2003). "Molecular Quantum Cellular Automata Cells. Electric Field Driven Switching of a Silicon Surface Bound Array of Vertically Oriented Two-Dot Molecular Quantum Cellular Automata". *J. Am. Chem. Soc.* 125(49):15250–15259.

Rahimi, Ehsan and Shahram Mohammad Nejad (2012). "Quasi-classical modeling of molecular quantum-dot cellular automata multidriver gates". *Nanoscale Research Letters* 7(274).1–13.

Ribou, Anne-Cécile, Jean-Pierre Launay, Michelle L. Sachtleben, Hu Li, and Charles W. Spangler (1996). "Intervalence Electron Transfer in Mixed Valence Diferrocenylpolyenes. Decay Law of the Metal–Metal Coupling with Distance". *Inorganic Chemistry* 35(13):3735–3740.

Rojas, F., E. Cota, and S. E. Ulloa (2002). "Quantum dynamics, dissipation, and asymmetry effects in quantum dot arrays". *Phys. Rev. B* 66(23):235305.

Santana Bonilla, Alejandro, Rafael Gutierrez, Leonardo Medrano Sandonas, Daijiro Nozaki, Alessandro Paolo Bramanti, and Gianaurelio Cuniberti (2014). "Structural distortions in molecular-based quantum cellular automata: a minimal model based study". *Phys. Chem. Chem. Phys.* 16(33):17777–17785.

Sturzu, I., J. L. Kanuchok, M. Khatun, and P. D. Tougaw (2005). "Thermal effect in quantum-dot cellular automata". *Physica E: Low-dimensional Systems and Nanostructures* 27(1–2):188–197.

Van Voorhis, Troy, Tim Kowalczyk, Benjamin Kaduk, Lee-Ping Wang, Chiao-Lun Cheng, and Qin Wu (2010). "The Diabatic Picture of Electron Transfer, Reaction Barriers, and Molecular Dynamics". *Annual Review of Physical Chemistry* 61(1):149–170.

Wang, Y. and M. Lieberman (2004). "Thermodynamic behavior of molecular-scale Quantum-dot Cellular Automata (QCA) wires and logic devices". *IEEE Trans. Nanotech.* 3(3):368–376.

Wasio, Natalie A., Rebecca C. Quardokus, Ryan P. Forrest, Steven A. Corcelli, Yuhui Lu, Craig S. Lent, Frederic Justaud, Claude Lapinte, and S. Alex Kandel (2012). "STM Imaging of Three-Metal-Center Molecules: Comparison of Experiment and Theory For Two Mixed-Valence Oxidation States". *The Journal of Physical Chemistry C* 116(48):25486–25492.

Yan, M. (2008). "Electric field measurement for quantum-dot cellular automata clocking circuits". *Surf. Interface Anal.* 40(12):1503–1506.

Printed in the United States
By Bookmasters